Latin American Films, 1932–1994

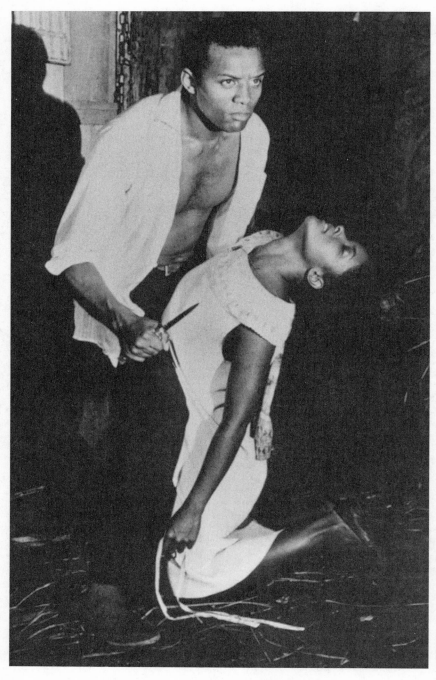

Bruno Mello as Orpheus has just stabbed Marpessa Dawn as Eurydice
in Marcel Camus' French-Brazilian coproduction, *Orfeu negro* (*Black Orpheus*, 1958)

Latin American Films, 1932–1994

A CRITICAL FILMOGRAPHY

by Ronald Schwartz

McFarland & Company, Inc., Publishers
Jefferson, North Carolina, and London

Once again, for my beautiful and wonderful wife
Amelia Fletcher,
my inspiration, my life,
my most cherished love.

And in memory of that explosion of fantasy,
energy and playful eroticism,
Carmen Miranda, whose Latin American charisma
triggered my interest in Latin American film.

British Library Cataloguing-in-Publication data are available

Library of Congress Cataloguing-in-Publication Data

Schwartz, Ronald, 1937–
    Latin American films, 1932–1994 : a critical filmography / by
Ronald Schwartz.
      p.   cm.
    Includes bibliographical references and index.
    ISBN 0-7864-0174-5 (library binding: 50# alkaline paper) ∞
    1. Motion pictures — Latin America — Catalogs.   I. Title.
PN1995.9.L37S38   1997
016.79143'75'098 — dc21   96-37416
                                             CIP

Manufactured in the United States of America

McFarland & Company, Inc., Publishers
 Box 611, Jefferson, North Carolina 28640

TABLE OF CONTENTS

ACKNOWLEDGMENTS

Latin American Films began as a sequel of sorts to my earlier book, *The Great Spanish Films*, although it is indeed uniquely different because of the very nature of the material and the geography it encompasses.

Once again, I thank many of my colleagues, especially Elio Alba, Julio Hernández-Miyares, Margaret Rockwitz Kibbee and Alfonso García Osuna at Kingsborough Community College of the City University of New York for their ideas and discussions with me about the gigantic theme of Latin American cinema.

The dedicated librarians at Kingsborough, particularly Angelo Trippichio and Coleridge Orr, were extremely helpful in tracking down through interlibrary loans many reviews and other vital information which have found their way into this book, and for that I would like to thank them.

At the Museum of Modern Art, Charles Silver at the Film Study Center was particularly cordial and helpful and Mary Corliss in the Film Stills Archive at MOMA was particularly generous with her time and skill, helping to provide the majority of stills found in this book.

At the Lincoln Center Library for the Performing Arts, I wish to commend once again that large group of librarians and staff on the third floor for their diligence and cooperation while I made use of their film clip files.

Also at City College of New York, I am particularly grateful to Jerry Carlson for exposing me to the virtues of several televised intellectual discussions as an occasional guest on the CUNY produced television series "Cinema Then, Cinema Now" and "CUNY Cinémathèque." I must commend Professor Carlson for his great interest in Latin American cinema, which finds its way into this book through his continued dialogues with me.

I am also grateful to Professor Carlson for his guest editorial debut with the celebrated New York–based literary magazine *Review: Latin American Literature & the Arts*, whose entire fall 1992 issue is devoted to Latin American cinema, a first for the publication and a celebration for Professor Carlson as guest editor and those of us who teach and proselytize for foreign language films.

I must once again thank my wife, Amelia Fletcher, for enduring yet another period of research and writing of another volume of film criticism. It was also through her expertise as a librarian and editor that I finally decided on the format this present volume would take to make it as useful as possible to the reader yet uninitiated to the subject of Latin American film.

Also, a special thank you goes to the memory of Paul Lenti, the *Variety* film critic for Latin America, for giving me access to his videos and for his conversation. As this book neared completion, Paul, author and Latin American cinema expert *extraordinaire*, passed away at age 45. He was a helpful scholar and good friend, whose presence is much felt in this book.

Also, special thanks go to Peter Besas, who writes the *Variety* Latin American Issue; to the staffs of *Variety* and the *New York Times*, for their extensive cooperation in securing film reviews for many of the films discussed forthwith; to Laura Kaiser at the UCLA Film & Television Archives, who provided me with stills and a copy of the catalogue "Mexican Film & the Literary Tradition"; to the staffs at the Museum of Modern Art and the Walter Reade Theatre during the summer of 1993 for their help during MOMA's special archival film shows on Latin America, its film retrospectives on Mexico entitled "Mexico and the Narrative Tradition," and the "New Trends in Mexican Cinema" retrospective at the Walter Reade. Thank you all!

I would like to honor the memory of another friend and translator, Gregory Kolovakos, who passed away several years ago in his early thirties. Gregory was particularly fond of translating Latin American short stories, novels and articles for the *Latin American Review Magazine* and his spirit stays with us in his work.

I would like to salute Tom Chang and Stephen Cirona among others of our Wednesday night group at "God's Love, We Deliver," an AIDS service organization. Their sensitivity, perceptions and conversations with me and my family about life, art and film have found their way into this book. Antonio Lombardi, my son Jonathan, and my wife Amelia continue to provide insights in our weekly work sessions that help us to serve a vital organization which delivers meals to homebound AIDS patients in New York City.

In the United States, we have had the great AIDS play on Broadway, Tony Kushner's brilliant two-part epic, *Angels in America*; we have seen the fascinating HBO film *And the Band Played On* and the equally riveting multi–Cesar award winning film, Christopher Collet's autobiographical French masterpiece entitled *Savage Nights*. Curiously, by 1995 nothing had yet surfaced in film on this theme from Latin America.

Two now-departed giants of the Latin American film world might appropriately be honored here. The famous Puerto Rican actor Raúl Julia passed away in the autumn of 1994 at the age of 54. Of the many films in which he appeared, several of which are featured in this book, I will remember him best for his strong performance as the heterosexual revolutionary in Hector Babenco's *Kiss of the Spiderwoman*. He was darkly handsome and all his performances were larger than life. He will be missed by theater patrons and filmgoers alike. In May of 1995, Latin America's foremost female director, Maria Luisa Bemberg, died in Buenos Aires. Although she came to cinema relatively late in life, directing her first film at the age of 59, she will always be remembered for her feminist œuvre and the Academy Award–nominated film *Camilla*, made in 1984. Her films will be greatly missed by Latin American filmgoers.

In July 1995, a 90 minute biography-documentary by Helena Solberg, *Carmen Miranda: Bananas Is My Business*, premiered in New York City, showing the actress not merely as the larger-than-life Brazilian virtual cartoon figure — a persona she created in her American films — but as a sensitive and influential interpreter of the samba before the exaggerations of her Hollywood career. A great entertainer who helped cement the wartime alliance between the United States and various Latin American countries in the forties, Carmen Miranda deserves mention as an inspiration of this writer but also as a victim of the cultural movement she embodied.

A special word of gratitude goes to Ron Illardo for his late in the process suggestions for improving the critical posture of this manuscript.

PREFACE

The idea for this book began in the mid-seventies, when foreign language enrollments were flagging and a new strategy to lure students back to language courses became necessary. One component of this strategy is the teaching of multi-cultural and film courses about Spain and Latin America. My first film course about Latin American film was simply entitled "Spanish 82 — Latin American Cinema," but the students quickly re-titled it "Revolution 82" because most of the films available in 16 mm dealt with political themes.

There were very, very few distributors of Latin American films (Embrafilm and New Yorker films were the leading ones in New York City in the mid-seventies) and the video revolution did not take place till the early eighties. *Cinéaste Magazine*, under the editorial leadership of Gary Crowdus, was the only one of its kind that dared to review Latin American film as well as other Third World cinematic efforts. *Jump Cut* also devoted occasional space to similar themes.

There were too few books being published that were dedicated exclusively to Latin American cinema. E. Bradford Burns' *Latin American Cinema: Film and History*, published by the University of California Press in 1975, was the first text I ever used, but even then, Burns was too immersed in the historical and political ideology to deal simply with the aesthetics of Latin American cinema.

With the arrival of the eighties, several publishers brought out various tomes in their "great films" series, but not a single volume (known to me) about the great Latin American films appeared in that decade. Latin American cinema, after Spanish cinema, is perhaps the second most neglected of the national cinemas by critics over the last thirty or so years.

In the 1990s, however, a spate of scholarly works on Latin American cinema and Third World film has appeared in English, notably John King's *Magical Reels* (in 1990) and Zuzana M. Pick's *The New Latin American Cinema: A Continental Project* (1993). The latter is particularly good. It explores six areas of inquiry: history, authorship, gender, popular cinema, ethnicity and exile — six of the institutional and aesthetic foundations of the New Latin American cinema.

Another volume that has recently made an appearance on this side of the Atlantic is a 1993 British Film Institute publication entitled *Mediating Two Worlds: Cinematic Encounters in the Americas*, a series of top-notch essays on Latin

1

American film by many of the writers already cited in this volume, treating Latin American cinema from the silents to the present, edited by John King and others and illustrated with fascinating difficult to obtain, one-of-a-kind stills.

Also certain Latin American countries have received recent attention in tomes devoted exclusively to their cinema. The most notable recent volumes are these: David Foster's *Contemporary Argentine Cinema* (1992), Randal Johnson and Robert Stam's *Brazilian Cinema* (1982), Michael Chanan's *The Cuban Image* (1986) as well as his *Chilean Cinema* (1976), Charles Ramírez Berg's *Cinema of Solitude: A Critical Study of Mexican Film (1967–1983)*, published in 1992, *The Mexican Cinema Project*, a series of essays about Mexican cinema 1919–1992 published by the UCLA Film & Television Archive and edited by Chon A. Noriega & Steven Ricci in 1994, and Carl J. Mora's earlier tome in its second edition also highlighting Mexico: *Mexican Cinema: Reflections of a Society (1896–1988)*, republished in 1989.

Two recent volumes published in Spanish should not be overlooked for they both contain worthy material: Luis Trelles Plazaola's *Cine sudamericano. English*, which is really a fairly helpful dictionary of South American filmmakers published by the University of Puerto Rico in 1989, and the exceptionally worthy *10 Años del nuevo cine latinoamericano* (*Ten Years of New Latin American Cinema*), by Teresa Toledo, published by the Cinemateca de Cuba in 1990, which celebrates the best films of Latin America in the decade of the eighties by giving useful and detailed film credits, plot outlines, and major themes as well as a perusal of most Latin American film festivals of this prolific period.

One should not overlook William Luhr's stupendous job as editor of *World Cinema Since 1945*, brought out by Ungar in 1987, especially its chapters on Argentine, Brazilian, Cuban, Mexican and Latin American cinema. And Michael Chanan's monograph, *Twenty-five Years of the New Latin American Cinema*, published by the British Film Institute in 1983 as well as Julianne Burton's *Cinema and Social Change in Latin America: Conversations with Filmmakers* (1983) should not be overlooked. There is also a wonderful doctoral dissertation, by Ana M. López entitled "Towards a 'Third' and 'Imperfect' Cinema: A Theoretical and Historical Study of Filmmaking in Latin America" (1986), which is worthy of publication. Most of these titles deal, however, with Latin American cinema as products of their social and historical milieus rather than with the films themselves and their own intrinsic and aesthetic values.

There have been two outstanding histories of Latin American cinema published to date: Guy Hennebelle and Alfonso Gumucio Dagron's *Les Cinémas de l'Amérique Latine*, published in Paris in 1981 in French, and a Spanish translation, *Historia del cine latinoamericano*, of Peter B. Schumann's original German text, brought out in Buenos Aires in 1987-1988.

Still eagerly awaited is a thoroughly researched history of Latin American film in English or perhaps a translation into English of one of the foregoing ground-breaking texts.

What I have chosen to do to fill this void is produce a reference work dealing exclusively with the great (and some of the lesser) Latin American films themselves, a compendium irrespective of country, commercial distribution or political impact. I wish simply to promote the films themselves, to make that "uncertain screen," Latin American cinema, *seen film by film.*

Although 1950 is considered the watershed year for all Latin American countries, when most Latino film directors stopped copying the Hollywood models and began using the Neo-Realist style borrowed from the late forties Italian cinema, the style of Rossellini, Visconti and DeSica, I decided to push my inclusion criteria back to 1932. North American consciousness of Latin American cinema became prevalent in the United States in the 1930s with the release (in 1932) of *Santa*, Mexico's first sound film. Realism became the operative style also for the new Latin American films of the late forties, fifties and sixties. And it is in this epoch that Latin American cinema began to flourish and capitalize on the notion of a "third cinema." Although the term "third cinema" appeared in the writings of the Argentine filmmakers Getino and Solanas in the late sixties and was not widely used until the mid-seventies, its indications and traces were felt as early as the early fifties. (I have included a dozen seminal films of the forties in this reference work since they deserve a place in the pantheon of great Latin American films and their importance and influence should not be overlooked.)

This volume, then, is a personal selection of significant Latin American films from 1932 through 1994. To be of greatest use to scholars, the films are presented in alphabetical order (with cross-references from alternate, particularly English-language, titles). Some readers might object to some seemingly "American" titles found in the filmography, such as *Missing, The Emerald Forest, Kiss of the Spiderwoman,* or *Under the Volcano.* These were included because the films were shot on location in Latin America or were made by a Latin American director or were filmed in a combination of Spanish, Portuguese, native dialects and English. These films deal with specific problems of various Latin American nations and give a more rounded, somewhat scholarly and certainly, up-to-date and illuminating perspective of the state of Latin American culture and politics. Films like William Dieterle's *Juárez,* Elia Kazan's *Viva Zapata!,* John Huston's *Treasure of the Sierra Madre* and *We Were Strangers,* and John Ford's *The Fugitive* were deliberately excluded because they were mostly studio-bound films, shot with a minimum of location shooting and tended to tamper with Latin American culture as viewed through a Hollywood filter.

My hope is that the reader will consider these films and their themes as a reflection of the particular Latin American country in which they were produced and that each film by itself may be found to exhibit an important thematic concern of the director and the nation he or she represents.

Some of these films are not masterpieces; others may even be considered mediocre even if commercially successful. But all reflect, in some way, the diversity and mentality of Latin American countries from the 1930s to the 1990s. Some of these films have never been exhibited in theatres beyond the borders of their own countries while others have been shown internationally and have appeared on video cassette.

This volume contains numerous film stills and other illustrations (some never before published), all reproduced with the permission of the Museum of Modern Art's Film Archive.

Some readers may note the absence of some of their favorite films and wonder at the inclusion of others. It would be nearly impossible to compile a comprehensive record of some sixty years or more of Latin American cinema. What I have sought to do is document the styles and genres of the most representative films of each country in each decade. One of the goals of this volume is to suggest the vastness, the variety and the eminence of Latin American cinema. The selection of films is a personal one and all of the entries are significant.

RONALD SCHWARTZ
*Professor of Romance Languages
and Film
Kingsborough Community College
of City University of New York
Spring 1996*

INTRODUCTION

A reader of the Films Listed Chronologically (see page 15) will notice I refer to films made as early as 1932 mostly produced in Mexico. Beginning in the fifties, other Latin American films invaded the social consciousness of critics and audiences in the United States, especially from Brazil, Argentina and occasionally Cuba.

Argentina, Mexico and Brazil had the most accomplished and extensive film industries in Latin America, from the days of silent cinema (*cine mudo*) to the most accomplished films of the nineties, which employ the same technology as in the United States. In terms of film production, Cuba ranks fourth.

Peru, Bolivia, Chile, Colombia, Venezuela, Nicaragua and Uruguay (ranked in descending order) have on occasion produced significant films. The reader will find the largest number of films to be from these eleven countries.

It is sad to say that films from this next group of countries have had only a minor impact on Latin American film in general, although sometimes single films have resonated abroad. One will, therefore, see the occasional film from Costa Rica, Ecuador, Guatemala, Haiti, Honduras, Jamaica, Martinique, Panama, Paraguay, Puerto Rico and El Salvador.

The "Chicano" film is still considered somewhat of an off-shoot of Latin American cinema; I discuss it briefly later in this Introduction.

* * *

My own special interest in Latin American cinema began with the spread of Mexican films into the United States in the 1930s and 1940s. In fact, the first sound film made in Mexico in 1932, *Santa*, played in the United States and was directed by Antonio Moreno, the boldly handsome silent film star of the twenties who appeared with Greta Garbo in many of her films, most notably *The Temptress*, made in Hollywood in 1926. Moreno was one of a number of "Latino" types to find success in Hollywood in the twenties, thirties and forties.

George Hadley-García, in his wonderful book entitled *Hispanic Hollywood: The Latins in Motion Pictures* (1990), traces the course of the Latino actor from the thirties through the eighties and highlights the careers of Dolores del Río, Pedro Armendáriz, Cesar Romero, Carmen Miranda, Tito Guizar, Gilbert

Roland, Rita Hayworth and others, performers who have made their "Latin" impact in American film. It is unfortunate he could not include María Félix, who never made an English-speaking film.

But it was María Félix in *Doña Bárbara* (1943) and *Enamorada* (1949) and Dolores del Río in *Flor silvestre* (*Wild Flower*) (1943) and *María Candelaría* (1944) who were my favorite Mexican heroines, and Pedro Armendáriz, who appeared with these actresses, was my favorite Latino leading man. I remember watching very old, poorly subtitled prints of these films with severely scratched soundtracks before my teenage years; they had a great impact on me.

When my mother took me also in the late forties to see a documentary about the fisherman of Patzcuaro at the Museum of Modern Art, *Redes* (*Nets*), made in 1934 and directed by Paul Strand (with Fred Zinnemann as an assistant director) and first shown in the United States in 1937 (the year I was born), I knew I was hooked on foreign cinema and films from or about Latin America as well. It was at MOMA in the fifties I also saw excerpts from Sergei Eisenstein's monumental 1932 unfinished documentary work, *¡Qué Viva Mexico!*, a fascinating excursion into the impoverished Mexico of the thirties.

The incursion of Latin American actors and actresses into the North reached its peak in the late 1940s and with it, the beginning of a kind of escapist-romantic cinema that has all but disappeared. But the American love affair with a new kind of Mexican realist cinema began with the films of Luis Buñuel in the early fifties. I remember watching *Él* (*This Strange Passion*) with Arturo de Cordova but never quite grasped the meaning behind his sexual obsessions or those of Archibaldo de la Cruz, the hero of another film by Luis Buñuel, *Ensayo de un crimen* (*The Criminal Life of Archibaldo de la Cruz*), which eluded my comprehension in the fifties.

Nevertheless, a new spirit from restless young filmmakers was on the rise, especially in the short films (*cortometrajes*) coming from Cuba and Argentina. In 1955, Tomás Gutiérrez Alea made a short entitled *El mégano* (*The Charcoal Workers*) about the terrible working and living conditions of coal miners in northern Cuba. The Batista regime found it so realistic that all prints of the film were destroyed. Fernando Birri in Argentina made two shorts also critical of Argentine society: *Tire die* (*Throw Dimes*) in 1958, about homeless youths on the dole who hang out in railroad yards begging for dimes from passengers, and *Los inundados* (*Flood Victims*) (1961), a quasidocumentary of "underdevelopment," showing how some feisty and impoverished Argentines cope with natural disasters.

Thus by 1960, a new realist cinema began developing in Latin America, perhaps a politically oriented one, sometimes based on Marxist ideology.

Tomás Gutiérrez Alea in Cuba, Fernando Birri in Argentina, Glauber Rocha in Brazil with his *Cinema Nôvo* movement all sought to portray the realities of life in their respective nations. The same social realism affected Miguel Littín in Chile, Jorge Sanjinés and Antonio Eguino in Bolivia, Humberto Solas in

Cuba and Fernando Solanas in Argentina. These directors are the true creators of the new Latin American cinema, where realist cinema gives way to political cinema which in itself becomes a "third" cinema, not one of entertainment or politics or realism but one of life itself.

What has now come to be called "third cinema" became an alternative to the Hollywood-style commercial film that had been copied by Latin American directors in their own productions of potboilers, bourgeois "white telephone" musicals or soap operas during the forties and fifties, which accounted for the only type of cinema widely made then, known as "first cinema."

"Second cinema" refers to the proliferation of films made in the late fifties and early sixties by the French New Wave or *Nouvelle Vague* cinema, the cinema of the *auteur* or director, "new cinema" which placed total responsibility upon the director for content and montage, creating a counterweight to the former consumer-oriented ideology posited by the Hollywood models of "first cinema."

"Third cinema" came into its own after the *Nouvelle Vague*, with its willingness to mix fiction with documentary, surrealism and history, social analysis and allegory, modernism and folklore in an effort to create a unique cinema, authentically nationalistic, reflecting the reality of each nation — revolutionary, intractable, even indigestible cinema.

Rooted in the social concerns of Italian Neo-Realism, the stylistic experimentalism of the French New Wave and even the Spanish surrealism of Luis Buñuel (because of his partnership with Mexican cinema of the fifties), "third cinema" owes a lot to the *Cinema Nôvo* movement in Brazil, with its anti-illusionism and baroque tropicalism, as well as to the Cuban revolution, because of that country's resulting ideological, propagandistic, self-critical and adventurous films which later spread to other countries like Argentina, Chile and Bolivia.

"Third cinema" contributed to but also transcended the political documentaries of Solanas and Guzmán, and later the careers and films of Littín, Sanjinés and Eguino. These directors produced ground-breaking films about their country's politics, and racial and neocolonial conflicts, using experimentation, visual flamboyance, the harrowing exposé techniques of social-realist cinema to rise above, or away from, mainstream commercial cinema, even auteurist cinema, by creating the provocative and authentically engagé films of Latin America.

With this new concept of cinema, a new type of *cinéaste* was born as well as part of a new strategy for responsive viewer participation and film distribution. "Third cinema" was not mainstream commercial cinema but became the mettle for newly created cinema clubs throughout Latin America. Some of the most vigorous Latin film features have now become part of popular cinema as it is generally known in the North and have been shown commercially in the United States and elsewhere. Some have even been promoted on video cassette and have consequently received international distribution. (I will indicate which titles are available on video cassette, in which format and where they may be purchased, for each entry in this book.)

I should mention here certain feature coproductions based upon fiction that have had an impact on "international" cinema, like Gregorio Nava's *El Norte* (1984) made in Guatemala, Mexico and the United States, about a family of émigrés who are vigorously pursued by the *migra* until they arrive in Los Angeles, or Marcel Camus' *Orpheu negro* (1958, Brazil), a French language film about the Greek myth of Orpheus and Eurydice, or María Luisa Bemberg's *Miss Mary* (1985, Argentina), about an English governess and her relationship with an aristocratic Argentine family, or Werner Herzog's *Fitzcarraldo* (1982, Brazil), about building an opera house in the wilderness and an impossible journey by "ship" across land; also Herzog's *Aguirre, the Wrath of God* (1972, Peru), about Pizarro's expedition and conquest of the Incas, Carlos Saura's *Antonieta* (1981, Mexico), a romantic love story about one French woman's search for the truth about the love affair and suicide of the woman of the title, and Saura's *El Sur* (1991, Argentina), about a Buenos Aires librarian's obsession with his family home in the south on the pampas, and Hector Babenco's *At Play in the Fields of the Lord* (1991, Brazil), about American evangelists instilling the Christian God into the Indians of Brazil and the Amazon.

Documentaries such as Jonas Mekas' *Compañeros y compañeras*, made in Cuba in 1970 about the effects of the Castro revolution and communism, Deborah Shaffer's *Dance of Hope* (1990, Chile), dealing with the aftermath of the broken Allende regime, Peter Lilienthal's *The Uprising* (1979), about the revolution in Nicaragua, Herzog's *Ballad of the Little Soldier* (1984), about the Miskito Indians engaged in warfare with the Sandinistas, and David Bradbury's *Nicaragua: No pasarán* (1984), about U.S. interests and intervention — the last three films shot in the actual locales of their stories in Nicaragua and all fascinating. Barbara Trent's Academy Award–winning documentary *The Panama Deception* (1992) is most revealing about Panama and the United States' invasion of it under the aegis of President Bush.

Fiction films made in and about Latin America but with documentary pretensions in languages other than English are Gillo Pontecorvo's *¡Quemada!* (1970), an Italo-Franco production starring Marlon Brando, about slavery on a Portuguese-controlled island of the Antilles, Haskell Wexler's *Latino* (1985), another fictional film about the rebels' changing sides and fighting with the Sandinista movement, filmed in Nicaragua, and Jean Pierre Dutileux' *Raoni* (1978), a French-and Indian-language feature about the adverse effects of progress upon the lives of the Indians of the Amazon.

Other fascinating American motion pictures filmed principally in Latin America in English and utilizing real locales are John Boorman's sensational *The Emerald Forest* (1985, Brazil), about the abduction of an American engineer's son by Amazon Indians, Roland Joffe's *The Mission* (1989, Brazil), starring Robert de Niro and Jeremy Irons, about mercenaries and missionaries and the local Indians who suffer at the hands of both Spanish and Portuguese imperialists, Costa-Gavras' *Missing* (1982, Venezuela, Mexico and Chile), starring Jack Lemmon, about the assassination of an American "student" (or government agent or provocateur?) by an autocratic regime ostensibly supported by the American government in Chile, Oliver Stone's *Salvador* (1985, El Salvador), starring James Woods, about a photographer's experiences during the U.S. intervention in the war there, Roger Spottswoodie's *Under Fire* (1983, Nicaragua), starring Gene Hackman and Nick Nolte, about a group of photographers covering the war in Nicaragua and risking their lives there, and John Huston's *Under the Volcano* (1984, Mexico), starring Albert Finney, an adaptation of Malcolm Lowry's novel about the alcoholism and death of a diplomat in Mexico.

I have addressed in the affirmative the question of whether to include the Caribbean cinema, singleton films such as Euzhan Palcy's *Rue Cases Nègres* (1983), about poverty and the lives of sugar cane workers filmed in French in Martinique, or Jimmy Cliff's *The Harder They Come* (1972), about a reggae singer's conflicts with American capitalism, filmed in English and patois in Jamaica, or even Rupert Roonaraine's *The Terror and the Time* (1979), about British colonialism in the Guyanas, which was filmed in English in Guyana and also is of importance.

The question of whether to include Chicano cinema also arose. To ignore or exclude such widely distributed films as Robert Young's *The Ballad of Gregorio Cortez* (1983), with Eduardo Jaime Olmos as a Mexican who killed a young American sheriff and eluded 600 officers of the law for about six weeks, or Herbert Biberman's *Salt of the Earth* (1975), about Chicano miners on strike in New Mexico, seemed improper.

In the main, however, I have analyzed films made exclusively in Latin America, in their original language, in either Spanish or Portuguese, films that were produced and directed in their country of origin by filmmakers native to that country. (Directors in exile whose films have been produced in countries other than their native land have also been included.) If other titles appear, the reason for their inclusion would derive from a necessity to demonstrate their great impact on Latin American cinema. There are no Latin American films originally released on or after January 1, 1995, included in this volume.

After reviewing hundreds of films from Latin America, from a great variety of places, Mexico to Patagonia, and from exiled Latin American directors all over the world (notably in France, West Germany and Canada), and after examining U.S. and foreign coproductions made in Latin America, I could not but conclude that Latin American cinema is one of the great cinemas of the world even though its films are still neglected by European, Asian and American markets.

There have always been a number of film programs and festivals of Latin American features throughout the world. Some of the best take place annually in Havana, Toronto, Rio de Janeiro, Chicago, Guadalajara and New York and many Latin American films compete at other international festivals at Berlin, Cannes and Venice. But sometimes politics takes the spotlight from artistic merit.

For example, on June 29, 1994, the *New York Times* reported the resignation of the director of the annual Havana Film Festival, José Horta, who dared to show Tomás Gutiérrez Alea's 1994 film *Fresa y chocolate* (*Strawberry & Chocolate*). Called a "tale of intolerance in Cuban society, the film has become a test of Fidel Castro's willingness to look the other way," wrote Michael Z. Wise in his *Times* article of January 22, 1995, entitled "In Totalitarian Cuba, Ice Cream & Understanding." *Strawberry & Chocolate* tells the story of a young male sociology student who enters into a friendship with an older, sophisticated gay man. It was screened at the 1994 New York Film Festival, the very first time the festival included a film from Cuba.

Strawberry & Chocolate was seen in Miami in 1994 and on pirated video cassettes elsewhere in America. Miramax, the courageous American distributor, always noted for taking chances on "arthouse" films, bought the rights and gave it an official United States release in January 1995.

In the aggregate, the films of Latin American cinema-producing nations are eclipsed by American productions (U.S. produced and directed) and, unfortunately, Latin American festivals are not very well attended by foreign audiences. No single Latin American film, perhaps with the possible exception of Alfonso Arau's *Como agua para chocolate* (*Like Water for Chocolate*), has had a successful long run internationally, a situation which has led Latin American film critics to decry "the colonization of North American cinema."

It is usually the worst of American film products that take the place of good Latin American, Spanish or other European films in Latin America's movie theatres. Clearly, it is the responsibility of every Latin American country to create their own commercial initiatives, with production and distributing systems ready and able to compete with the U.S. film industry. Coproductions should certainly be encouraged to increase competition with American film products.

Although video in Latin America has had a tremendous impact (in every country), accounting for a great loss of attendance at the box office (and there are on-going battles among cable companies for connections of diverse programming to single units or entire building sites), Latin American films are still taking a poor share of box office receipts compared to U.S.–made films. In *Variety's* March 1994 Latin American issue, Madrid-based correspondent Peter Besas made it quite clear that with the advent of video and satellite telecommunication, the nineties can only bring in an era of radical change for Latin American cinema.

Perhaps with the creation of a common audiovisual marketing strategy with assured distribution for all Latin American countries and with the development of a greater business sense in the multimedia industries, Latin Americans will be assured of a fair share of the cinema market — and a provision for them of a true cultural panorama will be accomplished by the close of the decade of the nineties.

It is clear that many more Latin American films should be accessible internationally. They are not just arthouse oriented or elitist cinema but true commercial successes everywhere, artistic works that show off cultural diversity and each country's national heritage.

A NOTE ON THE FORMAT

A typical entry in this book follows this design:

000. [a serial number, used in indexing] **Title of Film** [most common title, frequently Spanish] **(Alternate Title)** [or titles or translation of title into English]. Director. Country [both location and origin of production company or studio unless otherwise indicated], Year. Running time, Color or B&W. Language. ¶Commentary. ¶Notes.

The Commentary is generally a definitive plot outline which has been constructed not only from personal viewing but from many original source materials, especially the original press books.

Commentaries include quotations from critical reviews in order to present each film within its own time frame and context.

Notes included are relevant bits of information concerning the production, director, actors, or awards, and appear directly after the commentaries.

THE FILMS LISTED
CHRONOLOGICALLY

The following is a list of the films whose entries appear in this book, ordered chronologically as the entries themselves are alphabetical. Each item in the list shows the year the film was made, the *film title* in its original language (the film's country of origin), and the name of its director; availability on VHS video is then indicated with a V.

1932   *Santa* (Mexico) Moreno V
1936   *Allá en el rancho grande* (Mexico) Fuentes
1937   *Redes* (Mexico) Strand and Zinneman
1940   *Ahí está el detalle* (Mexico) Oro V
1941   *Cuando los hijos se van* (Mexico) Oro
1941   *The Forgotten Village* (Mexico/U.S.) Kline
1942   *It's All True* (Brazil/U.S.) Welles V
1943   *Distinto amanecer* (Mexico) Bracho
1943   *Doña Bárbara* (Mexico) Fuentes V
1943   *Flor silvestre* (Mexico) Fernández
1944   *María Candelaría* (Mexico) Fernández V
1945   *The Pearl* (Mexico/U.S.) Fernández V
1948   *Malclovia* (Mexico) Fernández
1949   *Enamorada* (Mexico) Fernández V
1950   *Los olvidados* (Mexico) Buñuel V
1951   *Las aguas bajan turbias* (Argentina) Carril
1951   *Una mujer sin amor* (Mexico) Buñuel V
1951   *Subida al cielo* (Mexico) Buñuel V

1951   *Susana* (Mexico) Buñuel V
1952   *El bruto* (Mexico) Buñuel V
1952   *Él* (Mexico) Buñuel V
1953   *Abismos de pasión* (Mexico) Buñuel V
1953   *El brazo fuerte* (Mexico) Korporaal
1953   *O cangaçerio* (Brazil) L. Barreto V
1955   *Ensayo de un crimen* (Mexico) Buñuel V
1955   *El mégano* (Cuba) Alea
1957   *La casa de Ángel* (Argentina) T. Nilsson V
1957   *La fièvre monte à El Pao* (Mexico/France) Buñuel
1957   *Raíces* (Mexico) Alazraki
1958   *Orfeu negro* (Brazil/France) Camus V
1958   *Tire die* (Argentina) Birri
1959   *La cucaracha* (Mexico) Fernández
1959   *Fin de fiesta* (Argentina) Torre Nilsson
1959   *Nazarín* (Mexico) Buñuel V
1960   *Barravento* (Brazil) Rocha
1961   *Macario* (Mexico) Gavaldón V
1961   *Piel de verano* (Argentina) T. Nilsson V
1961   *La rosa blanca* (Mexico) Gavaldón V

1961   *The Young One* (Mexico/U.S.)
Buñuel

1962   *El ángel exterminador* (Mexico)
Buñuel V

1962   *La bandida* (Mexico) Rodríguez

1962   *La cifra impar* (Argentina) Antin V

1962   *En el balcón vacío* (Mexico) Riera

1962   *Garrincha, alegría do povo* (Brazil)
Andrade

1962   *Los inundados* (Argentina) Birri

1963   *Deus e o diabo na terra do sol*
(Brazil) Rocha

1963   *Os fuzis* (Brazil) Guerra

1963   *La mano en la trampa* (Argentina)
T. Nilsson V

1964   *Crónica de un niño solo* (Argentina)
Favio

1964   *En este pueblo no hay ladrones*
(Mexico) Isaac

1964   *La fórmula secreta* (Mexico) Gamez

1964   *Las Poquianchis* (Mexico) Cazals V

1964   *Yanco* (Mexico) Gonzales V

1966   *Pedro Páramo* (Mexico) Velo

1966   *Terra em transe* (Brazil) Rocha V

1966   *Tiempo de morir* (Colombia)
Ripstein

1966   *Ukamau* (Bolivia) Sanjinés

1966–68   *La Hora de los hornos* (Argentina) Solanas

1968   *Antonio das Mortes* (Brazil) Rocha
V

1969   *O bandido da luz vermelha* (Brazil)
Sganterla

1969   *Don Segundo Sombra* (Argentina)
Antín V

1969   *Luzía* (Cuba) Solas

1969   *Macunaima* (Brazil) Andrade V

1969   *Martín Fierro* (Argentina)
T. Nilsson

1969   *Primera carga del machete* (Cuba)
Gómez

1969   *Tres tristes tigres* (Chile) Ruiz

1969   *Valparaíso mi amor* (Chile) Francia

1969   *Vidas secas* (Brazil) Santos

1970   *Canoa* (Mexico) Cazals

1970   *El chacal de Nahueltoro* (Chile)
Sanjinés

1970   *Compañeras y compañeros* (Cuba/
U.S.) Mekas, Stone and Stone

1970   *¡Quemada!* (Italy/France)
Pontecorvo V

1970   *El señor presidente* (Argentina)
Madanes

1971   *Como era gostoso o meu frances*
(Brazil) Pereira V

1971   *Los días del agua* (Cuba) Gómez

1971   *La Notte di San Juan* (Bolivia/
Italy) Sanjinés

1971   *El topo* (Mexico) Jodorowsky V

1971   *Yo soy Joaquín* (Mexico/U.S.)
Váldez

1972   *Primera crónica* (Chile) Guzmán

1972   *El castillo de la pureza* (Mexico)
Ripstein

1972   *Chiricales* (Colombia) Rodríguez
and Silva

1972   *The Harder They Come* (Jamaica)
Henzell V

1972–76   *Los hijos de Martín Fierro*
(Argentina) Solanas

1972   *Memorias del subdesarrollo* (Cuba)
Alea V

1972   *La muralla verde* (Peru) Robles
Godoy V

1972   *El rincón de las vírgenes* (Mexico)
Isaac

1972   *São Bernardo* (Brazil) Hirszman

1972   *Tupamaros* (Uruguay/Sweden)
Lindqvist

1972   *Yo soy chicano* (Mexico/U.S.)
Trevino

1973   *Juan Pérez Jolote* (Mexico) Burns

1973   *La tierra prometida* (Chile) Littín
V

1973   *Yawar mallku* (Peru) Sanjinés

1973–74   *El coraje del pueblo* (Bolivia)
Sanjinés

1973–79   *La batalla de Chile* (Chile)
Guzmán

1974   *Boquitas pintadas* (Argentina)
T. Nilsson

1974   *El chacal de Nahueltoro* (Chile)
Littín

1974   *De cierta manera* (Cuba) Gómez

1974   *¿No oyes ladrar los perros?* (Mexico/France) Reichenbach

1974   *El otro Francisco* (Cuba) Giral

1974   *Traidores* (Argentina) Grupo Cine
de la Base

1974   *La Tregua* (Argentina) Renan

1975   *Actas de Marusia* (Mexico) Littín

1975   *El apando* (Mexico) Cazals

1975　*Chac* (Mexico) Klein
1975　*La guerra de los cerdos* (Argentina) T. Nilsson V
1975　*Juan Vicente Gómez y su época* (Venezuela) M. de Pedro
1975　*Lição de amor* (Brazil) Escorel
1975　*El muerto* (Argentina) Olivera V
1975　*Renuncia por motivos de salud* (Mexico) Baledon
1975　*Salt of the Earth* (U.S.) Biberman V
1976　*Cantata de Chile* (Cuba) Solas
1976　*Cascabel* (Mexico) Araiza
1976　*Iracema* (Brazil) Brodansky V
1976　*Pedro Páramo* (Mexico) Bolanos
1977　*Raíces de sangre* (Mexico) Trevino
1977　*Aguirre, der Zorn Göttes* (West Germany/Peru) Herzog V
1977　*Alambrista* (U.S.) Young
1977　*Chuquiago* (Peru) Eguino
1977　*Doña Flor e seus dois maridos* (Brazil) B. Barreto V
1977　*El hombre de Maisinicú* (Cuba) Perez
1977　*Muerte al amanecer* (Peru/ Venezuela) Lombardi
1977　*La Patagonia rebelde* (Argentina) Olivera V
1978　*Allá lejos y hace tiempo* (Argentina) Antin V
1978　*Cadena perpetua* (Mexico) Ripstein
1978　*País portátil* (Venezuela) Feo and Llerandi
1978　*Raoni* (France/Brazil) Dutilleux
1978　*El super* (U.S./Cuba) Ichaso and Jiménez-Leal
1978　*La última cena* (Cuba) Alea V
1979　*El amor bandido* (Brazil) Barreto
1979　*Muerte de un burócrata* (Cuba) Alea V
1979　*Retrato de Teresa* (Cuba) Vega V
1979　*The Terror & the Time* (Guyana) Roonaraine
1980　*Bye, Bye, Brazil* (Brazil) Diegues V
1980　*Gaijín: Caminhos da liberdade* (Brazil) Yamasaki
1980　*El infierno tan temido* (Argentina) Torre V
1980　*El lugar sin límites* (Mexico) Ripstein

1980　*Perro de alambre* (Venezuela) Cano
1981　*Antonieta* (Mexico) Saura
1981　*Lúcio Flávio* (Brazil) Babenco
1981　*El amor bandido* (Brazil) L. Barreto V
1981　*Barravento* (Brazil) Rocha
1981　*Eles não usam black-tie* (Brazil) Hirszman V
1981　*Mojado Power* (Mexico) Arau
1981　*Muerte de un magnate* (Peru) Lombardi
1981　*Pixote* (Brazil) Babenco V
1981　*Tiempo de revancha* (Argentina) Aristarain V
1981　*Tiempo de morir* (Mexico) Triana
1981　*The Uprising* (Nicaragua) Lilienthal V
1981　*Zoot Suit* (U.S.) Váldez V
1982　*Alsino y el condor* (Nicaragua) Littín V
1982　*Cecilia* (Cuba) Solas
1982　*Los últimos días de la víctima* (Argentina) Aristarain
1982　*Eréndira* (Mexico) Guerra V
1982　*Fitzcarraldo* (West Germany/ Brazil) Herzog V
1982　*Journal inachevé* (Canada/Chile) Mallet
1982　*A Man, When He Is a Man* (Costa Rica/Chile) Sarmiento
1982　*Missing* (Chile/U.S.) Costa-Gavras V
1982　*Plata dulce* (Argentina) Ayala
1982　*Pubis angélical* (Argentina) Torre V
1982　*El Salvador: Morazán* (El Salvador) Zero a la Izquierda Film Coll.
1982　*Señora de nadie* (Argentina) Bemberg
1982　*Xica (da silva)* (Brazil) Diegues V
1983, 1986　*La república perdida, Partes I & II* (Argentina) Pérez
1983　*The Ballad of Gregorio Cortez* (U.S.) Young V
1983　*Gabriela* (Brazil) B. Barreto V
1983　*María de mi corazón* (Mexico) Hermosillo V
1983　*No habrá más penas ni olvido* (Argentina) Olivera V

1983 *El norte* (Guatamala/Mexico/
 U.S.) Nava V

1983 *Rue Cases Nègres* (France/
 Martinique) Palcy V

1983 *Sargento Getulio* (Brazil) Penna

1983 *Under Fire* (U.S./Nicaragua)
 Spotiswoode V

1984 *Ballad of the Little Soldier*
 (Nicaragua/W. Germany) Herzog

1984 *Camila* (Argentina) Bemberg V

1984 *Los chicos de la guerra* (Argentina)
 Kamin

1984 *Cuarteles de invierno* (Argentina)
 Murua

1984 *Evita, quien quiera oír que oiga*
 (Argentina) Mignogna

1984 *Mauvaise Conduite* (Cuba) Almendros and Jiménez-Leal V

1984 *Nicaragua, no pasarán* (Nicaragua/
 Australia) D. Bradbury

1984 *Pasajeros de una pesadilla* (Argentina) Ayala

1984 *Quilombo* (Brazil) Diegues V

1984 *Les Trois Couronnes du matelot*
 (Chile) Ruiz

1984 *Under the Volcano* (U.S./Mexico)
 Huston V

1985 *Amargo mar* (Bolivia) Eguino

1985 *La ciudad y los perros* (Peru) Lombardi V

1985 *Los días de junio* (Argentina)
 Fischerman

1985 *Doña Herlinda y su hijo* (Mexico)
 Hermosillo V

1985 *The Emerald Forest* (Brazil/U.S.)
 Boorman

1985 *Esperando la carroza* (Argentina)
 Doria

1985 *Frida: Naturaleza Vida* (Mexico)
 Leduc V

1985 *Gregorio* (Peru) El Grupo Chaski

1985 *Hasta cierto punto* (Cuba) Alea

1985 *El imperio de la fortuna* (Mexico)
 Ripstein

1985 *Kiss of the Spiderwoman* (U.S./
 Argentina) Babenco V

1985 *Latino* (U.S./Nicaragua) Wexler V

1985 *Miss Mary* (England/Argentina)
 Bemberg V

1985 *Perros de la noche* (Argentina)
 Kofman

1985 *Salvador* (U.S./El Salvador) Stone
 V

1986 *Acta general de Chile* (Cuba) Littín

1986 *Gerónima* (Argentina) Tosso

1986 *Hombre mirando al sudeste*
 (Argentina) Subiela V

1986 *Malabrigo* (Peru) Durant V

1986 *Malayunta* (Argentina) Santiso

1986 *The Mission* (U.K./Colombia,
 Argentina, Paraguay, Brazil)
 Joffe V

1986 *La noche de los lápices* (Argentina)
 Olivera

1986 *La película del rey* (Argentina)
 Sorín

1986 *Pobre mariposa* (Argentina) Torre
 V

1986 *Tangos: l'exil de Gardel*
 (Argentina/France) Solanas

1986 *Yo, la peor de todos* (Argentina)
 Bemberg

1987 *El amor es una mujer gorda*
 (Argentina) Agresti

1987 *La gran fiesta* (Puerto Rico) Zurinaga V

1987 *Un hombre de éxito* (Cuba) Solas

1987 *A hora da estrela* (Brazil) Amaral V

1987 *Lejanía* (Cuba) Díaz V

1987 *Mariana, Mariana* (Mexico) Isaac

1987 *Opera do Malandro* (Brazil)
 Guerra V

1987 *Sentimientos: Mirta de Liniers e
 Estambul* (Argentina) Cosica and
 Saura

1987 *Sur* (Argentina) Solanas

1987 *Tango, baile nuestro* (Argentina)
 Zaranda

1987 *Um trem para as estrelas* (Brazil)
 Diegues V

1987 *Vampirios en la Habana* (Cuba)
 Padron

1988 *La amiga* (Argentina/
 West Germany) Meerapfel

1988 *Apartment Zero* (Argentina/
 U.K.) Donovan V

1988 *La boca del lobo* (Peru) Lombardi
 V

1988 *Las cartas del parque* (Cuba) Alea
 V

1988 *El color escondido* (Argentina)
 Torre

1988 *A dama do cine Shanghai* (Brazil)
      Prado
1988 *Debajo del mundo* (Argentina)
      Feijoo and Stagnaro V
1988 *Juliana* (Peru) Espinosa
1988 *Milagros en Roma* (Colombia)
      Naranjo
1988 *Nadie escuchaba* (U.S./Cuba)
      Almendros V
1988 *Oriane* (Venezuela) F. Torres V
1988 *Rodrigo "D": no futuro* (Colombia)
      Gaviria V
1988 *Romance da empregada* (Brazil)
      B. Barreto
1988 *Tango Bar* (Argentina/Puerto
      Rico) Zurinaga V
1988 *Técnicas de duelo* (Colombia/
      Cuba) Cabrera
1989 *Barroco* (Spain/Cuba) Leduc V
1989 *Boda secreta* (Argentina) Agresti
1989 *Eversmile, New Jersey* (Argentina)
      Sorín V
1989 *Lo quelle pasó a Santiago* (Puerto
      Rico) Morales
1989 *Lola* (Mexico) Novaro
1989 *Mentiras piadosas* (Mexico)
      Ripstein
1989 *La nación clandestina* (Bolivia)
      Sanjines
1989 *Old Gringo* (U.S./Mexico) Puenzo
      V
1989 *¡Plaff!* (Cuba) Tabio
1989 *Santa Sangre* (Italy/Mexico)
      Jodorowsky V
1989 *El secreto de Romelia* (Mexico)
      Cortes
1989 *Últimas imágenes del naufragio*
      (Argentina) Subiela
1989 *El verano de sra. Forbes* (Mexico/
      Spain) Hermosillo V
1990 *Caídos del cielo* (Peru) Lombardi
1990 *Caluga o menta* (Chile) Justiniano
1990 *Los cuentos de Abelardo* (Puerto
      Rico) Casanova
1990 *Dance of Hope* (Chile/U.S.)
      Shaffer
1990 *Danzón* (Mexico) Novaro
1990 *Lo que vendrá* (Argentina)
      Mosquera V
1990 *Sandino* (Spain/Chile/Nicaragua)
      Littín

1990 *La tarea* (Mexico) Hermosillo
1990 *La tigra* (Ecuador) Luzuriaga V
1990 *Verónico Cruz* (Argentina) Pereira V
1991 *Adorable Lies* (Cuba) Chijona
1991 *Alicia en el pueblo de las maravillas*
      (Cuba) D. Torres
1991 *Ángel de fuego* (Mexico) Rothberg
1991 *At Play in the Fields of the Lord*
      (Brazil/U.S.) Babenco V
1991 *Cabeza de Vaca* (Mexico)
      Echeverría V
1991 *Como agua para chocolate*
      (Mexico) Arau V
1991 *Disparen a matar* (Venezuela)
      Azpurua
1991 *Jerico* (Venezuela) Lamarta
1991 *Un lugar del mundo* (Argentina)
      Aristarain
1991 *El mariachi* (Mexico/U.S.)
      Rodríguez
1991 *La peste* (Argentina) Puenzo
1991 *Sensaciones* (Ecuador) J.E. y V.
      Codero
1991 *El sur* (Spain/Argentina) Saura
1991 *El viaje* (Argentina) Solanas
1991 *Viernes de la eternidad* (Argentina)
      Olivera V
1992 *El bulto* (Mexico) Retes
1992 *Como agua para chocolate* (Mexico)
      Arau
1992 *Cronos* (Mexico) Toro
1992 *La cruz del sur* (Spain/Chile)
      Guzmán
1992 *Kino* (Mexico) Cazals
1992 *El lado oscuro del corazón*
      (Argentina) Subiela
1992 *Lolo* (Mexico) Athié
1992 *María Antonia* (Cuba) Giral
1992 *Mi querido Tom Mix* (Mexico) Agraz
1992 *Miroslava* (Mexico) Rangel
1992 *Modelo antiguo* (Mexico) Araiza
1992 *Mujer transparente* (Cuba) several
      directors
1992 *The Panama Deception* (Panama/
      U.S.) Trent
1993 *El acto en cuestión* (Argentina)
      Agresti
1993 *Bartolomé de las Casas* (Mexico)
      Olhovich
1993 *El caso de María Soledad*
      (Argentina) Olivera

1993   *Cronos* (Mexico) Del Toro V
1993   *8-A* (Cuba) Jiménez-Leal
1993   *Encuentro inesperado* (Mexico)
         Hermosillo
1993   *Funes, un gran amor* (Argentina)
         Torre
1993   *Matar al abuelito* (Argentina)
         D'Angiolillo
1993   *El muro de silencio* (Argentina)
         Stantic
1993   *Palomita blanca* (Chile) Ruiz
1993   *El patrullero* (Mexico) Cox

1993   *Perfume de gardenias* (Brazil)
         Prado
1993   *Reportaje a la muerte* (Peru)
         Gavidia
1993   *Secuestro: A Story of a Kidnapping*
         (Colombia) Motta
1993   *Señora Bolero* (Venezuela) Vera
1993   *Tanguito* (Argentina) Pineyro
1993   *La vida es una sola* (Peru) Eyde
1994   *De eso no se habla* (Argentina/
         Italy) Bemberg
1993–94   *Fresas y chocolate* (Cuba) Alea

THE FILMS: A–Z

Abelardo's Tales see *Los cuentos de Abelardo*

1. Abismos de pasión (Wuthering Heights). Luis Buñuel. Mexico, 1953. 90 min., B&W. Spanish.

COMMENTARY: Certainly very different from the 1939 William Wyler version produced by Samuel Goldwyn and starring Laurence Olivier and Merle Oberon, *Abismos de pasión* captures some of the spirit of the American version, with several Buñuelian plot twists that make it a more fascinating Mexican variation and at least in some ways closer to the original Emily Brontë novel.

Jorge Mistral plays Alejandro, an orphaned boy who lives with a wealthy Mexican family and becomes their servant. He falls in love with Catalina (played by Irasema Dilian), a wild-eyed romantic child-woman who loves to go wandering through the Mexican landscapes in search of love and Alejandro. But the Buñuel version begins where Alejandro has returned after many years, running away to amass a fortune so he could marry or be worthy of Catalina. The latter, believing Alejandro would never return, has married Eduardo (played by Ernesto Alonso). As soon as Alejandro and Catalina see each other, their smoldering passion ignites. But Catalina wants to keep her rich husband and her new lover, too. And so, Alejandro, dissatisfied with this arrangement decides to marry Eduardo's sister, Isabela (played by Lillia Prado). Alejandro's

revenge upon Catalina does not work and the latter falls ill during childbirth and dies. On her deathbed, both Alejandro and Catalina had confessed their real love for each other. Therefore Isabela is left to lead a morose existence as Alejandro pines away for the dead Catalina.

In a remarkable ending, Alejandro digs up Catalina's body, covered in a white shroud, and embraces it as Catalina's drunken brother Ricardo (Hindley in the novel) fires a shot and kills him, thus uniting the lovers in death. *Abismos de pasión* is such a far stretch from the Wyler American version as well as the original Emily Brontë novel that one should not try to use these yardsticks as a basis for comparison. *Abismos* exists on its own level.

The principals, Mistral (as the Heathcliff character), Dilian (as the Catherine Henshaw character), Alonso as her husband Eduardo (the Edgar Linton character in the original) and Prado as his sister, are all very good in their roles. As was the fashion of the fifties, most of the Mexicans have pencil thin mustaches and this leads to confusion between characters, especially between Mistral and Alonso. Dilian is the very image of a horsewoman and Prado is quite demure physically and so there is no confusion between them. And certainly there is no comparison between the arid Mexican countryside and Emily Brontë's moors of Yorkshire. But *Abismos de pasión* is certainly a Buñuel film

Jorge Mistral and Irasema Dilián collecting Mexican "heather" in *Abismos de pasión*, Luis Buñuel's version of *Wuthering Heights* (1953).

in every way since it does capture the darkness in the hearts of Alejandro/ Heathcliff and Catalina/Cathy and it does recapture the celebrated concept of free love (*amour fou*) that Buñuel and the Surrealists praised in their doctrines since the 1920s. Buñuel's version is a stark film, sometimes repellent and abrasive as compared to the sweet, nostalgic version of Wyler. But Buñuel's use of Wagner's *Tristan und Isolde* as source music on the soundtrack actually de-

tracts from the images on the screen, not reinforces them. In this one instance, the Alfred Newman score in the 1939 Wyler version is appropriate and sublime. *Abismos* is available on video cassette in the U.S. and is worth a viewing.

NOTES: *Abismos de pasión* represents one of the several films director Luis Buñuel made in the Mexican phase of his prolific career when he moved to Mexico City in 1945 and began shooting his first Mexican production, *Gran casino*, there in 1946. *Abismos* is the thirteenth of some twenty-odd Mexican films Buñuel made during the period 1946 through 1960 while residing in Mexico. He returned only once to Spain in this period and made the highly controversial film *Viridiana*, which won a Cannes Film Festival Gold Medal in 1961, but continued to live in Mexico while he filmed in France and Spain again until 1977, where he made his last film, *That Obscure Object of Desire*.

Born in Calanda (Aragon), Spain in 1900, Buñuel was educated there, spent several years in Paris, joining the Surrealist Movement, was in and out of Spain during the Spanish Civil War, and spent a few years in the United States before migrating to Mexico where he resided from 1945; he died there, in Mexico City in 1983. His autobiography, *My Last Sigh*, written in collaboration with screenwriter Jean-Claude Carrière, tells the entire fascinating story of his life.

The Act in Question see *El acto en cuestión*

2. Acta general de Chile
(**General Document on Chile**). Miguel Littín. Cuba, 1986. 215 min., Color & B&W. Spanish.

COMMENTARY: This is a made-for-television eye-witness report of the Pinochet military regime's dictatorship. Littín takes us through the cities and countryside of Chile, interviewing many people in places where the director himself grew up. For example, he walks and talks with famed poet Pablo Neruda near his home by the sea; he also interviews Fidel Castro and author Gabriel García Márquez, who both offer fascinating insights into the Chileans' plight in the face of dictatorship. Interviews with the relatives of the *desaparecidos* and a reconstruction of the death of Salvador de Allende are all fascinating segments of this emotionally disturbing documentary.

NOTES: Miguel Littín (b. 1942) is currently living in exile. He is known primarily for his first film, *The Jackal of Nahualtoro* (1970), but such other films as *Promised Land* (1973), *Letters from Marusia* (1976), *Reasons of State* (1978) and *Alsino and the Condor* (1978) have also received international acclaim.

3. Actas de Marusia (**Letters from Marusia**). Miguel Littín. Mexico, 1975. 115 min., Technicolor. Spanish.

COMMENTARY: Set in Chile in 1907 in the village of Marusia, famous for its saltpeter mines, the film tells the story of the famous massacre that took place there, finding significant parallels with the overthrow of the Allende government in 1973. It is the old story of exploited saltpeter miners who murder a brutal foreman and kill several soldiers, then go on strike to better their working conditions and fight the military and the foreign capitalists before they are dutifully crushed by the Chilean army. The film was made in Mexico with a cast of Indian unknowns, symbolic of the Chilean class struggle. Only Italian actor Gian Maria Volonte is singled out as the "intellectual" who speaks out against the exploitation of Chilean (really, Mexican) peasants in their struggle for survival against the military, the capitalists, and each other. Volonte acts as a union organizer but has little success as a leader or propagandist. In the film's final scene, three escaping workers are carrying away from the massacre the famous "letters from Marusia," which is a journal of the events written by the Volonte character, Gregorio.

The film is a lyrical historical epic, highly stylized with its statements about social and political strife. Nevertheless, it is director Littín's version of a fundamental episode of class warfare, "an episode that shows both the origins of the working class and the origins of Fascism and repression in Chile as well" (Littín).

NOTES: *Actas de Marusia* was nominated by the Academy of Motion Pictures Arts & Sciences as a candidate for the Best Foreign Language Film of 1975. Littín, a native Chilean born in Palmilla (Colchagua), began his artistic career in the theatre at the University of Santiago between 1959 and 1962. He wrote several experimental plays and in 1963–1965 was active as a television director, producing plays by Pinter, Miller and Brecht as well as other Latin American playwrights. However he reached his artistic zenith in the world of cinema, making his first amateur documentary, *Por la tierra ajena*, in 1965. Continuing his studies at the University of Santiago, Littín was director of "Chile Films" until the overthrow of Salvador Allende's government in 1973 and has lived and worked in exile ever since. His documentary on the life of Allende entitled *President, compañero* (1971) has never been shown in the United States.

NOTE: Gian María Volonte is no stranger to political cinema. Believing much like Littín that film directors should be "politically involved," Volonte is an Italian actor fond of appearing in Italian political cinema. His roles in *Investigation of a Citizen Under Suspicion* (1969) and *Open Doors* (1990) are the cinematic markers of a long, varied career that have included other "politically oriented" roles in such films as *Sacco and Vanzetti* (1971) and *The Working Class Goes to Heaven* (1972). *Actas de Marusia* was his first and only collaboration with Littín.

On December 6, 1994, Volonte died of a heart attack while making a film in Greece. His obituary in the *New York Times* highlights his militant leftist political leanings: "During labor unrest in Italy in 1971, he was arrested along with workers who were striking for higher wages and better working conditions. Many of his most noted film roles were inspired by political events or judicial cases in Italy and elsewhere."

We shall miss those chiseled features and militant leftist politics that left their mark on his film and theatre performances.

4. El acto en cuestión (The Act in Question). Alejandro Agresti. Argentina, 1993. 114 min., Color. Spanish.

COMMENTARY: The film is based upon Agresti's own novel of the same title written in Argentina in 1979. In an interview with Harry Hosman quoted in the film's press book, Agresti states: "The atmosphere in Argentina at that time formed the basis for the main character in *El acto en cuestión*, the magician Miguel Quiroga. He can make objects vanish and people." (Agresti refers to friends of his who kept vanishing off the face of the earth because of their political convictions.) But the book (and the subsequent film) look at the subject of disappearance more abstractly.

The film is a disjointed, surreal travelogue about a magician who discovers an obscure book of magic which changes his entire life — a vanishing formula that works for both objects and human beings. The most startling event in the films depicts the magician's rise to fame and a trick which causes the Eiffel Tower to disappear. More surreal is a dream Quiroga has about the loss of the book containing the "vanishing secret" and its reprinting en masse. Like Federico Fellini (e.g., in *La strada*, *8½*, and *Nights of Cabiria*), Agresti relies heavily on the metaphor of the circus and his male star, Carlos Roffe gives a terrific performance as Miguel Quiroga while Lorenzo Quinteros as Rogelio, who narrates the film, is excellent as the restorer and repairer of dolls who watches Miguel's demise. The film is a record of events covering thirty years in Miguel Quiroga's life. It describes his obsessive stealing of books each day and reading them every night in his search for a copy of the same magic book containing the "vanishing formula," which Miguel burned one night in a paranoic fit. He continually searches for another copy of the book, haunted by the thought that this book may exist and reveal the secret of his success. He continues to live a tortured existence, dreading the moment when someone will unearth his secret by bringing another copy of this book to light.

NOTES: Agresti was born in Argentina in 1961 and has been involved in the film industry since he was a child, beginning as a clapper loader and then developing into a distinguished cameraman. His first film, *The Man Who Looked for Reason* (1986), was reasonably well-received by the Argentine film critics. He has done post-production work in Holland with Kees Kasander of Allarts, who has become his constant collaborator. Agresti prefers to write his own screenplays based upon his novels and to direct the film versions. To date, he has succeeded admirably with *Secret Wedding* (1988) and *The Act in Question* (1993). He reveals that Charles Chaplin's film *Monsieur Verdoux* (1948) influenced the narrative structure of this film as did Vittoria De Sica's use of crane shots, which gave the sense of realism Agresti was looking for in *The Act in Question*.

5. Adorable Lies (later known as Mentiras adorables). Gerardo Chijona. Cuba, 1991. 100 min., Color. Spanish.

COMMENTARY: Developed as a script at Robert Redford's Sundance Institute, *Adorable Lies* is the director's debut film, an odd mixture of comedy, melodrama, pseudo–film noir and even "novella." The story as such is based upon a series of confusions, between a would-be screenwriter, Jorge Luis (played by Luis Alberto García) and a blonde named Sissy (played by Isabel Santos) whom he picks up at a film screening either to se-duce her or let her play the lead in his new film (or both).

The plot is a series of confusions between the real-life characters and the roles they are supposedly playing in Jorge Luis' screenplay. For example, Sissy acts the role of a wife whose husband is connected to the black market, and leads the audience on with this charade until we discover it is only part of the role she is playing. Also, since the pair gave each other false names when they met, neither knows the other is married. In fact, Jorge Luis' wife, Flora (played by Thaïs Valdés), believes her husband is having an affair with another man when he walks in on him and Sissy as he imitates a woman with a rose behind his ear, entertaining their young daughter.

The central theme of the film is duplicity — but the most unduplicitous revelation of the film is the realities of Castro's Cuba, showing food and fuel shortages, cramped housing and lack of medical supplies. The actors in the film are competing with these political realities and so it is not easy to laugh with them when they go through a tiresome script, which appears more sad than hysterical. If one had to compare this film to another comedy director's work, it would be Spanish director Pedro Almodóvar, a past master of Spanish "black" humor who dealt with formerly taboo themes, but like Chijona has lost his charm and wit in the forced frenzied comedic situations he created in *Tie Me Up, Tie Me Down* or *Women on the Verge of a Nervous Breakdown*. It is hard to imagine Chijona will ever have enough financial support or comedic talent to bring off even these very well-known but forced "campy" films.

Campy humor may be Chijona's forte, but there is something very melancholy about his work that suspends our belief in the carefree world he wants to create. Ditto Almodóvar. You just do not care about the situations or the characters he

(Chijona) creates on screen. Likewise Almodóvar. But the Spanish director has a greater track record. And his Spanish characters are all immersed in a liberal society that shows off a prosperous Madrid. Chijona's cast members are part of a Communist society that looks mean-spirited and drab, coping with problems of existence. They could not care less about humor, and after watching this film, neither could we. Perhaps the next film we see of his will be conceived in a more realist mode.

6. Las aguas bajan turbias
(Muddy Waters). Hugo del Carril. Argentina, 1951. 85 min., B&W. Spanish.

COMMENTARY: Set around the 1920s in the Province of Misiones, near the frontier with Paraguay, in a yerba maté plantation, a starkly realistic film, *Muddy Waters* is the story of two brothers who sign on to work at plantations where they apparently are treated worse than slaves by the bosses. Anyone who escapes is usually killed or tortured. Sometimes the body of a killed worker floats down the river. A foreman of one plantation is hiring workers (*mensues*) for the next harvest; the Peralta brothers accept, not knowing the bad working conditions. At a bar a drunk tries to rape a prostitute and one of the Peraltas defends her. They have a night of love before he goes away to the plantation. Life conditions at the plantation are miserable. The owner and his foremen (*capangas*) are soulless and cruel. The workers always owe money to the company; they even have to pay for their own boat tickets. Every time they weigh the maté, 25 pounds are stolen. Nobody complains, otherwise they are beaten.

The Peralta brothers are watched because of their rebellious nature. Santos Peralta (played by the director, Hugo del Carril) falls in love with a beautiful girl, the only daughter of an old man resigned to his fate. A party is organized; some of the workers drink too much. The bosses take the workers' women for themselves. One of the bosses has laid eyes on the old man's daughter and goes after her. Her father tries to defend her but the guards stop him. The girl is raped and she does not want to look Peralta in the eyes anymore. He does not understand what is going on. The old man goes blind. The Peraltas visit him and find the foreman trying to embrace the girl. Upon their arrival, the foreman leaves, upset.

The prostitute has fallen in love with the other Peralta brother and goes to the plantation looking for him. The foreman wants to keep her for himself, but she sees Peralta in secret. They are caught together and he is beaten up.

The workers read a letter from another plantation that has organized unions with good results. Meanwhile the old man dies, the girl becomes pregnant, and the Peraltas go to live with her. A group of workers decides to escape, but Santos Peralta stays with his wife and his brother who is still recovering. The runaways are captured and their leader is killed. The older brother is killed and the younger one and his "wife" escape from the plantation as the fervor of freedom spreads, the workers revolt and the plantation is burned. (Press book.)

NOTES: When *Muddy Waters* was first shown at the Venice Film Festival in 1953, it was received as a wonderfully realistic story indigenous to Argentina, where film directors had been turning out nonserious productions up to that point, mostly escapist cinema. This film treats the subject of impoverished workers with stark realism, plenty of suspense and a minimum of dialogue. It was photographed by a "naturalist" cameraman in realistic settings, abetted by a simple but fitting music score and played by actors who aided in accomplishing the director's goal: to tell a real story about real people. It is indeed a pity that *Muddy Waters* is so rarely shown in the United States and elsewhere.

Hugo del Carril was born in Buenos Aires in 1919 and died there in 1989. He became an admirer and protégé of dictator Juan Perón and starred with the latter's wife, Eva, in *The Circus Cavalcade* (1945). However he directed his first film, *Muddy Waters* in 1951, which was approved by the Perón regime, surprisingly since the film dared to show the exploitation of rural workers. When the Perón regime fell in 1955, Carril's career declined. Upon Perón's return to power in 1973, Carril was named head of the National Film Institute, but with Perón's death three years later, he was ousted. Carril made only a handful of films of some worth and *Muddy Waters* is his best. Other titles include *This Land Is Mine* (1960) and *I Killed Facundo* (1975).

7. Aguirre, der Zorn Göttes

(Aguirre, the Wrath of God). Werner Herzog. West Germany/Peru, 1977. 90 min., Color. German/Spanish.

COMMENTARY: A film of power and visual beauty, *Aguirre* is the story of the conqueror Pizarro (as played masterfully by Klaus Kinski) and his expedition along the Amazon River to find the fabled *El Dorado*, or the legendary Peruvian city of gold. It is also an epic tale of a leader gone mad, pushing himself and his men to win power and glory for them in the name of God. Their trek through the jungles is doomed from the beginning, as fever, natural hazards and the Indians themselves set upon the explorers.

Set in the sixteenth century, with Pizarro's supposed intentions to explore and evangelize, the film marvelously depicts Pizarro's descent into madness, greed, racism and religious intolerance. What really keeps the narrative alive is Herzog's marvelous photography on location in the jungles. Herzog also recreates the year 1560 and the intense feeling of Spaniards to explore the New World. He documents the petty squabbles and ambitions of the nobility and the soldiers who seek to distance themselves from each other and their king, Philip II, because of their greed for gold. In one scene, the legitimate commander of the expedition, Pedro de Ursua, and his mistress Inéz are murdered as Aguirre declares himself to be Emperor of Peru and El Dorado.

With provisions running low and under continual attack by the Indians, Aguirre will allow no retreat and unwittingly prepares his own and the group's destruction. In one of the film's final scenes, Aguirre's 14-year-old daughter is killed by an arrow and Aguirre himself is found alone on a raft with a huge group of chattering monkeys floating out to sea. What Herzog has done is to create a film about power, and an ambitious psychopath, admirably played by Klaus Kinski, who tries to build an empire and loses it. Like Carlos Saura's *El Dorado* (1988), it is certainly one of the best films in German to treat such a uniquely indigenous Latin American subject.

NOTES: Werner Herzog's career as a film director soared with the release of *Aguirre*; he became one of the leaders of the New German Cinema by utilizing a Latin American theme for his masterwork. He was to return to Latin America one more time, in 1982, to Brazil, where he made *Fitzcarraldo*, starring Klaus Kinski once again, about a man so determined to bring grand opera to the Amazon in Brazil that he attempts to haul a ship over the mountains. Once again Herzog was fascinated by South American locales as well as Latino obsessive behavior and tenacity. In fact, the documentary filmmaker, Les Blank, recounts Herzog's (and Kinski's) story of the *Fitzcarraldo* production in his own short film entitled *Burden of Dreams*.

Klaus Kinski made his career playing ferociously obsessive characters in many

Klaus Kinski in the title role of Werner Herzog's *Aguirre, the Wrath of God* (1977), madly caressing the hair of his daughter who has just been shot with an arrow by the Peruvian Indians as Aguirre tries to escape the onslaught down river.

of Werner Herzog's films. In one scene during the making of *Fitzcarraldo*, when Herzog demanded a retake of Kinski floating down a wild river on a ferryboat gone berserk, Kinski reputedly said he would shoot Herzog with a revolver if he even dared approach the actor to do the scene. Kinski died in 1991, having established himself as a brilliant but generally unbridled performer.

Aguirre, the Wrath of God see *Aguirre, der Zorn Göttes*

8. Ahí está el detalle (That's the Problem). Juan Bustillo Oro. Mexico, 1940. 112 min., Sepia. Spanish.

COMMENTARY: Pacita, the maid, asks her boyfriend, Cantinflas (Mario Moreno), to kill Bobby, a local gangster. Her bosses, Dolores and her jealous husband Cayetano, are arguing when they hear the shots. Cayetano lies about a trip he must take and departs. Cantinflas has really killed a dog named Bobby. Using the nickname of "El Fox Terrier," Cantinflas walks into the house and tries to blackmail Dolores with some letters. Cayetano returns with the police just in time to prevent a scene of "adultery." Pacita, the maid, hides Bobby and Cantinflas in the pantry, while the latter drinks and smokes a cigar. When Cantinflas is discovered, Dolores tries to explain his presence by saying that he is her brother, Leonardo, who is looking for her to claim a bequest. Cantinflas is happy until Clotilde, Leonardo's wife, arrives on the scene with her eleven children. Cayetano asks Cantinflas to marry Clotilde, but the wedding is interrupted when the police arrive looking for the real Leonardo, who they believe has killed the gangster, Bobby. During the trial, Cantinflas admits he killed Bobby (the dog), contradicting the arguments of his own attorney. He is given a death sentence but is saved at the last moment when the real Leonardo shows up and confesses his crime, having killed the real gangster. (Press book.)

At times hilarious and confusing, *Ahí está el detalle* may not be everyone's brand of comedy, it is representative of the Cantinflas character and style (see Notes).

NOTES: Mario Moreno "Cantinflas" (1911–1993) was one of Mexico's enduring stars and made about fifty films. Starting out as a song and dance man in the mid–1930s, he then gained popularity as a circus clown, acrobat and buffoon. *Ahí está el detalle*, his second film, made him a national success, but Cantinflas is known more internationally for his role as Passepartout in Mike Todd's *Around the World in 80 Days* (1956) and *Pepe* (1960). He made his last film appearance in 1978. Cantinflas attributes his success to the character he created in Mexican cinema — the *pelado*, a native of Mexico City's slums, a humble, streetwise character who relies on wit and guile, an astute person with an open heart who uses language to obfuscate, confuse and turn the tables against the rich and law-abiding. Cantinflas demonstrated a gift for verbal invention, improvising fully on every script, creating the verb "cantinflear," which means talking a lot but saying absolutely nothing. A perfect example is the nonsensical, infectious double talk in the courtroom scene of *Ahí está el detalle*. Cantinflas was an original talent. No other actor approached his craft with such exceptional gifts.

9. Alambrista (The Illegal). Robert M. Young. United States, 1977. 90 min., Color. English/Spanish.

COMMENTARY: *Alambrista* is a drama about a Mexican illegal, his experiences in the United States, his humiliations, and his final deportation, all of which mark him bitterly for the rest of his life.

The film develops slowly as we observe Roberto (Domingo Ambriz) leaving his wife, child, mother and his own farm in Mexico to find employment in the United States Expecting to send back money every six months after securing a job, he is forewarned by his mother of his father's bad experience. Roberto goes from one negative event to another; he works extremely hard and receives little pay. He has a clandestine affair with a waitress who picks him up on the street. Caught by the *migra*, he is sent back to the border awaiting deportation. After being smuggled back into the United States, he watches his long-lost father die at a strike-breaking rally and realizes the latter had married an American woman and deserted his own family for her.

NOTES: *Alambrista* is a very famous small film, a forerunner of the newly formed Chicano school of cinema, films that deal with the Chicanos and their problems in the Southwest, California and along the Mexican border. Its director, Robert M. Young, is mainly known as a maker of documentaries but is also responsible for some of the finest docudramas in American cinema, including *The Ballad of Gregorio Cortez* (1983), another fascinating film on a Chicano theme.

10. Alicia en el pueblo de las maravillas (Alice in Wonder Town). Daniel Diaz Torres. Cuba, 1991. 93 min., B&W. Spanish.

COMMENTARY: Produced by ICAIC, the governmental cinema organization of Cuba, *Alicia en el pueblo de las maravillas* is a modern satire about a young woman bureaucrat who is sent to a small town called Maravillas ("wonders") to do her job. The town is indeed very strange — snakes and monkeys wander about the center of town; in her hotel, swarms of cockroaches besiege Alice at night. Her bathroom opens into a room next door, where she witnesses a man shaving. Moreover, the people that Alice (played convincingly by Thais Valdes)

interviews are mostly officials who have been fired from their jobs. The film is full of surreal images. The credits for the film are placed against illustrations from Lewis Carroll's *Alice in Wonderland*, but the film has nothing to do with these drawings. Clearly, this is an in-Cuba film whose allusions will be better understood by Cubans than by a mass audience. Although the film is beautifully produced and directed, it had one limited showing in Miami Beach; it has since become a sought-after pirated videotape.

NOTE: In an article published in the *New York Times* on June 29, 1991, "A Film Is Banished, but Its Sly Grin Still Lingers," correspondent Howard W. French writes from Havana that "lines wrapped around entire city blocks" to see this film. He adds: "Toward the end of the film, when 'Viva Fidel!' is chanted repeatedly, ... viewers are left with doubt over whether the spectacle is meant as an endorsement of Cuba's leader of 32 years or a risque, if ambiguous, slap." The director said the movie was intended as "shock therapy...to rouse Cubans from their double-standard morality, indolence, self-importance and nonrevolutionary attitudes." Whatever the reason, the film was yanked from theatres without explanation after four days of screenings.

Alice in Wonder Town see *Alicia en el pueblo de las maravillas*

11. Allá en el rancho grande (Way Down on the Rancho Grande). Fernando de Fuentes. Mexico, 1936. 95 min., B&W. Spanish.

COMMENTARY: Fernando de Fuentes is a practitioner of the old-style Mexican musical. This 1936 film stars Tito Guizar, who made his reputation singing Cole Porter's "Begin the Beguine" in the United States. However, in Mexico he is very well known as a dramatic actor with a musical talent as a leading tenor and guitarist. In this film he plays a ranch foreman who conceals his love for Esther Fernández, an orphan who lives with a shrewish vixen. Before he loses the heroine to his rival, Guizar sings many melodies against a fairly realistic background of life on a big hacienda. Of course, he gets the girl and the film ends on a happy note.

NOTE: The director decided to remake the very same film in 1949, with Jorge Negrete in the Guizar role and Lilia del Valle as the orphaned girl, Cruz. But this time, Fuentes used Cinecolor. The best features of this enterprise are Negrete's renditions of songs like "Alla en el rancho grande," and "Ojos tapatíos." There is also a splendid rendition of the old favorite, the Mexican hat dance — "El jarabe tapatío" — as well as a real old-time cockfight, all except the kill. This remake surprises us by its great attention to folkloric detail and certainly bolsters our view of Mexico of the late forties.

12. Allá lejos y hace tiempo
(Far Away and Long Ago). Manuel Antín. Argentina, 1978. 91 min., Color. Spanish.

COMMENTARY: This film is a poetic rendering of an autobiographical novel by Guillermo Hudson — about the memories of his childhood and the images of the mysterious Argentine pampa, its gauchos, its women, its witchcraft. Hudson is the protagonist whose youth and deep friendship with old gauchos places him on the threshold of life.

We learn about his fascination with nature and the mysteries of the human soul. Hudson himself was a dedicated naturalist and a master of English prose. (He was the author of *Green Mansions*, a spirited tale about Rima, the girl of the Amazon jungle who meets an adventurer in his quest for truth and beauty.)

The director, Manuel Antín, has created a film with a pristine, impressionist style in a nostalgically revealing vein. The film stars Juan José Carrero as Hudson, with Leon Ormanso, Dora Baret, Walter Santana and Susu Pecoraro in various roles. Fortunately, the film is available in the United States on video cassette.

NOTES: Manuel Antín was born in 1926 in Argentina. He began his career in the arts as a playwright, wrote some scripts for short films and began to direct in 1960 with his first fictional feature, *La cifra impar*, based on Julio Cortázar's short story "Cartas a Mama." The majority of his films deal with Argentine literary works and themes. They are *Circe* (1964), *Psique y sexo* (1965), *Castigo al traidor* (1966), *Don Segundo Sombra* (1969), *Juan Manuel Rosas*, *La sartén por el mango* (1972), *Allá lejos y hace tiempo* (1978), and *La invitación* (1982), based on the works of Julio Cortázar, Roa Bastos, Ricardo Guiraldes, Guillermo Hudson and Beatriz Guido. Antín is the author of several volumes of verse and plays and continues to live and work in Argentina.

Alsino and the Condor see *Alsino y el condor*

13. Alsino y el condor (Alsino and the Condor). Miguel Littín. Nicaragua, 1982. 89 min., Color. Spanish/English.

COMMENTARY: *Alsino* is based on a wonderful short novel of the same name by a Chilean novelist, Pedro Prado, in which a boy with a hunchback finally attains the kingdom of heaven when wings sprout from his infirmity and he flies heavenward, only to plummet to earth like Icarus. This *Alsino y el condor* is yet another variation on the Icarus myth.

Alsino is a twelve-year-old peasant boy living with his grandmother on a farm in a mountain village in Nicaragua. He has been friendly with Lucia, a peasant girl his own age who is the daughter of Manuel, a guerrilla leader. The time is the 1980s. Nicaragua is torn by war, and this particular village is harshly ruled by government soldiers. Frank (American actor Dean Stockwell) is a military advisor based there. Frank befriends Alsino, whose dream is to fly freely, like a bird, perhaps in Frank's military helicopter, a Condor. But Frank's experimental flight with Alsino is to no avail. Alsino prefers to leap off the branch of a tall tree instead, is seriously injured and becomes a hunchback.

As Alsino gets older, he is constantly tormented and deluded by whores and swindlers of the town. Hungry and impoverished, he seeks out Manuel to join the guerrillas, observing death and misery all around him. The guerrillas adopt him into their community. Alsino finds Manuel's dead body floating in a nearby river; his grandmother also dies of starvation and illness. The villagers, with the aid of Frank, try to assuage their grief with one last all-out offensive against the military that has ruined their lives.

Alsino y el condor is a maddening blend, a politically angry film with the style of a mournful fable. It is not as gripping as the political films of Costa-Gavras (*Missing*, for example), but it educates as it entertains, chiefly because of the performance of Alan Esquivel. It also highlights the real events behind the fiction film — the leftist Sandinista rebel overthrow of the dictator Anastasio Somoza in 1979. The story of this young boy who wants to fly is expressed in a symbolic parallel between the magical flight of Alsino and the real Condor (the North American military professional), set against the background of the war. The film gives us an idealized view of guerrilla movements in Latin America and often transcends its immediate goals

because of its extremely sophisticated style and acting.

NOTES: *Alsino y el condor* was the first fiction feature film made in Nicaragua. It was a Mexican-Cuban co-production. Littín said of it, "We had no money, only $60,000 for raw stock and some technical things. The rest was human effort you cannot buy with dollars. With more money the picture might have been easier to make, but it would have been less passionate. Every day was a struggle, and many times I thought we would never end the movie. But when it was finished, I was sorry."

Dean Stockwell's career received a tremendous boost when he appeared in this film. Known primarily as a child actor of the 1940s in American cinema, Stockwell's venture into foreign locactions has served him well; he made *Sons and Lovers* in England, *Rapture* in France and *Alsino* in Nicaragua, transcending his image of adorable American boy to become a multi-faceted actor willing to take chances in international productions. In America he most recently played a deranged saturnine homosexual in David Lynch's *Blue Velvet* (1986) and a comical Mafia don in Jonathan Demme's *Married to the Mob*, for which he received a Supporting Oscar nomination in 1988.

14. **Amargo mar** (Bitter Sea). Antonio Eguino. Bolivia, 1985. 96 min., Color. Spanish.

COMMENTARY: *Amargo mar* is a fascinating film based upon the Pacific War of 1879, one of the most tragic episodes in the history of Bolivia, when neighboring Chile invaded that country and took possession of its coastline. The film deals with both political and social implications of this event. Although the film has several actors in starring roles, the characters they play seem to recreate many diverse political points of view — duplicitous military men, pompous politicos, evil industrialists, Chilean sympathizers. The film leads us into confrontations between all these groups in some fabulous natural geographical settings, all to fine effect.

NOTES: Antonio Eguino is one of the original members of the Ukamau group of Bolivian directors, founded by Jorge Sanjinés in the mid–sixties. He collaborated with the Sanjinés on two of his most famous films, *Yawar Mallku* and *El coraje del pueblo*. But Eguino is primarily known for three films: *Pueblo chico* (1974), *Chuquiago* (1977) and *Amargo Mar*. A flawed filmmaker, Eguino has inspired political intentions that sometimes exceed his gifts as a practitioner of commercial cinema, producing fascinating, yet often mishandled, uninspired results on the screen.

15. La amiga (The Girlfriend).

Jeanine Meerapfel. Argentina/West Germany, 1988. 108 min., Color. Spanish.

COMMENTARY: Very similiar to other films that deal with Argentina's *desaparecidos* (literally "disappeared ones" or missing persons), *La amiga* begins in Buenos Aires in 1945. Two girlfriends swear everlasting friendship and promise to become actresses as they dangle their legs on a bridge overlooking the Rio de la Plata.

The scene shifts to twenty years later, where Raquel (Cipe Lincovsky), who has indeed become a famous Argentine actress meets María (Liv Ullman), who lives in the same neighborhood and is married to an electrician, Pancho (Federico Luppi), with three children.

The scene shifts again to 1976, the military takeover of Buenos Aires. María's eldest son, Carlos, has been abducted by a special commando. As she searches for him, she tries to use the influence of her actress girlfriend, Raquel. The latter is also threatened by a bomb attack and is forced to return to Berlin, the city she had to leave as a child

when Hitler came to power. Meanwhile, María joins the group called "Mothers of the Plaza de Mayo," searching for her lost son.

Maria and Raquel meet again in Germany, when María traces the whereabouts of the still missing Carlos through a friend of his. Although their old friendship is there, the political events that have shaped their lives have changed the two women.

The scene shifts once again to December 1983. The military dictatorship is at an end, and Raquel returns from West Germany. She urges María to accept the possible death of Carlos, but the latter refuses. The women represent two voices from two countries torn apart by dictatorship. Some women want to forgive and to forget; but others, like María, insist on remembering the past. The women continue their friendship, abetted by their losses and their memories.

Liv Ullman is extremely moving as María, and newcomer Cipe Lincovsky is also excellent. Lincovsky herself experienced exile under Argentina's military dictatorship and was forced to live in Spain for five years.

NOTES: Although this film has received little world distribution, its subject was close to the heart of Liv Ullman, who is a diplomat for the international children's relief organization UNICEF.

Cipe Lincovsky is a native Argentine actress who began her career in Argentina's Yiddish theatre. She has done many one-woman shows there and in Europe.

The director, Jeanine Meerapfel, was born in Buenos Aires but has lived in the Federal Republic of Germany since 1964, studying at the Film Institute there. *La amiga* is her seventh film, and her first international feature among other documentary films she has directed since 1980.

16. El amor bandido (Bandit Love or Outlaw Love or Beloved Lover). Bruno Barreto. Brazil, 1979. 95 min., Color. Portuguese.

COMMENTARY: The first film made after Barreto's extremely succeessful *Doña Flor e seus dois maridos, El amor bandido* stars Paulo Garnieri as Toninho, a taxi driver, hustler and killer, and Cristina Ache as Sandra, a prostitute shill who lures fares with Toninho to kill cab drivers and split the profits (and the sex) after he dispatches them.

Sandra's father, Galvão (Paulo Gracindo), is a detective assigned to the case in pursuit of this São Paulo lowlife punk and accidentally runs across his accomplice daughter while on the job. Galvão's reaction to Sandra, as he sees her dance in a strip-joint, is a mixed one — part lust, part caring, all senseless. This film recalls Paul Schrader's 1978 film *Hardcore* starring George C. Scott, about a wayward Michigan girl who ends up in porno films in Los Angeles. Here the focus is on Toninho, but why the director chose to make a film about a hustler and a prostitute in Rio de Janeiro is beyond anyone's guess.

The film does have some graphic softcore sexual sequences, and Barreto aptly captures the grittiness of the city and the lowlifes who populate it. The plot can be twisty — for example, Sandra first meets Toninho after his lover, a male transvestite, has committed suicide. There is an instant sexual attraction between them — "outlaw love" — and the stars' passionate moments practically melt the screen.

El amor bandido carries no moral weight as a film about 1970s Brazilian life. Nobody in the film has feelings of guilt or remorse. There are some tender scenes beautifully played between father and daughter, but the lead characters are unapologetic; they were spawned in a dog-eat-dog society and, to paraphrase Rita Hayworth's great song in the 1946 Charles Vidor film *Gilda*, "they do what they do."

The real star of the film is Lauro Escorel Filho's camera, as it weaves through Copacabana and its sleazy atmosphere, its heavy air filled with the terror of murder and the desperation of its degenerates compelled to kill for cash. *El amor bandido* is a chilling slice-of-life film set in a place where there seems to be no choice beyond "kill or be killed".

17. El amor es una mujer gorda (Love Is a Fat Woman). Alejandro Agresti. Argentina, 1987. 80 min., B&W. Spanish.

COMMENTARY: Agresti's film is the story of a journalist, José (Elio Marchi), who loses his job with a visiting American film company and wanders the street, sleeping wherever he can, in search of his *desaparecida* girlfriend. It is yet another film about the bold contradictions and absurdities of Argentine society. Agresti's style is very much Wellsian in approach to his material. He uses oddly angled shots, extremely stylized camera angles, carefully framed black and white compositions, even geometric camera movements and an elliptical style to tell a simple story — limned with vitriolic humor and sarcasm — of a loser who cannot deal with Argentina's complacency after suffering the trials and tribulations of a fascist dictatorship. His wanderings become a sort of political and spiritual pilgrimage. On the streets of Buenos Aires, he meets a blind man, a tango player, an American movie director and an intellectual — all symbolic characters who are blind to Argentina's past. Much like the picaresque adventures of a Tom Jones, but without the sexuality or ribaldry, José's wanderings serve the denunciatory tone of the film. There is disillusionment and futility everywhere, as well as a heroic dimension to the character which Agresti catches beautifully.

José cannot accept deceit on any level. For example, he loses his job because he objects to the film the American company is making, a fradulent picture about Argentine misery. He prefers to live on the periphery of society, searching for a woman whose death he cannot accept as he discovers himself an amnesiac longing for a society rooted in his past.

NOTES: Alejandro Agresti made this film, his second feature, when he was 26 years old. Fond of stories that deal with the past and themes of memory, Agresti said of himself: "The street is my real inspiration. I was raised on the streets; everything I put in my films is based on my experience of life on the streets." This film was financed partly by the Dutch firm Allarts and was processed in Holland because Agresti sought exile there after offending the Argentine dictatorship.

And So It Is see *Ukamau*

18. Ángel de fuego (Angel of Fire). Dana Rotberg. Mexico, 1991. 90 min., Color. Spanish.

COMMENTARY: *Ángel de fuego* was first shown in the United States as part of a film series entitled "New Trends in Mexican Cinema," which followed a fascinating retrospective, "Mexican Film and the Literary Tradition," presented by UCLA in 1991 and then by New York's Museum of Modern Art in 1992. Rotberg's film certainly represents the culmination of Mexican talent and indicates the "new trends" and directions of contemporary Mexican cinema. The press book calls the film "a colorful contemporary fable of a young female fire-eater" that "explores the underbelly of society, dealing with strong themes such as incest, fanatical religion, power."

The circus is Rotberg's principal metaphor to tell the story of Alma (Evangelina Sosa), a trapeze artist and fire-eater, abandoned by her mother and involved in an incestuous affair with her father, who leaves her pregnant just before he dies. Alma becomes an itinerant carnival worker, traveling to poor neighborhoods. She joins a marionette theatre and promptly falls in love with the owner's son, Sacramento (Roberto Sosa, the star's real life brother). But before she can think of marrying Sacramento, she must undergo a rigorous purification ritual for her blasphemy and incest. The film moves relentlessly toward an astounding conclusion: Alma's total immolation and purification as she literally becomes the "angel of fire" of the title. The color camera work is excellent, and Evangelina Sosa gives a riveting performance as a woman who seeks retribution through death. Many Old Testament tales are presented as the circus and marionette troupes act them out, giving a multi-level dimension to a rather simple morality tale sometimes complicated by many shifts of time frame. Incest and women's rights had never been addressed so openly. Rotberg's entertaining but thought-provoking film is a new and welcome direction for the modern Mexican cinema.

19. El ángel exterminador (The Exterminating Angel). Luis Buñuel. Mexico, 1962. 95 min., Spanish.

COMMENTARY: *El ángel exterminador* should be considered a kind of rehearsal film for Buñuel's great 1972 French masterpiece, *The Discreet Charm of the Bourgeoisie*. Made exactly ten years earlier on location in Mexico City, the story concerns a group of upper-class guests at a high-society party at the Nobile mansion who suddenly discover that they are unable to leave the room for days on end. As food and drink dwindle, so does their civilized behavior. For every guest at the party, there is a different plot or subplots in the film. Some plots concern adultery, greed, lust, lack of free will, death and conformity.

As the guests realize they are trapped, some of them react with various degrees of boredom, annoyance and hostility. One man has a heart attack, and his body is hustled discreetly into a closet. An engaged couple try to sneak in a little lovemaking in another cramped closet. When they become frustrated because of interruption, they commit suicide. Another couple, an incestuous brother and sister team, fight with the host for a secreted box of morphine. Conditions gradually worsen, and no one can escape the isolation or the abulic nature of his own personality.

The only character who is a real free spirit is Leticia (played by the beautiful blond Silvia Pinal), who holds the key of the mystery to end the group's bondage in the mansion. By suggesting to everyone that they resume their places at exactly the moment they became trapped, she frees the group. However, Buñuel has one last trick up his sleeve. Thankful for their freedom, the guests celebrate their joy at the local Catholic church — and become trapped once again as shots are heard in the street (a revolution has begun mysteriously) and a group of sheep streams into the church.

El ángel exterminador has some wonderful performances, especially by Silvia Pinal, Enrique Rambal, and Claudio Brook, but it is Gabriel Figueroa's wonderful realistic photography and the lack of a music score that make the film a riveting experience. Buñuel's later *Discreet Charm* had color, CinemaScope and the sweetness of the French language, but its message about conformity and revolution is exactly the same. Both are bizarre films; available on video cassette, they deserve a comparative viewing.

Angel Hair see *Pubis ángélical*

Angel of Fire see *Ángel de fuego*

Another Dawn see *Distinto amanacer*

20. Antonieta. Carlos Saura. Mexico/France/Spain, 1981. 104 min., Color. French/Spanish.

COMMENTARY: Filmed in Paris and Mexico City, *Antonieta* tells the story of a journalist seeking an explanation for the suicides of women, and in particular, the suicide of the Mexican aristocrat Antonieta Rivas Mercado, who killed herself in the Notre Dame cathedral in February of 1931. Jean-Claude Carrière's excellent screenplay presents Isabelle Adjani as Antonieta, frustrated by love, art, politics, but always sensitive to the era and the society around her. Hanna Schygulla is the reporter who probes for answers to the mysterious suicide, reflecting on Mexican society of the 1920s, watching film clips about Mexican history, interviewing people who were acquainted with Antonieta. We discover, after nearly two hours of film, that Antonieta had written a series of 87 love letters to Manuel Lozano, a homosexual painter, to whom she will always remain faithful. The film is a compilation of semidocumentary and pseudodramatic events based loosely upon this woman's extraordinary suicide in Notre Dame. Although the actresses Adjani and Schygulla give credible performances, one wonders why the Carrière-Saura screenplay meanders over this subject, which at times seems disjointed because of extraordinary time shifts between the 1920s and the present. Saura's talent as a director has been to film wonderful screenplays about memory, such as *Sweet Hours*, *Elisa, vida mía*, *La prima Angélica*, and *Raise Ravens*, all excellent Spanish films of the seventies and eighties. Although the film does have wonderful production values, beautiful sets, excellent camera work and beautiful Eastmancolor, overall the viewer is left frustrated by the lack of

Revolutionary violence in Glauber Rocha's film *Antonio das Mortes* (1968), in which Mauricio do Valle (left foreground) plays the fabled outlaw of the title.

real insight into the life and death of Antonieta.

NOTES: Much like his contemporaries, Michelangelo Antonioni (*Red Desert*), Wim Wenders (*Paris, Texas*), and José Luis Borau (*Rio abajo*), Saura has filmed abroad, in Mexico for the first time, making a distinctly European/ Latin American film depicting a Mexican woman's life and death against the background of her own country and history. Saura would attempt to repeat this experiment twice more, in the late eighties in Costa Rica for the filming of *El Dorado* and in Argentina in the early nineties with *El sur* (*South*). He struggles to seek new locations and extend his Spanish vision of the world into Latin American locales.

21. Antonio das Mortes (Anthony of the Death). Glauber Rocha. Brazil, 1968. 100 min., Color. Portuguese.

COMMENTARY: Antonio das Mortes was a retired hunter who tracked down and killed two of the most famous outlaws (*cangaçeiros*) in Brazilian folklore, Lampiao and Corisco, in 1938. With their deaths came the end of an epic age of lawlessness, when the outlaws roamed the northeast backlands (*sertão*) of Brazil. The entire action of the film is set against the mystic and folkloric traditions of Brazil. After killing the outlaws and seizing power and property in the name of the nation, Antonio then undergoes a mystical transformation, becoming an advocate for the dispossessed; he later embraces and foments revolution against the landowners.

There is much sex and violence in *Antonio das Mortes*, intercut with dances and songs that give the film a cathartic power and a feeling of timelessness that together assuage the classic struggle between life and death. The violence is at times lyrical, abetted by a true revolutionary fervor that suggests future chaos if radical political change is not in the offing. Mauricio do Valle gives the performance of his life as Antonio, the fanatic killer whose real conversion to law and order is the basis of this film.

Critic Burns Hollyman says that *Antonio das Mortes* uses color, style and character to present an amalgam of Brazil's "Tropicalist" image. Rocha himself said the stylistic elements were "very important in Brazilian civilization," possibly because this film holds up a mirror to Brazilian cinematic reality that accurately reflects the aesthetic and political concerns of the country in 1968, under control by a repressive military regime. This was Rocha's last radical cry before he went into exile for ten years. Like other *Cinema Nôvo* filmmakers, Rocha wanted to project a visage that would place Brazil in touch with itself on an unconscious national level.

On another level, Rocha manipulates and disrupts traditional "classic cinema" by incorporating a number of diverse cinematic influences in several sections of the film. Eisenstein, Godard and Brecht are utilized and reworked in a Brazilian setting. Neo-Realism is also represented, for instance by the long takes of dancing masses, since *Cinema Nôvo* directors wanted to portray reality as accurately as possible. As a result, the film, shot on location in the northeast (Milagres), is as authentic as it can be. Although folk dances and music undercut the cinematic reality of the film, Rocha feels that by inventing a rough and new narrative structure which incorporates these elements, he has created a new mode of cinematic expression, imperfect but appropriate for his purposes. Rocha said, "It is better to have a form that is badly polished but new."

NOTES: Born in Bahia, Brazil, in 1938, Rocha began his career as a promoter of films and film clubs. He later became a film critic and then a maker of short films until he produced and directed his first effort, *Barravento* (*Tempest*) in 1962. He is primarily known as the spokesman for the *Cinema Nôvo* movement, favoring a "poor" cinema as the medium by which to interpret reality and foment social change. Some of his outstanding films examined in this book are *Deus e o diabo na terra de sol* (*Black God, White Devil*) and *Terra em transe* (*Land in Anguish*). He is also remembered for several books about Brazilian cinema, and especially for his leadership in the *Cinema Nôvo* movement. Said Rocha in a 1971 interview: "Whenever one finds a director willing to film reality and to oppose hypocrisy and repression of intellectual censorship, there one will find the living spirit of *Cinema Nôvo*. Wherever there exists a director of whatever origin or age willing to place his art and work at the mighty causes of his day, there one finds the living spirit of *Cinema Nôvo*." He died prematurely in 1980 before the showing of his last film, *A idade da terra*, which was presented at the Venice Film Festival of 1981.

22. El apando (The Heist or Solitary). Felipe Cazals. Mexico, 1975. 90 min., Color. Spanish.

COMMENTARY: The program notes for *El apando* call it "a prison film unlike any other. In fact, as a result of the film's unrelenting depiction of a prison in which student activists were incarcerated after the 1968 uprising, the prison Lecumberri (the Black Place) was finally closed by the government. The film's author, José Revueltas, one of a family of political activists and intellectuals in Mexico, was more than familiar with the subject matter: Revueltas was a political prisoner at Lecumberri, a prison which was designed to hold the most incorrigible and hardened criminals in the entire Mexican penal system." (Program

Notes.) The film is based on Revueltas's novel of the same name.

El apando is a story about corruption behind the walls of the Lecumberri prison. The *apando* is a two-by-two foot punishment cell. The film deals with three criminals sharing an *apando*. During their confinement in this tiny space, the prisoners reflect on dope trading, corrupt guards, body searches of female visitors and homosexual acts in which they were forced to participate. We never know the reasons for the prisoner's internment, but we watch them often brutalized by the vicious attacks of their jailers. Not for the squeamish, *El apando* is good melodrama, but has very little to say about prison reform. It prefers to revel in its excesses of brutality.

NOTES: Director Felipe Cazals is primarily known in Mexico and abroad for his seventh film, *Canoa* (1975), an incisive docudrama based upon a real event that took place in the village of San Miguel de Canoa, dealing with antistudent hysteria. He continues to direct films within a spirit of freedom usually approved by the Mexican government.

Cazals was born in Mexico in 1937. He studied filmmaking at IDHEC in Paris and on his return to Mexico made many fairly forgettable short films. His first full-length feature was *La manzana de discordia* (1968), which he made independently. He founded, together with Arturo Ripstein, the Cine Independiente de Mexico, a cooperative of young filmmakers which produced one film, *Familiaridades*, in 1969. By 1970, Cazals had entered the mainstream Mexican film industry, directing *Emiliano Zapata*, then *El jardín de Tía Isabel* (1971) and *Aquellos años* (1972), all dealing with Mexican historical figures. In *Los que viven donde sopla el viento suave* (1973), he returned to the form of the documentary, making *Canoa* in 1975, *El apando* in 1976 and *Las Poquianchis* shortly thereafter.

23. Apartment Zero. Martin Donovan. Argentina/Great Britain, 1988. 124 min., Color. English/Spanish.

COMMENTARY: *Apartment Zero* owes much of its appeal to its excellent actors: Colin Firth as a repressed proprietor of an arthouse cinema in Buenos Aires, and Hart Bochner as his tenant who may be a member of a death squad financed by the American government. Yet the stunning locale, Buenos Aires, is the real star of the story. Most of the film is a cat-and-mouse tale dealing with repressed homosexuality and the discovery of Bochner's real identity. It has a unique twisted ending, very reminiscent of Alfred Hitchcock's great thriller, *Psycho*. Some allusions are made to the current Argentine political context of *desaparecidos*, serial murderers and foreign intervention by mercenaries, but the film is basically a love story between two men — love and betrayal set in exotic Buenos Aires, still an ominous, fascinating city full of living ghosts.

NOTES: Martin Donovan is an Argentine who has lived many years in the United Kingdom. *Apartment Zero* represents his best effort to date on international screens as producer, director and scenarist.

Ascent to Heaven see *Subida al cielo*

24. At Play in the Fields of the Lord. Hector Babenco. Brazil/U.S., 1991. 185 minutes, Color. Niarunian dialect/English.

COMMENTARY: Hector Babenco, who internationally is known primarily for *Pixote* (Brazil) and *Kiss of the Spiderwoman* (Brazil/Argentina/U.S.), made this grandiose epic in the Amazon rain forest in Brazil. The subject is American missionaries seeking to convert the Niarunian indians to Christianity. Using Peter Matthiessen's massive novel for his screenplay, Babenco tells several stories simultaneously, about the Christian couples, John Lithgow and Darryl Hannah and Aidan Quinn and Kathy Bates, all Quakers who have just arrived in the jungle from the United States. The most fascinating tale is about Moon, played by Tom Berenger, who is half American Indian; his loss of faith in Christian ideals has prompted him to live among the Niaruna while searching for his true identity. But the real star of the film is the jungle locations, whether seen from aerial views or at ground level. And the Niarunian performers are very sympathetic, especially during the scenes of illness and contamination. *At Play in the Fields of the Lord* is really about preserving the life and beauties of the rain forest, a dazzling paradise wonderfully recorded by the Brazilian photographer Lauro Escorel. Matthiessen's novel is worthy of the grand production it has received, and the film deserves to be seen for its spectacularly photographed, mystical milieu alone.

NOTES: Born in 1946 to Jewish immigrants in Buenos Aires, Hector Babenco traveled extensively internationally before settling in Brazil. He worked as an extra in spaghetti westerns made in Italy and Spain before he attempted his own first film, *Pixote* (1981), which brought him international success. His other best known films are *Kiss of the Spiderwoman* (1985) and *At Play in the Fields of the Lord*. Despite the star power of Jack Nicholson and Meryl Streep, his first American film, *Ironweed* (1987), was a critical disaster.

Bad Connection see *Malayunta*

25. Ballad of the Little Soldier.

Werner Herzog. Nicaragua/W. Germany, 1984. 45 min., Color. Spanish/German.

COMMENTARY: Another surprisingly short but incisive documentary that tells of the tragedy of the Miskito Indians of Nicaragua, *Ballad of the Little Soldier* is mainly an interview film shot in refugee camps, where these Indians tell of murder, torture and pillaging in their first-person, placidly stoic manner.

The "little soldiers" are the ten- or twelve-year-old boys who comprise the army. These young commandos express their willingness to fight the good fight and die for their country — but for which country? The Miskitos were allied with the Sandinistas against the dictator Somoza, but now they are warring with the Sandinistas, who want to keep them prisoner, with no guarantee that they will ever be free to pursue their own cultural imperatives.

The film shows how these brave Miskito Indians have been caught in the crossfire of two politically unsound groups and have suffered extreme losses as a consequence — losses of their crops, their villages, their very lives. This led to the 1981 "Red Christmas" atrocities — the murder-mutilation of seven government soldiers, followed by the forced resettlement of several Miskito villages after the Indians tried to retaliate. Literally thousands of Miskitos have been slaughtered. But the film is remarkable because it shows, for the very first time, that not since the Spanish conquest had any tribe of Indians carried out armed resistance until this era of the Miskito in Nicaragua.

The filmmaker, Werner Herzog, shows the Indians as pawns of the Somoza regime, the marxist military junta and even the Sandinistas, who were once allies of the Indians but justified their relocation because they momentarily supported the guerrillas. In this tangled web of history and intrigue, it is the children of the Miskitos, being trained as commandos in an unidentified base in Honduras, who are the real pawns in an ideological battle beyond their comprehension. They have been brainwashed, which reminded Herzog of the kind of ideological brainwashing the Nazis performed on their youth during World War II — a point well made. Herzog concludes that war, and this particular war, is idiocy, but he has sought to capture the glow of the persistent human spirit despite such incredible adversity.

26. The Ballad of Gregorio Cortez. Robert M. Young. U.S., 1983. 99 min., Color. Spanish/English.

COMMENTARY: Another "Chicano film" very different from Young's earlier effort, *Alambrista*, *The Ballad of Gregorio Cortez* recounts a real event that took place in Texas in June 1901, when the protagonist murdered a sheriff after Cortez misunderstood a question the law officer had asked him. At a trial, it was revealed the sheriff had turned the question into a threat which prompted Cortez's response and caused the latter to flee some 450 miles, pursued for 11 days by a 600-man posse led by Texas Rangers. Cortez gave himself up when he realized his family had been arrested and were being held as hostages.

The film is divided into two parts. The first is reminiscent of the *Rashomon* structure of flashbacks, with witnesses recounting different views of the same event. The second comprises the jury trial and the *fait accompli* of Cortez's guilt.

Young's film version of this real event emphasizes Texas's discrimination against Mexicans — the inhumane treatment Cortez received once captured, and the predictable outcome of his trial. In reality, Cortez served twelve years of a fifty-year sentence and was pardoned by the governor of Texas. Both the trial and the sentence were unjust. Eduardo Jaime Olmos plays Cortez with honesty and depth, moving among the authentic settings with a grace and sadness that renders his character more humane than the stereotyped Texans, who seem to be participating in a historical recreation of a miscarriage of justice rather than a blood-and-guts story with real feelings. Only Olmos's moving performance and Young's treatment of the Old West (with occasional spurts of violence) save the film from the tedium of its predictable but important message. The film has been very popular in the United States and abroad because it is the authentic tale of an American ethnic folkhero.

NOTES: The script for this film was developed during the 1981 workshops at Robert Redford's Sundance Institute in Utah together with the actors, Eduardo Jaime Olmos and Tom Bower, who play victim and sheriff respectively. The inspiration for the screenplay also came from the popular *corrido* or ballad sung today along the Mexican border entitled "The Ballad of Gregorio Cortez," which was recently recorded by Linda Ronstadt.

27. La bandida (The Female Bandit). Robert Rodríguez. Mexico, 1962. 110 min., Eastmancolor. Spanish.

COMMENTARY: Set during the Mexican Revolution of 1910, *La bandida* is another love triangle in which the major star, María Félix, has to fight off the attentions of two leading men, Pedro Armendáriz and Emilio Fernández. The plot involves Félix as the owner of a brothel who is forced to choose between the two ex-soldiers.

The film contains much Mexican folkloric color — cockfights, songs, whippings, feminine histrionics and even a suspenseful Russian roulette scene. At the conclusion, Fernández kills Armendáriz for Miss Félix's attentions but rides off into the sunset to rejoin the revolution when he hears a report that the new president has been killed.

NOTES: Born María de los Ángeles Félix Güereña in 1915, this beautiful Mexican actress conquered Mexican and French cinema but never made one American film. As she approaches the age of eighty, she has survived several marriages, eclipsed only by Dolores del Río, her rival in Mexican cinema. Presently residing in Cuernavaca, she has starred in over fifty films and represents all the glamour and sophistication of the forties and fifties. She retired from the screen in 1970, but her best-known films all date from the forties and fifties, among them *Doña Bárbara* (1943), *Enamorada* (1948), *La belle otero* (1954), *French Can-Can* (1955) and *Sonatas* (1959). She has worked mainly in Mexico, with occasional forays into France and Argentina, but never in the United States.

Her co-star, Pedro Armendáriz, born in 1912, first arrived on Mexican screens in 1934 and appeared with Dolores del Rio in some of the greatest Mexican films of the forties, notably *María Candelaría* and *The Pearl*. He died in 1963 of cancer, probably a result of filming on radioactive locations in Nevada with John Wayne and Susan Hayward in the former's Mongol epic, *The Conqueror* (1956). He also played in many John Ford productions, notably *Three Godfathers* (1949), and is known mainly in America for his last role in the James Bond thriller *From Russia with Love* (1963) in which he portrayed a Turkish villain. He is survived by his son, Pedro Armendáriz, Jr., also a contemporary actor in Mexican films, who is his spitting image.

Emilio Fernández is best known for his direction of some of Mexico's best films of the forties, *María Candelaría*, *The Pearl*, and one of María Félix's best films, *Enamorada* (1946). He also made his reputation as an actor in Mexican and American cinema, appearing mostly in Sam Peckinpah westerns such as *The Wild Bunch* (1969) and *Bring Me the Head of Alfredo García* (1974). When he died in Mexico in 1986, many retrospectives of his films took place internationally. His most popular films today are those of the forties, which reflect the socioeconomic conditions under which he lived as a youth.

28. O bandido da luz vermelha (The Red Light Bandit). Rogerio Sganterla. Brazil, 1969. 92 min., B&W. Portuguese.

COMMENTARY: This first feature by a then, 22-year-old Brazilian film director is based on real events and police files about a famous bandit from São Paulo, dubbed the "Red Light" Bandit because of his criminal associations with prostitutes, gambling, night clubs and brothels. However, the film reeks with obvious bad taste, a campy send-up of all those trashy Carmen Miranda musicals of the forties filled with exotic palm trees, plantains, pineapples, and the erotic sounds of boleros, sambas and tangos, peppered with soap-opera-style dialogue and vulgar acting.

The film is filled with sensational headlines, crude acts that take place in dirty nightclubs, break-ins into seedy apartments which promptly call attention to the "Red Light" Bandit, making him the equivalent of a Clyde Barrow. Paulo Villaca plays the campy *bandido* with slicked-down hair, in zoot-suit style complete with patent leather shoes, revealing his slum roots. As in every morality tale, our bandit is tracked down and killed by the police.

The film is an imperfect first effort, part of the *Cinema Nôvo* movement of the sixties, full of cynicism, tropical exaggerations, vulgarity and melodrama. The camera technique is, at times, unfocused, vapid, noir, intentionally delineating the corrupt world of Boca do Lipo, a region unheard of before the making of *O bandido da luz vermelha*.

NOTES: Rogerio Sganterla was born in Brazil in 1946. Together with another filmmaker, he founded his own production company, Bel-Air, to make very personal films, iconoclastic cinema called *cinema sujo* or "dirty cinema." Beginning as a documentary filmmaker, he became one of the initiators of an underground movement known as *udigrundi*, and *O bandido da luz vermelha*, his debut film of 1968, alternates with another style of film called *lixo*, like his next production, *A mulher de todos* (1969), and *Betty Bomba, a Exibicionista* (1978). Between his *cinema sujo* and *lixo* phases, he made two films in 1975 entitled *Carnaval de lama* and *Copacabana mon amour*. He continues to live and work in Brazil.

The Bandit see *O cangaçerio*

Bandit Love see *El amor bandido*

Baroque see *Barroco*

29. Barravento (Tempest). Glauber Rocha. Brazil, 1960-61. 110 min., B&W. Portuguese.

COMMENTARY: Presented at the very first New York Film Festival in 1963, the story is about Firminio (Antonio Sampaio), part revolutionary, part devil, and his efforts to free the fishermen in his native Bahian village from capitalist exploitation and religious superstition that impedes social change. Shot in black and white, the film recalls Eisenstein's *¡Qué viva Mexico!* but also brings to mind Flaherty's *Moana* and especially, Murnau's *Tabu*. Reflecting the best ideals of the *Cinema Nôvo* movement, the director integrates Brazilian folklore, music and dance, commenting on the narrative.

The story deals with Firminio's return from the city to the primitive life of Bahia. An interloper who disturbs the emotional life of the natives, he makes love to a beautiful negress, Cota, while he secretly covets the attentions of Naina, who is loved by Aruan. Firminio asks the gods for a curse against Aruan.

Firminio tries to help the fishermen survive even though he has cut their nets. Because the fishermen are unable to work, the people experience intense hunger and suffering. A storm comes upon the Bahian village, and Aruan goes out to sea on a raft to pray for his people and their livelihood. Firminio believes Aruan's faith in witchcraft will not solve the problems of the people, so he tricks Cota into seducing Aruan. When the storm hits, Cota drowns after the seduction; Firminio denounces Aruan's perfidy, which ends in a violent *capoeira* fight. Since Firminio is the victor, he has proven Aruan is not a god. Aruan is now freed from the old superstitions and becomes a man of courage who will fight for better days for the fishermen, as well as for the love of Naina. Aruan goes to the city to earn money for new nets so his village can survive.

Barravento is a film which not only depicts a fisherman's life in a community full of superstition but also shows how African religion and mysticism operate as forces to move the community of Bahia to escape from the exploitation and miseries of underdevelopment.

NOTES: Rocha said of this film: "When men revolt and expel the gods from the earth, a tempest explodes.... Tempest means a turbulence in the weather and also a change in the minds of men that destroys their old superstitions." (Press book.)

Barren Lives see *Vidas secas*

30. Barroco (Baroque). Paul Leduc. Spain/Cuba, 1989. 115 min., Eastmancolor. Spanish.

COMMENTARY: The press book synopsis of this film suggests the difficulty of summarizing its action: "The dawn breaks out over a Mexican hacienda. A middle-aged man with Latin-American features meditates, smokes, drinks, imagines. At his side lies a music score:

"Moctezuma-Storia per Musica." A Caribbean mulatto, his friend, majordomo and accomplice, hums the tune of one of the latest popular songs from the new world and in so doing, asks himself a question with no possible philosophical answer, which is phrased in such a way that it is virtually untranslatable: 'Mama, yo quiero saber de dónde son los cantantes...' (Mama, I want to know where the singers are from...) These two characters embark on a journey which takes them through Mexico, Cuba, the Caribbean, Europe, in both time and music, the self-same question returning to them constantly... ¿De dónde son los cantantes?" (Press book.)

Leduc's musical film is about the baroque imagination, which plays with the images of history. With this film, Leduc felt he had initiated a new form of filmmaking, begun in an earlier work entitled *Frida: naturaleza vida*.

It is unfortunate that film critic Peter Besas of *Variety* did not appreciate Leduc's experiment, calling it "seemingly long, self-indulgent...consisting of a succession of scenes apparently set in Latin America during colonial times." It is indeed a pity that Leduc never identifies any of the historical personages, but lets his rambling camera dwell on folkloric dances and music. Besas presumes the film is some kind of allegory, a put-down of the Spaniards, as Leduc jumps ahead in time to the Spanish Civil War and then into a Madrid discothèque of the late eighties. Admittedly, *Barocco* is a "turgid exercise in obscurity," as Besas called it, and the reviewer was correct in his prediction that it would never reach the light of commercial screens. However, probably because of its star power — Francisco Rabal and Angelina Molina — and because of its literary inspiration (it is supposedly based upon Cuban novelist Alejo Carpentier's *Concierto Barroco*), the film has surfaced on video cassette here and abroad.

NOTES: Paul Leduc was born in Mexico in 1942 and studied architecture and theatre. Becoming a film critic in the 1960s, he entered IDHEC in Paris and returned in 1967 to Mexico, where he produced seventeen documentaries for the World Olympic Committee. His most famous films to date include *Reed: Mexican Insurgent* (1973),the biography of John Reed; *Ethnocide: Notes on Mezquital* (1978), about the extermination of Latin-American natives; *Forbidden Stories* (1979); *Petroleum Conspiracy* (1981); and *Frida* (1985), the biography of artist Frida Kalho. It was this last film which supposedly triggered Leduc's "reconstruction of Latin American history" as the basis for *Barroco*.

31. Bartolomé de las Casas.
Sergio Olhovich. Mexico, 1993. 120 min., Color. Spanish.

COMMENTARY: In this film, based upon Jaime Solom's play, *Bartolomé de las Casas: A Bonfire at Dawn*, José Alonso plays the role of the famous Spanish missionary who defended the Mexican Indians and their human rights against the cruelties imposed upon them by Hernando Cortez and his Spanish conquerors. The film follows the life of Bartolomé as he goes from enlightened despot, champion of Spanish evangelization, to revisionist advocate for human rights. The film also takes a different spin on traditional interpretations of colonization, with its contemporary anti-racist view within present-day Christian society. While the film deals with the mistreatment of the indigenous population of Mexico, it is long on rhetoric and short on spectacle. Nevertheless, it is an interesting transposition of art — from play to film, especially since the director, who did both stage and screen versions, deliberately bookends the film with the actors in the studio, as we watch the cameras roll and the action begins with them in period

THE PASSIONS OF A PEOPLE DIVIDED...

A NATION ON THE BRINK OF CIVIL WAR...

The Battle of Chile

Produced by Patricio Guzman
and the Equipo Tercer Año
with the collaboration of
the Cuban Film Institute and Chris Marker

"A landmark film...none of the new Hollywood movies can match the suspense packed into these frames." —SAN FRANCISCO CHRONICLE

"A beautiful, heartbreaking work...deeply moving." —IN THESE TIMES

Poster art for Patricio Guzmán's documentary *La batalla de Chile* (*The Battle of Chile*, 1970–79).

settings and costumes. Olhovich is insisting upon our attention to reality by highlighting the artificiality of the soundstage locations and the settings — perhaps a comment on his own "style" of theatre or cinema.

32. La batalla de Chile (partes 1, 2 & 3) (The Battle of Chile [Parts 1, 2 and 3]). Patricio Guzmán. Chilean/Cuban, 1973–79. 287 min., B&W. Spanish.

COMMENTARY: A fascinating three-part documentary detailing the radicalization that led to the coup of Salvador Allende, Patricio Guzmán's *La batalla de Chile* was edited in exile in Cuba. Guzmán filmed every day for seven months with borrowed equipment, gaining access to all sectors of Chilean society and witnessing the class struggle first-hand. After the coup aided by the CIA and the forces of General Pinochet, he smuggled all the film stock out of the country into Cuba. At ICIAC, he edited the final work over a four-year period into three parts: "The Insurrection of the Bourgeoisie," "The Coup d'Etat" and "The Power of the People." There are voice-overs that offer background information, and protagonists in the film give testimony that is either complemented or opposed by the images on the screen from this turbulent and tragic period. It is the most important documentary work ever to come out of Chile, since it gives insight and real testimony to the events during the Allende coup as well as meaning to the notion of solidarity. Beginning with its Marxist leanings, the documentary tries to be objective, but at the same time, it is analytical and critical of Chile's leftist forces. Overall it presents an uncompromising but informed view.

Viewers of this film might call it biased, pro-revolutionary, even monotonous and long, but still, it is profoundly moving and disturbing, an epic of sorts, with Salvador Allende viewed as some sort of remote, symbolic hero. At times the documentary tries to simplify very complex events. Although the first two parts realistically recount the sorrowful events of the coup, there is awareness on the part of the workers, especially in Part 3, when they give testimony and we see through their eyes the awesome proportions of civil disorder throughout the country and how the nation struggles to survive this disorder. We witness the creation of the organisms of "popular power" to distribute food; occupy, guard and run factories and farms; oppose black market profiteering; and link together in community zones grass-roots social services. These activities are documented through the same man-on-the-street interview technique and emphasize a strategy for worker control of the nation's economy. All this is caught by Guzmán's fluid camera work, panning, zooming incessantly, reframing, editing and reediting his images to emphasize the extraordinary spectacle. Thus Guzmán creates a film work of monumental proportions, analogous to the Argentine epic *La hora de los hornos* (*Hour of the Furnaces*) by Fernando Solanas. Like *La hora*, it is a profoundly moving film work, humane and courageous.

NOTES: Born in 1941, Guzmán was a well-known documentary filmmaker, beginning his career in the early sixties, working in black and white with a 16mm camera. His first feature-length documentary is *Primer año* (1971), after which he made *October's Answer* (1972) and finally the three-part *Batalla de Chile*. He has been living in exile in Cuba for many years. His last film is entitled *Rose of the Winds*, a Cuban-Venezuelan-Spanish co-production made in 1983.

Guzmán was helped in the enormous task of filming this epic work by French documentary filmmaker Chris Marker, who is said to have collaborated with him on the thematic organization of the material.

The Battle of Chile see *La batalla de Chile*

Beloved Lover see *El amor bandido*

Bitter Sea see *Amargo mar*

Black God, White Devil see *Deus e o diabo na terra do sol*

Black Orpheus see *Orfeu negro*

Black Shack Alley see *Rue Cases Nègres*

Blood Feast see *Fin de fiesta*

Blood of the Condor see *Yawar mallku*

33. La boca del lobo (The Lion's Den). Francisco J. Lombardi. Peru, 1988. 122 min., Color. Spanish.

COMMENTARY: The literal translation of this film's title is "mouth of the wolf," but "lion's den" is certainly more appropriate, since the film deals with Peruvian army decisions made by men who are isolated in a climate of violence, prisoners of their own loneliness, trapped in an Emergency Zone, isolated by the Shining Path movement. Based upon a real event that took place in 1947 in Chuspi, a small town in the Andean highlands, the film depicts a massacre of 47 peasants by the army — 47 men, women and children suspected of communist-inspired terrorist activities. Rather than attempting to explain the conditions under which the peasants live, the film chooses to dramatize the moral disintegration of the members of the army detachment assigned to root out the members of the Shining Path and annihilate terrorism, or any subversive activities by communist guerrillas, at any price.

The film's story develops around the changes in one recruit, Vega, who has volunteered for assignment in the terrorist-dominated Emergency Zone hoping to win an appointment to officer training school. However, with the arrival of a brutal new commander, Lieutenant Roca, Vega must decide whether to follow orders (executing all villagers who witnessed Roca's fatal beating of a man who protested the rape of an Indian woman) or his own conscience.

Luna refuses to use gunfire on the peasants and is disillusioned by the brutal, irrational war. The director is commenting not only on the political oppression of the Peruvian Indians but on the macho ethos of the army as well. The soldiers come off as a sadistic gang of liars, thieves, rapists and killers. There is a final confrontation scene between Vega and Roca, a Russian roulette scene that owes much of its inspiration to Cimino's film *The Deer Hunter*. At the conclusion, Vega wanders off into the communist-infested foothills, profoundly affected by the devastating violence of the massacre of Peruvian peasants, a damning indictment of grotesque government policy. Honest, caring, innocent soldiers were most certainly trapped in a brutal "lion's den."

NOTES: Francisco José Lombardi was born in Tacna, Peru, in 1950, studied filmmaking in Argentina and wrote film criticism for several magazines and features before making some short films and features. His first feature was *Muerte al amanecer* (1977), also inspired by a real event, the execution of the so-called "monster" of Almedariz in 1957. It was his most succesful film in Peru until *La boca del lobo*. He also directed *Muerte de un magnate* (1980), *Maruja en el infierno* (1983) and *La ciudad y los perros* (1985, based upon the novel by Mario Vargas Llosa). He has been active in Peruvian televison and has been involved in the creation of new laws governing film production in Peru.

34. Boda secreta (Secret Wedding). Alejandro Agresti. Argentina, 1989. 95 min., Fujicolor. Spanish.

COMMENTARY: Another film about the *desaparecidos* and vaguely reminiscent of Luis Puenzo's *La historia oficial*, *Boda secreta* is a fantasy love story about a man called Fermín, found running naked through the streets of Buenos Aires, suffering from amnesia. He had disappeared thirteen years before and is now in search of Tota, the woman he has always loved. Their romance is rekindled in a politically repressed town outside of the capital, although she fails to recognize him. Changing his identity to "Alberto," Fermín befriends Pipi, a rebel whose causes have all but disappeared, an ex-torture victim who has given up his ideals. However, Pipi is pro-democratic and believes in freedom of speech, especially when confronting the hostility of the townspeople he encounters. Once again, the director is critical of the hypocrisy and bigotry of Argentine society and has made an incisive political parable set against the background of a heartbreaking, highly original love story.

35. Boquitas pintadas (Painted Lips). Leopoldo Torre Nilsson. Argentina, 1974. 120 min., B&W. Spanish.

COMMENTARY: Basing his film upon the Manuel Puig bestseller *Heartbreak Tango*, director Torre Nilsson has made a successful commercial film about a young man, Juan Carlos, who has defined the memories of his youth through the vehicle of soap opera. The story involves several characters over the period 1935 to 1968. Juan Carlos, the lothario, is involved with several women over this period, but mainly with Nene, who is his intellectual equal and resists his advances because she is no longer innocent. During their courtship, Juan Carlos develops tuberculosis and is sent into the country to recover. When he returns, he continues his courtship of Nene, only to discover that she is promised to marry another man who offers her the prospect of living a sophisticated life in Buenos Aires, the capital. Nene now becomes the focal point of the story, since, at long last, she has realized the error of her marriage. She returns to the small town where Juan Carlos had died several years before, recovers from this sentimental shock and lives the rest of her days listening to soap operas, which help to blur the memories of her own youthful sexuality. Although there are other characters whose stories are revealed to us in similiar sentimental fashion, one feels that the Juan Carlos–Nene affair is a true mirror of Argentine romanticism during that 33-year period.

NOTES: Torre Nilsson (1924–1978) lived his entire life in Buenos Aires and was married for many years to novelist and screenwriter Beatriz Guido. He made 27 films throughout his career, mostly artistic rather than commerical successes. Among his best known films are *La casa de Ángel* (1956), *Piel de verano* (1961) and *Martín Fierro* (1968). He also produced films and wrote poetry and prose fiction.

36. El brazo fuerte (The Strong Arm). Giovanni Korporaal. Mexico, 1953. 85 min., B&W. Spanish.

COMMENTARY: Made in Mexico by an Italian-Dutch director, *El brazo fuerte* is an excellent morality tale about an engineer (Claudio Morell) who comes to a small town to do surveying for the Mexican government. At first, he is mocked and scorned by the townspeople, but later they regale him as a hero for some "acts of heroism" whose exact nature is never revealed to the audience. Based upon his newfound fame, he marries the richest girl in town and becomes a ruthless exploiter of the townspeople. At last he receives his just desserts in a riding accident. In his very first film, director Korporaal succeeds very well in presenting his condemnation of small town life and politics as he also takes potshots at corruption, backwardness and selfishness. Because the film was so incisive in its critiques, it was censored in Mexico and shown at the Locarno Film Festival in Italy in 1961. It has recently been rediscovered and given worldwide screenings.

Brickmakers see *Chiricales*

The Brute see *El bruto*

37. El bruto (The Brute). Luis
Buñuel. Mexico, 1952. 93 min., B&W.
Spanish.

COMMENTARY: If the concept of
"camp" had been known in the fifties,
this film would certainly conform to the
definition of high camp. *El bruto* is way
over the top in its melodramatics, and
the plot is deceptively simple.

"El Bruto" (played movingly by
Pedro Armendáriz) is hired by a landowner (Fernando Soler) to bring some
pressure to bear on a tenant group's
leader, Carmelo, so that the landowner
can sell the property for a huge profit to
the Mexican government. Bruto works
in a slaughterhouse and does not know
his own strength. He attacks the tenant leader, and Carmelo collapses and
dies — actually from a tuberculosis in-
fection he has had for several years. The
tenant group rallies and sets out to pun-
ish Bruto.

Meanwhile, the landowner, Cabrera,
tells Bruto to leave the slaughterhouse
and work for him and his wife, Paloma
(Katy Jurado), in their butcher shop.
Paloma falls for Bruto, attracted by his
great strength and masculinity. After
some hedging, she finally lures him to
her bed in the house they all share.
Cabrera is more of a father figure for his
wife, but Bruto represents vigor, youth
and enormous sexual power.

Hearing about the death of the tenant leader, Bruto tries to discover the
truth behind his encounter and meets
Carmelo's daughter, Meche played by
Rosita Arenas (who played another
Meche in Buñuel's *Los olvidados*). Bruto,
chased by an angry mob, stumbles into
Meche's apartment. She kindly removes
a nail from Bruto's back, and they fall in
love. When the landowner hears about
the mob attack, he sequesters Bruto,
"getting him out of town," so to speak,
where Bruto carries on an affair with

Meche. While Bruto is working as a
watchman, Paloma decides to surprise
him at his new dwelling, and finds
Carmelo's daughter there. Enraged with
jealousy, she informs on Bruto to the police, telling them his whereabouts and
that he is the real murderer of the tenant leader. She then tells her husband
that Bruto raped her. Her clothes are
torn, her brassiere exposed; her lipstick
is smeared, and her arms look bruised.

Cabrera sends for Bruto and accuses
the latter of assaulting his wife. Bruto
pleads not guilty, but the old man becomes abusive and brandishes a gun;
Bruto is forced to break his neck and
stomp him to death. When Paloma finds
her husband dead, she sends the police
to Bruto's hiding place, and as Bruto says
goodbye to Meche, the police trap him.
He climbs over a wall, and they shoot
him dead. Paloma comes to the scene,
raging that justice has been done.

The film is not just a revenge melodrama that is sexually motivated. Buñuel
is also concerned with political corruption on the part of the government, tenant's rights, the civilizing of brutal instincts, and the passive nature of religion
as it tends to (or does not) meet man's
needs. There is also a suggestion that
Bruto may be the illegitimate son of the
landlord Cabrera, who seems to take an
inordinate interest in this slaughterhouse
worker. Apparently Bruto's mother was
a former maid of Cabrera's and he might
have had an affair with her, producing
this illegitimate son. But it is Katy Jurado as Paloma who brings out all of the
animal instincts in Bruto, and Meche
who humanizes him just before he is
killed.

Although Jurado is the female star, it
is Armendáriz's performance as Bruto
that is truly memorable and mesmerizing. He plays Bruto as a lusty man, a bit
slow, but respectful of authority and
childlike. He should never have been
victimized by the lusty Paloma or her

corrupt landowner husband, Cabrera. One would have preferred a happy ending, where Meche and Bruto live happily ever after, but Buñuel acceded to commercial needs and made the script into a potboiler for popular consumption. Yet there is always some artistic merit in this film — especially Buñuel's use of a statue of the Virgin Mary, placed just outside, but looking on and into the "slaughterhouse." Obviously the church is witness to all sorts of slaughter but passively looks on — another interesting Buñuel anti-religious touch. *El bruto* is on video cassette in the United States and is worth at least one viewing. It has some wonderful noir-like photography by Agustín Jiménez and a pounding score by Raúl Lavista that telescopes all the actions of the characters. It is a very diverting film for all of its 93 minutes.

38. El bulto (Excess Baggage).
Gabriel Retes. Mexico, 1991. 114 min., Color. Spanish.

COMMENTARY: According to the program notes, *El bulto* is reminiscent of such films as Penny Marshall's *Awakenings* and Mike Nichols' *Regarding Henry*, since this is a tale of a modern Rip Van Winkle's efforts to integrate himself into society after waking from a twenty-year coma. The story concerns Lauro, a leftist journalist who falls into a coma when clubbed on the head during the 1971 student riots in Mexico City. Suddenly awakening twenty years later, he finds that his wife has taken a lover, his children are all grown and his radical friends now work for the government. Lauro is referred to as the "excess baggage," which could have been easily discarded by pulling the plug on him. With his awakening, Lauro undergoes painful physical therapy and a deadly slow recovery. Hardest for him is to come to grips with his wife's infidelity, his children's demand for a father to respect and his daughter's flagrant sexual relation-

ship with her current beau. Retes, the actor and director, prefers to tell the human story of an anachronistic man coming to grips with his new reality rather than dealing with the political ramifications of such a story — selling out sixties idealism in favor of the politics of the nineties. *El bulto* is part of the New Wave of Mexican cinema immersed in a new sense of freedom and exploration of the past, free of censorship and ideological barriers, free to explore formerly forbidden themes. It will be interesting to see what direction Retes's career will take in the future.

Burn! see *¡Quemada!*

39. Bye, Bye Brazil. Carlos
Diegues. Brazil, 1980. 110 min., Eastmancolor. Portuguese.

COMMENTARY: Meet Andorinha, King of Muscle; Salome, Queen of Rumba; and Lorde Cigano, the Emperor of Magicians and Clairvoyants. These and other itinerant artists make up the Rolidei Circus Caravan, whose travels make up the wandering plot of *Bye, Bye Brazil*. In the course of the film, they encounter a young accordionist named Cico and his pregnant wife. Cico becomes desperately smitten with Salome and will stop at almost nothing in his attempt to get hired by the circus group, which continues to travel as Brazil seems to change all around it.

The film is a naturalistic tale, following the tatty caravan as it works its way through the grim *sertão* of northeastern Brazil. Ever conscious of their petty foibles, their emotional involvements, their own glittery magic, the entertainers wander through the deserted country, bringing some semblance of refreshing entertainment and joy to the backwaters of Bahia. Although *New York Times* film critic Vincent Canby considered the film "a psychological inventory of a country on the verge of extraordinary economic

Carlos Diegues perches on top of the truck of the Caravana Rolidei in a rare behind-the-scenes shot from *Bye, Bye Brazil* (1980).

and industrial development, a travelogue through a nation that doesn't yet exist," and Richard Corliss in *Time* called it "a naturalistic tale to a bossa nova beat," the film is really nothing more nor less than colorful entertainment. Nevertheless, Carlos Diegues, its director, sees *Bye, Bye Brazil* as "representing the possibility of a new tropical civilization by living the adventure of this dream, towards the twenty-first century with no prejudices." Diegues, like most of his *Cinema Nôvo* contemporaries, is trying to discover, through his films, a real Brazil in which the modern coexists with the archaic, misery with abundance, tragedy with beauty, past with future. Within the present soulless and geographical decay of the twentieth century, Diegues' character creations are searching for the euphoria of change in a world currently out of control. Material progress has destroyed the rain forest and the culture of the Amazon Indians. Diegues is searching for a return to those lost values.

NOTES: Carlos Diegues was born in Maceio, Brazil, in 1940 and began his film career in 1962 with *Cinco vezez favela*, a serial film about poverty. Becoming one of the major theoreticians of *Cinema Nôvo*, he made several other short films. But it was his first full-length feature, *Xica da Silva* (1976), that brought him international success. *Bye, Bye Brazil*, *Quilombo* (1984) and *Um trem para as estrelas* (1986) have brought him further renown. He is also a poet, journalist and film critic.

40. Cabeza de Vaca. Nicolas Echeverría. Mexico, 1991. 111 min., Color. Spanish.

COMMENTARY: Based upon Cabeza de Vaca's 1542 memoir entitled *Shipwrecks*, this film is set during the period

1528–1536, when the famed Spanish explorer roamed from the Florida coast across the American Southwest into Northern Mexico. "Shipwrecked off the coast of Florida in 1528, he walked for eight years across America to the Pacific coast of Mexico. During his quest for survival he lived with now lost Indian tribes, experienced the secrets of their mystical ways and performed medical wonders like reviving the dead. When finally reunited with the Spaniards, he viewed the conquest in a different light." (Press book.)

Spanish actor Juan Diego captures the loneliness of Cabeza de Vaca's geographical and spiritual odyssey. We watch him learn to communicate with the Indians, develop the mystical powers of the shaman who holds him prisoner abetted by an armless dwarf (who weeps when the shaman sets Cabeza de Vaca free), and finally reunite with the Spaniards, who have been evangelizing and destroying the same Indian tribes from whom Cabeza de Vaca has learned so much.

The style of the film is usually straightforward, but occasionally it is hallucinatory. It has many documentary details of the tribal life of the Indians and emphasizes the violence of their existence. Our hero is treated harshly, with contempt, and finally with reverence as Cabeza de Vaca assumes the role of shaman with great healing powers.

Juan Diego acts the principal role in a broad, somewhat dreamy, vacant manner. We never feel close to Cabeza de Vaca, although he might be one of the first white men who enjoyed the mind-expanding pleasures of peyote. Diego does emphasize Cabeza de Vaca's reverence for the Indians and their powers — a reverence that dismays his fellow Spaniards, who wish to stamp out their healing expertise. *Cabeza de Vaca* is an unusually long film for a very small subject but of admittedly epic proportions.

It will probably be seen in shorter abbreviated versions in the United States and elsewhere.

NOTES: Nicolas Echeverría was born in Nayarit, Mexico, in 1947 and studied architecture and music before making contact with the Millennium Workshop in New York in 1972, where he first experienced filmmaking. He is primarily a documentary filmmaker; *María Sabrina* (1979) and *Rural Poets* (1980) represent the early efforts that preceded this first full-length feature.

41. Cadena perpetua (In for Life). Arturo Ripstein. Mexico, 1978. 95 min., Color. Spanish.

COMMENTARY: Based upon the crime novel *Lo de antes* (*Same As Before*) by Luis Spota, Ripstein's film stars Pedro Armendáriz, Jr., as Javier Lira, an ex-convict who tries to live a normal life but is impeded by a corrupt police official, Commandant Burro Prieto (by Narciso Busquets). Just as "Tarzan" Lira is succeeding at a new job, Prieto brings him in for questioning or blackmails him to keep him out of jail. The director has presented a very dark view of police corruption and brutality. Ripstein himself said that the work "is kind of a film noir. ... You cannot make a film that speaks openly about Mexican police brutality...to denounce police methods.... I wanted to speak publicly about the misuse of the police's power." (MOMA program notes.)

Variety called the film a "grim tale of an ex-con, one-time pimp and thief, who has gone straight, ... hounded back to criminality by a venal blackmailing detective..." The critic also felt Pedro Armendáriz, Jr., lacked the forcefulness of his father's ability to make the ex-con a more complex character than the macho lout who is too easily undone by the detective. Another issue at hand is the ex-con's responsibility to his boss, who could have helped him with this predicament.

Ripstein's film is more than just a commentary on corruption; it is a sad and well-meaning film, but obviously a footnote to the director's prolific career.

42. Caídos del cielo (Fallen from the Sky). Francisco J. Lombardi. Peru, 1990. 127 min., Color. Spanish.

COMMENTARY: Intertwining three different stories set in inflation-ridden Lima, *Caídos del cielo* is a long film which offers a metaphorical rendering of the crises affecting Peruvian society by viewing three different social classes and their respective problems.

First there is an elderly couple, so determined to build themselves a magnificent tomb that they sell all their furniture and mortgage their home, making themselves indigent and ending up in an old people's hospital. Then there is a blind old woman who becomes so obsessed with a pig she deems valuable that she continues to fatten it up to the detriment and ill health of her own grandsons. Finally we have the story of a lonely, facially scarred radio announcer who saves a beautiful girl from jumping off a cliff, only to be rejected by the girl because of his ugliness. All three stories are linked by coincidences and bizarre events that unfold gradually to reveal the parable concocted by the writer-director.

43. Caluga o menta (Toffee or Mint). Gonzalo Justiniano. Chile, 1990. 100 min., Color. Spanish.

COMMENTARY: After dealing with the frustrations of middle-class youngsters in two earlier films, the director now turns his attention to the squalid lives of tenement children living in a grey environment. Niki (Mauricio Vega), Nacho (Aldo Parodi) and Manuela (Patricia Rivadeneira) and their friends are hopelessly caught in an abulic life with their families and their jobs. They turn to petty crime and then to drug running in order to relieve their boredom. Manuela's appearance signifies some future hope and choices between toffee or mint, life or death, heaven or earth — but the reality of Chilean life offers only gritty realism and a pessimistic future for all concerned.

NOTES: *Caluga o menta* is this young Chilean director's third film. His earlier ones, especially *Children of the Cold War*, tend to depict Chile's wayward youth.

44. Camila. María Luisa Bemberg. Argentina, 1984. 105 min., East-mancolor. Spanish.

COMMENTARY: Based on the real lives of the Jesuit priest Ladislao Gutiérrez and the young, aristocratic Catholic socialite Camila O'Gorman, *Camila* tells the story of their love, forbidden by the Juan Manuel de Rosas regime, and its consequences (death for both by the firing squad in 1847).

We witness the sexual attraction between the lovers (beautifully played by Imanol Arias and Susu Pecoraro), their escape from the prejudice which plagues Buenos Aires society, their short-lived happiness in the provinces pretending to be husband and wife, their sexual joy (intimately shown on screen), their capture by the military, their imprisonment, the revelation of Camila's pregnancy, their bloody execution.

Under the new democratic freedoms permitted film directors with the ousting of the former military dictatorship, María Luisa Bemberg was able to film a love story and emphasize the political malaise of the Rosas regime as well as the recently departed one.

Besides the principal actors, Hector Alterio gives a superb performance as Adolfo O'Gorman, Camila's father, who would rather see her dead than have her defy him, the church or the politics of the Rosas regime. Elena Tasisto, who plays Camila's grandmother, exiled by her son into the provinces because she

Susu Pecoraro taking communion from Imanol Arías, her soon-to-be lover in a scene from María Luisa Bemberg's *Camila* (1984).

dared to love outside of her class, represents the true romantic spirit of women's liberation incarnated in Camila. *Camila* is a beautiful film to watch: intelligent, pictorially stunning, deeply moving. Moreover, the director had the courage to attack, albeit obliquely, the abuse of political power, arbitrariness and repression — in short, the overturned regime which she had just survived.

NOTES: Born in 1917, María Luisa Bemberg has been an Argentinian scriptwriter and founder and producer of the Teatro del Globo. She came to write and direct films in her seventies. Her most famous features are *Señora de Nadie* (1982), *Camila* and *Miss Mary* (1986). She feels that "*Camila* is the first real film she made with complete freedom at the time the government of President Raúl Alfonsín ended censorship along with many other repressions. And the extent to which it has been taken by the Argentines as a symbol of freedom is reflected in the fact that five to six baby girls born each day in Argentina are now named Camila." (Press book.)

45. O cangaçeiro (The Bandit). Lima Barreto. Brazil, 1953. 105 min., B&W. Portuguese.

COMMENTARY: Heralded as the first Brazilian film to be shown in the United States (in 1954), this is an eye-filling adventure story about a band of outlaws who terrorize the northern countryside. One day, they capture a beautiful young schoolteacher, bringing her to their hideout. One of the men, the chieftan's lieutenant, falls in love with her and spirits her back to town. The leader, enraged by the abduction and his man's betrayal, kills a whole group of militia who slow his pursuit of the couple, although he is too late to recapture them.

Milton Ribeiro is excellent as the fanatical, violent bandit chief, and Alberto Ruschel plays effectively as his rival in love with Olivia, the schoolteacher admirably played by Marisa Prado. There are wonderful scenes of the bandits at work (pillaging) and play (dancing and singing), and suspenseful scenes of the brutal rebel chief tracking down the young escaped couple, leading to a final showdown that results in the death of his defecting lieutenant. This story of pursuit is a poetic adventure set against beautiful scenery and a background of pulsating Brazilian folk music. It has many action scenes and brutal moments that remind one of the American western; like them, it is completely thrilling and enjoyable.

NOTES: Lima Barreto was born in São Paulo in 1902 and died in a nursing home in Campina in 1982. He spent his entire life in Brazil as a scriptwriter, actor, photographer, journalist, author of several books and a filmmaker of documentaries, then feature films. *O cangaçeiro* is his best-known film, winning him a special prize at Cannes in 1953. His other feature, *A primeira missa* (1961), was not as eagerly received since it did not have the same charged atmosphere of the "outlaw epic," one of the most outstanding genres of Brazilian cinema.

46. Canoa. Felipe Cazals. Mexico, 1976. 115 min., Color. Spanish.

COMMENTARY: The MOMA program notes called *Canoa* one of Felipe Cazals' most important films to date, noting that the script was penned by Tomás Pérez Turrent, a prestigious Mexican film critic. The program described the film's structure as "a compromise between documentary cinema, direct cinema and the classical form."

Played with sincerity, *Canoa* is a revisionist film that seeks to expose all sorts of injustice, alleged or true. The film is based upon a real incident that took place in the town of San Miguel Canoa on September 14, 1968, when a group of five male hikers, employees of the University of Puebla, were caught by a thunderstorm in this small village dominated by a dictator-priest figure who accused them of being communist student subversives. Milking local gullibility and employing his religious faith to secure his own financial ends, the film's priest incites the villagers to attack the group, claiming that they were going to desecrate the church. Two of the students are hacked to death by machete along with a villager who tried to shelter them. The others are dragged to the main square of the town, about to be lynched, but they are saved by the opportune arrival of the Mexican police.

The film makes a vivid comment about anti-student hysteria generated by the Mexican government and press preceding this incident. It also stresses the naivete and lack of education of suburban Mexicans, prey to provincial forces in the hinterlands and the disparities in the educational process between city and rural populations.

47. Cantata de Chile (Song of Chile). Humberto Solas. Cuba, 1976. 119 min., Color & Scope. Spanish.

COMMENTARY: In 1907, the nitrate workers of northern Chile organized a vast strike designed to improve the living conditions of thousands of miners' families, who were mercilessly exploited by the British-owned nitrate companies. The response of the Chilean oligarchy went down in history as the Iquique Massacre (1907), a mass strike, a savage episode that failed to crush the militancy of the Chilean working class.

These events serve in the film as a bridge that links up the whole Chilean historic process as one of steadily mounting struggle. The film, with the Iquique events as its point of departure, presents the most vital moments of the struggle, whose roots go back to the heroic resistance of the Araucanian Indians against the Spanish colonists and whose expression by 1976 could be found in the Chilean people's struggle against the fascist junta that took such a heavy toll of lives. *Cantata de Chile* is a tribute to all those fighters who made that country's history such a vital part of the Latin American and worldwide struggle for liberation. (Press book.)

The film employs a potpourri of styles to unfold its solidarity-party line. Stressed is the propaganda regarding the Spanish takeover of Latin America, British imperialism and the slaughter of Chileans by the military, all events interspersed with music, poems, myths — a blend that has been described as "Bertolt Brecht combined with Diego Rivera." *Cantata* is a highly stylized film, full of theatrical tableaux, shifting back and forth in time, utilizing the same performers in all epochs of Chilean history, underlining the links between Chile's past and present. Music and dance and the recitation of Pablo Neruda's poem "Cantata de Chile" are used to effect the transitions between realism and surrealism; the techniques and striking styles of Latin American painters, especially the Mexican muralists, bring the film to vibrant heights. A prize-winning film, *Cantata de Chile* is a worthwhile experience if the viewer can separate the propaganda from the artistic merits of this sometimes overlong, over-didactic film work.

NOTES: Born in December 1942 in Havana, Humberto Solas is still a leading figure in contemporary Cuban revolutionary cinema. At age fourteen, he dropped out of school to aid in the struggle against the Batista regime. Under Fidel Castro, he joined the Cuban film institute in 1959; there he has made a number of documentaries and features. Besides *Cantata de Chile*, some of his best know films are *Cecilia Valdes* (1982) and *Un hombre de éxito* (1986). However his international reputation was secured in 1968 with the award-winning film

Lucía, the story of three women who trace various important phases in Cuban history — Solas's most brilliant film to date.

48. Las cartas del parque
(Letters from the Park). Tomás Gutiérrez Alea. Cuba, 1988. 93 min., Color. Spanish.

COMMENTARY: The story takes place in Matanzas, one hundred kilometers from Havana, in 1913. Two very young people, each in love with the other but each unaware that the love is mutual, solicit the services of a scribe to write letters for them. Slowly, the scribe begins to impose his own personality on the letters, which reveal one eternal truth: love conquers all.

The film is divided into four parts, according to the seasons. Juan, who works in a pharmacy, is writing to María, the other client of the scribe named Pedro. They are really writing to each other! However, Juan ceases in his affections for María, being dazzled more by aviation and balloons than by her romantic attitudes. Pedro tries to keep the romance between them afloat by sending postal cards from around the world signed by Juan. María soon realizes the deception and falls in love with Pedro.

This is a small, charming film, reminiscent of Rostand's *Cyrano de Bergerac* and Ernst Lubitsch's film *The Shop Around the Corner*, but totally Cuban in conception, recreating the old turn-of-the-century Cuba. It is a light, delightful work from the maker of many well-known political dramas. *Las cartas del parque* has been shown nationally in the United States on public television and also can be found on video cassette.

NOTES: Born on December 11, 1928, in Havana, Tomás Gutiérrez Alea has been a supporter of communism and Marxism throughout his youth. Together with his fellow student Nestor Almendros, he began making short films. Unlike Almendros, who left Cuba, Alea was caught up in the 1959 Castro revolution, making his first documentary feature film for the Castro government, entitled *Stories of the Revolution* (1960). However his best films were yet to come. They are *La muerte de un burócrata* (1966), *Memorias del subdesarrollo* (1968), *La última cena* (1976), *Hasta cierto punto* (1984) and *Fresa y chocolate* (1993). Alea continues to reside and make films in Cuba.

49. La casa de Ángel (The House of Angel / End of Innocence).
Leopoldo Torre Nilsson. Argentina, 1957. 75 min., B&W. Spanish.

COMMENTARY: When this film was first presented at the Cannes Film Festival in 1957, it was considered the first truly important film to come out of Argentina in decades. It was the director's sixth film, and it marked both his entry into European art film circles and his first close collaboration with novelist and screenwriter Beatriz Guido.

La casa de Ángel (or *End of Innocence*, as it was known in its initial American release) is a subtle and delicate study of adolescence, a tale told against the background of wealth, ignorance, political turmoil and corruption in Buenos Aires of the 1920s. Brought up within an atmosphere of stifling puritanism heavily charged with hellfire religion, its sheltered 16-year-old heroine, Ana Castro (Elsa Daniel), is the victim of an unpremeditated seduction by a man older than herself named Julián (Lautaro Murua). The entire film is an extended flashback from the present, when Ana tries to cope with the realization that her ideals and her youth have been ruined. The experience marks her for life since her first sexual experience is one of rape. The claustrophobic and sexual tension of Argentine society of the twenties as presented in the film is formidable. As Ana struggles with her own sexual awakening, she is surrounded by class restrictions, nannies who preach hellfire and brimstone, a mother's religious bigotry, a father's womanizing, fears of her own sensuality and body (she bathes in a robe). The recreation of the period is brilliant and the oppressive social background illuminatingly presented. One can feel the atmosphere of moral decay, the prurience, the eroticism mingled within the girl's claustrophobic life and spirit. *La casa de Ángel* is a bold, vivid, complex film that uses a deeply subjective, personal story to illuminate a whole time and place. Torre Nilsson's favorite films are those that explore the decline of the Argentine upper-class and genteel bourgeois society, the relationship between innocent adolescents and the world of adults that corrupts them, and the total lack of communication between characters. The corruption of innocence in youth and adolescence, the effects of an enclosed upbringing in a cynical society, the ever-present influence of Catholicism tempered by a mood of nostalgic pessimism, and a retreat to the world of fixed social and sexual taboos, all expressed through a photographic style heavy with high angle shots, looming close-ups and sudden stabs of music, give *La casa de Ángel* its artistic edge and greatness.

NOTES: Leopoldo Torre Nilsson was born in Buenos Aires in 1924 and died there in 1978. He was married to screenwriter and novelist Beatriz Guido. Their collaboration made for some of their most successful films, beginning with *La casa de Ángel*. They made 27 films together in a marriage that lasted some twenty-five years. Torre Nilsson himself comes from a filmmaking family — his father was a director and producer during the 1940s in Argentina. But it was the son who produced and directed at least a dozen films to establish his own reputation internationally. Among his best are *Fin de fiesta* (1959), *La mano en*

la trampa (1960), *Piel de verano* (1961), and *Boquitas pintadas* (1974).

50. Cascabel (The Rattlesnake).

Raúl Araiza. Mexico, 1976. 108 min., Color. Spanish.

COMMENTARY: Dealing with the social responsibility of a filmmaker, *Cascabel* tells the story of a director of documentaries who wants to make a short film exposing the conditions of the Lacandonian Indians in Chiapas. However, he is fired for trying to make the film his own way, and another director is hired. The replacement films an Indian birth scene against the government's will, which leads to talk of government exploitation of the Indians. Meanwhile, the previous director, while in a sleeping bag on location, is bitten by a rattlesnake (symbolic of the government's will) and probably dies since the serum to save him arrives too late. Although there is some harrowing suspense in the snakebite scene, the film makes a mild attempt at showing societal progress through the use of documentary filmmaking in Mexico. However, the original director's jumbled motives for achieving truth, like those of filmmaker Araiza, are superficial. Nevertheless, *Cascabel* initiated a populist trend in Mexican filmmaking whose goal is a national cinema focusing on Third World themes, developing autonomously and recognized internationally as a quality product.

51. El caso de María Soledad (The María Soledad Case). Hector Olivera. Argentina, 1992. 125 min., Color. Spanish.

COMMENTARY: María Soledad Morales was a real-life high school girl whose murdered, mutilated body was found on the outskirts of Catamarca in the Andes. Director Hector Olivera tells María's story in fragments, using flashbacks, intertwining television coverage, using narrators on camera, creating hypothetical situations, imagining testimony, and adding real location shooting in an effort to solve the crime which is, to date, unsolved. It was Argentina's most shocking murder in years and had political implications since the sons of certain political leaders had a rendezvous with María at a local disco. A cover-up of the crime began as soon as the names of the politicos were mentioned. Evidence was destroyed, witnesses were intimidated, a smear campaign began defaming María for participating in an orgy, and then her former lover was accused of the murder. Only her classmates in a Catholic girl's school, along with their head, Sister Martha Pelloni, defended Maria. The girls staged a silent march to protest the handling of the case. However, the principal suspect was freed, Sister Pelloni was transferred to another school, and the filmmakers could only comment on the "psychopathic excesses" of a corrupt political regime, nothing more. In reality, the president of Argentina did force the resignation of the governor of the province of Catamarca, but the crime remains unsolved, surrounded with suggestions of political complicity to obfuscate police and juridicial efforts to solve the case.

NOTES: Hector Olivera was born in Buenos Aires in 1931 and with writer Fernando Ayala founded the film company Aries Cinematográfica in 1956. He began in the Argentine film industry as a producer and since the late sixties has directed many films, the most notable of which are *La Patagonia rebelde* (1974), *Los viernes de eternidad* (1981), *No habrá más penas ni olvido* (1984) and *La noche de los lápices* (1988). Beginning as a documentary filmmaker, he has tried to combine testimonial cinema with a narrative style that has proven commercially successful in Argentina and abroad.

52. El castillo de la pureza

(**Castle of Purity**). Arturo Ripstein. Mexico, 1972. 114 min., Color. Spanish.

COMMENTARY: Owing much to the directorial style and black humor of Spanish director Luis Buñuel, *El castillo de la pureza* is the story of Limas (Claudio Brook), who sequesters his wife (Rita Macedo) and his three children for eighteen years in a large old house in Mexico City while they manufacture rat poison to earn a living. Limas is the only member of the family permitted to leave the premises to sell his homemade product when the family needs money. Based upon an actual event that occurred in Mexico City some years before, the film forgoes any documentary intentions for the sake of dramatic and thematic unity. Our director is more interested in the moral and spiritual contamination threatening the isolated family from outside their sealed world. Gabriel Limas continually exhorts his family to stay pure, free of taint and corruption from the outside world. However, somewhat tragically, he does not realize that corruption and sin are implicit in the human condition. Although he has named his children Utopia, Willpower and Future, their allegorical names and Lima's self-enclosed world of idealism and repression cannot ultimately prevent the intrusion of the outside world.

In an ending that recalls the Buñuel film *El ángel exterminador*, the family is freed from their isolation. Gabriel Limas is arrested, and the family has the opportunity to enter the outside world, determining their own freedom. However, the wife and children return to their former reclusive existence, habit and ritual triumphing over reason, thereby preserving the insularity — the purity — of this dysfunctional family.

Some critics have found the film a poetical destruction of the "sacred family" unit; others find it a story of suspense, moral and interior. The film is

An unidentified Tzeltal Indian woman from Southern Mexico in Rolando Klein's film about Mayan rituals, *Chac* (1974).

open to all interpretations, but the internal Mexican character of the film is undoubtable as it passionately examines those totemic figures of Mexican society: the Father and the Mother, before whom the rebellion of the children can take place. What one remembers in *El castillo* is not just the family's eighteen-year confinement, but the film's allegorical representations — the film as an image of the paternalism of the Mexican government, as a criticism of the macho double standard, as a metaphor for rationalist Christian society, as pretensions derived from the film works of Buñuel and Cocteau. Whatever the provenance, Ripstein is an original *auteur*.

Castle of Purity see *El Castillo de la pureza*

53. Cecilia. Humberto Solas. Cuba, 1982. 159 min., Color. Spanish.

COMMENTARY: Adapted from the "telenovela" of seven hours' length and the popular nineteenth-century novel by C. Villaverde, *Cecilia* stars Daisy Granados in the title role and Spanish actor Imanol Arias as her lover. It depicts Cuban society of the 1800s, stressing the class distinctions between whites, mulattoes and blacks. Although slavery by this time had been abolished in Spain and Britain, it was still rife in Cuba, the center of the island's economy. After a slave revolt in nearby Haiti, there was fear in Cuba of the same sort of rebellion. Thus, in the film, tension hangs in the air; violence and atrocities against black slaves persist. There are some graphic scenes in beautiful set pieces like a nineteenth-century sugar mill (Solas did this before in his film *Lucia*, but in black and white), and the director evokes lovingly his portrait of nineteenth-century Cuban society. Some may prefer to see the complete seven hour film, since Solas is an expert at pictorial depiction of societal panoramas. (*Lucia* was half as long; a strong indictment of the Spanish colonials and Batista, the film was decidedly pro–Castro.) A complete video version is available for those who prefer the raw details and not the emotional gloss of the three-hour version.

54. Chac (Chac: A Mayan Tale of Ritual and Magical Power). Rolando Klein. Mexico, 1974. 95 min., Color. Spanish/Tzeltal/Mayan.

COMMENTARY: An isolated village suffers a terrible drought. The shaman predicts rain. The villagers plant, but the rain does not come. Rumor spreads that a certain diviner, who lives alone in the mountains, can bring rain. Some say he is a witch, and the chief refuses to call him. Nevertheless, the elders insist that he should be summoned. Reluctantly the chief and his captains journey in search of the diviner. The latter agrees to help them but demands their full trust. Instead of returning to the village, he takes them far into an unknown land, in search of some sacred water needed for his ceremony. Now certain the diviner is a witch, the chief and his two captains abandon him in fright. Finally the diviner and the nine remaining captains return to the village, where they prepare an elaborate rain ceremony. In spite of the devotion, the rain fails to come. The diviner says rain will come after three days and then departs. On the first day, a boy of the tribe falls ill for no apparent reason; on the second day, he dies. On the third day, the chief, reassuming control over the village, charges that the diviner used wicked powers over the boy, causing his death. The chief and his villagers then head for the mountains to kill the diviner in revenge for the boy's death. They find him already dead, and in horror, they throw his bundled body down a deep well to rid themselves of evil spirits. Instantly the rain breaks with all its might. (Press book.)

Filmed entirely on location with an Indian cast — the Tzeltal villagers of Tenejapa (Chiapas) of southern Mexico — *Chac* is a beautifully made documentary in a glossy, picturesque style reminiscent of National Geographic photographic layouts. Director Rolando Klein shows real ability to obtain simple, direct, unselfconscious performances from his actors. *Chac* is incantation, spell, simple and direct in its content, elegiac in its imagery but complex in its form. In a literal sense, it is about the search for a rainmaker. But its search encompasses faith, belief, endurance, perserverance. The film belongs to the cinema of myth and ritual along with Flaherty's *Nanook of the North*, Jodorowsky's *El topo*, Kurosawa's *Seven Samurai* and Eisenstein's *Ivan the Terrible*. There is a timeless, legendary quality to the work which makes it fascinating. And the scenery is absolutely awe-inspiring.

NOTES: Chilean-born Rolando Klein

studied film at UCLA. His first documentary was *The Green Bridge* (1971), about a prisoner on Terminal Island in San Pedro, California. He moved to Mexico in 1972 and began filming *Chac* in 1974.

Chac: A Mayan Tale of Ritual and Power see *Chac*

55. El chacal de Nahueltoro (The Jackal of Nahueltoro). Miguel Littín. Chile, 1970. 95 min., B&W. Spanish.

COMMENTARY: Always trying to foment political change, director Miguel Littín based this film on an actual incident. A Chilean peasant, José (expertly played by Nelson Villagra), for no apparent reason kills a widowed farm woman and her five children. He is hunted, captured and jailed for the crime. While incarcerated, he converts to Catholicism, learns life's values, and masters reading and writing just before he is duly executed by a firing squad. Littín builds up our expectations that the criminal will be pardoned, giving the film some suspense and emotional depth. But when the "jackal" is executed, Littín blames the institutions — the church, the penal system, not the poverty or ignorance that the Chilean government perpetuated before the election of Salvador Allende. To create authenticity, Littín shot the entire film on location where José was imprisoned. He even used direct quotations from interviews with the "jackal" himself. However it is the denunciation of injustice of the penal system and the irony of José's illumination that leads him to literally sign his own death warrant after learning how to write, and to die as a Catholic within his newly acquired faith. *The Jackal of Nahueltoro* certainly belongs in the pantheon of great revisionist cinema and stands as one of the first and best of Littín's politically

A scene from Miguel Littín's *El chacal de Nahueltoro* (*The Jackal of Nahueltoro*, 1974).

inspired films. The allegorical *Alsino y el condor*, *La tierra prometida* and *Sandino* are all worthy politically inspired films by this exiled Chilean director.

The Charcoal Worker see *El Megano*

56. Los chicos de la guerra

(The Children of the War). Bebe Kamin. Argentina, 1984. 107 min., Color. Spanish.

COMMENTARY: Based on the lives of four boys, Pablo, Fabian, Santiago and Marcelo, all of different social classes and psychological makeup, this film tries to reflect through them the political history of Argentina during the years leading up to the Malvinas War. The film puts the blame squarely on the shoulders of the older generation, who send the kids into a war they do not want and for which they are ill prepared.

The four *chicos* were born in a country with no civil liberties, no human rights, and no possibility of free speech or opinion — an authoritarian society that does not have much to offer except repression and frustration. The script presents a series of flashbacks, the past of the youngsters, from their first days in school to their mobilization and final defeat. The boys were born in 1962 and entered primary school in 1968; two began high school in 1976. One boy is artistic, one headstrong, one rich, one poor. In addition to tracking the lives of the boys, the film shows grownup attitudes ranging from middle-class indifference to upper-class militaristic elitism to the ignorant nationalism of the blue-collar sector.

The director also presents her views of political corruption and manipulation, the brutality of mindless terrorism and media-driven brainwashing. Speaking

Unidentified youngster from the Castaneda family lugging bricks, part of the hard life of the youth in Colombia in Marta Rodríguez and Jorge Silva's film *Chiricales* (*Brickmakers*, 1972).

about the film, Bebe Kamin said in an interview: "Its purpose is not to judge or condemn in advance, but to bring back the need for creative freedom that can allow us to gradually define our own identity." The film shows us the repressed lives of four youngsters, growing up in an authoritarian society that frustrates their potential and mutilitates them by sending them into an unnecessary war. *Chicos* is a strong film that one hopes might point the way for Argentines to redefine their own national identity.

Children of the War see *Los Chicos de la guerra*

57. Chiricales (Brickmakers).
Marta Rodríguez and Jorge Silva. Colombia, 1972. 42 min., B&W. Spanish.

COMMENTARY: A marvelous short film, *Chiricales* follows the Castaneda family in its daily labor: the artesanal production of clay bricks. In doing so, the film explores the culture of poverty that is the way of life for millions of Latin Americans, landless peasants living on the fringes of major cities. According to the MOMA program notes, the film took six years to make and was shot without synchronized sound. The result of the directors' craftsmanship is "a denunciation of the conditions of indentured servitude under which a once-rural populace now struggles vainly to survive.... [The film] begins in an explicitly political and sociological register but then becomes something quite different — subjective, introspective, fantasy-based — when a young girl's first communion celebration is elided with

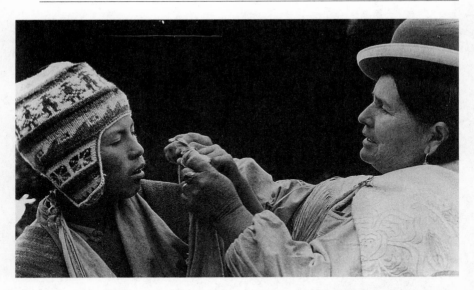

Nestor Yuria (left) plays Isico, the young boy apprenticed to the unidentified old Peruvian Indian woman (right) in Antonio Eguino's multi-episode film, *Chuquiago* (1977).

scenes of widowhood and mourning. Poised between observation and interiority, this film recapitulates the cinematic strategies of the 1960s and anticipates those of the eighties." (MOMA program notes.)

Chronicle of a Boy Alone see *Crónica de un niño solo*

58. Chuquiago. Antonio Eguino. Bolivia, 1977. 87 min., Color. Aymara/ Spanish.

COMMENTARY: The film tells the story of four main characters who live in the city of La Paz — or Chuquiago, as the city is called in Aymara, one of the Indian languages of Bolivia. (La Paz is the name bestowed by the Spanish conquerors.) Each character's social class is determined by the topography of the city: the higher the altitude of the character's residence, the lower the class. Each of the characters is involved in a process of alienation and shaped by the contradictions within the society. (Press book.)

The first episode deals with Isico, a young Indian boy who is brought to La Paz by his parents and apprenticed by them to an old woman working in the local marketplace as a coffee vendor. Isico drifts into the life of a street urchin, probably to become like one of the drunken Indians who torment him as he wanders about La Paz. Meeting a woman who sells fruit, Isico gets a job carrying loads of fruit on his back for lady shoppers in the market, an occupation that will condemn him for the rest of his life.

The second episode is about Johnny, an Indian teenager. His parents, a hardworking bricklayer and his wife, embarrass their upwardly mobile son. Johnny, frustrated by the life around him, is desperately seeking to escape his milieu. He becomes a school dropout and enters into a life of petty crime. He is last seen running (probably after committing a minor theft as a means of getting out of the country) after being conned by an employment agency that promises work in the United States, another exploit that results in further frustration.

The third episode is about Carlos, a middle-aged civil servant who works in a government office where bureaucracy has become an art. Well on his way to joining the middle class, he has five children, is in debt and has few aspirations except to spend Friday evenings out "with the boys," his only enjoyment. Carlos' way of life is described in a series of scenes that contradict what is said about Carlos and what he really does. Although congenial, Carlos is really a parasite in the social structure. The true banality of his life expresses itself in an outburst of machismo in an evening of drink, dice and whoring.

The fourth and last episode is about Patricia, a pretty, young upper-class university student, a pseudo-radical always flirting with university activism, much to her mother's dismay. She covets a profession but gives in to her parents by marrying the man of their dreams — a man she does not love who promises to be a replica of her father, perhaps even worse. Her decision to marry comes when the university is shut down by the government. Patricia decides to leave her previous activities as a romantic remembrance.

All the episodes are depressingly bleak, but the director has achieved fine performances from his actors: Nestor Yuria, Edmundo Villaroel, David Santalla and Tatiana Aponte. Eguino has also presented a scathing indictment of Bolivian society, its economic and social system, in his slice-of-life view of four people. Although these characters never even meet in the film, through some clever editing Eguino achieves remarkable continuity. At the conclusion, there is a chance encounter between Isico, loaded with a bundle on his back, and Patricia, who is leaving on her honeymoon trip. They exchange glances, nothing more, and the film is open-

ended. For Eguino, daily life is a continual process of illusion and frustration, reflecting the contradictions within Bolivian society.

NOTES: *Chuquiago* is the director's second feature. Although his first orientation into filmmaking was as a still photographer in the late fifties, Eguino first studied filmmaking at City College (CUNY) for one year in the mid-sixties. Originally part of the Ukamau group of filmmakers created by Jorge Sanjinés in the mid-sixties, Eguino began his film career as the director of photography on Sanjinés's early films, *Yawar mallku* and *El coraje del pueblo*. His first film was *Pueblo chico* (1974). His 1984 *Amargo mar* (*Bitter Sea*) dealt with the War of the Pacific and its disastrous consequences for Bolivia.

59. La cifra impar (Odd Number). Manuel Antín. Argentina, 1962. 86 min., Color. Spanish.

COMMENTARY: Based upon Julio Cortázar's short story "Letters to Mother" from his collection entitled *Las Armas Secretas*, this film deals with a young couple now living in Paris who receive letters from the husband's mother in Buenos Aires. She talks of another son (a painter, now dead, who was the wife's former lover) as if he were alive and announces his imminent arrival in Paris. In adapting this Cortázar story, the director hauntingly evokes the disintegrating reality of the couple and the phantom of obsession that comes between them. Starring María Rosa Gallo and Lautaro Murua, *La cifra impar* is Antín's first highly successful fiction feature.

NOTES: Manuel Antín was born in Las Palmas, Argentina, in 1926 and was first an author of novels and plays before he entered the world of cinema as a scriptwriter, then a director. He made his first early films with Rodolfo Kuhn based upon his own scripts and then in

1962 directed *La cifra impar*. His subsequent films are based upon literary themes — *Don Segundo Sombra* (1969), *Allá lejos y hace tiempo* (1978) and *La invitación* (1982) are based upon the novels of Ricardo Guiraldes, Enrique Hudson and Beatriz Guido, respectively. An extremely personal and creative director, Antín has been working for Argentine television since 1983.

The City and the Dogs see *La ciudad y los perros*

60. La ciudad y los perros
(**The City and the Dogs**). Francisco J. Lombardi. Peru, 1985. 138 min., Color. Spanish.

COMMENTARY: Based upon Mario Vargas Llosa's 1962 international bestseller, this is director Lombardi's fourth film. Ostensibly about the moral corruption of military cadets, the film also underscores the reality of military corruption in Peru and the end of a dictatorship. The cadets represent a cross-section of Peruvian society. There is Poet (Pablo Serra), the narrator of the film, who stands for decency and fair play. He becomes the arch enemy of Jaguar (Juan M. Ochoa), a blonde, Nazi-like leader who controls a small gangster clique that deals in forbidden liquor, cigarettes, pornography and stolen exams. The essential conflict exists between Poet and Jaguar. Another student, Slave, is "accidentally" killed during war maneuvers for ratting on a student who cheated during exams, and Poet brings charges against Jaguar through a secret report to Lt. Gamboa (Gustavo Bueno). The top brass want to bury the shooting incident as quickly as possible. Gamboa promises to defend Poet but is penalized himself, posted to a faraway barracks as recompense for a clear conscience. Poet leaves the military academy, and Jaguar is drummed out of the corps. Lt. Gamboa may represent the mentality of the military at its best, but he is roundly defeated by the officer class that constantly undermines moral decision-making in favor of cover-ups and machismo. There are some minor subplots dealing with each boy's longing for sexual experience with a local girl named Teresa and the military's use of blackmail to bury Poet's accusations against Jaguar since Poet wrote some pornographic stories.

Nevertheless, director Lombardi has taken an unwieldly novel with many stylistic time shifts and made a fairly blunt, literal film with narrative force, richly detailed at times, but with few surprises. If the film had pretensions of an allegorical dimension, it escaped this viewer completely. Of inordinate length, the film could use some sharp cutting. The fact that it was made at all constantly surprises since it could only be filmed after the military regime that ruled Peru until the mid-eighties was thrown out of power. Many films have been set in military academies, where traditions and loyalties are both served and violated, where brutality and machismo surge forth as principal values. But few films are as good as this at dealing with the collapse of the authoritarian system and the loss of innocence of members of the academy. *La ciudad y los perros* deserves much praise for its attempts to grapple with these problems and provide some limited insights into the Peruvian nation.

Classic Model see *Modelo Antiguo*

61. El color escondido (Hidden Color).
Raúl de la Torre. Argentina, 1988. 92 min., Color. Spanish.

COMMENTARY: The Argentine director Raúl de la Torre probes the psyche of a young woman's life, one who is struggling particularly with an Electra complex. Instead of using dialogue, however, de la Torre relies upon a wordless story, advancing our revelation of Helena (remarkably played by Carola Reyna) through her own actions, dreams, imaginings and recollections.

One evening, while on her way home from work, she imagines she is being raped on the train by three macho youths — but we follow her real life in other thoughts about her husband (who betrayed her with another woman), her current lover, her boss and even a peeping Tom. As she relives some of these fantasies and realities, three women acting as the Three Graces serve Helena as a wordless chorus, emphasizing her thoughts. There is much nudity and sex in the film as the tale of Helena's complex comes to a predictable conclusion. The film would have been better if it were half of its length and had the look of a super first-rate production, rather than a glossy sex manual or video, despite its beautiful photography which rarely serves the scenario.

62. Como agua para chocolate (Like Water for Chocolate). Alfonso Arau. Mexico, 1992. 144 min., Color. Spanish.

COMMENTARY: A magical and enchanting film based upon the fictional experiences of a Mexican family that enjoys life intensely, the movie captivates this viewer with its magical realism, its supernatural and also realistic screenplay (written by Laura Esquivel, based upon her novel of the same name).

The film is a family saga whose main theme is forbidden love. It is the story of Tita (played beautifully by newcomer Lumi Cavazos), who has always had the power of mixing food with herbs that create strong emotional responses. Her mother (Regina Torne) has gone through much hardship and wants her youngest daughter to take care of her in her old age. However, Tita has other ideas. She meets Pedro (Marco Leonardi), falls for him wildly and wants to marry him, but she is denied his offer of marriage by Mama Elena, who persuades him to marry Tita's elder sister, Rosaura (Yarell Artizmendi). Pedro agrees to the marriage, realizing this is the only way he can stay close to Tita, still his beloved. Poor Tita has to prepare their wedding feast. But with the help of the elderly cook, Nacha (Ada Carrasco), Tita's tears flow into the food and as a result, the wedding guests are overcome with the frustration of Tita's lost love and all become ill at the wedding, mourning for their own lost loves.

In one of the film's most imaginative episodes, Tita pricks her finger on thorns, then prepares a sauce that is a physical embodiment of her desire for Pedro. The effect of this sauce is so great that Tita's other sister, Gertrudis (Claudette Maille), feels her body temperature rise and rushes outdoors to cool off. The shower catches fire with her body heat, and she is rescued nude on horseback by a revolutionary, one of Pancho Villa's soldiers, who has fallen under Gertrudis's spell. Of course, Mama Elena disowns her daughter for life.

Tita's life continues to be one of misery; she cries herself to sleep nightly and knits blankets to ease her pain. Her mother finally dies, and Tita is relieved. Because of her hatred for Mama Elena, Tita's love for Pedro has grown even stronger, despite the fact that her mother sent Pedro and Rosaura to live in Texas. Nevertheless, in one spectacular scene, Pedro and Tita make love and thereby drive away the ghost of Mama Elena forever — some magical realism here. Rosaura becomes ill after giving birth to her second child. She has also become obese because of digestive problems. Fearing that she is losing Pedro, she asks Tita to help win him back. Since Tita may now marry John Brown (Mario Iván Martínez), an American Indian doctor, Tita agrees to help her sister. But Rosaura dies, and she and Pedro are united.

The film moves twenty years ahead in time to a party scene. An older Pedro and Tita are embracing each other; Gertrudis and her soldier husband are equally fulfilled. Chenca, the maid, feasts on the food Tita has prepared with "love and lust." After the guests have eaten, everyone rushes off to fulfill the sexual desires inspired by the cuisine. Finally, after twenty-two years, Pedro and Tita indulge in their most passionate lovemaking scene, where he dies in her arms. Their torrid, slow-burning affair has never ceased in all that time. Tita then takes a blanket she had knitted and covers herself and Pedro with it. Eating grains of matches with the fire inside, flames ignite Tita from within and she dies, ending her own life, lying on top of Pedro, covered by the flames and heat of passion their bodies expelled...incredible.

Como agua para chocolate is a stunning film to watch, beautifully photographed, excellently acted, brilliantly written and directed. It should have won the Best Foreign Film Oscar for 1993, but it seems the Spaniards had sewn up that political scene and the Academy gave the award to that insipid, beautifully photographed but poorly allegorical film, *Belle Epoque*. The latter film had a very short run in New York City, while *Chocolate* continues to tantalize audiences in the third year of its first run. Who said a film combining food and the spirit could not succeed commercially?

NOTES: In the United States, Alfonso Arau is primarily known as a Mexican actor in American films, playing usually the villain (*The Wild Bunch*, *Posse*, and *Romancing the Stone*). However, in Mexico, he is primarily known as the director of *Como agua para chocolate* as well as the 1980 production *Mojado power*. He is married to screenplay writer and novelist Laura Esquivel.

63. Como era gostoso o meu frances (How Tasty Was My Little Frenchman). Nelson Pereira dos Santos. Brazil, 1971. 80 min., Color. Portuguese.

COMMENTARY: Set in sixteenth-century Brazil, the film is about a French soldier (Arduino Colassanti) who escapes his officers and is captured first by the Portuguese and then by a tribe of Indian cannibals. Because the Indians mistake him for one of their enemies, the Portuguese, they decide to kill the Frenchman for his crimes and eat him for his powers. But he is given a long period of reprieve and privilege, during which he marries a local widow and gives counsel to the chief, finally showing the Indians how to use cannons and gunpowder. Though he helps them to win a fight against a local tribe, our Frenchman is on the menu for a victory feast. He discovers a buried treasure and trades it for gunpowder to lengthen his life, but he is finally eaten after he tries to escape with the gold. His wife is seen munching on a part of him after the Frenchman has died with some dignity as a result of her coaching.

The film begins as a comedy but is not really all that humorous. It is a moving but uneven treatise on the primitive versus the modern and the transfer of power. The tribe believes that the slave, the Frenchman, is their enemy, who must first fight with the tribe and then be killed and eaten to become part of the chieftan's body as an offering to the gods, so that those souls who have fought beside the chief will rest in a pleasant place. The cannibalistic act takes on the significance of the Eucharist. However, the Catholic clergy are more interested in gold than in the magical mysteries of transubstantiation or overt cannibalism as a symbolic act. Yet the entire film turns on the premise that the sacrifice of the Frenchman is a moment of supreme faith and beauty,

totally in opposition to the religious solution of Europeans who lust for gold
and power. By sacrificing himself, the
Frenchman has conquered death and
will achieve nobility, living the lives of
his ancestors in a pattern of eternal return.

It is fascinating that *Como era gostoso
o meu frances* was turned down as an
entry into the Cannes Film Festival of
1971 because of extreme frontal nudity
by both sexes, even though the film is
an ethical, morally sound, innocent, un-
exploitive and profoundly serious work
by a director who explores the melding
of different cultures and religions and
gives us a unique, totally enticing view
of pre-colonial Brazil ripe for territorial
exploitation. Although some critics may
scorn the director for using middleclass
white Brazilians in garishly reddened
body makeup as substitutes for real Indians, or sneer at the phony set piece of
a model Portuguese galleon in the harbor, the film contains wonderfully convincing performances and a bold attempt at versimilitude in recreating an
Indian village and society of the early
sixteenth century. Although the story
may meander at times, the director has
made a fascinating film in the spirit
of classic Brazilian cinema, culturally
thrilling and consistently entertaining.

NOTES: Nelson Pereira dos Santos
was born in São Paulo in 1928 and is
considered one of the most important of
the *Cinema Nôvo* directors in Brazil
today. He began his own career in film,
making documentaries — *Rio 40 graus*
(1955) and *Rio, zona norte* (1957), preferring to accentuate the sociological and
psychological aspects of cinema rather
than the neo-realistic. He helped edit
Glauber Rocha's *Barravento* (1962) and
made his debut feature in 1964 with
Vidas secas, for which he gained international recognition. He continued to
make films into the late eighties, but
none had the international success of
Vidas secas or *Como esa gostoso o meu
frances*.

64. Compañeras y com-
pañeros. Adolfas Mekas, Barbara
Stone, David C. Stone. Cuba/U.S.,
1970. 140 min., Color. Spanish.

COMMENTARY: The press book calls
this "a film about Cuba's youth: the student, the worker, the peasant, the
teacher, the soldier. A portrait of the
new third world consciousness." In
1969, in four of Cuba's six provinces, an
American crew spent several months living with and filming five different
groups of young people, representing a
cross-section of Cuban youth. In each
section of the film, the young people are
shown in their daily activities — school,
work, entertainment. They discuss the
revolutionary society and their place in
it; their political thinking; the violence
of the urban guerrillas; and their feelings about Che and Fidel.

The film tells the story of Cubans ten
years after the revolution in their own
words, without narration. It is a unique
record, capturing the vitality and verve
of what the Cuban Revolution was really all about. Jonas Mekas said of it: "It
succeeds where most of the political documentaries fail: it succeeds in making
the filmmaker invisible: the people of
Cuba present their own truth." It may
be a nice change to see Cubans talking
about work, pride, loyalty and patrio-
tism rather than movies, restaurants, life
insurance, medical plans and the like,
but the film is pure propaganda and
shows only interviews with people who
follow the party line. There is no adverse criticism, no skepticism, no anti-
social attitude, only conformity and an
undiluted belief in the illusions of the
Cuban Revolution. It is worthwhile only
as a filmed document of Barbara and
David Stone and Adolfas Mekas, who
were given permission to film between
July and October of 1969 and who

Unidentified miner in a scene from Jorge Sanjinés's *El coraje del pueblo* (*The Courage of the People*, 1973-74).

present this record of their accomplishments seemingly in total agreement with the goals of the Castro government. Perhaps an update of the film today might help the producers to revise their original thinking about this 1970 work.

65. El coraje del pueblo
(The Courage of the People). Jorge Sanjinés. Bolivia, 1973-74. 95 min., Color. Spanish.

COMMENTARY: *El coraje del pueblo* is a brilliant film which recreates the tragic events in Bolivia in June of 1967 at the Siglo XX mines, when the military put its tin miners under siege in an attempt to restore law and order in the face of communist infiltration. It reenacts the massacre in detail and suggests the military had the support of United States observers. As close to docudrama as he can be, Sanjinés intermingles fact and fiction, using testimony from survivors

of that infamous Noche de San Juan as well as recreations of past events. For example, we see women forming groups to protest the lack of food at company stores. After their clandestine meeting, many of them disappear. Men who ask their whereabouts are beaten, sometimes to death. Then the armed military burrows into the mining town and shoots the people down. Sanjinés is very succesful in recreating the collective memory of persecution and resistance by using survivors of the massacre as actors in the film. Multiple narrators tell the story of what happened on that fateful Night of San Juan. Sanjinés lets the witnesses speak directly into the camera, openly. Sanjinés imposes none of his own views on what really happened but simply creates an atmosphere of freedom where the narrators reveal their own history. The film, as good and accurate as it is, was not shown in Bolivia until ten years after its production because of the military's return to power.

NOTES: Born in 1937 in La Paz, Jorge Sanjinés studied film at the University of Chile and in 1963 made his first documentary, *Revolución*. Subsequently, he formed Ukamau Films and produced and directed several films that have achieved international acclaim: *Ukamau* (1963), a bleak realistic tale of rape and vengeance which was also Bolivia's very first feature film; *Yawar mallku* (1969), a piercing outcry against sterilization of unsuspecting peasant women as part of a wholly deceptive, American-guided birth control program enacted by the Peace Corps until their eventual ouster in the 1970s; and *El coraje del pueblo*. Outside of Bolivia while in exile, he directed *The Principal Enemy* (1974); *Get Out of Here* (1977) and *Flags of Dawn* (1984). As always, Jorge Sanjinés returns to his essential preoccupation: the plight of the Bolivian Indian and his social and ideological transformation. Sanjinés is one of the leading practitioners of militant cinema.

The Courage of the People see *El coraje del pueblo*

The Criminal Life of Archibaldo de la Cruz see *Ensayo de un crimen*

66. Crónica de un niño solo

(**Chronicle of a Boy Alone**). Leonardo Favio. Argentina, 1964. 80 min., B&W. Spanish.

COMMENTARY: A debut film for Leonardo Favio, who owes much to François Truffaut (*The 400 Blows*), Hector Babenco (*Pixote*), Robert Bresson and the Italian Neo-Realists as he tells the story of a boy in a children's home who experiences a severe regime of brutality and hunger as well as suffering the imaginative and perverse whims of other inmates. A young street kid, Polín (Diego Puente), is arrested and placed

in a juvenile corrections center from which he later escapes, fleetingly, into the streets of Buenos Aires to join his mother at his home somewhere in a shady part of the great metropolis. He is caught and returned to the detention center. There is only one lapse in the otherwise stark nature of the film — a bucolic section where Polín goes to swim in an unidentifiable river. But even this serene moment is broken as he is accosted by a *pandilla* of other tough kids, making fun of his institution-shaved head. The director's view is very pessimistic. Favio sees no way out of these sordid conditions. Poverty will drive Polín back to juvenile hall, and Favio merely acts as an unsentimental observer of the harsh realities, with candid tight shots of the reformatory, labyrinthine patterns of slum dwellings and impressionistic street scenes executed beautifully in black and white by ace cinematographer Ignacio Souto.

NOTES: On October 14, 1987, when *Crónica* was first seen in New York at the Museum of Modern Art in an Argentine film series, a *Variety* film critic called this first film of Leonardo Favio a "fine example of the 'gaucho nuevo cine movement'" of the sixties and seventies and saw the film as a powerful statement about juvenile delinquency.

67. Cronos. Guillermo Del Toro.

Mexico, 1993. 92 min., Color. Spanish/ English.

COMMENTARY: *Cronos* is a wonderful revival of the vampire film, in color and imbued with a sense of humor and visionary style of the director, elevating it into something more exotic and meaningful than the Bela Lugosi *Dracula* and the newest Francis Ford Coppola CinemaScope version of the old stake-through-the-heart story. It stars Argentine actor Federico Luppi as Jesús Gris, an elegant antique store proprietor who comes across a mysterious statue in his collection that contains the "chronos device," an ornate clockwork instrument that has the power to grant eternal life by giving its user a thirst for life-sustaining human blood. Sometimes we see the inside of the chronos instrument, a pulsating mixture of gleaming gold and mechanical parts, full of beetles and roaches, elegant and ghoulish. It fastens its claws like a crab onto the arm of Gris and transforms him instantly into a vampire. The chronos is also desperately sought after by a dying millionaire industrialist, Dieter de la Guardia (Claudio Brook), who sends his son, Ángel de la Guardia (played in high thug style by the American actor Ron Perlman), to procure the chronos either by purchase or thievery. Ángel, however, wants to gain immortality by stealing the chronos for himself. The film ends with an unsettling conclusion, for all the protagonists are dispatched to their respective deaths, including our sympathetic antiques-dealer-turned-vampire. But the real star of the film is the ghoulish vampire makeup by a firm called Necropia, apparently jointly owned by the director and Dick Smith, the famous American makeup artist of many modern horror films.

NOTES: Guillermo del Toro is thought to be one of the most promising youthful Mexican film directors today. He studied screenwriting with Jaime Humberto Hermosillo, one of Mexico's most respected and outrageous contemporary filmmakers, and also learned the art of special effects and advanced makeup with expert Dick Smith. He headed the film department at the University of Guadalajara and is the author of a definitive volume on Alfred Hitchcock. In 1985, he founded his own film production/special effects/stop-motion and clay animation company, Necropia, which also produces commercials in Mexico for Kodak, Kraft and other companies. Other films to del Toro's credit are

Invasión (1990) and *Caminos de ayer* (1990), with three others that have never been seen in the United States. *Cronos* is his first international success.

68. La cruz del sur (The Southern Cross). Patricio Guzmán. Spain/Chile, 1992. 80 min., Color. Spanish.

COMMENTARY: Made as a three-part television documentary, *La cruz del sur* is a blend of historical scenes with interviews and documentary footage about conflicts between ancestral Latin American religions and Christianity. Opening with the first historic contact between the Spanish invaders and Latin American natives, the director then cuts to modern-day Guatemala and daily military drills. He juxtaposes ancient religious concerns with present-day ongoing military occupation. Much like a stream-of-consciousness novel, the film is freewheeling in form. Guzmán tosses in many theological and ideological questions but offers few answers. His faith rests in the individual, whose own personal religious practices will survive despite the prevailing onslaught of Catholicism. Edited with the zest of a true documentary approach, Guzmán's film is unclear at times when he does not identify certain countries and particular faiths practiced there. But his prime interest is resurrecting the concept of the soul, and the body afterwards. A new and somewhat strange direction for the politically inspired filmmaker of the sensational three-part documentary *La batalla de Chile*.

69. Cuando los hijos se van (When Children Leave Home). Juan Bustillo Oro. Mexico, 1941. 127 min., B&W. Spanish.

COMMENTARY: One of the most popular films of all time in Mexico and throughout Latin America, *Cuando los hijos se van* is a family melodrama that has been remade twice (in 1957 and 1969) and also has become the basis for a contemporary *telenovela* (television soap opera), the equivalent of the British *Upstairs, Downstairs* but reflecting the best nationalistic qualities of Mexican cinema.

The plot concerns an upper-middle-class family: domineering father Don José Rosales (Fernando Soler), his soft-hearted wife, Doña Lupita (Sara García), and their problematic children, Amalia (Marina Tamayo), Raimundo (Emilio Tuero), and José (Carlos López Moctezuma).

Amalia has decided to elope with a wealthy older man, a wolf old enough to be her father, without consent from her parents. Raimundo, the father's favorite, is mistakenly thought of as a troublemaker. José is the real villain who casts blame upon Raimundo. He makes a play for the erring wife (Gloria Marín) who has just given him a good job, and Raimundo is blamed for this indiscretion. What saves the film from the dreariness of these melodramatic events is the humor of Don Casimiro, the steadfast friend of the family (played with boundless energy by Joaquin Pardave).

The story proceeds to unravel through two years of Christmas celebrations. At the conclusion, Amalia has left her husband and returns home, repenting her disobedience. José also returns home, confessing his misdeeds, and is forgiven by his father, who learns that Raimundo, now dead, was the really good son. Amalia is reunited with an old boyfriend, who seems to have waited for her enlightenment, and the family unit continues to adjust, bearing their pain and persevering towards an indefinite future. The acting is reminiscent of Hollywood's silent era — Don José is too righteous and repentant as the head of the family; Doña Lupita is too sympathetic as the long-suffering mother; the boys display equal amounts of goodness and scorn befitting their characters. Only Gloria Marín as the erring wife projects provocative emotion and sexuality with real conviction and intensity as the flirtatious paramour of Carlos López Moctezuma. Although the film may have the reputation of a shameless, tear-jerking melodrama sprinkled with occasional comedy scenes, the moral ups and downs of the children redeemed through self-sacrifice give it universal appeal despite much beating of breasts, tortured facial expressions and milking of emotional scenes to the last melodramatic drop. Despite its drawbacks, the film deals with the major themes of classical Mexican cinema: capitalism, patriarchy, machismo, woman as virgin-whore-wife-mother, the church and class. In this context it should be seen as most revealing of the mores of 1940 Mexico.

70. Cuarteles de invierno
(Winter Headquarters). Lautaro Murua. Argentina, 1984. 120 min., Color. Spanish.

COMMENTARY: Based upon a novel by Osvaldo Soriano, this film is set in a small town outside of Buenos Aires in 1980. The military-occupied country is in the last months of brutal repression. Two men have been detained to be used by the military as an example for the troops of the outpost, presenting an image of unity on behalf of the townspeople. But as the men are interrogated, their attitudes change and they resist the will of the military, which results in their probable deaths.

Another political film made very much in the style of Jorge Sanjinés, *Cuarteles de invierno* benefits from the documentary approach and the wonderful acting of Oscar Ferrigno, Eduardo Pavlovsky, Ulise Durant, Arturo Maly and Enrique Almada in stellar roles, as well as the crisp photography of Aníbal

Gonzáles Rodríguez and a delicious musical score by tango artist Astor Piazzolla. Like Sanjinés, Murua is a believer in revisionist political cinema, always seeking societal change through his films.

NOTES: Lautaro Murua was born in Chile in 1927 but is primarily known as an Argentine actor and director although he did act in one Chilean film, *El paso maldito* (1947), before his arrival in Buenos Aires ten years later. It was in Buenos Aires that he became very well known, starring in several Torre Nilsson films such as *Graciela*, *La casa de Ángel*, *La caída* and *Fin de fiesta*. He began directing in 1960 and made *Shunko*, about the problems of illiteracy in the provinces and far-flung rural regions of Argentina. That film had a wonderful screenplay by Paraguayan novelist Augusto Roa Bastos. In 1975, he filmed *La raúlito*, an innovative film about psychosocial casework and investigations. He followed this up with another version made in Spain called *La raútio hoy*, made in 1977. But because of his overtly political films like *Cuarteles de invierno*, he was forced into exile, having survived a bomb attack on his home during the 1980s.

71. La cucaracha. Ismael Rodríguez. Mexico, 1959. 89 min., Eastmancolor. Spanish.

COMMENTARY: Set during the Mexican Revolution with a fascinating cast of all-star actors — María Félix as Refugio, Dolores del Río as Chabela, Pedro Armendáriz as Valentín, and Emilio Fernández as Antonio — *La cucaracha* is the tale of a peasant, General Valentín, torn between the loves of two women — the hard but feminine warrior Refugio and the sedate widow Chabela. Armendáriz finally chooses the widow but fathers an illegitimate child with Refugio before dying in battle and leaving the two women trudging on in the revolution together. The conclusion is very remi-

niscent of von Sternberg's *Morocco* and "El Indio" Fernández's *Enamorada*, in which the women survive their men or follow them into battle to their eventual deaths. The best to be said for *La cucaracha* is that it is an atmospheric film with a wonderful feeling for the era and excellent re-creation of the historical settings, although the script and acting are both conventional. We have seen this sort of historical panorama before — but with the wonderful camera work of Gabriel Figueroa and the film's star power, it is a worthwhile entertainment.

72. Los cuentos de Abelardo (Abelardo's Tales). Luis Molina Casanova. Puerto Rico, 1990. 82 min., Color. Spanish.

COMMENTARY: Few films from Puerto Rico are ever shown internationally, and *Los cuentos de Abelardo* is the first Puerto Rican effort to be shown in America since the eighties. It is also the director's debut feature and comprises three separate stories, based upon the works of Abelardo Díaz Alfaro, about simple folk living in rural towns whose main occupation was listening to the radio and passing along gossip during the decade of the forties.

The first tale, "Don Procopio el despedidor de duelos," is about a good-natured, happy undertaker haunted by his awareness that one day he will need similar services. The second tale, "Peyo Merce enseña inglés," deals with a country schoolteacher who teaches English so badly that it eclipses his students' proper knowledge of Spanish. The final tale, "Bagazo," is about an old sugar cane cutter who is unsympathetically fired by a new field boss.

The film moves quickly and is pleasantly acted by a group of unknown players who use the *jíbaro* (mountain) dialect for folkloric flavor and authenticity. But because of the unevenness of the stories and the themes, the film seems more like a faithful literary transposition of its material than a truly enjoyable cinematic experience. We hope to see other new film productions from Puerto Rico in the coming years.

73. A dama do cine Shanghai (Lady from the Shanghai Cinema). Guilherme de Almeida Prado. Brazil, 1988. 115 min., Color. Portuguese.

COMMENTARY: A parody of the American gangster films of the 1940s, *A dama do cine Shanghai* is about Lucas, an ex-boxer selling real estate who finds himself in a local cinema one evening, escaping from his job duties. While watching a gangster film, he is lured by a *femme fatale* in the audience who looks suspiciously like an onscreen heroine. In a plot reminiscent of the American films *Pennies from Heaven* and *Purple Rose of Cairo*, in which actors walk off the screen into the audience and participate in the lives of real people, Lucas (Antonio Fagundes) is whisked away by Suzana (Maite Proenca), a dame who leads him into a maze of danger, violence and crime. Lucas assumes a Bogart role and Suzana plays his Bacall in this complex parody of American forties film noir, resulting in a Brazilian cult film that deserves international exposure.

74. Dance of Hope. Deborah Shaffer. Chile/U.S., 1989. 75 min., Color. Spanish.

COMMENTARY: Through intimate portraits of eight women, *Dance of Hope* tells the story of the human and social costs of sixteen years of military rule in Chile. Many of the women are members of the Association of the Relatives Detained and Disappeared. Their "dance of solitude," based upon the sensuous *cueca*, Chile's national dance, was the basis for the theme song by Sting, "They Dance Alone." (Press book.)

This film opened just two weeks before the historic December 14, 1989,

elections in Chile — the first since the 1973 military coup that began Pinochet's sixteen-year dictatorship. The film itself interweaves intimate portraits of eight Chilean women, opening with the stark testimonies of women whose relatives disappeared. It examines the issues of human rights and social policy in contemporary Chile as the Chilean people attempt to reclaim their democratic heritage. We watch the women dance alone, symbolic of the irrevocable loss of their male partners. We watch them demonstrate in the streets of Santiago, brutally dispersed by the police with tear gas and water cannons. We even watch them dig in the desert sands of northern Chile in search of their relatives, murdered by high military officials in October of 1973. Their tragedy symbolizes the tragedy of other Latin American nations who seek their loved ones under similar circumstances. Daily the women experience violence and progressive impoverishment in Santiago's poor neighborhoods, where three million people struggle with hunger, lack of housing, unemployment and disillusionment. Like Trojan Women, these women become the collective conscience of Chile, in their "dance of hope" seeking truth and justice to insure human rights and a correct social policy that will be the central issue for the newly elected government.

Shaffer uses no voice-over to narrate what she has photographed. She prefers the on-camera interview as most revealing of the insights of the Chilean women she has chosen for the film. Although the interviews are sometimes spoken in a monotone, there is an immediacy, an informative urgency to their testimony that gives this film a hardened, truthful edge. The film also includes footage of the Amnesty International concert across the border in Argentina, where Sting and Peter Gabriel performed to publicize the Chilean women's cause.

75. Danzón. María Novaro. Mexico, 1990. 120 min., Color. Spanish.

COMMENTARY: Every Wednesday evening for six years, Julia (María Rojo) and Carmelo (Daniel Rergis) have met each other at the Colonial Dance Hall. Their passion for dancing turned them into *danzón* contest winners. For Julia, the *danzón* is not merely a simple dance, but a whole world's outlook and an art form.

Julia, a short, stout, mature woman, lives with her daughter, Miriam. Both work as telephone operators. One day, Carmelo does not show up at the dance hall. Perplexed, Julia realizes she knows little about Carmelo — just that he is from Vera Cruz, is single and is a local cook at a nearby restaurant. She knows she misses their weekly dancing. After hearing some gossip from a friend that Carmelo has left because he is being falsely accused of a robbery, Julia sets herself a goal: to save Carmelo. Although she has not been outside of the capital in 38 years, she now leaves on a trip to Vera Cruz. There she runs across a world of prostitutes, sailors, mulattoes, palm trees, street dancing, night clubs — and Rubén, a young, attractive man with whom she has a love affair.

Julia returns to Mexico City more beautiful and full of life, impregnated with the fragrances of the sea and the harbor. She heads off to her beloved Colonial Dance Hall, where she again finds Carmelo. Their bodies are in tune with each other, and they dance to perfection. Julia knows that in the arms of Carmelo, she is the queen of *danzón*.

NOTE: *Danzón*, a fine style of ballroom dancing, originated in Haiti, gained popularity in Cuba in the mid-nineteenth century and traveled to Mexico by way of Vera Cruz. The film honors this tradition of dance as it examines the female soul. (Press book.)

Danzón has been roundly applauded by American film critics, who consid-ered it an unusual work of Mexican feminism, with sweetness and eloquence, deeply satisfying, sensual. Director Novaro taps into what is to be female in a landscape so distinctly shaped by gender. Much like the Australian dance film *Strictly Ballroom*, *Danzón* is a love story utilizing the dance as its centerpiece, abetted by colorful characterizations, fascinating rhythms, beautiful photography, infectious charm and superb acting. María Rojo as Julia is just about perfect in the role of the romantic telephone operator in search of her partner, Carmelo, a great mover on the dance floor, but as Julia discovers to her chagrin, no more than a friend.

NOTES: María Novaro was born in Mexico City in 1951 and obtained a degree in sociology from UNAM before deciding on a career in filmmaking. Having made both short and medium films since 1982, her first real feature film was *Lola* (1989), and *Danzón* directly followed. She was a member of the Women's Collective for Cinema from 1979 to 1981. With Dana Rotberg (*Ángel de fuego*) and Marisa Sustach (*Los pasos de Ana*), María Novaro is currently considered one of the three leading women directors of Mexican cinema.

Days of Water see *Los días del agua*

76. De cierta manera (One Way or Another). Sara Gómez. Cuba, 1974. 79 min., B&W. Spanish.

COMMENTARY: Essentially a propaganda film for the Castro regime, *De cierta manera* tells the story of a post–Revolution romance between two factory workers, a macho mulatto mixed-up guy named Mario (Mario Balmaseda) and a formerly middle-class schoolteacher now liberated by the revolution (Yolanda Cuellar) who meet cute, fall in love while working in a bus assembly factory and discover the class prejudices in each other's backgrounds. Their relationship is funny, provocative, occasionally touching. Yolanda returns to teaching, but Mario is not sure if women should work at all, let alone be professionals. Yolanda believes discipline and education are the new hope for the poor Cuban people to rehabilitate their lives. But Mario is nostalgic for the old days of shantytown, when men played dominos and women served them. The couple argue throughout the film. This is not just a romance but a dialectic. When the lovers walk off into the sunset arguing, it is a happy ending. Intercut with the romance filmed in a gritty black and white style is documentary footage showing the building of a new Cuba.

Our director's intention was to take a conventional love story and subvert it by intercutting interviews, voice-overs and *cinéma vérité* shots to confront the situation of building a new Cuba. But what is most off-putting about the film is that because it is a propaganda piece, the characters are subsumed into the surroundings — love giving way to politics, emotions to dogma. And yet, the film works on a very elementary level.

NOTES: It was too bad Gómez died of an acute asthma attack shortly after the film's initial release. *De cierta manera* is the first Cuban film to be directed by a woman who confronts the problems of being both female and black in the Third World. We would love to have seen which direction this 31-year-old woman, an accomplished pianist and journalist, would have taken in the future. In 1961 she gained most of her experience in film working for Tomás Gutiérrez Alea on *Memorias del subdesarrollo* at the Cuban Film Institute. There she made ten documentaries with titles like *Local Government, People's Power* and *On Overtime and Voluntary Work* until 1973. *De cierta manera* was filmed in Cuba in 1974, the only feature film we have of this promising director who died so tragically young.

77. De eso no se habla (I Don't Want to Talk About It). María Luisa Bemberg. Argentina/Italy, 1994. 105 min., Color. Spanish.

COMMENTARY: Directed by Argentina's leading woman director, *De eso no se habla* is a quirky comedy set in a small Argentine town during the 1940s. Luisina Brando plays Leonor, a rich widow and mother of a dwarf, Charlotte (Alejandra Podesta). Leonor is determined to marry off her daughter to a successful suitor. Marcello Mastroianni plays Ludovico D'Andrea, the most eligible bachelor available. Leonor eyes him for herself, but he prefers Charlotte, whom he marries. They live happily until a circus comes to town, delighting in Charlotte's dwarfish presence.

Watching this film about obsessive passions, we wonder how the triangle of amorous relationships will be solved. If Buñuel had made this film, it would have been perversely pathological. If Jodorowsky had written or directed this screenplay, the film would have gone over the top surrealistically. If Marco Ferreri had control of this scenario, the excesses à la *Grande bouffe* would have been extraordinary.

Rather than making the film in any of these modes, Bemberg is more concerned with the struggle of an unusual woman for her rightful place in society. She has chosen to make the film as a fairy tale, not funny or ferocious in Buñuelian style nor scary like Tod Browning's *Freaks*, but a romantic tale styled after Goethe's novel *The Sorrows of Young Werther*, from which she borrowed the name Charlotte for her heroine. But the film is also about Charlotte's mother, Leonor, an arrogant and possessive woman who is for the director a representation of repression and intolerance. Thus *De eso no se habla* also has a political subtext, since Leonor could represent any of a number of Argentine or South American dictators.

In a *New York Times* article published on September 25, 1994, entitled "Political Subtext in a Fairy Tale from a Feminist," Bemberg herself declared that women "are connected with feelings ... and we are just as different and contradictory as men artists." Admittedly, most of Bemberg's films deal with women who defy convention — *Camila* and *Yo, la peor de todos* among others — and who pay the price for their defiance. *De eso no se habla* is another worthy film from Bemberg's cadre of feminist Latin American filmmakers. It is rather tragic to know that this was director Bemberg's last film work in a late career that offered such promise and gave her audiences such real emotional pleasures, in Argentina and elsewhere. She will be sorely missed in Argentina and abroad.

The Dead One see *El muerto*

Death of a Bureaucrat see *La muerte de un burócrata*

Death of a Tycoon see *Muerte de un magnate*

78. Debajo del mundo (Under the World). Beda Docampo Feijoo and Juan Bautista Stagnaro. Argentina/Czech, 1988. 105 min., Color. Spanish.

COMMENTARY: Breaking new ground, *Debajo del mundo* was the first Argentine film in many years that dealt with a totally un–Argentine theme — the Holocaust and a Polish family escaping the Nazi onslaught — and it was also shot on location in Czechoslovakia. Apparently based upon the real-life account of one of the film's producers, Leo Mehl, the story is a graphically detailed, straightforward account of how the Mehls survived by pure ingenuity —

fashioning burlap garments when their clothes rotted, hiding under an ice house just a few feet away from a Nazi barracks, living essentially underground, sometimes just below the earth's surface, scavenging for food, stealing potatoes, and living in their excrement. They dealt with deluges of slime when it rained, lice from their filthy existence, claustrophobia and their ultimate horror of being discovered. It is a miracle the six Polish Jews survived, a tribute to their daring and resourcefulness. A *Schindler's List* the film is not — it is not essential viewing to understand the meaning of the Holocaust; yet it does emerge as a righteous document about one Jewish family's survival of the war, Nazis, anti–Semitism, the Holocaust and the resilience of the human spirit.

Sergio Renan as the father, Nachman, and Barbara Mugica as his wife, Liba, are superb, as is the rest of the cast. The film should not be compared to the excellent documentaries *The Sorrow and The Pity* or *Hotel Terminus* or *Shoah*, which are philosophical, intellectual and exhaustive works that examine the nature of evil of the German spirit. But *Debajo del mundo* does have emotional power and is brutally honest in its presentation of the alarming facts that comprise its real and fascinating story.

NOTES: Both directors are better known here in the United States for their brilliant screenplay of María Luisa Bemberg's 1985 Argentine film *Camila*. Their link to directing *Debajo del mundo* was obviously their co-producer, Leo Mehl, whose family really spent three years, beginning in September 1942, escaping daily Gestapo roundups of Jews and were finally liberated by Soviet troops in 1945.

Beda Docampo Feijoo also directed and wrote the screenplay for another Argentine film, *Los amores de Kafka* (1988), with *Camila*'s star, Susu Pecoraro. That film concerns an Argentine director who arrives in Prague in 1983 with a script entitled *The Loves of Kafka*, which intersects with another story (the script itself), a biography of the real Franz Kafka and his life in Prague circa 1920. Unfortunately the film never was seen theatrically in America.

The Debt see *Verónico Cruz*

Demonio y carne see *Susana*

La deuda interna see *Verónico Cruz*

79. Deus e o diabo na terra do sol (Black God, White Devil).
Brazil, 1963. 120 min., B&W. Portuguese.

COMMENTARY: This film, Glauber Rocha's second feature, is about a peasant who has murdered his master. He turns first to a *beato* (wandering holy man), who prophesises a golden future; then to a *cangeçeiro* (bandit). Neither can help him; both are killed. He runs symbolically towards the sea to the strains of a song that declares: "The land belongs to man / And is neither God's nor the devil's." The peasant becomes an outlaw whose code is triumph through bloodshed.

Essentially, the film is dialectic between God and the devil, symbolized by the beatific priest and the ruthless outlaw, all rooted in the misery of the people who inhabit northeast Brazil. The basic themes are the unconscious search for meaning in life; love and the tragic impossibility of loving in a context of violence; superstition; and death. The film is also an intoxicating synthesis of symbolism, realism and popular culture, often evoking the styles of the westerns of John Ford, the theatricality of Eisenstein in his *¡Qué viva Mexico!*, the choreography of its violence as in Kurosawa's best epic *Seven Samurai*, even Pasolini's *Porcile*, which evokes some of Rocha's compositions of men in action in the *sertão* (desert backland). Clearly, Rocha is a director of violence. He resurrected Antonio das Mortes, the hero of his first film, to save the peasant and his wife by killing the henchmen of a paid killer, mowing them down in a hail of bullets. Scenes like this, as well as the ritualized stabbing of the priest in a candle-lit chapel, make the film visually overwhelming. Also, the music of Heitor Villa-Lobos and the music of Bach used together with folk songs from the region make the film an electrifying, dynamic, almost hysterical display of directorial pyrotechnics from this fascinating Third World director. The performances of Geraldo del Rey and Yona Magalhes (the peasant and his wife) together with Othon Bastos, Lidio Silva and Mauricio de Valle (the priest and outlaws, respectively) are all excellent and work cohesively for the director to spin out his dialectic, his "romance," his delirious ballad, his coherent drama, his fable, his work of art.

Devil and the Flesh see *Susana*

80. Los días de junio (Those Days in June). Alberto Fischerman. Argentina, 1985. 90 min., Color. Spanish.

COMMENTARY: In the midst of the war for control of the Malvinas Islands, the Pope visits Argentina. The day before the pontiff's visit, Emilio, an exiled Argentine actor, returns to the country to take the main role in a theatrical production. While there, he meets old friends — Jorge, José and Alberto — and brings them together again to resolve a test from their childhood, an oath of loyalty and affection. Says the press book: "Apart from the pranks and regressive games, the violence of their meeting reveals open scars, obscure betrayals, postponed ideals and absences. Dictatorship has branded these friends, and now they confront each other."

Los días de junio is part of a series of "New Argentine Films" of the 1980s whose theme is the return of the Argentine exile from abroad. The exile (Norman Briski) confronts not only his past but the present. His friends talk and reminisce about the recognized and unrecognized compromises of their relationships with families, friends and work; their talk is presented against a backdrop of the last days of the military junta, now engaged in the Malvinas War and hosting the Pope. The four protagonists, representing different political responses to the military's current repression, try to recapture their idealism of the past. But Emilio is cruelly reminded of the present as he and his friends are "disappeared" and then let go by the military police. The film conveys the fragility of daily life under the dictatorship — in particular, the anxiety produced by treading too close to the limits of permissible conduct without knowing exactly when that line might be crossed, or the finality of such a misstep.

Spanish actor Norman Briski is excellent in the role of Emilio, and with the arrival of democracy in Argentina under the Alfonsín government, the Argentine cinema is in a state of recovery. *Los días de junio* is just one of the films serving as evidence of the new vigor that will return Argentina to its former status as one of the leading producers of international cinema.

81. Los días del agua (The Days of Water). Manuel Octavio Gómez. Cuba, 1971. 105 min., Color. Spanish.

COMMENTARY: *Los días del agua* tells the story of Antonia Izquierdo, a woman known as "the saint," who in Valle de Vinales in 1936, in the Cuban province of Pinar del Rio, healed sick people with water, alleviating the desperation they suffered from the miserable conditions under which they lived. It was believed that Antonia worked with the guidance of God and the Virgin Mary after receiving a visitation. Sick people from near and far canonized her and went to her house in search of relief from their pain, their misery, their impotence.

In the film her home becomes a sanctuary, and also quite legendary because of all the attention she receives from the local press who sensationalize the most elementary cures. Local businessmen profit from the hordes of people who come for the waters. Her popularity is quickly exploited by commercial charlatans and political demagogues. The local doctor, pharmacist and priest, seeing their positions threatened, accuse Antonia of murder when one of the sick men she tried to cure dies. A lawyer who is running for the position of governor of the province obtains her freedom, but in exchange he uses her popularity to win the election. Once in office, he decides her activities hurt his own interests and sends the army against her. Obviously, politicians are profiting from the popularity of the miracle worker and her ability to attract voters and votes. Unconsciously Antonia becomes an instrument for the worst elements of the government. In the end she tries to defend herself with her water and her followers, some of whom respond quite violently to the army's violence. By basing his story on real events and by trying to recapture the dialogue and feeling of the era by using actual testimony from the case, our director has created a bold production. The film is exuberant, with a flamboyant visual and narrative style that illustrates the social origins and distorted uses of popular culture. It also offers a trenchant critique of Cubans exploited by both religious fanaticism and political opportunism. Idalia Anreus as Antonia gives a remarkable, sympathetic performance, a "saint" overwhelmed by forces she does not understand. The director also shows himself to be a master of the crowd scene. Hysterical and fanatical mobs are beautifully controlled by the director's will for the purpose of capturing on film one of the most difficult contradictions of Cuban life — the conflict between religion and politics in the communist state. Religion wins out here.

82. Disparen a matar (Shoot to Kill). Carlos Azupurua. Venezuela, 1991. 90 min., Color. Spanish.

COMMENTARY: Very reminiscent of the pseudo-documentary kind of film made in America by Louis de Rochemont in the late 1940s, more particularly with a plot very much like the James Stewart–Richard Conte film *Call Northside 777*, *Disparen a matar* is a political drama about a man unjustly accused of killing, whose mother goes to a reporter to initiate an investigation. The reporter reveals an police cover-up of the crime and how the law can intimidate the victim's mother, family and the reporter himself. But unlike the American film, political corruption wins out over real justice. Amalia Perez Díaz as Mercedes, the poor working-class mother who continues her fight against the police, is excellent in her role, whereas Jeancarlo Simancas as her son, victimized by the police in their sweep of the poor working-class neighborhood, is merely effective. But Daniel Alvarado as Castro Gil, the corrupt cop, is outstanding as the embodiment of villainy. Apparently, recent political events in Venezuela make this a particularly relevant film. Made as part of the political thriller genre, *Disparen a matar* has received several top awards in 1991 at both the Havana and Cartagena film festivals.

83. Distinto amanecer (Another Dawn). Julio Bracho. Mexico, 1943. 108 min., B&W. Spanish.

COMMENTARY: Loosely based upon Max Aub's novel *La vida conyugal* and beautifully photographed by Gabriel Figueroa, the film takes place at Mexico City's huge central post office. The union leader, Armando Ruelas, has been assassinated on his way home to obtain some documents that compromise a corrupt governor, General Vidal. It is now up to Octavio (Pedro Armendáriz) to get the documents. But Octavio is followed by Jorge Ruiz, a secret agent of Vidal who wears dark glasses. In order to avoid him, Octavio walks into a movie theatre and finds Julieta (Andrea Palma) there. Julieta helps Octavio to escape and takes him to her house, where she lives with her husband, Ignacio (Alberto Galan), and her brother Juanito (Nariciso Busquets). Octavio, Julieta and Ignacio were all students together at UNAM, where they fought for autonomy and student rights. Ignacio is now a bureaucrat in the government and has become an embittered writer. He earns too little, and his relationship with Julieta has soured. The old romance between Octavio and Julieta flares up again. They nearly elope in one of the film's final scenes set in a railroad station, but in the end Octavio goes off alone, clutching those much sought-after documents.

There are many scenes in Mexican nightclubs with the requisite musical extravaganzas and an especially affecting song by Agustín Lara entitled "Cada noche un amor." We move in the milieu of gangster-owned cafés, bars and powder rooms that suggest many famous American gangster films or *films noirs* of the mid–1940s. Andrea Palma, the *femme fatale*, has a languorous acting style very reminiscent of Marlene Dietrich. Although Pedro Armendáriz gives a very strong, convincing performance, his mustache and Mexican-looking features remind us of no crime iconography in either American or Mexican cinema. The film however, has the look of the great *films noirs* in America because of the highly nuanced, beautiful black and white photography by Gabriel Figueroa, and the story maintains a fair atmosphere of suspense. It is the noir style and capable directing by Julio Bracho that save this gangster melodrama from the turgidity of similar Mexican films of the same era.

Do You Hear the Dogs Barking? see *¿No oyes ladrar los perros?*

Dogs of the Night see *Perros de la noche*

84. Don Segundo Sombra.
Manuel Antín. Argentina, 1968. 100 min., Color. Spanish.

COMMENTARY: Based on the famous 1926 gaucho novel by Ricardo Guiraldes, which was considered by critics the most accurate document on life in the pampas and most insightful into the "gaucho character," the film version is true to the spirit of the novel, if not exactly faithful to the written word. Adolfo Guiraldes, a nephew of the author, plays the title role; Juan Carballido, also of the Guiraldes family, plays the part of Fabio at age 18; Luis de la Cuesta, who enacts the role of Fabio at age 14, is yet another family member. The remainder of the cast consists mainly of non-professional actors from rural areas.

Don Segundo Sombra represents a paean to life on the pampas and presents a uniquely Argentine character: the gaucho. Like the novel, the film succeeds in capturing the essence of the gaucho and his Argentine spirit. Antín, the director, has also presented the physical and metaphysical aspects of the gaucho and his traditions, as we watch the young gaucho age through many key experiences in his life. Antín does something extremely unusual by having the elder Fabio at times seen in the same frame as the younger one, remembering his experiences, giving the film a literary resonance never before seen on the Argentine screen.

The film captures authentically the folkloric traditions of the gaucho, his work, his songs and dances, his values and sense of humor. It is beautifully photographed with some fascinating pictorial scenes and contains a first-class musical score by Adolfo Morpurgo. This is also the debut of camerman Miguel Rodríguez, who came to Argentine cinema from the commercial advertising field. It is a very serious work, not to be compared with the gaucho hokeyness of Rudolph Valentino's performance in Rex Ingram's 1921 silent film *Four Horsemen of the Apocalypse* or Rory Calhoun's "western gaucho" role in Jacques Tourneur's totally Hollywood (and wooden) 1952 production called *Way of a Gaucho*. Antín has made the definitive gaucho film with his version of *Don Segundo Sombra*.

85. Doña Bárbara.
Fernando de Fuentes. Mexico, 1943. 138 min., Color. Spanish.

COMMENTARY: With a screenplay written by Romulo Gallegos based upon his own novel of the same name, *Doña Bárbara* is florid melodrama, about an extremely arrogant woman (sensationally played by María Félix) whose hatred of society is the result of her rape as a young woman by six sailors as well as the death of her young boyfriend.

Set in Mexico in the early twenties, the story begins when Santos Luzardo (Julián Soler) comes from Caracas to take over his property. He visits his cousin, Lorenzo (Andrés Soler), who is a victim of Doña Bárbara's debauchery, a drunkard. Santos also meets Marisela (María Elena Márquez), who is, in reality, the daughter of Doña Bárbara. Believing the girl has lived in a semi-wild state, Santos decides to educate Marisela and takes her to live with him. Doña Bárbara, however, has other plans for Santos. She tries to seduce him and steal his lands, but really falls in love with him

María Félix (left) in the title role of Fernando de Fuentes's *Doña Bárbara* (1943), talking with her daughter, Marisela (María Elena Márquez) reflected in the mirror.

and returns to him the lands she formerly stole. Santos rejects Doña Bárbara when she insinuates there is something sexual going on between Marisela and him. At this point, mother and daughter fight for Santos' love. Doña Bárbara orders Santos kidnapped, but her men desert her when they realize how driven she is by passion and murder to achieve her goals, i.e., to win all the lands that surround her, along with Santos' fidelity and love. Now completely defeated, Doña Bárbara finally gives up her lands (and even some supposed powers of "witchcraft" to force people's wills to hers) and leaves her daughter and Santos, who have now fallen in love, to live in conjugal bliss.

María Félix has the role of her life as the scenery-chewing Doña Bárbara, acting out male fantasies of power and domination even though at heart she is a simple woman caught by nostalgia and longing for the love of Santos Luzardo. According to the MOMA program notes, "it was *Doña Bárbara* which established María Félix as the 'diva' of Mexican cinema. So great was her power that she became known as 'La Devoradora,' the devourer of men." The film is acted in high style by all the players and is certainly one of the most colorful and entertaining Mexican films to come to America during the mid-forties. *Doña Bárbara* is pure melodrama, but on another level, it represents the melodrama of "continental regionalism" that Gallegos inserted in his novel, a novel replete with verbal folklore, barbarism, and caricature. Gallegos's intention was to use the characters of his novels as symbols: Santos Luzardo representing the "holy" light of bourgeois civilization; Doña Bárbara representing the barbarousness of the human spirit; Marisela incarnating the free, wild life; and other characters embodying the dangers of Yankee imperialism. Gallegos's novel succeeds, as does the film version, which lifts these symbols off the page and brings them forth cinematically in a dynamic, hysterical, colorful bit of film.

Doña Flor and Her Two Husbands see *Doña Flor e seus dois maridos*

86. Doña Flor e seus dois maridos (Doña Flor and Her Two Husbands). Bruno Barreto. Brazil, 1977. 106 min., Color. Portuguese.

COMMENTARY: Based upon the romantic international bestseller by Jorge Amado, *Doña Flor e seus dois maridos* is a bewitching fable, a sort of Brazilian *Blithe Spirit*, but without Noel Coward's stinging wit. It represents the wish-fulfillment of every wife who has wanted to trade her imperfect husband for a new, improved model. The plot is intriguing: In Bahia on Carnival Sunday, Doña Flor's husband, Vadinho (José Wilker), is dancing exhuberantly in the streets when he is felled by a fatal heart attack. At his funeral, friends and neighbors remember him as a scoundrel, a gambler, a lothario, and even as a great man.

The grieving widow (Sonia Braga) continually reminisces about her life with Vadinho, which we see in a number of flashbacks. Clearly, Vadhino was less than a model husband — he even slipped out of bed on their wedding night to visit the local brothel with his drinking buddies — but even so, Doña Flor loved him deeply, and he returned her love with equal passion.

Eventually, at the urging of her friends, Doña Flor marries again. Her new husband, Teodoro (Mauro Mendoca), is completely the opposite of Vadinho — a quiet, respectable pharmacist,

so methodical that he even makes love on schedule (Wednesdays and Saturdays).

Flor and Teodoro celebrate their first anniversary with a party. Afterwards, Flor goes to her room. There, sprawled happily on the bed, is Vadinho. Flor is pleased, thinking she will be able to have a long talk with the husband she has missed so much. However, Vadinho prefers to initiate a bout of lovemaking. Shocked, Flor rejects his advances, so Vadinho wanders off to find his friends, who succeeded wildly at roulette with his help.

Vadinho continues his overtures to Flor, and eventually she gives in, to find complete fulfillment in the love of her two husbands.

Reportedly outgrossing the Steven Spielberg film *Jaws* in Brazil, *Doña Flor e seus dois maridos* set in the 1940s, has charm, sensuality, a folksy fable quality, and a necrophilia twist proving that there is sex after death. Sonia Braga is excellent as the widow, playing her role with a certain primness and passion; José Wilker, the dissipated first husband who dies at age 33, brings a feeling of sexiness and lust to his role; Mauro Mendoca is just right as Teodoro the pharmacist, the innocent, inexperienced wimp of a second husband. At age 42, he is a caricature of respectability (he wears yellow pajamas on their wedding night). He promises Flor eternal fidelity and even sets up a savings account for her (unlike Vadinho, who stole Flor's money to carouse). Teodoro is the most poignantly moving character in a film that otherwise celebrates sensuality and seduction, against a background of bossa nova music. The images of *Doña Flor* are abetted by soft-focus photography that accentuates the Brazilian myths of sexuality and potency in an atmosphere of gaiety and abandon. Without its exoticism, artfulness, sensitivity, wit and disarming morality, the film might have ended up on the soft-porn circuit.

Ramón (Arturo Meza, left) is jumping rope at home as Doña Herlinda (Guadalupe del Toro) rides her exercise bicycle in Jaime Humberto Hermosillo's *Doña Herlinda y su hijo* (*Doño Herlinda and Her Son*, 1985). The third party in the gay ménage, Doña Herlinda's son, is not shown in this scene from the film.

Although Doña Flor is searching for a life inspired by confidence and stability, her need to return to the *mas allá*, the beyond, is her fantasy (as well as ours)—a dream that makes this film one of the most beguiling art films to come from Brazil in many years.

NOTES: Born in Brazil in 1955, Bruno Barreto grew up during the explosion of *Cinema Nôvo* in Brazilian culture. Son of a film producer, he began making short films in the sixties. However, *Doña flor e seus dois maridos* (1977) was his first feature of international fame. He quickly followed this success

with *El amor bandido* (1979), *Luzía* (1981) and the filming of another Jorge Amado novel, *Gabriela* (1983). He has since made other films outside of Brazil, notably *A Show of Force* (1990), and returned to Brazil to make *The Story of Fausta* (1992). He is the father of a child by American actress Amy Irving, who starred in his only American film.

Doña Herlinda and Her Son see *Doña Herlinda y su hijo*

87. Doña Herlinda y su hijo
(**Doña Herlinda and Her Son**). Jaime

Humberto Hermosillo. Mexico, 1985. 90 min., Color. Spanish.

COMMENTARY: "Ramón (Arturo Meza), a young music student, and Rodolfo (Marco Antonio Trevino), a well-to-do doctor, maintain a secret, amorous relationship. Rodolfo's mother, Doña Herlinda (Guadalupe del Toro), pretends not to know about his affair. Nevertheless, she wants her son to be happy. She arranges for Ramón to move out of his boarding house and into her home and into Rodolfo's bedroom.

Doña Herlinda also wants her son to be married to a girl of a good family. Her choice is Olga (Leticia Lupersio), and soon she has Rodolfo engaged to be married. Ramón is upset at this development, but Doña Herlinda and Rodolfo persuade him to stay with them as part of their family.

Soon Olga and Rodolfo are married and a child is on the way. Now, with Ramón, Rodolfo, Olga and the baby under her roof, Doña Herlinda's happiness is complete." (Press book.)

The first gay domestic comedy ever to be produced in Mexico, this is the fascinating tale of a *menage à cinq*, a story that pleases all audiences because it presents sex, all kinds, as a natural part of life without resorting to rigid role responses. Obviously, Doña Herlinda and the director, Jaime Hermosillo, want to have their cake and eat it, too. They are successful because viewers generally enjoy the characters in the film, all of whom are extremely likeable. Although some viewers may be put off by the graphic male sex scenes as well as the graininess of the 35mm blowup from the 16mm original print, the film succeeds admirably as entertainment as part of the New Wave of Mexican cinema, dealing with outrageous and heretofore forbidden themes. Doña Herlinda also suggests a recent Tawainese film of 1993, entitled *The Wedding Banquet*, dealing with a Chinese family who wants their accountant son (openly gay and living with a man in Soho) to marry the requisite Chinese girl so that they may have an heir. Although the ending of *The Wedding Banquet* differs from *Doña Herlinda y su hijo*, homo- and heterosexuality on screen are vividly represented and in vogue.

NOTES: Jaime Humberto Hermosillo is an openly gay Latin American film director. His films are usually explorations of character as well as indictments of hypocrisy and the petty foibles of the Mexican bourgeois. He studied at UNAM's film school in the late sixties and made the obligatory film shorts before his first feature-length film, *The True Vocation of Magdalena*, debuted in 1971, immediately followed by *The Lord of Osanto* (1972) based upon a novel by Robert Louis Stevenson. His more significant films came later: *The Passion According to Berenice* (1975), about a disturbed woman; *Matineé* (1976), about two movie-struck children; *María de mi corazón* (1980), adapted from a García Márquez novel about the ruinous aspects of romanticism; and finally *Doña Herlinda* (1985). He continues to make compassionate, inventive films that are serious, outrageous and provocatively engaging.

Dueling Techniques see *Técnicas de duelo*

Earth Entranced see *Terra em transe*

Easy Money see *Plata dulce*

88. 8-A. Orlando Jiménez-Leal. Cuba, 1993. 83 min., Color. Spanish.

COMMENTARY: "8-A" is the code name for General Arnaldo Ochoa Sánchez, one of the highest-ranking generals of the Cuban Revolution and commander-in-chief of the Angolan campaign, who was tried and executed in 1989 for drug trafficking. Of course, the arrest was a hoax: General Sánchez had expressed his dissent with Fidel Castro's political, social and economic policies, and Castro tried him on trumped-up charges to silence his dissent.

The trial was shown on national Cuban TV, and General Sánchez and other members of his power elite supposedly confessed to the charges against them (charges that compromised the dignity and honor of the country) and expressed repentance for "betraying the fatherland and the revolution." While focusing on the media event of the trial, the documentary also raises startling questions about human rights in Castro's dictatorial regime. Director Jiménez-Leal constructed this orderly and stimulating film from trial tapes made available from RAI, the Italian TV organization. Although in structure and tone the film resembles the work of Costa-Gavras, Jiménez-Leal is no stranger to the documentary. He has made other thrilling works about the violation of civil liberties in Cuba, including _The Other Cuba_ (1983) and _Mauvaise Conduite_ (1984).

NOTES: The director Orlando Jiménez-Leal is a Cuban exile who has had a successful career in New York, primarily as a spokesman against the Castro regime. Forming an advertising agency with publicist Emilio Guede, he began making feature films such as _El super_ (1980), a fictional work about a Cuban apartment building superintendent, living in Queens who has problems adjusting to New York society and dreams of returning to Cuba one day but settles for Miami Beach instead. But Jiménez-Leal's chief success was in his collaboration with Nestor Almendros, the Cuban photographer, when they made the remarkable documentary film _Mauvaise Conduite_ (1984), a real indictment of the lack of human rights in Castro's Cuba.

89. Él (This Strange Passion / Torments). Luis Buñuel. Mexico, 1952. 82 min., B&W. Spanish.

COMMENTARY: _Él_ is a deceptively simple story about a woman, Gloria (played by Delia Garcés in her debut role,) who marries a pathologically jealous man, Francisco (played brilliantly by Arturo de Cordova), who eventually tries to kill her. The story itself is mainly told in flashbacks, when Gloria was courted by Francisco, who had no remorse in stealing her away from Raúl, her fiancé. It is Raúl who saves Gloria in the end from the pathological excesses of Francisco. After beating Gloria, subjecting her to other extreme physical and mental cruelties and nearly throwing her from the top of a bell tower, Francisco experiences a breakdown and is sent to a retreat, where he spends the rest of his life in seclusion as a somewhat "disturbed" acolyte. Gloria, newly married to Raúl, visits Francisco with her son, also named Francisco, in tow.

_Él_ is a fascinating psychological melodrama about the mental deterioration of a puritanical bourgeois (Francisco), obsessed carnally by a woman he meets in church (Gloria); because of his jealous state of mind, he degenerates into an irreversible psychotic state.

Beneath the surface of the film is a brilliant analysis of a paranoid's distorted outlook on reality as well as offering bitter indictment of Christianity and bourgeois morality. The film is filled with Buñuel's characteristic erotic imagery, black humor and moments of undeniable terror. (Press book.)

In an interview Buñuel said the following: "[_Él_] is one of my favorites.... It satisfies me above all for what it brings as truthful document of a pathological case.... But all the minute detailed, documented exposition of the psychopathic process of the personality seemed improbable to the large public that would laugh frequently during the film's showings. That confirms for me the fact that common, traditional, current cinema has cultivated in the public a great attachment to the conventional, in the common superficial and false sense.... The final intent of the film is more humorous than anti-clerical. Nevertheless the man is pathetic. He moved me, this man of such jealousy, of so much loneliness and anguish inside, with so much interior violence. I studied him like an insect...."

No one who has seen the film is likely to forget Francisco's urge to repair Gloria's virginity with alcohol, needle and thread, or the scenes in church where Francisco feels everyone is laughing at him, or his zig-zag walk, indicating his demented state at the film's conclusion. *Él* is probably Luis Buñuel's most brilliant Mexican film after *Los olvidados* (1950) and should be considered one of the greatest works of Mexican *and* Latin American cinema.

NOTES: Although Luis Buñuel was a Spaniard born in Calanda in 1900, he died in Mexico City in 1983 and spent part of his life in exile with his wife and family in Mexico during the 1940s and 1950s, always opposed to General Franco's fascist regime. He had a triple-pronged career: In Spain and France, he made some wonderful surrealist films and documentaries (*Un Chien andalou, L'Âge d'or, Las hurdes*) in the twenties and thirties, but he hit his stride in Mexico in the fifties with *Los olvidados, Él* and *Nazarín*. He then returned to Spain, where he made the wonderful *Viridiana* in the sixties and *Tristana* in the seventies. However, he could no longer consider Spain his home and preferred to work for the remainder of his career in France, directing some of the greatest films in his career: *Diary of a Chambermaid, Belle du jour, The Discreet Charm of the Bourgeoisie* (an Academy Award winner for Best Foreign Film of 1972). He made his last film in France, *That*

Obscure Object of Desire, before retiring to Mexico to spend the rest of his days. Buñuel was an original, one of the greatest filmmakers in the pantheon of artists. He deserves immortality, and he has achieved it on film.

90. El Salvador: Morazán.

Zero a la Izquierda Film Collective. El Salvador, 1981. 45 min., Color and B&W. Spanish.

COMMENTARY: Made by a collective of Salvadorean filmmakers sympathetic to the anti-government rebels, this film shows how remarkably well organized is this civilian-military community of peasants and armed rebels of Morazán. We watch rebel commanders instructing peasants in the use of sophisticated weaponry — how to manufacture bombs, mines and hand grenades in their fight for liberation. Although none of the issues of liberation are ever mentioned, they are parenthetical to scenes of preparation for future victory. The film deserves to be seen because it is a documentary record of an era as well as propaganda for El Salvador's drive for national liberation.

91. Eles não usam black-tie

(They Don't Wear Black Tie). Leon Hirszman. Brazil, 1981. 120 min., Color. Portuguese.

COMMENTARY: Reminiscent of the social-problem films made by Warner Bros. in the 1930s, *Eles não usam black-tie* is a story about strikes and strike-breaking set in Brazil of the eighties. It is about a young worker who marries his pregnant fiancée. Son of a union organizer who was jailed and is still involved in organizing further strikes during his layoff, our youthful protagonist believes it is better to work from inside the system to foment changes. Nevertheless, the father brings off the strike, which fails miserably, and the fiancée tells off her lover, vowing never to see

Two scenes from Luis Buñuel's *Él* (***This Strange Passion***, 1952): Arturo de Cordova looks truly disturbed (upper) as he plots to choke his "unfaithful" wife (Delia Garcés) atop a cathedral bell tower in the middle of Mexico City (lower).

him again because of his strike-breaking activities. The father also disowns his son, who favors the plight of the owners.

There are some fascinating scenes of secret police shooting militant strikers and a heartrending funeral for a strike organizer who was shot down. Although the film ends quite predictably, it is well meaning; perhaps it is a signal to the audience that repressive measures against workers in Brazil are on the wane. All the leading actors — Fernanda Montenegro, Gianfrancesco Guarnieri and Carlos Alberto Ricelli — enact their roles with appropriate style and sympathy, evoking the right notes in this tale of the workers' lives, abetted by fine characterization, substituting real, human, socially acceptable values for straight melodrama.

NOTES: Born in Rio de Janeiro in 1938, and one of the founders of *Cinema Nôvo*, Leon Hirszman was mostly an expert at making short, rigorous and cold documentary films. Not until the release of his second feature, *They Don't Wear Black Tie*, did he achieve worldwide renown. His first feature film, *São Bernardo* was released in Brazil in 1972 to less than enthusiastic reviews. It was a pity he died at age fifty, cutting short a promising career.

92. The Emerald Forest.

John Boorman. Brazil/U.S., 1985. 113 min., Color. English/Spanish.

COMMENTARY: *The Emerald Forest* is based upon a true story about a Peruvian architect whose son was apparently abducted by Brazilian Indians along the Amazon River. The architect (in the film an American engineer, played by Powers Boothe) and his wife (played sympathetically by blue-eyed Meg Foster) spend many years looking for the son (played by the director's own son, Charlie Boorman) and finally meet up with him when the boy is in his late teens and about to marry into a tribe.

The director, John Boorman, has chosen to emphasize the details about growing up in the wilds, man's return to nature, the slow erosion of the rain forest, the perils of living in the jungle with other marauding tribes and above all, the encroachment of civilization in the Amazon jungle. Against this setting, Boorman spins his tale about the abducted boy's recovery by his parents, and their subsequent recognition that their child is no longer their own physical and spiritual son and must go back to the rain forest. Moreover, our engineer has some doubts about bringing civilization into the jungle for merely a profit motive and returns stateside with his wife, leaving his son to live his life as a warrior in the Brazilian jungles.

The real star of the film is the photography (by Phillipe Rousselot) of the fabulously lush settings. The ravishing location settings evoke the story of the Indian tribes, their folklore and ceremonies, echoing the best visualizations of the works of either Ruth Benedict or Margaret Mead. For viewers, the film's ultimate fantasy is placing yourself in the position of the abducted boy and wondering if you could meet the challenges facing this noble savage. Once again, an English director has made fascinating use of a Latin American location in a story that could only be filmed in Brazilian jungles with Amazonian Indians — a real tour de force.

NOTES: In the world of cinema, John Boorman is primarily known for his insistence on using location shooting around the world. *Hell in the Pacific, Deliverance*, and *Emerald Forest* brilliantly illustrate this modus operandi. In fact, on *Emerald Forest*, he published a diary entitled "Money Into Light," about the three adventurous and traumatic years he and his family spent in the rain forests making the film. He returned to the British homefront (he was born in London in 1933) to make a somewhat autobiographical film about World War II entitled *Hope and Glory* in 1987.

93. En el balcón vacío (On the Empty Balcony). Jomi García Ascot. Mexico, 1962. 60 min., B&W. Spanish.

COMMENTARY: Primarily known because it was the first film of its kind to be thought of in Mexico as "experimental cinema," made in 16mm and totally financed by its director and the author of its screenplay, Emilio García Riera, *En el balcón vacío* is a small film that deals with the memories of its leading protagonist, Gabriela (played as an older woman by María Luisa Elio and as a younger woman by Nuri Perena). We first see her in Spain, but war (the Spanish Revolution) leads her family to flee and seek refuge in neighboring France before they finally settle in Mexico.

Gabriela returns to Spain as an older woman. She recaptures memories of her loneliness in France, but only in Mexico is she able to remember her life in Spain. The director intersects Gabriela's bouts with memory with newsreel footage that interrupts her dreamy, reminiscent narration of her story. *Balcón* is an extremely short, personal, intimate film revealing the interior life of an impressionable young Spanish woman and is beautifully written and directed despite the production's obvious lack of resources.

94. En este pueblo no hay ladrones (There Are No Thieves in This Village). Alberto Isaac. Mexico, 1964. 82 min., B&W. Spanish.

COMMENTARY: Much like its predecessor, *En el balcón vacío*, this film was thought to represent a turning point toward a "new" Mexican cinema, bringing refreshment to a stagnant film industry.

Based upon a story by Gabriel García Márquez, the film deals with a thief named Damaso (brilliantly played by Julio Pastor) who breaks into a local pool parlor and steals the billiard balls. His crime, a thoughtless act perpetrated out of boredom and mischief more than for economic gain, throws the town into a brouhaha of accusations, xenophobia and violence. A bypassing stranger is charged with the crime when caught trying to pick someone's pocket in a local movie house. He discovers the billiard balls are worth money and envisages setting up a gang to steal the balls from another town, since the mostly unemployed men here cannot survive their boredom without a daily game of pool. The stranger's stratagem never comes to pass; instead he gets involved with a local prostitute and is thrown in jail for stealing her money. The filmmaker blames ignorance (the impoverishment of minds) as well as the generally poor state of the economy for the crimes perpetrated in the town.

The film is widely known because it contains many cameo performances by leading directors and writers, among them García Márquez, Juan Rulfo, Arturo Ripstein and above all, Luis Buñuel making his acting debut as a sermonizing priest. *En este pueblo no hay landrones* is a highly inventive piece of cinematic fluff, a breath of fresh air in Mexico of the sixties.

NOTES: Alberto Isaac is known primarily as an avant-garde director. *En este pueblo no hay ladrones*, his first film, is in keeping with his own philosophy of "seeking some new thing." In 1974, Isaac directed *Tivoli*, reviving the cabaret film of the 1950s; it is about the last days of a burlesque house in Mexico City. In 1976, he directed his first film about a historical figure, Belisario Domínguez, entitled *Cuartelazo* (*Barracks Mutiny*), which received less than enthusiastic praise from the critics.

95. Enamorada. (Emilio "El Indio" Fernández). Mexico, 1949. 100 min., B&W. Spanish.

COMMENTARY: A scintillating effort from the fruitful collaborations between stars María Félix and Pedro Armendáriz, director Emilio Fernández and photographer Gabriel Figueroa, *Enamorada* is another of those tempestuously romantic melodramas tailored for the talents of Félix, whose scene-stealing is notorious in Mexican cinema. Reminding us very much of William Shakespeare's *The Taming of the Shrew*, the plot has been transposed to a new time and setting: Mexico during the Revolution of 1910.

Felix plays the spoiled but educated daughter of a very wealthy ranch owner, and Armendáriz is the illiterate but very macho general who wants to seduce her first, marry her later. The general also has intentions of stealing Félix's land by murdering her father in the name of the revolution. He relents and recants when Félix also tones down her stubborn attitudes, and through a go-between, the priest (Fernando Fernandez), both parties gradually learn to love and care for each other, as did Katherine and Petruchio in the Shakespeare comedy.

There is a wonderful scene very reminiscent of Josef von Sternberg's immortal Gary Cooper–Marlene Dietrich collaboration, *Morocco* (1931), when Dietrich, realizing she would rather be with her man and scorn the existing society, decides to follow Cooper with the French Foreign Legion into the desert, becoming his enslaved camp follower. Likewise, Félix follows behind Armendáriz's horse, carrying food and water, smiling, with danger all around as he attempts to win the entire Mexican Revolution. Sublime. It would have been interesting to have seen the planned American version of *Enamorada*, with Paulette Goddard in the Félix role and Armendáriz again playing "el general."

96. Encuentro inesperado
(**Unexpected Encounter**). Jaime Huberto Hermosillo. Mexico, 1993. 80 min., Color. Spanish.

COMMENTARY: This is Hermosillo's eighteenth feature film, and a tour de force it is for María Rojo, the star of *Danzón*, and newcomer Lucha Villa, who plays the role of a famous ranchero singer modeled on the life of Pilar Landeros. It seems that Pilar had abandoned her dying husband (seen in flashbacks and played by Ignacio Retes) and daughter Estela (played by María Rojo) in order to reach the top of her profession. Pilar has just returned from a vacation trip abroad and finds Estela at her home in a maid's uniform, begging for a job. But Estela is actually a newspaper reporter looking for an interview, as well as Pilar's long-lost, abandoned and bitter daughter. The women eye each other suspiciously, vying for control. Hermosillo suggests Pilar may be a dominatrix (Estela finds whips and handcuffs in her closet) and that Estela may be playing out a fantasy by masquerading in a servant's costume. Neither woman is totally sound mentally, and Hermosillo accentuates their dementia with his use of confined space that reveals their inner claustrophobia. The film is vaguely reminiscent of an earlier (1982) Hermosillo film called *Confidencias*, a two-character drama about a manipulative woman and a submissive maid. Both films, however, contain the requisite tension and melodrama to entertain their audiences. Not as outrageous as some of Hermosillo's earlier efforts, the film's lack of spontaneity and comedic force renders *Encuentro inesperado* a domestically bound production without international resonances.

End of Innocence see *La casa de Ángel*

End of the Party see *Fin de fiesta*

97. Ensayo de un crimen
(The Criminal Life of Archibaldo de la Cruz). Luis Buñuel. Mexico, 1955. 90 min., B&W. Spanish.

COMMENTARY: Based upon a fascinating novel by Rodolfo Usigli, *Esayo de un crimen* was Luis Buñuel's first "breezy" black comedy in years. Starring Ernesto Alonso as the irreverent Archibaldo and Miroslava (Stern) as Lavinia, it is a delightful comedy about obsessional behavor.

Archibaldo is rich, well-born, handsome, sensitive, and a bit disturbed by a childhood trauma. It seems at age five, when Archibaldo was a child growing up during the Mexican Revolution, he witnessed the death of his governess-nurse by a stray bullet. Before her death, she had caught him in a closet dressing up in his mother's corset. Feeling guilty, he wished (upon a music box with supposed magical powers) that his governess would die. No sooner had he made the wish than the governess was killed.

His obsession with death grows and is always associated with this music box, which he reclaims in an antique store after it was lost during his childhood. His obsession with the music box and death affects all his subsequent relationships with women; he plans their demise, but does not succeed. When he reflects upon the death of his governess, we see her lying dead on the carpet, her skirts above her upper thighs, blood smeared on her face — an image that made an everlasting impression on the boy, who, as an adult, goes through life confusing love, death and sexuality.

He wants to be jailed for crimes against women he never did commit. For example, there is Patricia, the drunken wife of a gambler who lusts after Archibaldo. He refuses her advances and she dies tragically, killed by her equally drunken and jealous husband. Archibaldo may have wished her dead, but he did not kill her. Again, when recuperating from an illness in a hospital, he deters the advances of a nun probing into his secrets, also wishing her dead. The nun runs out of Archibaldo's room after an altercation with him and into an empty elevator shaft to her demise. He finally meets a tour guide and model, Lavinia, is attracted to her and sculpts a life-size model of her. It is she who finally brings Archibaldo out of his fantasy world. Instead of killing her, Archibaldo immolates his sculpture, throws his music box in a nearby lake and ultimately marries the model, who was formerly promised to another man. For Archibaldo, the future holds promise of happiness.

Buñuel himself has described this film as a "comedie noire." Archibaldo has embarked upon the career of a great criminal, only to have his every attempt at homicide thwarted by ill luck or his own incompetence; the more industrious and elaborate his preparations for ensnaring his victims, the more spectacular the concatenation of events which robs him of his prey. The Buñuel film reminds one of Charles Chaplin's great classic, *Monsieur Verdoux*, the old Bluebeard story. The boating scene where Chaplin tries to dispatch Martha Raye is probably one of the all-time greatest moments of almost-comedic murder in screen history. However, Buñuel, unlike Chaplin (or Claude Chabrol in his film *Landru*, which documents the pathology of a serial murderer of French women), uses his main character to comment upon corrupt Mexican society. Buñuel is against the obvious hypocrisy and materialism of the world in which Archibaldo moves.

At one point in the film, Archibaldo is engaged to Carlota (beautifully played by Ariadna Weler), a pseudo-religious woman who wants to ensnare Archibaldo for his wealth. Although Archibaldo sees her as a perfect symbol of purity who prays at her own household shrine, she is in reality carrying on an affair with a married man, Alejandro (Rodolfo Landa), who shoots her dead on the same altar where she and Archibaldo were to take their final vows. Perhaps Carlota is killed in a "dream" of Archibaldo's. But once again, Buñuel is attacking the bourgeois mentality, the church ideals of faith and chastity, the duplicity of women, the contrived nature of the love relationship between Carlota and Archibaldo. Obviously, Buñuel is a partisan of free love, and love without guilt. In Archibaldo's relationship with Lavinia, he achieves the freedom in love that Buñuel has extolled his life long as one of his guiding principles.

98. Eréndira. Ruy Guerra. Mexico, 1982. 103 min. Color. Spanish.

COMMENTARY: Based upon a short story by Gabriel García Márquez, this film capitalizes upon the author's trademark excess and wild imaginings and even goes over the top because of the operatic direction of Brazilian director Ruy Guerra.

Eréndira (Claudia Ohana) is a fourteen-year-old waif prostitute who lives with her witch of a grandmother, also her madam (Irene Papas). Wherever they go, life follows them, carnivals and marketplaces springing up around them. Eréndira, exploited by her grandmother, accepts her fate until a blonde-haired juvenile angel named Ulysses arrives (Oliver Wehe). Carrying oranges filled with diamonds and Sir Francis Drake's gun, he sets Eréndira free from a life of bondage and prostitution.

Conceived somewhere in the canon of magical realism, the sets of the film (as well as some of the performances) are quite hallucinatory. The sets were designed, executed and filmed by artists with flamboyant visual imaginations. The director creates a real world within a fantastic one, the mystery within

human relations, oppression, rebellion, the kind of world common to any small Latin American town where real love is reborn. We see a great house filled with paper flowers, flammable bric-a-brac, pet ostriches, exotic sedan chairs, frenetic furniture. When the carnivals come to town, there are snake charmers, games of chance, musicians, food sellers, all bathed in the fantasy world of the set designer's imagination.

One of the most imaginative scenes occurs at the very beginning of the film, when Eréndira accidentally leaves some candles burning after going to bed and the huge house belonging to the grandmother is transformed into an inferno. The latter says: "My poor darling, your life will not be long enough to repay me." And the matriarch then leads Eréndira into a life of prostitution. After being set free by Ulysses, Eréndira demands that the angel fulfill his destiny by dispatching the old woman. The fairy tale ends here, with Eréndira fulfilling her murderous desires.

Greek actress Irene Papas gives a big, broad, comic performance as the grandmother, although her accent is more Mediterranean than Mexican, and Claudia Ohana is suitably charming and winsome as the long-suffering Eréndira. Although the physical production is appropriately fantastic, it is sometimes difficult to decode the symbols and meanings of the original story and the film. Nevertheless, *Eréndira* is unquestionably a worthwhile cinematic experience.

NOTES: Another key director of Brazil's *Cinema Nôvo* movement, Ruy Guerra was born in Mozambique in 1931 and educated in Paris, where he attended IDHEC, the famous French film institute. He is best known for his second feature film, *Os fuzis* (*The Guns*, 1964), a violent vision of Brazilians living in the *sertão* (backlands) of the northeast. Leaving Brazil because of political reasons in the mid-sixties, he settled in Mozambique and continues to film there as well as around the world on foreign locations. Other films he is known for are *A queda* (1976, a sequel to *Os fuzis*) and *Opera do Malandro* (1986). Guerra also founded and presently directs the National Institute of Cinema in Mozambique.

99. Esperando la carroza
(**Waiting for the Pallbearers**). Alejandro Doria. Argentina, 1985. 95 min., Color. Spanish.

COMMENTARY: Elderly Mama Cora has four children: Sergio, Jorge, Antonio and Emilia. Mama lives with Jorge and his wife Susana. But living together is difficult because the old woman, wishing to be useful, makes matters worse through her clumsiness and lack of memory. Susan, already under a great deal of stress in their small, financially straitened household, has to bear Mama Cora's "help" as an extra burden. The situation explodes one Sunday as a result of an incident between Mama Cora and Susana. In a frenzy, Susana goes to her relatives' house and begs them to temporarily take care of Mama Cora. Their tense conversations show the hypocrisy and lack of solidarity of the other members of the family towards Susana and Jorge's request for help.

When Susana and Jorge return home, they can't find Mama Cora. Worried about her absence, they start inquiries which lead them to the morgue. There, they are shown the dead body of an old woman who has committed suicide by throwing herself under a railway train. Full of sorrow, the couple declare that this is, indeed their mother's dead body. Later, returning from her walk, Mama Cora makes a sudden appearance at her own wake, causing great commotion and joy among her afflicted children, who try to conceal the real motive of this infrequent family reunion. (Press book.)

The second most popular film at Argentina's box office in 1986, *Esperando la carroza* is a black comedy because it demystifies the timeworn concepts of reverence for the Latina mother, respect for the elderly, and above all, the notion of the extended family, whose members should care for the elderly even though some are harridans, as Mama Cora appears to be. The film pretends to be a broad comedy, but it is really an incisive view into Argentine family life, especially in a family already plagued with infighting and family intrigues that lead to chaos. Even the title gives away the director's premise. Apparently, when two Argentines get together, you already have three differing opinions. Doria is satirizing the whole nature of the Argentine middle-class, who leap to conclusions without the requisite knowledge and duck responsibilities whenever they can. (Why wait for the pallbearers when there is no death in the family?) There is also a soap-opera quality inherent in the plot of this film that reminds one of the Argentine characters in the early novels of Manuel Puig. However, where Puig's creations can resort to nostalgia and reminiscence to give their lives calm and substance, Doria's protagonists are raw caricatures, caught in the pettiness of their minor intrigues. Although this film comes at a propitious time for Argentine cinema, the *apertura* (opening) with the arrival of the Alfonsín government, its minor critique of Argentine life hardly paves the way for new inroads into a profound Argentine cinema of social problems. It is incisive, but it fumbles the ball in its critique of the Argentine bourgeois, because Doria could have fleshed out the characters of many other family members who still remain undeveloped in the background. However, when you examine the thematic ground it is trying to cover — false piety, hypocrisy, bourgeois vested interests, problems of old age, family appearances and contradictions in human feelings —

the film is certainly courageous in its attempt to depict Argentine society of the mid-eighties.

NOTES: Alejandro Doria was born in Buenos Aires in 1936 and majored in business administration before he decided to make filmmaking his career. He worked in Argentine television for ten years before making his first feature film in 1974 entitled *Los años infames* (later retitled *Proceso a la infamia*). Other films include *La isla* (1979), *Los miedos* (1980), *Los pasajeros del jardín* (1982, based on a famous novel by Sylvia Bullrich), *Darse Cuenta* (1984), and *Sofía* (1986). He continues to live and film in Buenos Aires.

100. Eversmile, New Jersey.

Carlos Sorín. Argentina, 1989. 94 min., Color. Spanish.

COMMENTARY: Fergus O'Connell, a dentist (played by Daniel Day Lewis), travels by motorcycle through Patagonia, offering dental care advice to anyone in need. He gives free treatment and urges the unconcerned population to take care of their teeth. On the road, he meets the daughter of a tow-truck driver (Mirjana Jokovic), about to be married, who travels along as his dental assistant. She first stows away, then reveals herself to him. She offers him sex, but since he is married, he refuses. Their relationship comes alive when a chance tooth extraction on the road reveals the young woman's talents for dentistry. Finally, the two travelers do become a couple in this comedic Argentine road film. The title of the film refers to the name and location of the sponsoring foundation for the dentist's trip, a foundation he can no longer contact by telephone. He has also lost contact with his wife. There is something quite surreal in this screenplay, written by Jorge Goldenberg, about a dentist losing all contact with society on the great plains of Patagonia, but even with the acting talents and star

power of Daniel Day Lewis, this film is unlikely ever to take off commercially. And yet, there is a video cassette available; at the unheard-of price of $89.98, one can own this travelogue of Patagonia, with its rugged landscapes beautifully photographed by Esteban Courtalon.

NOTES: Carlos Sorín is primarily known in Argentina for directing a wonderful satire on filmmaking called *La película del rey* (*A King and His Movie*, 1985), which won the Opera Prima Award at the Venice Film Festival that year. He continues to make films in his homeland.

101. Evita (quien quiera oír que oiga) (Evita — Who Wants to Hear May Hear). Eduardo Mignogna. Argentina, 1984. 90 min., Color and B&W. Spanish.

COMMENTARY: Part documentary, part reenactment, *Evita*, the film by Eduardo Mignogna, contains both archival footage and new interviews with those who knew or watched Eva Duarte as she grew from a child to a legend — the legend of Eva Perón, "Evita." Mignogna also uses reenactments to tell the story. According to the U.S. Film Festival program for 1988, "the restrained reenactments are subtle enough to count as home movies that were never made: Evita in her first school plays, Evita at play, Evita trying out for her first roles." Leading from these reenactments into actual footage from the Perón era, Eduardo Mignogna's film succeeds in capturing the myth that was Evita, from her youth, through her early second-rate actress days, her marriage to Juan Perón, her days as an idol adored by the Argentine masses and her untimely death by cancer. It is the director's first film, and he perseveres in revealing unknown data about his subject, at the same time providing wide sympathetic response without resorting to the ad copy style of other political documentarists.

His use of interviews that sometimes conflict provides the viewer with fascinating insights about Evita. Some intellectuals felt that people "were idiots to believe in Evita," that her "illegitimate origin justifies her social rancor," that "she was resentful, full of hate," but that "she was a woman chosen by the gods: she got all that she wanted and she died young." Although some philosophers believe that no individual alters the course of history, one columnist opined that if Evita had not died so early, Perón would not have been ousted from power during his second term. Ironically, Eva Perón's myth was revived by Andrew Lloyd Weber and Tim Rice in their politically charged musical version of her life, starring Patty Lupone and Mandy Patinkin, simply called *Evita*. Faye Dunaway also played Evita in a dramatized miniseries of her life on NBC. Although both actresses were later ousted from Lloyd Weber's musical of *Sunset Boulevard* in 1994 (Lupone because of her height and Dunaway because of her singing voice), both made successes of our B-player, Eva Duarte.

Evita — Who Wants to Hear May Hear see *Evita (quien quiera oír que oiga)*

Excess Baggage see *El bulto*

Exterminating Angel see *El ángel exterminador*

Fallen from the Sky see *Caídos del cielo*

Far Away and Long Ago see *Allá lejos y hace tiempo*

Feelings: Mirta from Linares to Istanbul see *Feelings: mirta de Linares a Estambul*

The Female Bandit see *La bandida*

Fever Mounts on El Pao see *La Fièvre monte à El Pao*

102. La Fièvre monte à El Pao (Fever Mounts on El Pao or Republic of Sin). Luis Buñuel. Mexico/France, 1957. 97 min., B&W. Spanish/French.

COMMENTARY: Gerard Phillipe plays the role of the small-time government administrator, Ramón Vásquez, who is about to lose his job because the governor was just assassinated. He may also lose the sexual favors of the governor's wife, Ines (María Félix), with whom he has had a long-standing affair. However, as fate would have it, Vásquez replaces the governor. He is immediately challenged by his rival, Alejandro Gual (Jean Servais), for the position. Vásquez tries to improve the lot of political prisoners but to no avail. Fascism is all around him in this unidentifiable Latin American country. Gual begins to take over Vásquez's power, and Ines must fend for herself. First she tries a striptease to win Gual's attentions; then she nearly kills him with a pistol; and finally she reverses herself, pulling Gual down on top of her in a devouring sex scene that fades out leaving little to the imagination.

However, Gual becomes a victim when Vásquez incites a prisoner uprising and takes control of the island. The former is taken prisoner and shot, while the latter is troubled by the concept of death without a trial. Ines and Vásquez have become assassins themselves. Vásquez takes control again, frees the political prisoners and tries to end the tyranny. But danger lurks everywhere when one is trying to improve a totalitarian regime from the inside. Free, but inept, Vásquez plays into the hands of his new fascist enemies and becomes enmeshed in a system of government beyond his capacity to control.

Although Gerard Phillipe brings the right kind of sensitivity to the role of Vásquez, he is outdone by María Félix's scene-stealing and histrionics. The themes of the film are relevant today, and the basic Buñuel touches are there — his sardonic comments on lust, greed, hypocrisy, cruelty and political power — but the film suffers, as Buñuel himself said, from the compromises he had to make for a co-production. Yet *La fièvre monte à El Pao* is still an interesting Buñuelian exercise as a study of revolt and compromise, completely made on Mexican soil with French artistry and finances.

The film is really part potboiler, part trenchant political analysis. The fact that individuals have to keep in line in the system is the basis of Buñuel's unique commentary about life in this Latin American country. Although the film is plainly cynical in its message, Gerard Phillipe (whose last film this was) projects little more than Gallic charm; he simply wrinkles his brow when the ideas become profound or beyond his reach. The film still had the wonderful camera work of Gabriel Figueroa and a fascinating Paul Misraki score.

103. Fin de fiesta (End of the Party or The Blood Feast or The Party Is Over). Leopoldo Torre Nilsson. Argentina, 1959. 107 min., B&W. Spanish.

Set in the 1930s in a puritanical household, *Fin de fiesta* is a story about a boy's adolescence spent in the shadow of political tyranny. Braceras (Arturo García Buhr), a veteran political boss, has moved from the gaucho class to a position of wealth and power maintained by terror and rigged elections. His decline is witnessed through the eyes of his grandson, Adolfo (Leonardo Favio), a sullen, highly sexed, directionless boy whose hatred of Braceras is complicated

by his growing affection for the old man's worldly henchman, Guatavino (Lautaro Murua). Braceras is very hard on his grandson, even as the old man loses his control of the political scene through corruption while Adolfo assumes the social consciousness and mantle of the family.

Leonardo Favio perfectly expresses Adolfo's brooding sensuality and constraint, and his scenes with Lautaro Murua have the terseness of the best kind of graphic photojournalism. The director has an excellent feeling for the era, and he throws in a few comic scenes as well. For example, there is a fancy dress-rehearsal for a ball, a girl's bathing party, a visit by a group of snobbish aunts — scenes whose family-album quality is as rich in atmosphere and suggestion as the all-pervading violence in the film (Braceras uses hoodlums who extort money to gain political favors). The kind of violence seen in the film was based on actual events linked with a definite chapter in Argentine history. Although the violence is quite evident, the director preferred to emphasize the literary qualities of the screenplay written by his favorite collaborator, novelist Beatriz Guido.

First Charge of the Machete see *Primera carga del machete*

First Chronicle see *Primera crónica*

104. Fitzcarraldo. Werner Herzog. W. Germany/Brazil, 1982. 157 min., Color. German.

COMMENTARY: Resembling in many ways his earlier film *Aguirre, The Wrath of God*, this work took Werner Herzog once again to Latin America, using the spectacular locales of Peru and Brazil (particularly locations along the Amazon River and in Manaus, Brazil) to tell his epic fairy tale of Brian Sweeney Fitzgerald, or Fitzcarraldo, who so far has failed to achieve his dreams: building a Trans-Andean railroad through the jungle and

Claudia Cardinale plays Molly, the madam of an elegant bordello in the Peruvian Amazon, who supports the dreams of her lover, Fitzcarraldo (Klaus Kinski), in Werner Herzog's *Fitzcarraldo* (1982).

an ice factory without paying customers (shades of Paul Theroux's *Mosquito Coast* here). Now Fitzcarraldo (brilliantly played by Klaus Kinski) dreams of erecting an opera house in the middle of the jungle to welcome his idol, Enrico Caruso. Securing the money for such an undertaking through Molly (Claudia Cardinale), Fitzcarraldo takes an option on land in hostile Indian territory with rubber trees, then buys a converted passenger ship and hauls it over a mountain to an adjoining river, opening up this new territory for rubber exploitation. His creditors are so overjoyed that they celebrate their new prospects with an opera performance.

Fitzcarraldo is an extraordinary film, an adult daydream, a delightfully mad fantasy from start to finish, using fully its extraordinary South American locations and several tribes of Brazilian and Peruvian Indians. As the press book says: "Like most Herzog heroes, [Fitzcarraldo] wins and loses. But for the audience, it is all triumph.... *Fitzcarraldo* is the thinking man's epic."

NOTES: Along with *Fitzcarraldo*, one should also see Les Blank's marvelous short documentary on the making of this film, *Burden of Dreams*, which documents the whole hazardous nature of Herzog's expedition, the illness of his original star, Jason Robards, and Kinski's assuming the title role, somewhat chagrined by the whole experience.

The Flood Area see *Los inundados*

Flood Victims see *Los inundados*

105. Flor silvestre (Wild Flower). Emilio "El Indio" Fernández. Mexico, 1943. 90 min., B&W. Spanish.

COMMENTARY: Another of those wonderful Mexican dramas depicting hardship and suffering during the Mexican Revolution of 1910, this time told in flashback! Dolores del Río plays the beautiful Esperanza, who remembers her marriage to José Luis Castro (Pedro Armendáriz), the son of a wealthy landowner, and the losses she suffered over the years because of the revolution with the overthrow of the Porfirio Díaz government.

Charles Ramírez Berg, in his book *Cinema of Solitude*, calls *Flor silvestre* "Mexican provincial melodrama at its best." Among the conventions Berg notes are the hero as *charro*, embodiment of the pure revolutionary ideal, and his conflict with the wicked *hacendado* (landowner), who stands in opposition to the revolution. In *Flor silvestre*, the character José leaves his father's wealth and status behind in order to serve the revolution. The serious side of this story, Berg notes, is combined "with the music and broad comedy of the 'comedia ranchera.'"

It is too bad that most American critics do not appreciate this kind of film, characterizing Dolores del Río as beatific but wooden and Pedro Armendáriz as lacking expression. The director, Emilio Fernández, gives his usual signature performance as Rogelio Torres, a friend of the masses.

The Forgotten Ones see *Los olvidados*

106. The Forgotten Village. Herbert Kline. Mexico/U.S., 1941. 65 min., B&W. English.

COMMENTARY: *The Forgotten Village* was filmed on location in Mexico during a ten-month period. Its "script" was written by John Steinbeck and spoken on screen by actor Burgess Meredith. It is an admirable effort to tell the story of real people caught in their birth-life-death struggle against poverty and disease.

Made in an unidentified village with all native actors, the film identifies its essential conflict: superstition and witchcraft versus the power of education and modern scientific advances. We watch the daily lives of the Mexican peasants unfold before our eyes — their work, sense of humor, dignity, anguish, pain.

Esperanza, the mother, calls in Trini, a midwife, to help her deliver her child (she cannot even imagine a doctor's help in this primitive part of rural Mexico). For a fee, Trini mixes potions and predicts the baby will be a boy. Two weeks later, the baby arrives. Trini wraps Esperanza in a shawl, and two other Indian women aid her in guiding the newborn baby into the world, although the actual birth is not shown.

The death of Esperanza's son Paco seems to take place immediately after the birth of the baby. It's not the "bad airs," but the waters contaminated with typhoid. Trini's potions are of no help. Paco dies, but his brother Juan Diego spirits his sick sister away from the family to the local town, where he has her injected with a vaccine that saves her life.

The photography by Alexander Hackensmid is excellent, as is the provocative music score by Hans Eisler. Although the film shows many negative aspects about the Mexican government, the project was wholly supported by them. *The Forgotten Village* is not really an original documentary. Luis Buñuel did the same sort of thing, without narration, in 1932 when he went to an equally desolate region in Spain, Las Hurdes, and made that terrific documentary called *Land Without Bread*. Unfortunately, the Spanish government took exception to Buñuel's portrait of poverty, starvation and illness and exiled him from the country. The Mexicans, however, welcomed Steinbeck, Klein and crew, since they were sincerely interested in education, reform and the future prosperity of the nation.

107. La fórmula secreta (The Secret Formula). Rubén Gamez. Mexico, 1964. 45 min., B&W. Spanish.

COMMENTARY: *La fórmula secreta* is a personal expression of certain aspects of life in Mexico in the sixties and evokes the oppression and poverty of the people who live in the provinces. The film is based upon a story by surrealist author Juan Rulfo (author of the novel *Pedro Páramo*) and features music by Vivaldi, Stravinksy and Leobardo Velasquez. The cast consists of non-professional actors "who depict rural Mexico's underprivileged classes. These images are juxtaposed with urban Mexico to create a powerful metaphor for the drama and the struggle of rural, poor Mexicans coping with a foreign world in their own land. Yet who is really to blame for this seemingly eternal struggle?" (Press book.)

Critics have indubitably noted its overall surreal style, reminiscent of Buñuel's feature film *L'Âge d'or*, as well as some truly astonishing specific images — the scaffolding of priests and seminarists, the latter chewing the hands of the former until the blood runs and they fall to the ground like ripe pears. Also, the director has a truly Mexican obsession with death, and his images show an anti–Yankee violence of rare intensity.

This ground-breaking experimental feature was shown in 1991 at UCLA's marvelous Mexican film series entitled "Mexican Film and the Literary Tradition," which moved to New York's Museum of Modern Art in the summer of 1992.

NOTES: The film was primarily the work of the director, Rubén Gamez, inspired by the reading of a poem by Jaime Sabines, the script of Juan Rulfo, all in collaboration with a group of non-professional actors. The Mexican director, now in his sixties, made short films for advertising before directing *La fórmula secreta*, his first medium-length film, which won first prize at the Festival of the Experimental Film in Mexico City in 1966.

108. Fresa y chocolate (Strawberry and Chocolate). Tomás Gutiérrez Alea and Juan Carlos Tabio. Cuba/Mexico/Spain, 1993-94. 110 min., Color. Spanish.

COMMENTARY: David (Vladimir Cruz), a sociology student in his 20s, meets Diego (Jorge Perugorria), a gay man in his 40s, at an outdoor ice cream parlor. Though he is heterosexual, David is drawn to the remarkable Diego, who in turn finds David a true soulmate. "To call this new film by Tomás Gutiérrez Alea ... — co-directed with Juan Carlos Tabio — ground-breaking doesn't nearly do it justice: for Cuba, it's off the political seismic scale. Rather, it's simply one of the most humane and deeply felt love stories of the year." (New York Film Festival program notes, 1994.)

Having much in common with Alea's *Letters from the Park* (based upon short stories by García Márquez), *Fresa y chocolate* is a sweetly lyrical love story about two men intellectually adrift in postrevolutionary Cuba. Although they develop an odd friendship much like the William Hurt–Raúl Julia characters in Babenco's *Kiss of the Spiderwoman*, this film is much lighter in tone, and certainly more humane since the main characters are not in prison, though they do argue about politics as they fall in love with each other in an atmosphere of governmental gay intolerance.

Although there are more cloying moments as the friendship takes wing, and David realizes Diego is somewhat of a name-dropping gay iconoclast ("Do you know Oscar Wilde, André Gide, García Lorca, even Truman Capote?"), the two men establish their ideological and political stances without resorting to campy swishing of hips or lecherous sensual gazes as they embark on the sexual side of their friendship. Jorge Perugorria is just perfect as the gay counter-revolutionary, and Vladimir Cruz as David, just jilted by his fiancée, is equally adept in his role of a young, heterosexual Communist who is ready for a new kind of relationship.

Beautifully photographed in color by Mario García Joya as a love story against a candy-colored backdrop and punctuated with a fine musical score by José María Vitier, *Fresa y chocolate* is a sumptuous treat for the eyes and also the mind, since it is the first film about a gay hero that is also a critique of Castro's gay intolerance. (Compare the reviews that deal quite vicerally and voraciously with the same subject.)

Fresa y chocolate was released in the United States and worldwide by Miramax Films in January of 1995. It has already gained much notoriety because of its malicious swipes against the Castro regime. But the film succeeds especially at its conclusion, when the straight, passionate Cuban communist revolutionary, David, embraces the effeminate, gay, artistic Diego in a final hug. The story is told with a good deal of humor and wit and should be a huge commercial success in America and abroad, especially with audiences who enjoyed *The Wedding Banquet*, another gay love story. *Fresa y chocolate* is just content with its love story and some mild satirizing of some of the sacred tenets of Cuban communism — no more, no less. It does not go even as far as Hermosillo's *Doña Herlinda y su hijo*, but is another humorous addition to Latin American cinema, with homoerotic overtones. It is a provocative sex comedy, made with intellect and taste, that is sure to please its audiences internationally.

NOTES: It is rumored that Tomás Gutiérrez Alea, the directorial superstar of the Cuban Film Institute since the Castro takeover in the fifties, has taken up permanent residence in Mexico City since finishing this film. He was reportedly "ill" when Juan Carlos Tabio, a resident director, took over his directorial duties and finished the film for him.

Frida see *Frida: naturaleza vida*

109. Frida: naturaleza vida
(Frida). Paul Leduc. Mexico, 1985. 107 min., Color. Spanish.

COMMENTARY: Known as the flamboyant wife of Diego Rivera, Frida Kahlo was an artist, a surrealist painter in her own right. Her life and her paintings are inseparable. The latter consist mostly of self-portraits that evoke her romantic and political passions as well as the physical and spiritual agonies that shaped her life. *Frida* is a series of elegant tableaux, painted in the artist's own hothouse palette, and structured as memory fragments recalled upon her deathbed. Relying upon a minimum of dialogue, the film recreates the exotic lives of Kahlo, husband Diego Rivera and their friend (and Kalho's lover), the exiled Leon Trotsky. Before her short life ended, Kalho earned a reputation as Latin America's greatest woman artist, political activist, and feminist. The film traces on screen the interior and exterior pathways of its protagonist and examines her relationships with both her famous Mexican muralist husband and her Russian revolutionary-in-exile lover. (Press book.)

Director Paul Leduc has succeeded in recreating Kalho's passionate existence, especially her pain, which began at age eighteen when her spine was fractured, her pelvis crushed and one foot broken. (A few months before her death, her right leg had to be amputated.) Surrounding herself with mirrors, she began a series of self-portraits, some of which show her physical pain, sometimes in a very surreal way. The director observes no sense of chronology, moving forwards and backwards in time as Frida grows younger or older, scene by scene. We watch her argue with Rivera about his illicit affair with her sister; we witness an early miscarriage; we watch her argue with David Siquieros, the painter, about extending her hospitality to Trotsky; we observe Kalho marching at communist demonstrations, rallying behind hammer-and-sickle flags. Frida herself was to die at the age of 44 with some 200 amazing self-portraits as testament to her years of joy and sorrow.

Ofelia Medina, the actress who plays Frida, is perfectly cast and gives a vibrant, heroic performance. She certainly has all the requisite energy the real Frida had for several love affairs, painting huge canvasses and participating in political rallies. Medina, who won the Best Actress Award at the Havana Latin American Film Festival for her portrayal, bears an uncanny resemblance to the real Frida, with her striking black eyebrows linked in one singular black line, the faint, strangely erotic hint of a mustache and piercing dark eyes that could penetrate any pretension. The exotic face is complemented by her vivid Mexican costumes, set off by fabulous pre–Columbian jade beads, grand loops of colonial earrings, baroque rings, ribbons and flowers braided through her hair — and often, a spider monkey clinging to her neck. Frida was a woman who made herself a work of art. Medina captures the hearty, hungry spirit of Frida, who felt "nothing is worth more than laughter. It is strength to love and to abandon oneself, to be light. Tragedy is the most

ridiculous thing." The film is an excellent homage to a woman with an extraordinary gift for life.

Fridays of Eternity see *Viernes de la eternidad*

Funes, a Great Love see *Funes, un gran amor*

110. Funes, un gran amor
(**Funes, a Great Love**). Raúl de la Torre. Argentina, 1992. 115 min., Color. Spanish.

COMMENTARY: Another "tango" epic melodrama from Argentina told in flashback, *Funes, un gran amor* stars Italian actor Gian Maria Volonte as the owner of a bar-cum-brothel outside of the slaughterhouse district of Sarate, the hometown of the director. The film is narrated by Pepe Soriano, now living in an old age home, who remembers how the bar owner beat a corrupt politico at poker, slept with prostitutes and finally fell in love with the pianist of a tango band (Graciela Borges). Although the plot is strictly minor and unconvincing, the film serves as a showcase for many tango musical attractions — songs like "Naranja en flor" — and many bandoneon soloists like Daniel Binelli and tango dancers such as Juan Carlos Copes. There have been many other tango films of recent vintage coming from Argentina and elsewhere, better in their quality of entertainment, scripting and editing. *Funes* suffers from overacting and general disjointedness of plot and script. It is far from the best work of Raúl de la Torre, but it is worthwhile as entertainment to see the stars perform.

NOTES: Raúl de la Torre was born in Buenos Aires in 1938. He began in the film advertising world before making his first feature, *Juan Lamoglia y señora*, in 1970. Some critics say his work is reminiscent of the films of Italian director

Michelangelo Antonioni because he explores the existential boredom and ennui of bourgeois lives and loves to explore feminine psychology. His favorite leading lady is actress Graciela Borges, who has appeared in at least three of his films. His best known works in America are *Pubis angélical* (1982) and *Pobre mariposa* (1985, a historical epic with a script by Aida Bortnik). His films with Graciela Borges are mostly commercial ventures like *Crónica de una señora* (1971, following Antonioni's style), *Heroína* (1972) and *Sola* (1976).

A Funny, Dirty Little War see *No habrá más penas ni olvido*

111. Os fuzis (The Guns). Ruy Guerra. Brazil, 1963. 110 min., B&W. Portuguese.

COMMENTARY: "Encouraged by the words of a holy man, the peasants of northeastern Brazil follow a sacred ox in the belief that it will bring rain to the drought-ridden area. Soldiers are sent to the nearby town of Milagres to protect the mayor's food supply from the starving people. One of the soldiers, Mario, falls in love with a local girl, Luisa, but her mistrust of the troops inhibits her from returning his love. When another soldier, Pedro, kills a peasant in a thoughtless accident with a rifle, the matter is quickly hushed up. On the day of the food lorry's departure, Gaucho, a truck driver and ex-soldier, is enraged by the apathy of the peasants in the face of deprivation and, seizing a gun, opens fire on the troops. He is pursued and shot, and the truck moves away. Meanwhile, in defiance of the Holy Man, the peasants kill the sacred ox and share and devour its meat." (Press book.)

Os fuzis is a small film that disturbs the viewer because of its larger implications. Through the sun's glare and heat, the sweating peasants, with eyes shaded and dusty, must confront their hunger and the failure of religion, the military and other supposed leaders to resolve their problems. Only through revolution or the violence of their own initiative are they able to transcend their static existence, made doubly bleak and oppressive by the choice they face: starve, or abandon the restrictive shibboleths of organized religion and live.

French critic André Delvaux thought *Os fuzis* was "a major work in any language ... particularly important because, together with Rocha's *Black God, White Devil* [*Deus e o diabo na terra do sol*] and Dos Santos' *Barren Lives* [*Vidas secas*], it introduced *Cinema Nôvo* to the outside world." Ruy Guerra, the director, said of the film: "What distinguishes *Os fuzis* ... is its structure ... various aspects of northeastern life are introduced as if at random and then gradually drawn together towards the film's climax ... the failure of the peasants, who defy religious taboo, turn on their useless god-figure and eat it, ... exploding with violence, reflecting the Brazilian character."

Os fuzis is a tough, violent, implacable film that makes no concessions, but its human, political and aesthetic resonances touch us profoundly. *Os fuzis* is more than a western, a documentary or a war film. It is a tragic film, since it has its origins in one of the lands where people still die of hunger. The film offers no solutions, but telling the whole truth is in itself a revolutionary act in a country where illiteracy, ignorance, intolerance and lethargy are rife due mainly to poor working conditions, the scarcity of food, the tyranny of tradition, religious fanaticism — all circumstances that prevent the Brazilian northeasterner from completely grasping the nature of his existence. *Os fuzis* also offers the expression of a manic lyricism, a savage cruelty, where the appetite to live clashes with harsh necessity. The film is at times operatic, hysterical, reveling in its excesses — the expression of the agonies of

Brazilian soldiers retreating from starving peasants in Ruy Guerra's *Os fuzis* (*The Guns*, 1963).

heat, starvation and unbearable suffering. *Os fuzis* is monumental because it shows a change in consciousness by its climactic act of blasphemy, implying that within the violent, iconoclastic act of slaying the ox lies the key to social revolution and future change for Brazil. *Os fuzis* is a masterwork, comparable to the best social films of Sergei Eisenstein. It won the Silver Bear at Berlin's 1964 Film Festival and deserves to be seen internationally.

112. Gabriela. Bruno Barreto.
Brazil, 1983. 102 min., Color. Portuguese.

COMMENTARY: Based upon Jorge Amado's internationally best-selling novel *Gabriela, Clove and Cinnamon*, this was probably the most expensive film made in Brazil in 1983, costing over three million dollars. The Brazilian television soap opera starred Sonia Braga, and that actress repeats the title role with Marcello Mastroianni as her lover, Nacib.

The story is very, very slight. The time is 1925; the place, the small town of Ilheus. Gabriela, a mulatto migrant worker, is first introduced in the film as a beautiful but bedraggled creature caked with blue mud. She and some fellow Bahians have wandered into town in search of water during a drought. Gabriela's sweet nature becomes apparent to Nacib, the foreign-born tavern keeper, who hires her to cook for his establishment. Soon enough, Gabriela has added other "services" to her work regimen. Gabriela is a free, generous spirit, performing household chores like washing Nacib's laundry with a lecherous smile. Sonia Braga plays the role in skimpy outfits, a character whose libido cannot be confined by clothes or even the respectability of marriage. Nacib realizes Gabriela's sexual attraction to every man in the town and decides to marry her. Because the townspeople are bringing social pressures to bear, marriage is the best route for Gabriela to gain respectability. But respectability means Gabriela must wear modest clothes, keep them on and sleep apart from Nacib until their wedding day. However, the uninhibited Gabriela can do none of these things and breaks the strictures of societal conventions.

As in her earlier film, *Doña Flor e seus dois maridos*, Sonia Braga is a bouncy eyeful, eager for nudity, sexuality and love, and she plays Gabriela with an innocent impishness. Mastroianni plays the Turkish barkeep as a physical wreck of a man, sallow, sweating, paunchy, with lust in his eyes. When Gabriela licks her lips as she eyes Nacib, she almost destroys our credibility in the film because mooney-eyed Mastroianni projects loony irascibility, not lust. By the end of the film he is weakened by Gabriela, vulnerable, a cuckold in love, a middle-aged friend-to-all who is acutely lonely.

Gabriela was filmed entirely on location in Parati, Brazil, a coastal hamlet renowned for its Portuguese architectural style. The once-thriving port juts into a picturesque bay of tropical islands. During the seventeenth century, Parati was known for its gold trading and its cobblestone streets. Parati serves the director well as a substitute location for Bahia, the original setting of the novel. But Brazilian film critics have excoriated the director for using the Parati location as well as leaving out Amado's rich description of the political conflicts and social tensions during the 1920s, reducing the novel to a love affair between a wealthy bar owner and his young attractive employee, despite his fine direction of Mastroianni and Braga. Because of so much tampering with the original novel, the motivations of the characters and their behavior seem inexplicable in this reduced screenplay. The production values, however, are excellent, and Antonio Carlos Jobim has provided the film with a beautiful score.

Gaijín: A Brazilian Odyssey see *Gaijín: caminhos da liberdade*

113. Gaijín: caminhos da liberdade (Gaijín: A Brazilian Odyssey). Tizuka Yamasaki. Brazil, 1981. 105 min., Color. Portuguese/Japanese.

COMMENTARY: "Gaijín" means "outsider" and this Brazilian film is the story of migrant workers imported from Japan, confronting an alien and often hostile culture. Like its predecessors, John Ford's outstanding *The Grapes of Wrath* (about dust-bowl emigrants of 1930 in America's southwest) and Robert M. Young's searing *Alambrista* (dealing with migration from Mexico in the mid-seventies), *Gaijín* is based upon a true story, in this case told to director Yamasaki by her grandmother. It is the account of eight hundred Japanese who left for Brazil during the coffee-production boom in 1908 and their harrowing experiences to survive.

The film begins in São Paolo in 1980 and flashes back to the Japan of 1908. Since Brazilian emigration authorities preferred that coffee plantation workers be married, we see Yamada (Jiro Kawarasaki) take a young bride, Titoe (Kyoko Tsukamoto). When they arrive in Brazil with many other young and old couples, they are placed on a plantation dominated by a very wealthy family and ruthlessly controlled by a murderous overseer. All the Japanese immigrants realize they are now slaves. An Italian anarchist and labor leader, Enrico (Gianfrancesco Guarnieri), tries to organize the Japanese workers and is murdered by machete-wielding Brazilian henchmen of the wealthy landowners. The Japanese still remain isolated from unionizing efforts, preferring to commit suicide or die from malaria or the elements. A Brazilian plantation accountant, Tonho (Antonio Fagundes), secretly in love with Titoe, helps her and her family to escape the marauding overseers on horseback. Titoe survives the death of her husband and moves to the big city. The film returns to the present, and we see Titoe in a chance meeting with Tonho, the accountant, who also escaped from the clutches of the landowners. Tonho's sympathy was always with the Japanese, many of whom now have assimilated culturally into factory jobs in an urban setting.

According to the director, Titoe was a fictional representation of her grandmother, and much of the film is drawn from the old woman's memories of those early days. *Gaijín* is a film of exceptional beauty, luminous and unfailingly moving. It is director Tizuka Yamasaki's debut film.

NOTES: Born in Porto Alegre, Brazil, in 1949, Ms. Yamasaki obtained a bachelor's degree in communications with a major in cinema. She worked with directors Nelson Pereira dos Santos and Glauber Rocha on their films during the seventies while continuing her career as a photographer and journalist for the magazine *Luz e Acao.*

A third-generation Brazilian herself, she spent her childhood within the Japanese community of São Paulo and spoke no Portuguese until she was fifteen. Although she always thought of herself as Japanese, when she went to Tokyo to hire several of the cast for *Gaijín*, she suddenly felt Brazilian. Thus displacement is a central theme in her life as in her film. Yamasaki always understood that her family was involved in a class struggle. It was their initial alientation by Brazilian society that forced even the most docile Japanese to break out of their isolation and create a community of their own in Brazil. This is the story *Gaijín* relates — an autobiographical one for the director, who feels her film "uncovers a chapter in the early history of colonialism whose pattern endures little changed in much of Latin America."

Her second film, *Parahyba, muljermacho* (1983), is another historical project, dealing with the 1930 revolution in Brazil. It is a love tragedy as well as a true story, relating the life of Anayde Beiriz, an intellectual poet from Parahyba who committed suicide because she could not face the repression of society. Yamasaki's last film, *Patriamada* (1984), was a love story integrated into the political events of Brazilian life of the early eighties. It was screened at the Toronto Film Festival, and Julianne Burton did an interview with the director in an issue of *Film Quarterly*, but the film has never been seen in the United States.

114. Garrincha, alegría do povo (Garrincha, Hero of the People). Joaquim Pedro de Andrade. Brazil, 1963. 66 min., B&W. Portuguese.

COMMENTARY: Offering interesting insights into the Latin American enthusiasm for sports, especially soccer, *Garrincha* is not just another filmed biography of a soccer player but a documentary that will appeal to fans internationally because of its storyline and its footage of

Brazil's World Cup victories of 1958 and 1962. We trace Garrincha's rise from his days as a poor factory worker to his professional stardom as one of soccer's most highly paid athletes, idolized by the Brazilian population. There are some excellent montages of Garrincha in action, capturing the sports-arena atmosphere, and an amusing biographical note on the soundtrack about our superstar, father of seven daughters and wishing number eight would be a son. Recent documentaries about the Argentine Maradona and Brazilian Pelé, in color, have been equally competent recapitulations of their lives as soccer players, but none have been as diverting as Garrincha's story.

NOTES: A Brazilian by birth, Andrade entered the movie industry in the fifties, first serving as assistant director to Santos Pereira, then founding his own company, Saga Films, which produced mostly short documentaries. *Garrincha* was his first feature-length documentary, made in 1963. Other films include *O padre e a moca* (1966), *Macunaima* (1970), *O homem do Pau-Brazil* (1981) and *Vida mansa* (1984). He also made an outstanding documentary on the *Cinema Nôvo* movement for German television entitled *Improvisiert und Zielbewurzt* in 1967.

Garrincha, Hero of the People see *Garrincha, alegría do povo*

General Document on Chile see *Acta general de Chile*

115. Gerónima. Raúl Tosso. Argentina, 1986. 96 min., Color. Spanish.

COMMENTARY: Based upon a true story, this film folows the life of Gerónima Sande, a Mapuche Indian from the southern province of Patagonia (Trapalco). With her four children, Gerónima ekes out a living from a desolate land. A visiting health inspector sees that her living situation is intolerable, but while "civilized" society may be capable of defining Gerónima's problem, it has no method of solving it.

Gerónima and her children are taken to a hospital in the city of General Roca to be treated for malnutrition. Gerónima becomes mentally ill in the hospital, which becomes her hostile environment. (It was the Hospital de Glauber Rocha in the province of Rio Negro in Southeastern Argentina.) Furthermore, her children catch whooping cough, and three die.

The film is punctuated by haunting recordings made in the 1970s of Gerónima being interrogated by a doctor, probably the real Argentine Dr. Jorge Pellegrini. While the doctor accumulates information on her way of life, the filmmaker mounts a critique of the notion of judging one's culture by the standards of another.

Gerónima first began as a 40-minute short in 16mm; later, because of festival exposure, it was given commercial treatment, using extended footage and blown up to 35mm. Luisa Calcumil gives an extraordinarily sensitive performance as Gerónima, being of part Mapuche Indian descent herself. Some viewers may consider this film an anthropological work, but the director does not seem to cast blame or perpetuate any particular ideology; rather, he presents Gerónima's story in an unsentimental way. The story of Gerónima itself is an emotionally overwhelming experience.

NOTES: Raúl Alberto Tosso was born in 1953 in Buenos Aires. Although he has a degree in business, he began filmmaking in 1977 with an experimental documentary entitled *Zoo la plata*. In 1980, he filmed another documentary about his hometown of Avellaneda before making *Gerónima* in 1982 and reworking it into a commercial feature for 1986 release.

The Girlfriend see *La amiga*

Cordelia Gonzáles and Daniel Lugo play star-crossed lovers in one of the many sub-plots of Zurinaga's *La gran fiesta* (1987).

116. La gran fiesta. Marcos Zurinaga. Puerto Rico, 1987. 101 min., Color. English/Spanish.

COMMENTARY: The film stars Raúl Julia, E.G. Marshall and a host of Puerto Rican actors who participate in a melo-dramatic account of personal and polit-ical intrigue set in Puerto Rico in 1942. The period sets recreate the era beauti-fully as we witness the last grand ball in the Casino at Old San Juan on the eve of the city's takeover by United States Armed Forces. The film has a limited re-lease in America but was eclipsed by the more serious entertainment, *Tango Bar*, by the same director, which received more favorable notices than this film, his first effort. However, it does show off Puerto Rico to fine advantage.

It was bruited about that Puerto Ricans were hoping for an Academy Award for the island's first full-length feature film, but despite its being a well-polished evocation of a decisive moment in Puerto Rican history and a love story amid World War II intrigue, the plot overwhelmed the audience with tedious detail, sometimes over-explaining its characters, other times rendering them and their concerns unintelligible. Nev-ertheless, the movie should be consid-ered a first stop in a drive to create a Puerto Rican film industry.

The story set against the historical background is about a pair of star-crossed lovers, José (Daniel Lugo) and Raquel (Cordelia Gonzáles). José works in the governor's reform office and is the son of an old-guard Puerto Rican family. He is engaged to a wealthy landowner's daughter but falls passionately in love with his co-worker, Raquel. Like the House of Montague in *Romeo and Juliet*, José's family faces ruin since certain political factions are plotting against his father and only a correct alliance can save his own position. The story of José's choice between love and duty is resolved on its last scene, stolen from Michael Curtiz's 1942 melodramatic noir *Casablanca*. Otherwise, the plot is sacrificed to the beautiful depiction of rumbas, sambas, Spanish ballads about unrequited love, and American swing of the early forties.

Miguel Ángel Suárez plays Vászuez, a scheming district attorney, trying to wrest political control from José's father, Don Manolo (Luis Prendes), a Spanish *criollo* expatriate whose business has fallen on hard times and who is relying on his son's marriage to the wealthy Rita Inéz (Laura Delano), daughter of the liberal bureaucrat Don Antonio (Julián Pastor), to save him financially. Cameo appearances by E.G. Marshall as the scheming American Judge Cropper and Raúl Julia as a drunken poet add some real spice and professional acting ability that lifts the film into a first-class production. *La gran fiesta* does show off San Juan as a beautiful locale, and Zurinaga, as director, screenwriter and photographer, has produced a remarkable-looking debut feature.

The Green Wall see *La muralla verde*

117. Gregorio. F. Espinoza, S. Kaspar, A. Legaspi, M. Barea, S. Pastor or the Grupo Chaski. Peru, 1985. 85 min., Color. Spanish.

COMMENTARY: Perhaps modeling their work on Hector Babenco's heartwrenching 1981 film *Pixote* (a documentary-like, graphic and depressing account of a boy's life on the streets of a Brazilian metropolis), the Chaski Group

of directors (originally formed in 1982) made *Gregorio* with a group of child actors who experience similar angst but in a more genteel setting — the barrios of Lima, not of Rio.

The story is still one of family disintegration, as Andean peasants are forced off their land and must earn a living in the city, without any education or skills. Whereas *Pixote* was filmed in a visceral, graphic, hard-hitting fashion, *Gregorio* is a more lyrical and impressionistic movie.

We first watch Gregorio playing naked in the Pacific surf, free, independent, a child moving from the mountains into the urban setting of Lima. Gregorio's father works night and day for his family's survival until he collapses from exhaustion and dies. The widowed mother depends upon Gregorio's meager earnings as a *limpiabotas* (shoeshine boy) but takes up with another man after her husband's death, to the consternation and jealousy of her son. Gregorio begins to live on the streets, joins a gang and becomes alienated from his mother, with whom he can no longer communicate. Here the film greatly resembles Hector Babenco's, since we meet many other boys, see their faces and listen to their confessions about why they have run away from home. (The children in *Pixote* tell why they have run away from both their homes and the corrupt reformatory.)

Gregorio is a strong film and makes its points about delinquency and family disintegration calmly, stylishly and realistically. It will not overwhelm the viewer (as does *Pixote*), but it is provocative and deeply moving.

118. La guerra de los cerdos (**The Pig's War**). Leopoldo Torre Nilsson. Argentina, 1975. 90 min., Eastmancolor. Spanish.

COMMENTARY: Based upon a novel by Adolfo Bioy-Casares, *La guerra de los cerdos* is about the generation gap in Buenos Aires. Though it does not retain the sinister style of the original novel, the film is a realistic, brutal and harsh drama about one youth, played by Emilio Alfaro, who labels all old people "pigs" and feels that because they receive pensions, eat food, occupy domiciles, have possessions and have no real place in an already overpopulated society, they deserve to be done away with.

Led by Alfaro's character, a gang of older teens and men in their twenties starts to mill about affluent Buenos Aires neighborhoods, using chains to beat, maim and kill elderly citizens. The older citizens realize there is a problem, but the police do not help, and so it is up to the strongest among them to confront the problem and try to remediate it.

Interestingly, the older generation is depicted as pretty much worthless themselves. The men especially do very little except sit around all day in bars, play cards, have an occasional sexual fling and talk banalities. Still, they certainly don't deserve to be murdered. Finally, a middle-aged man (José Slavín) is spared by the group, only to learn that his own son runs with the gang, maiming and killing old men. All the older actors — Slavín, Miguel Ligero, Luis Politti and Zelmar Guenol — play their roles admirably, while the younger ones, especially Alfaro, are appropriately menacing.

But the film seems to go nowhere. The crimes against old men seem to end as mysteriously as they began. Perhaps the film is a parable about the persecution of minorities or how young people run amok if treated badly by their elders. It is hard to judge what Leopoldo Torre Nilsson and his screenwriter wife, Beatriz Guido, had in mind when this film was made. Sad to say, both these talents are ebbing in their careers. They made their best films in the fifties and sixties. So no matter how good the music score by Gato Barbieri or the camera

work of Aníbal di Salvo, regardless of the wonders of Eastmancolor, *The Pig's War* is a flat transposition of art in which a fairly well-known novel has become a graphic, somewhat hysterical exercise not even worthy of its creative team. Sadly, it is one of the few Argentine films available on video cassette in the United States. It does have some good location shooting in Buenos Aires neighborhoods, some good acting, but little else to recommend it.

The Guns see *Os fuzis*

Hand in the Trap see *La mano en la trampa*

119. The Harder They Come.
Perry Henzell. Jamaica, 1972. 105 min., Color. English/Patois.

COMMENTARY: The first indigenous film to come from the island of Jamaica, *The Harder They Come* has become a kind of a cult film in America, usually playing to midnight audiences. It is essentially about an honest and ambitious young man, Ivan (played with enormous charm by singer Jimmy Cliff), who is pushed into a world of crime and is shot down by the Jamaican police at the conclusion.

In something of a fairy tale, Ivan comes to the big city after his grandmother's death and tries to get work as a singer of rock ballads. He finally lands a job with a harsh preacher (Basil Keane), who is protective of the virtue of his beautiful ward, Elsa (Janet Bartley). Ivan falls in love with Elsa and they run off together. Their romance is connected to a subplot in which Ivan makes a record for an unscrupulous producer who seems to control the whole island, including the running of drugs. Ivan's record becomes a sensational hit, but Ivan cannot reap the profits. So he returns to drug-running, kills a policeman, becomes a cult-pop hero of sorts and is shot down by police while running into the ocean to escape.

Better than the sum of all the James Bond films ever made on the island, this work by Perry Henzell shows off the beauty not only of Jamaica, but of the people themselves — their wit, their music, their language (which is sometimes translated by subtitles), their elegance, grace and charm. Jimmy Cliff is a real find, a jaunty actor with sex appeal. The director also makes use of local color in his depiction of the rage of the protagonist during the whipping he receives as punishment for running off with the girl and in the knife fight before Ivan meets his maker in the film's predictably moral conclusion.

The director shows much promise; *The Harder They Come* combines taut action sequences with genteel love scenes that show much visual flair. The reggae score is actually blended into the framework of the film, especially songs like "You Can Get It If You Really Want It" and "Sitting in Limbo." Henzell tells us so much about Jamaica and its people in this florid tale that viewers who liked this film can hardly wait for the resurrected Jimmy Cliff— singer and actor — in his next Jamaican vehicle.

120. Hasta cierto punto (Up to a Certain Point). Tomás Gutiérrez Alea. Cuba, 1983. 88 min., Color. Spanish.

COMMENTARY: *Hasta cierto punto* has been shown in three different versions in the United States with three different running times. All three make the same point— that Cuban men must rule the roost, with or without communism.

Perhaps somewhat autobiographical, the film presents two central characters. Oscar (Oscar Álvarez) is a successful screenwriter, a middle-class intellectual who is filming a documentary about *machismo* for the government, using a series of video-taped interviews to make

his points. He is married to a woman who supports his views impeccably. However, while doing research for his project, Oscar meets Lina (Mirta Ibarra), a strong, self-supporting worker, pretty, independent, mother of a ten-year-old son who works on the docks as a checker. They begin a torrid love affair, but Oscar cannot squarely face the reality that Lina is a truly liberated woman and that he must make a choice between her and his wife, Marian (Coralia Veloz).

The best part of the film is contained in the video interviews we get to see on screen, especially with a burly, black dock worker who believes he will never be comfortable with the idea of a truly liberated woman even though he believes almost 87 percent in the concept, and another stevedore whose wife stayed at home, not liberated, but fell in love with another man, thus destroying their marriage. Machismo is still favored today in Cuba, even though the party line prefers a progressive, egalitarian and revolutionary society. What Alea's film indicates is that the social aims of the revolution are not being achieved — that indifference to the party line exists and that in this area of *machismo*, perhaps the revolution is a failure. No wonder the film was seen in so many versions! Alea's directorial talent is there, and his incisive interviews hint at underlying weaknesses in the revolution. However, because he still lives and makes films in Castro's Cuba, he must put up with the usual abuses of communist censorship — but up to what point?

The Heart's Dark Side see *El lado oscuro del corazón*

The Heist see *El apando*

Hell Hath No Limits see *El lugar sin límites*

Mirta Ibarra as Lina, one of the strong, liberated Cuban women working on the docks in Tomás Gutiérrez Alea's *Hasta cierto punto* (*Up to a Certain Point*, 1983).

Hidden Color see *El color escondido*

Highway Patrolman see *El patrullero*

121. Los hijos de Martín Fierro (The Sons of Martín Fierro).

Fernando Solanas. Argentina, 1972–76. 90 min., B&W. Spanish.

COMMENTARY: Fernando Solanas began making this film in Argentina in 1972, but while shooting on location in 1974, he was forced to suspend production because of the government's return to fascist policies, and Solanas had to finish the film in Germany and France in exile.

Basing the film upon the gaucho myth of Juan Hernandez's nineteenth century epic poem "Martín Fierro," Solanas sought to recreate the contemporary history of Argentina by transposing it to the level of a poetic gaucho myth. Myth and history would intermingle. Solanas uses the gaucho to unravel the complex political events of Argentine history, from 1945 to 1973. The new gaucho is Juan Domingo Perón, a reincarnation of Martín Fierro. Through voice-overs and flashbacks, we witness the birth of Peronism, the years of prosperity, the fall of Perón, the death of Eva, the return of Perón, several military coups and the definitive return of *peronismo* in 1973.

In this film — another in a long line of documentaries that Solanas utilized to fight Argentina's military regimes — the director was fairly successful in his searing indictment of the military, just as he succeeded in his earlier collaborations with Octavio Getino on behalf of the Peronist movement. Perón is the heroic gaucho of the pampas. The film is Solanas' propagandist farewell to Juan Perón and his left-wing supporters.

NOTES: Fernando E. Solanas was born in Buenos Aires in 1936. He studied law, drama and music there until his total involvement in filmmaking came about in the early sixties, when he began making short political documentaries: *Seguir andando* (1962) and *Reflexión ciudadana* (1963). In 1966 he joined the Cine Liberación collective, a group of pro–Peronist filmmakers, and with Octavio Getino, a young Spaniard and fellow student, they made their monumental three-part film entitled *La hora de los hornos* (1968), which took them two years to complete. Solanas left Argentina after Peron was ousted in 1976 and lived in Paris till 1983. He has since returned to Argentina and continues making films there. Other than *La hora de los hornos*, some of his better-known works are *Perón: acutalización política doctrinaria para la toma del poder* and *La revolución justicialista* (1971), two pro-Peronist documentaries made in Argentina; *Le Regard des autres* (1979), made in France after he finished *Los hijos de martín fierro* in 1976; *Tangos: l'exil de Gardel* (1985), also made in France; and *Sur* (1988) and *El viaje* (1992), both Argentine productions. Since the eighties, Solanas has been making feature films, entertainments that deal with nostalgia and his Argentine past. His documentary days appear to be over.

122. La historia oficial (The Official Story). Luis Puenzo. Argentina, 1984. 112 min., Color. Spanish.

COMMENTARY: Set in Buenos Aires in 1983, the story revolves around a female history professor, Alicia (a towering, luminous performance by Norma Aleandro); her husband, Roberto (Hector Alterio); and their adopted daughter, Gaby (Analia Castro). Alicia confronts the possibility that her adopted daughter might be the child of a *desaparecida* woman abducted by the military dictatorship several years earlier. Her life begins to collapse around her as she investigates. Her husband tells her a vague tale about having bought a newborn baby and urges his wife, somewhat angrily, to forget about the matter. But Alicia persists, overpowered by a moral instinct to investigate and discover the truth — that Gaby is really the grandchild of Sara (Chela Ruiz), whose own daughter disappeared during the military junta's counterinsurgency campaigns of the 1970s, and that Roberto has grown rich through his links with the military junta and foreign businessmen profiting from the corruption in power circles.

"I always believed what I was told," says Alicia as she witnesses the rallies of the Mothers and Grandmothers of Plaza de Mayo. After discovering the real parentage of Gaby and suffering torture and beating by Roberto (he locks her arm in a closing door and squeezes hard), Alicia leaves home, totally disillusioned with her counterfeit marriage and the loss of her child, resigned to leading a separate life as the current political regime under Galtieri tumbles around her.

La historia oficial is a strong film, excellently scripted by Aida Bortnik and the director. It won the Academy Award for Best Foreign Film of 1985. It has superb performances by Norma Aleandro (who won a Best Actress Award at Cannes the same year), and by Hector Alterio as her husband, who holds a "potential" for violence and who, when finally acting upon his fascistic instincts, asks his wife, "What am I, a torturer?" Coincidentally, Hector Alterio, a wonderful Argentine actor, spent most of his professional life in Spain because of a self-imposed exile from the dictatorship so roundly criticized in this film. The film's golden moments occur when

Hector Alterio torturing Norma Alejandro in Luis Puenzo's Oscar-winning Argentine film *La historia oficial* (*The Official Story*, 1984).

Alicia becomes politicized, realizes her own complicity, exposes her husband's violence and witnesses the disintegration of her life with terror, poise, sophistication and the realization that she is a survivor and will carry on. Although the film makes no direct pitch for "human rights," the film's implicit ethical statements are overpowering.

NOTES: *La historia oficial* is Luis Puenzo's debut film as a director. Little is known about his biography, except that he was probably born in Argentina around 1945, that he filmed some 800 commercials while working in advertising in Buenos Aires, and that he made one short episode ("Light of My Shoes") in a film entitled *Las sorpresas* (1974) before becoming internationally famous with *La historia oficial*. The film was also a first for Argentina since *La historia oficial* was the first Argentine film (with an extraordinarily low budget of

$300,000) to win the Academy Award for Best Foreign Film. In 1989, he came to the United States to direct a version of Carlos Fuentes' novel, *Old Gringo* with Gregory Peck and Jane Fonda, a modest failure. Since then, he has returned to Argentina and directed a version of Albert Camus' famous novel *The Plague* (*La peste*, 1992).

Holy Blood see *Santa sangre*

123. Un hombre de éxito (A Successful Man). Humberto Solas. Cuba, 1986. 110 min., Color. Spanish.

COMMENTARY: Humberto Solas is a film director whose screenplays are conceived as large panoramas of Cuban life. In this vein, *Un hombre de éxito* is another successful recreation of Cuban life, from the early thirties up until the Castro Revolution of the late fifties.

Set in Havana in the 1930s, the film

Poster art for Humberto Solas's *Un hombre de éxito* (*A Successful Man*, 1986); Daisy Granados stands between two unidentified actors.

revolves around a theme of ambition and social climbing, through seduction and unscrupulous behavior. After the fall of the dictator Gerardo Machado in 1933, the protagonists move in more powerful circles, and as each decade passes, they become more successful politically. However, all around them, the real values of family and goodness are collapsing as one of the brothers contrives his societal rise through opportunism and treachery.

The story is about two brothers, Javier (nicely played by César Evora) and Dario (suitably performed by Jorge Trinchot), their student days, and the promise of the future. Javier has faith in politics and wants to play the game and move up in the bourgeois hierarchy under Batista, but Dario is a self-styled revolutionary, spreading leaflets, planting bombs, hopelessly caught up in anarchy that leads him to a tragic end.

Solas asks the question, "What makes for a successful man?" The male leads, one representing innocence and purity, the other corruption, try to give us the answers. But the plot of the film is banal, and the director compromises his male characters with cliché-ridden dialogue. (There are, however, some wonderful performances by the female leads, actress Daisy Granados as Rita and Raquel Revuelta as Raquel.) But in every Solas film, there is fine attention to pictorial detail and the recreation of the lost world of 1930s and 1940s Cuba. It is here that Solas succeeds the most as a director of panoramas, and here that his film becomes a succesful story of characters caught in the vortex of bourgeois opulence and simplistic revolution.

124. El hombre de Maisinicú (The Man from Maisinicú).
Manuel Pérez. Cuba, 1974. 124 min., B&W. Spanish.

COMMENTARY: Cuban audiences responded enthusiastically to this film, marking it as a significant standout among revolutionary feature films. Set in the early sixties, this true story begins with the discovery of a body. The dead man is Alberto Delgado, a farm administrator at Maisinicú in the Escambray mountains, then a counter-revolutionary stronghold where desperate men terrorized the population and recklessy tried to make contact with the CIA. The film then jumps backwards in time and follows Delgado through the 14 months preceding his death, slowly unraveling his mysterious relationship with the counterrevolutionary movement.

"Like many Cuban films, this one both utilizes and subverts a traditional narrative genre — here the adventure film, complete with subversives, spies and counter-spies. The choice of Sergio Corrieri, so acclaimed for his performance in *Memorias del subdesarrollo*, for the title role is particularly appropriate since the actor has spent the intervening years organizing, directing and acting in a people's theatre in the same Escambray mountains where the film is set. Many secondary parts are, in fact, played by members of the local community who participated in breaking up the counterrevolutionary stronghold." (Press book)

The first film by 37-year-old Manuel Pérez, *El hombre de Maisinicú* does generate some realistic suspense as we try to penetrate the mysteries of the dead man's identity. Was he a Castro loyalist or an undercover counterrevolutionary? Who really killed him, Castro's militia or the CIA? Much offscreen narration and many confusing flashbacks and flashforwards obscure the mystery of the man's death as well as the political message of the director, characterized by A.E. Weiler in the New York Times as "elliptical Marxism."

Although the film has a wonderful *cinéma-vérité* look and an excellent performance by Sergio Corrieri, we never really come to conclusions about the

The Man from Maisinicú

A film by Manuel Pérez

A political thriller of espionage and counter-intelligence activity during the early years of the Cuban Revolution

Produced by the Cuban Film Institute (ICAIC)
With Sergio Corrieri, Reinaldo Maravalles, Adolfo Llauradó & Raúl Pomares

Presented by Tricontinental Film Center & the Center for Cuban Studies

Poster art from Manuel Pérez's spy thriller *El hombre de Maisinicú* (1974).

mystery man's death — whether he was a hero or a traitor — mainly because of the bewildering style of the director. One can "subvert the traditional narrative genre" with purpose, as Alain Resnais or Jean Luc Godard have done in master-ful films like *La Guerre est finie* or *Vivre sa vie*; but Pérez has not profited from these masters, and consequently, the film suffers both dramatically and politically. However, Manuel Pérez is certainly a Cuban director to watch in the future.

125. Hombre mirando al sudeste (Man Looking Southeast / Man Facing Southeast). Eliseo Subiela. Argentina, 1986. 105 min., Color. Spanish.

COMMENTARY: "Dr. Denis (Lorenzo Quinteros) is a weary psychiatrist in charge of a section at a Buenos Aires neuropsychiatric hospital. He suffers along with his patients as he listens to their pathetic stories. Recently divorced, he lives alone in a small apartment, where in his off hours he watches home movies of his children and plays a plaintive melody on the saxophone.

"One day, a routine hospital check reveals an extra patient. Dr. Denis finds the man named Rantes (played luminously by Hugo Soto) in the hospital chapel, where he is expertly playing the organ. Rantes introduces himself and tells the doctor that he has traveled from another planet to study the inhuman behavior of earthlings. Denis figures Rantes to be a simple case of paranoid delusion, but cannot help being intrigued by the charismatic intelligence of this man with no recorded identity.

"As the story proceeds, Rantes continues to insist on his extraterrestrial origins, and the doctor is slowly brought into the web of delusion. Is Rantes insane, or does he really come from another planet? Each day Rantes stands in the hospital courtyard facing southeast in order to send the information he is recording in strange cryptograms to his home planet. Little by little, the other patients begin to follow Rantes as he becomes their only source of hope within the confines of the asylum.

"One day Rantes receives a young woman visitor, Beatriz, the saint (Inés Vernengo), whom Dr. Denis pulls aside to find out more information about the would-be extraterrestrial. Denis is attracted to Beatriz; she holds valuable information about Rantes as well as being sexually alluring. An odd triangle of relationships is formed between the doctor, the patient and the woman.

"Denis is pulled further into the obsession to find out who Rantes really is. He begins to take liberties with hospital rules and takes Rantes and Beatriz to an outdoor symphony concert. In the middle of a wonderful symphonic waltz, Rantes moves to the podium and takes over the direction of the orchestra, eventually rousing the entire audience in a grand finale of Beethoven's "Ode to Joy." But the moment of liberation turns sour when the hospital simultaneously erupts with patient revolt. Hospital authorities order immediate sedation for Rantes — the dreaded inhuman cure of earthlings, according to the man from another world.

"As medication proceeds, with Dr. Denis washing his hands of any involvement, Rantes begins to deteriorate. He can no longer keep up the daily transmissions. Dr. Denis suffers along with Rantes and reaches out for Beatriz to help him. After an almost desperate interlude of lovemaking, Beatriz reveals to Denis that she, too, is an agent from the same world as Rantes.

"The earthbound cure of the hospital eventually leads to Rantes' death and the complete disillusionment of Dr. Denis. The psychiatrist's world of the sane vs. the insane, of reality vs. nonreality, no longer makes sense to Denis. As the film closes, the patients stand silently in the courtyard awaiting the arrival of a special spaceship that will take them all to the home of Rantes." (Press book.)

Hombre mirando al sudeste is reminiscent of *E.T.*, *The Man Who Fell to Earth* and *One Flew Over the Cuckoo's Nest*, in varying degrees. It is a remarkable film, though it does not seem particularly Argentine; rather it weds the stylistic inventiveness of the European art film to the social and theological consciousness that has long defined Latin

Hugo Soto (foreground) in the title role of Rantes, the man facing southeast, and Lorenzo Quinteros (background) as his psychiatrist in Eliseo Subiela's *Hombre mirando al sudeste* (*Man Looking Southeast*, 1986).

American cinema. The combination of the film's fantasy premise and its intellectual content, plus the overtones of religion and social consciousness, makes it an irresistible international art film. It is a gripping, piercingly intelligent fable about faith, madness and medicine. The film never hops the track, becoming a Christ allegory or a hermetic art work, but deftly makes its points, especially about societal repression of exceptional talent, intelligence or brilliance when it disturbs prevailing notions. Of the film itself, Subiela said: "I wrote the film continuously from beginning to end. ...When I arrived at the concert [scene], I felt the need for an explosion of light, liberty, freedom. I happened to be listening just then to Beethoven's Ninth. I thought, "¿Por qué no?— Why not?" (*New York Post* interview.)

Subiela's film is the hope and promise for new excitement in the Argentine cin-

ema, demonstrating the complexity of Argentine culture in this postrepression moment of its cultural history.

NOTES: Born in the late 1940s, Eliseo Subiela lives and works in Argentina primarily as a film director. His idea for *Hombre mirando al sudeste* came from his very first twenty-minute documentary, which he shot on location in the Borda Hospital outside of Buenos Aires. Other interesting films to date include *Ultimas imágenes del naufragio* (1989), the director's Pirandellian exploration into the creative impulse, and *El lado oscuro del corazón* (1992), a self-explanatory title about human nature. Subiela believes the most dangerous weapon in the world is human stupidity, and like one of the characters in his movies, he wants to stay informed but resists all innovations to do so. "I do not even have an answering machine in my house...only the dog has the telephone."

Homework see *La tarea*

126. A hora da estrela (The Hour of the Star). Suzana Amaral. Brazil, 1985. 96 min., Eastmancolor. Portuguese.

COMMENTARY: Based upon the novella by Clarice Lispector, Suzana Amaral's film version is as close a transposition of art as you can possibly get. Recapturing the Chaplinesque sadness of her lead protagonist, Amaral proceeds to tell the story of Macabea (sensitively played by Marcelia Cartaxo), an unworldly young woman — a naive, doomed innocent working as a typist in Rio de Janeiro, living with several roommates, wiping her nose on the collar of her blouse, changing her clothes under her bedcovers, standing next to strange men while taking subway rides to assuage her desperation for companionship. Like Fellini's Cabiria (so wonderfully incarnated by his muse, the wonderful Giulieta Massina), Macabea finally finds the man of her dreams, a vain, ignorant metalworker ironically named Olímpico (José Dumont). But the ultimate tragedy of her life is her incurable romanticism and her dream to be a movie star. Her ignorance about life sometimes tries our credibility, and her aspirations are even more heartbreaking. Macabea is so plain, so unsophisticated, so sad as the film comes to its heartrending conclusion in her death. But at last, in dying, she has the ultimate starring role. Her secret vision of herself as a movie queen breaks the chains of a deprived person whose life was preordained to boredom and frustration, the bland embodiment of a socioeconomic stereotype. Millions of Brazilian women are just like Macabea, their very existence going unnoticed because they are unaware themselves, superfluous creatures nobody cares for. Most infuriating to viewers is Macabea's inactivity; she may want to work, understand, embrace society, but she does not struggle, takes no initiative. She simply lives out her routine existence — a metaphor for the underdeveloped peoples of her nation — until her relationship with Olímpico, a brutal, pathetic man, leads to her death.

As silent star Norma Desmond (played by Gloria Swanson in *Sunset Boulevard*) achieved stardom again in life after killing her lover and set the newsreel cameras rolling, the fortune-teller Madame Carlota (played by famous Brazilian stage actress Fernanda Montenegro) sets the scene for Macabea's ascension in death to a kind of Hollywood-style heaven in an operatic contrivance that sends *A hora da estrela* over the top as art cinema. A terrifically intelligent and poignant first feature about guilt, alienation and redemption from a woman director in her late thirties (compare the career of Argentine María Luisa Bemberg) who raised a family with nine children and began her film career late in life.

127. La hora de los hornos (The Hour of the Furnaces). Fernando Solanas. Argentina, 1966–68. 260 min., B&W. Spanish.

COMMENTARY: Directed and edited by Fernando Solanas and co-written by Octavio Getino, *La hora de los hornos* is a three-part film, a pace-setting masterpiece of the political documentary.

Part One, "Neo-Colonialism and Violence," is about the history of Argentina; Part Two, "Act for Liberation," tells of the struggles for liberation on behalf of the Argentines; Part Three, "Violence and Liberation," deals with the meaning and use of violence in the process of liberation.

Made clandestinely in Argentina, it is an assemblage of stock footage, scenes from other documentaries, interviews and new material from contemporary newsreels. Solanas bombards us with didactic material from the films of

A still showing Argentine military in action in Fernando Solanas' brilliant Argentine documentary *La hora de los hornos* (*The Hour of the Furnaces*, 1966-68).

Fernando Birri, Leon Hirszman, Humberto Rios, Joris Ivens. He uses songs, poetry, interviews, intertitles and a zooming camera to indict people and nations responsible for colonialism in Argentina. He composes a mosaic, a filmed polemic, a pamphlet.

Part One is agit-prop, pure propaganda, jolting the audience from its torpor and alienation. Solanas analyzes the current "Argentinian situation" in thirteen observations, concluding that "daily violence is practiced on the people, in their economy, in their culture." Part One ends with the death of Che Guevara, a devastating close-up of his face for two full minutes, hammering home the fact that this entire film is dedicated to all those who have died for liberation of Latin America.

Part Two follows the irresistible rise, then the fall of Peronism, the first movement of the Argentinian masses. Solanas extols the rise of the proletariat and the violent decade (1955–65), condemning the most significant activities of the resistance.

Part Three is dedicated to the new man born in that war of liberation. Letters of soldiers, witnesses, reporters all give testimony. The film remains open to all those who join the struggle.

As Louis Marcorelles, the critic for *Le Monde*, stated: "*La hora de los hornos* is not a masterpiece. It is something else: an open work, in which each spectator has a particular role to play, is in effect almost a co-creator. I readily consider it a superb example — along with the films of Emile de Antonio of the U.S. ... of this cinema of the spoken word that is overthrowing established notions. This is a cinema which writes history." (Program notes, MOMA, 1970.)

Above all, the film is an emotional assault, inevitably compared to Leni Riefenstahl's *Triumph of the Will* and even Frank Capra's *Prelude to War*. In 1979, *Cahiers du Cinéma* called it "probably the greatest historical film ever made."

Hour of the Furnaces see *Los hora de los hornos*

Hour of the Star see *La hora da estrela*

House of Angel see *La casa de Ángel*

How Tasty Was My Little Frenchman see *Como era gostoso o meu frances*

I Am Chicano see *Yo soy chicano*

I Am Joaquín see *Yo soy Joaquín*

I Don't Want to Talk About It see *De eso no se habla*

I, The Worst of Them All see *Yo, la peor de todos*

The Illegal see *Alambrista*

128. El imperio de la fortuna (The Realm of Fortune). Arturo Ripstein. Mexico, 1985. 135 min., Color. Spanish.

COMMENTARY: Basing his film upon a Juan Rulfo story, "The Golden Rooster," Arthur Ripstein has made a tragicomedy of an ignoble peasant who turns his back on simple goodness and destroys himself and his family. The film depicts the seventeen-year rise and fall of a small-town gambler, Dionisio Pinzón, and his family. It focuses on the hard life of rural Mexico, particularly the arid region of San Miguel del Milagro, where survival is an ordeal and one makes a life anyway he can. The story introduces us to the interior life of these human beings, prisoners of their destiny, forced into cataclysmic changes. Their dreams and ambitions, their desire for affirmation and freedom, will help them to make their fortune, realize their ideals, through luck, a most vital element to attain all of this.

Because of a crippled hand, Pinzón (Ernesto Gómez Cruz) is incapable of physical labor; poverty and lack of education have closed off his options in life, and, sheltered by his sickly mother, he leads a wretched existence. But Pinzón has a powerful voice, and as the town crier, he announces all public events. When a fair comes to town, he is recruited to call the winners of the cockfights. After one of the fights, he begs for a wounded bird, which, now crippled, is deemed useless as a fighter.

His virtue revives the bird, which becomes a champion and his lucky charm for the future. His success brings him fame, fortune and a beautiful woman, "La Caponera" (Blanca Guerra), who becomes his second lucky charm and who brings him into a world of gamblers, power and greed, resulting in the eventual destruction of his benefactor, Benavides (Alejandro Parodi), himself and his family.

Sometimes considered the spiritual heir of Luis Buñuel (with whom he worked on several films), Arturo Ripstein has made a startlingly beautiful and grotesque film in Buñuelian fashion. All the ingredients are there: obsession, mystery (a withered hand wrapped in a rag), lust, violent and irrational behavior, chance, superstition, greed and exasperation. In this black comedy of the fortunes of Dionisio Pinzón, Ripstein takes us on a bizarre journey to a sordid, oppressive, almost hallucinatory world of passionate men and women who have nothing to lose. When Pinzón's fortunes are in decline, his once-glamorous wife wanders around their house in a shabby sweater, so neglected she talks to herself. Their teenage daughter escapes into promiscuity. Pinzón himself is a banal man masquerading as an eccentric.

Ripstein shows us a new Mexico with a contemporary perspective. It is no longer the colorful land of the past, for economic depression has taken its toll and the demands of the urban middle class have uprooted traditions. The lustre of wealth shines brightly only for the few. Those unprepared for it will sacrifice all that has made them what they are (Pinzón's story), selling off their future for a small piece of the present.

NOTES: Juan Rulfo's story is popular; this is the second time it has been filmed. What distinguishes Ripstein's version is his modern sixties view of Mexican society as well as a marvelous mariachi score featuring Lucha Vila, a major interpreter of the style.

Improper Conduct see *Mauvaise Conduite*

In for Life see *Cadena perpetua*

In This Town There Are No Thieves see *En este pueblo no hay ladrones*

129. El infierno tan temido
(So Feared a Hell). Raúl de la Torre. Argentina, 1979. 113 min., Eastmancolor. Spanish.

COMMENTARY: Filmed in Buenos Aires in color and with a delicious tango score by Astor Piazzolla, *El infierno tan temido* is a love-hate story of a relationship between an older man (Alberto de Mendoza) and a woman (Graciela Borges), a relationship soured by the latter's lover. The older man cannot understand his girlfriend's attempt to end the relationship with her previous lover by sleeping with him. Mendoza's character, a firm believer in *machismo* and very conscious of his dignity, is incapable of believing that his girlfriend was just testing to see if she still felt anything for her former lover. He throws her out, and she bombards him with nude photographs of herself *in flagrante* as a kind of moral punishment through the mails. The best that can be said for this film

(based upon a story by Juan Carlos Onetti) is that it features very capable performances by the principal actors. The director does maintain an interest in both male and female psychology. Why the woman sends pornography through the mail as a reaction to Mendoza's male-chauvinist attitude is still a mystery by the end of the film. However, the film remains on a high level intellectually, even with its daring amount of nudity, because the director has preserved the literary aspect of the story and not catered to prurient tastes. The city of Buenos Aires is also a star, rich in atmosphere, stunning as a backdrop for this story of love and loss.

130. Los inundados (The Flood Area / Flood Victims). Fernando Birri. Argentina, 1961. 85 min., B&W. Spanish.

COMMENTARY: In his second film, a mixture of documentary and fiction, Fernando Birri shows how people cope with a natural disaster and even maintain a sense of humor. Winner of the Opera Prima prize at Venice in 1962, *Los inundados* profits from excellent ensemble acting and becomes a social comedy in the face of a disaster.

The story is deceptively simple. The Gaitan family is washed out of its house by a flood and becomes the responsibility of the state. They are put on a train, which becomes their home for many, many weeks before they are finally given real housing. However, because of their naivete and the greed of local politicians, they are done out of their new home and return to the rails to travel aimlessly about Argentina until they are rediscovered. "We are all Argentines, but some people have played us for fools," says the father poignantly. Meanwhile they are seeing the country and we are watching the ravages of flood and other natural disasters with them, witnesses to poverty, bureaucracy and governmental sloth. With realism and satire, Birri has created a social documentary showing real people living on the edge of hunger and danger from flood conditions.

The family members play their roles effectively, showing their own foibles and innocence. It is the viewer who becomes cynical, even bitter, because of the continual perpetuation of human error and bureaucracy that is so common in Latin America. But the director does not dwell on these emotions. Rather than pulling us down into the mire of the situation, he emphasizes the humor, wit and graciousness of the innocent family that finally finds a place in the world.

NOTES: Born in 1925, Fernando Birri was first a poet, then a puppeteer; he finally became a filmmaker after going to film school in Italy in the fifties. Because of politics, he left Argentina and has resided in Cuba where he is the director of the Film Institute of the Americas. Beginning his career as a documentary filmmaker, he is primarily known for *Tire die* (1958-59), *Los inundados* (1961) and *La pampa grande* (1963). He has made other political films such as *Residente: Nicaragua* (1984), *Mi hijo, el Che* (1985) and one fiction feature that has been seen internationally, *Un señor muy viejo con unas alas muy grandes* (1988), based on a García Márquez short story.

131. Iracema. Jorge Brodansky. Brazil, 1976. 90 min., Eastmancolor. Portuguese.

COMMENTARY: Unlike the filmmakers of the *Cinema Nôvo* movement, who have generally insisted their films have some social importance, Jorge Brodansky and Orlando Senna have made an entertaining but jaundiced view of the great Brazilian dream — represented by the trans–Amazon highway and the journey to the junk heap by the central character, Iracema. Iracema is a fourteen-year-old prostitute from the Amazon, trying to make her fortune in the city of Belem. Almost as in a picaresque novel, her adventures along the road and with a truck driver named Tiaco are the essence of the film. We travel with them as Tiaco talks about the greatness of the country but all around him sees the jungle being burned off, wildlife slaughtered and the Amazon Indian population left to languish in despair.

Iracema will enjoy a similar fate if she continues to believe that hitchhiking and whoring will get her somewhere — for she always remains in the same place. Iracema is continually deflowered, defoliated, depressed by the men who discard her without even paying for her services. The film is a story of overwhelming despair, a sprawling picture of Brazil's outback, revealing in its frankness the ignorance and heartbreak of its chief victim, Iracema, who does not know that she is a victim.

The film has wonderful performances by Edna de Cassia as Iracema and Paulo César Perejo as Tiaco the truck driver. Lushly photographed in blazing color, it is a handsome film, full of turquoise and tangerine, but it also paints a degrading portrait of the pillage of the Amazon. It is here that the director Jorge Brodansky is ultimately successful. *Iracema* was not shown in Brazil for many years because of its critical posture.

NOTES: Jorge Brodansky has made one other film to date, *The Third Millennium*, about a yearly state visit to the Amazon by politicos from the Brazilian senate. This 90-minute documentary follows Senator Evando Carreira on his whistle-stop tour of the Amazon to study the lives of his constituents.

132. It's All True (It's All True: **Based on an Unfinished Film by Orson Welles**). Orson Welles. Brazil/U.S., 1942. 89 min., Color and B&W. English/Spanish/Portuguese.

Commentary: In 1942, Orson Welles, after just having directed *The Magnificent Ambersons*, was sent by Nelson Rockefeller to make a film about Latin America as part of the war effort to promote the United States Good Neighbor policy in the Americas.

The film was made in three parts. First was the "My Friend Bonito" section, directed by Norman Foster, about a Mexican boy's pet bull spared from his fate in the ring. Welles oversaw the location shooting of "Bonito" in Mexico for several weeks. Although it is a slight tale, it has that wonderful black and white cinematography, ennobling the faces of peasants, that is seen in some of Brazil's *Cinema Nôvo* films of the early sixties.

The second part, "The Story of the Samba," was shot in color during Carnival in Rio. The Technicolor sequences are glorious as we watch dancers wind their way through the crowded, float-filled streets. But most of the filmed material in this episode is formless, especially when Welles turns his cameras on to the *favelas* (slums) of the people in his search for the real roots of the samba. RKO executives who were producing the film did not consider Welles' portrait of poor black people a good way to proselytize for President Roosevelt's Good Neighbor policy.

The last section, "Jangadeiros," is the most complete and fascinating part of *It's All True*. Based upon a real-life incident, it tells the story of four very poor Brazilian sailors who take their raft from their hometown and sail to Rio without a compass, many thousands of miles away, risking their lives to bring the attention of the president of Brazil to their state of poverty and poor working conditions. Jangadeiros is the name of the fishermen or raftsmen who sailed. The episode is also referred to as "Four Men on a Raft" and is the longest, best and most beautifully photographed of all the episodes we have from this unfinished film. This section clearly recalls the best work of Murnau's *Tabu* or Eisenstein's *¡Qué viva Mexico!* "Jangadeiros" also has the look of the famous Glauber Rocha film *Barravento*, about the lives of poor fishermen, made in Brazil in 1961. Funeral processions in both films rival one another in terms of form, content, composition and spirituality. Welles was a master in black and white filming, and one wonders what he would have done with all this raw material had it not been confiscated by RKO.

Luckily, Richard Wilson, an associate of Welles, rediscovered cans of film of *It's All True* and has just assembled an 89-minute film (now available on video cassette), resurrecting Orson Welles' 1942 lost work. Miguel Ferrer narrates the Paramount film written by Bill Krohn, released in 1993 in the United States. The most remarkable sequence is still "Jangadeiros," fantastically photographed by George Fanto. It is wonderful to have men of vision like Richard Wilson, who brought *It's All True* to its most definitive version and enhanced our own vision of the great artist-director. It is also interesting to footnote here that film scholar Robert Carringer has reconstructed Welles' original version of *The Magnificent Ambersons*, the film they would not let the director himself cut because they wanted to send him to Brazil. Such irony — but Welles has been redeemed through Wilson's and Carringer's fantastic film expertise and scholarship.

The Jackal of Nahueltoro see *El chacal de Nahueltoro*

133. Jerico. Luis Alberto Lamata. Venezuela, 1990. 90 min., Color. Spanish.

COMMENTARY: Cosme Cortázar plays Santiago, a Dominican priest who in the early sixteenth century was sent by Spain

Cosme Cortázar as the Dominican priest Santiago embracing an Indian in Luis Alberto Lamata's Venezuelan film *Jerico* (1990).

to evangelize the South Americans. Instead of bringing God to the tribes, he has to deal with the cannibalism and greed of his own people — the supposedly civilized Spaniards. Frustrated at every turn while trying to organize and initiate a Catholic mass, he is taken by force by local Indians and inducted into a cocaine ceremony. Very much like characters in Indian revisionist films like *Dances with Wolves* or *Black Robe*, Padre Santiago sheds his clothes and becomes a member of the tribe before the Spaniards come for him.

In *Jerico*, his first feature film, director Lamata is trying to recreate the pre–Colombian world of the sixteenth century. Because of the wonderful use of color and the expert camera work of Andres Agusti, he has succeeded admirably. What is more startling is his presentation of the Indians as noble savages, contrasted with the brutality of the Spaniards. Not until recently have we seen Indians talking on screen in their native languages. Lamata capitalizes on this aspect of Indian life as well, presenting a beautifully delineated portrait of a sensitive priest in a remarkably frank pro–Indian film. *Jerico*'s release coincides with the five hundredth anniversary of the discovery of America and should do very well at the box office as another anthropological view of the Spanish Conquest.

134. Journal inachevé (Unfinished Diary). Marilu Mallet. Canada/Chile, 1982. B&W. Spanish.

COMMENTARY: Despite its French title, *Journal inachevé* is most certainly a Latin American film, directed by Chilean exile Marilu Mallet, who has spent most of her life in Quebec since 1973. The film itself is extremely personal, neither a complete documentary nor a fictional story, but comprised of private correspondence and diary entries together with a series of images, the director's photographs, her mother's photographs, from Mallet's infancy to adolescence in Chile, including scenes of the *coup d'état* and her emigration to Canada.

The film is spoken in three languages: Spanish, the director's mother tongue; English, the language of her husband; and French, with Mallet's infant and during her daily life at work and at play. Her voice in these languages drifts over black and white images of the past, photos, tableaux, rotogravures, images of interiors of houses, souvenirs, *objets d'art*, as well as images of exteriors, cold, vast empty spaces in both Canada and Chile. In the aggregate, these images make up an autobiographical story — some of it fact, other parts fiction.

Mallet has said of the film: "The biographical aspect of the film was another challenge to overcome, because to show one's self and to assume one's own reality demands courage: how to confront one's self as an exile, without roots, a woman or second class citizen, mother of a child, wife of a filmmaker, and on top of that speaking in three languages." ["Women in Cinema from Quebec."] Zuzana M. Pick, in her 1993 book *The New Latin American Cinema*, gives an excellent review of *Journal inachevé*, concluding with two marvelous insights that sum up Mallet's work: "[The film] makes use of the private environments and urban landscapes of exile to stage how emotions are stifled and creativity is inhibited by cultural difference. ... [Mallet] has imagined exile as a scrapbook on which memory is constantly being recomposed. In this way the authority of the film as a document on Chilean exile is displaced toward the critical reconstruction of conflict and crisis." (Pick, p. 167.)

NOTES: Marilu Mallet was born in Santiago, Chile, in 1944, studied architecture and film and was exiled in 1973, taking refuge in Quebec. She made two short films in Chile in 1971 and 1972 and had the opportunity of working with Patricio Guzmán on *The First Year* (1972) before going into exile. She also made *One Must Not Forget* (1975) and *The Pilgrimage to Solentiname* (1979). Her best films are inspired and defined by her immigrant status. Besides *Journal inachevé*, *Los Borges* (1978), about the experiences of a Portuguese immigrant family in Montreal, and *Memories of a Child in the Andes* (1986), about life in a Peruvian village seen through the eyes of a little girl. She has also published two collections of short tales.

The Journey see *El viaje*

La joven see *The Young One*

Juan, the Chamula see *Juan Pérez Jolote*

135. Juan Pérez Jolote (Juan, the Chamula). Archibaldo Burns. Mexico, 1976. 95 min., Color. Spanish/ Tzotzil.

COMMENTARY: A surprisingly poetic movie, *Juan Pérez Jolote* is a slow-moving but often touching chronicle of life in a small village of the Chamula tribe, one of the surviving Mayan groups. Focusing on one man, Juan Pérez Jolote, it is spoken in the Tzotzil language (a contemporary Mayan dialect) and features the music of the Chamula. Although it is based on a novel by Ricardo Poza, it uses a semi-documentary approach. No fewer than three cameramen photographed the sparse story, which reads like a poem while it informs like an anthropological study — reflecting the background of its director, a leading anthropologist. Though we hear about how little Juan ran away from home, was traded for local brandy, and did military service, we first see him at the point of his return home to his native village and family. The film then follows him through his courtship, wedding ceremony, the birth of his child, the death rites of his father, and various fiestas and Indian pow-wows. Candido Coeto, a professional actor, plays Juan, but all the other actors are natives from the village. The director has thrown in lots of folklore, and the film contains an important anthropological message — the "deep social conflicts" caused by the juxtaposition of "tribal traditions which predate the Spanish context ... with modern national economic imperatives." (UCLA program notes.) Nevertheless, it is more than a travelogue or an anthropological document; it is also a moving and successful piece of filmmaking.

Juan Vicente Gómez and His Era see *Juan Vicente Gómez y su época*

136. Juan Vicente Gómez y su época (Juan Vicente Gómez and His Era). Manuel del Pedro. Venezuela, 1975. 88 min., B&W. Spanish.

COMMENTARY: Very few documentaries have surfaced from Venezuela, especially about one of their famous dictators, Juan Vicente Gómez, who ruled the country with an iron hand during the first thirty years of the twentieth century. But director Manuel del Pedro has made a fascinating documentary about the country and its dictator. Trying for impartiality, he presents both sides of Gómez' politics and character. Consequently, the viewer must decide about the man's foibles and virtues: whether he was benevolent or merely ruthless.

With the use of excellent newsreel footage, life in the city of Caracas comes alive for us. We see the sophisticated high life of social events — society balls, Lindbergh's visit, horse races, public audiences — as well as the horrors of executions, the military quelling of public outbursts, the devastation of the jails. Most especially interesting are the director's interviews of some of the descendants of the dictator, who cautiously pick their words as if the ghost of Juan Vicente might smite them for an unfavorable comment. The director's sense of editing is superb, skillful and thoughtful, and he has put together a lively paced film work that ranks with the best of Patricio Guzmán and Fernando Solanas.

137. Juliana. Fernando Espinoza and Alejandro Legaspi. Peru, 1988. 97 min., Color. Spanish.

COMMENTARY: The film cooperative Grupo Chaski produced, wrote and directed this movie, which sensitively explores a socially relevant theme: children living on the strets in modern-day Lima. Though reminiscent of their 1984 production *Gregorio*, about the transition of a migrant family to Lima and their depressing disintegration and dysfunctional behavior, *Juliana* is far more upbeat, with more fully developed characterizations, better acting and humorous, even poetic moments.

Rosa Isabel Morfino plays the title role of the poor adolescent girl, constantly verbally abused and physically beaten by her ne'er-do-well, lazy father. Juliana decides to run away rather than endure her miserable life at home. Dressing up as a boy (remember how Katharine Hepburn did it in the 1935 film by George Cukor entitled *Sylvia Scarlett!*), she goes with her brother to join a group of street thieves (more pandering to a plot device right out of Dickens' *Oliver Twist* as visualized by David Lean) before they are caught by the authorities and sent back home.

The film does have some poetic, poignant moments when Juliana, lit only by candlelight, explains her dreams to her runaway brother, giving the camera and the audience a mesmerizing closeup.

Otherwise, the film is business as usual, like *Pixote* and its predecessors. It is still another social revisionist film by the Chaski Group, but worth our attention for ninety-odd minutes.

Killing Grandad see *Matar al Abuelito*

A King and His Movie see *La película del rey*

The King's Movie see *La película del rey*

138. Kino. Felipe Cazals. Mexico, 1992. 120 min., Color. Spanish.

COMMENTARY: Part of the New Mexican Cinema series that came to the United States in 1993, *Kino* is the story of the epic exploration of the life of Francisco Eusebio Kino (1645–1711), better known as Padre Kino, early missionary to the territory of California.

Most of the footage is spent on Padre Kino's determination to explore California, and there is much discussion about it with the military, but not with church prelates, who are more mindful of Padre Kino's religious duties than of his role as an explorer. Nevertheless, after much verbiage, we reach an emotional climax when the good father does indeed come upon Baja, California, originally thought to be an island but really a peninsula belonging to the land known as California.

Enrique Rocha is excellent in the role of Padre Kino, and his florid acting is in keeping with the overpowering screenplay, which treats him with great reverence, making him almost godlike. The outstanding panoramic photography by Ángel Goded sweeps gorgeously over northern Mexico's great plains, and the music score is imitative of John Williams, reaching crescendos that suggest an epic quality. However, in reality, it is a small story, given over-zealous treatment by a director whose really exciting film experience is more on a par with important social themes than less-than-significant biography.

139. Kiss of the Spiderwoman. Hector Babenco. Brazil/U.S., 1985. 119 min., Color. English.

COMMENTARY: Despite location filming in Brazil, *Kiss of the Spiderwoman* is really an Argentine work, made by an Argentine-born director, Hector Babenco (who made his home and career in Brazil), and based upon a novel by Argentine writer Manuel Puig. It is played by American, Puerto Rican and Brazilian actors in English. It contains the Academy Award–winning performance of William Hurt as Molina, a homosexual hairdresser whose acting goes way over the top in this film.

"In a prison cell somewhere in Latin America, two very different men warily confront each other. Molina (William Hurt) completes his morning toilette by wrapping his head in a towel in the shape of a turban, as Valentín (Raúl Julia), bearded and classically macho in appearance, watches with a mixture of fascination and revulsion. On the walls behind Molina's makeshift dressing table are pinups of Rita Hayworth, Lana Turner and Marlene Dietrich. On Valentín's face are deep cuts and bruises, and a large scar as yet unhealed.

"A complex story of friendship and love, *Kiss...* explores the enforced relationship — through imprisonment — of two men with radically different perspectives on life. Molina, a window dresser by profession and openly homosexual, entertains his revolutionary cellmate with fanciful narratives drawn from some of his favorite movies. Valentín, a political prisoner who has been systematically tortured, is at first diverted by Molina until he realizes that the movie being "told" (which the audience sees in black and white) is a Nazi

Raúl Julia (right) plays a macho revolutionary and William Hurt (left) a gay hairdresser in a complex story of friendship and love in Hector Babenco's *Kiss of the Spiderwoman* (1985). In this rare production still, Babenco (center) directs the two actors.

propaganda film about which Molina knows or cares nothing! When challenged to a story point by Valentín, he defends himself by saying, "I don't explain my movies; it ruins the emotion." Later, Valentín warns him that "fantasies are no escape," and thereupon are drawn philosophical swords for skirmishes on fundamental issues dealing with identity and personal responsibility. Along the way, a remarkable relationship evolves." (Press book.)

The story continues to show how the macho, narrow-minded Valentín learns humility and becomes more of a man because of his close relationship to Molina. Molina, on the other hand, falls in love with Valentín, and they consummate their relationship in bed and even with an onscreen kiss. Molina has become more "masculine," more self-respecting, and is willing to carry a message to Valentín's political activist friends on the outside when his prison term is up, even if it results in his death. It is unfortunate that the last words Molina hears are, "You fucking fag" as they throw his body on a pile of garbage in an empty lot. In a death reminiscent of the ending of Buñuel's *Los olvidados*, Molina winds up on top of the garbage heap, but he dies for an ideal — keeping faith with Valentín to deliver that unknown message and thereby keeping alive their love no matter what the cost. At the conclusion of the film, Babenco narrows the margins of sexuality — what it is to be really masculine or really feminine, and what is the real meaning of love between men, between women, between humans? Sonia Braga plays several roles in the film —first as Valentín's girlfriend, an agent of the revolutionary activist group, then as Denise Dumont, the glamorous French double agent in Molina's Nazi film rendition, and finally as "the Spiderwoman" who unites with Molina in death, freeing him from physical bondage as a homosexual transvestite and elevating their future existence on a higher, moral, idyllic plane, beyond reality, webbed and wedded together in their ultimate love fantasy. Here is where Babenco, the filmmaker, with images and dreams, and with the aid of remarkable performances from Hurt, Julia and Braga, achieves transcendence over Puig's written words. He has brought off the ideal bonding of the three major characters in a combination of reality and fantasy. Bravo!

140. El lado oscuro del corazón (The Heart's Dark Side).
Eliseo Subiela. Argentina, 1992. 127 min., Color. Spanish.

COMMENTARY: Set in Buenos Aires and Montevideo in the nineties, *El lado oscuro del corazón* is a surreal tale that asks its viewers to indulge its intellectual and sexual fantasies towards solving the riddle of achieving immortality through sex in a real environment.

Starring Dario Grandinetti as Olivero, a poet who is trying to survive in a nonpoetic environment — the streets of Buenos Aires — by selling bits of poems for money or food, the screenplay, somewhat disjointedly, follows Olivero and his friends in their bohemian existence. Of his two cronies, Pierre Reguerraz as the Canadian sculptor of giant penises and buttocks is most engaging, and film director André Melancón is excellent as a bohemian enthralled with the *paisaje* (countryside) of Argentina and Uruguay. Sandra Ballesteros has the interesting role of Ana. After numerous sexual affairs with women, whom he ejects into

oblivion after he is done with them, Olivero meets Ana, a prostitute working in a local cabaret. Their affair takes off, and so does his career. Though he could not find a job earlier, suddenly Ana becomes his lucky charm. Olivero accepts work doing commercials so he can afford spending $100 for each session with Ana. Their lovemaking grows in passion, and soon they start levitating over the sheets, eventually flying over the cities of Buenos Aires and Montevideo. Through his newfound career and their furious love affair, Olivero admits to Ana that she has enlightened the dark side of his heart.

Hugo Colace, the cameraman, should be commended for his wonderful photography, framing thrilling locations in gorgeous color. Marcela Sáenz did a wonderful editing job on the somewhat fragmented dialogue and parts of poems that suit the images. Most outstanding is the music directed by Osvaldo Montes, a romantic score with fleeting passages of tango. Cabaret singer Dalia gives a wonderful performance as do María Martha Serra Lima and the Trio Los Panchos, all doing fascinating boleros. But it is Dario Grandinetti as Olivero, tired of sex but hungry for love, whose rapturous, sexy looks and sardonic commentary give the film its complexity, its artistic pose, and its best performance.

Subiela's films are always an experience to behold. Like the earlier *Hombre mirando al sudeste*, *El lado oscuro* shows that the director is never conventional, always stimulating and forever difficult to grasp completely.

The Lady from the Shanghai Cinema see *A dama do cine Shanghai*

Land in Anguish see *Terra em transe*

Annette Cardona as Marlena and Robert Beltrán as Eddie Guerrero play the lovers in Haskell Wexler's film about love and war in Nicaragua, *Latino* (1985).

The Last Days of the Victim see *Los últimos días de la víctima*

Last Images of the Shipwreck see *Últimas imágenes del naufragio*

The Last Supper see *La última cena*

141. Latino. Haskell Wexler. U.S./Nicaragua, 1985. 108 min., Color. English/Spanish.

COMMENTARY: Nicaragua is the battleground where location shooting for this film took place. Ace cinematographer Haskell Wexler wrote the screenplay as well and had the rare opportunity to clear up the confusion coming from untrustworthy news sources in the country. However, Wexler missed this opportunity, because *Latino* is nothing more than a love story, set against the background of the Sandinistas fighting against the United States–backed Contras.

Roberto Beltrán plays American Eddie Guerrero, a Vietnam war veteran who has come to help the Contras fight the leftist Somoza regime. After many action scenes, depicting the usual gamut of war brutalities (death and torture of women and children; the capture of teenage boys to force them into service of the Contras), Eddie meets Marlena (Annette Cardona), who converts him to her pro–Nicaraguan political views and searches his conscience. *Latino* becomes a personal story for Eddie's search for love and dignity with the Spanish forces of liberation. While the conflicts of war surround him, his love affair with Marlena provides the excuse for him to leave the military.

The film remains an action-filled war drama, but it is uninformative and conveys none of the urgency of the Nicaraguan war. Nor does it fill in the gaps of our political knowledge about the country or what the Contras or Sandinistas stand for. Perhaps the director just gave up and concentrated on the atrocities and the love story, simplifying the very complex political situation by not even trying to explain it. He does succeed in conveying his anti-war message, having Eddie, a former Chicano Green Beret assigned to the United States Special Forces, rebel against the senselessness of war while fighting a covert action in war-torn Nicaragua.

NOTES: Haskell Wexler is widely known internationally as a director of photography, having won the Academy Award in 1966 for his work on *Who's Afraid of Virginia Woolf?* He also has ambitions of producing, directing and writing his own films. *Medium Cool* (1969), about violence in America, was the first film over which he had almost total control and the best one he ever made in his triple role as producer, director and writer. Over the years he has worked as a photographer on some of the truly great films to come out of Hollywood, including *One Flew Over the Cuckoo's Nest* and *Bound for Glory*. His latest documentary is entitled *The Rolling Stones at the Max* (1992).

142. Lejanía (Parting of the Ways). Jesús Díaz. Cuba, 1985. 90 min., Color. Spanish.

COMMENTARY: "A psychological drama from Cuba — and the first film to deal with the complicated and controversial issue of Cuban exiles returning to visit the families they left behind. Susana (played by Veronica Lynn), an attractive middle-aged woman, left Cuba and her 16-year-old son, Reinaldo (played by Jorge Trinchot), ten years ago for Miami. (Males of draft age were not permitted to emigrate.) Arms laden with gifts (electric coffee pots, designer jeans, portable radios), she walks into an explosive situation." (Press book.)

The director tries to describe the current relationship between Susana and Reinaldo after her years of exile and her return. The film gives an excellent portait of Havana of the 1980s but does little to explain why the son, Reinaldo, took to boozing and hanging out with the local toughs. Now happily married and about to become an engineer, Reinaldo does not feel the irresistible tug of a mother-son relationship. Having heard his father died in exile, Reinaldo wonders why he married a divorcee who is part black.

Emotional dislocation is the main theme of the film. Susana should realize that you can't go home again, especially to a Havana of the past. Only in one very long, convincing scene does Susana realize she is an expatriate in her own country, more of a capitalist Miami matron than a returning Cuban exile. She cannot give up her materialism. Reinaldo says at one point, "I won't stand for her waving dollars in my face." Reinaldo also looks much wiser and older than Susana, with a bearded face and a strong contempt for his mother's capitalist materialism.

At a recent film festival in India, Jesús Díaz won the Best Director award for this film. Yet in Cuba, the film has been the focus of much controversy: some feel the son should not have allowed a visit from his mother who abandoned him, while others criticize his restraint. According to the director, they feel "no Cuban would reject gifts, especially from his mother!" Ironically, the director has been attacked by certain quarters in his native country for trading as extensively as he does in ambiguities, for admitting that some contemporary Cubans can be seduced by the supposedly superficial attractions of "decadent" American society. Yet the film is still considered a sharp satire. It does capture the atmosphere of a run-down bourgeois home, like so many in Havana, where feelings unfold in the chiaroscuro of tropical interiors or explode on a rooftop open to the city. At the film's conclusion, we are still disconcerted by Susana's visit, and Reinaldo's wife makes the declamation, "We are still puzzled by what you did, lady!" Although the camera dwells on all of the actors in gorgeous close-ups, the photographic intimacy does not reveal what is going on inside the minds and hearts of the actors. We're close but not deep. More flawed in the script than in the direction, *Lejanía* has the makings of a serious, politically conscientious drama, but teeters dangerously on the edge of sit-com because of its over-extended emotional moments, which are gratuitous and sadly unrevealing.

Letters from Marusia see *Actas de Marusia*

Letters from the Park see *Las cartas del parque*

143. Lição de amor (Love Lesson). Eduardo Escorel. Brazil, 1975. 75 min., Color. Portuguese.

COMMENTARY: Based upon a 1927 novel by Mario de Andrade entitled *Love, Intransitive Verb*, *Lição de amor* is a costume drama set in the 1920s in Rio. A German governess is hired to teach the sons of the wealthy their lessons in academics as well as in love, so they will not learn about sex from "women of the street" and will understand the real meaning of love.

This is an old, old story; Ernst Lubitsch did it better and with more wit and charm in 1945 when he made the Twentieth Century–Fox Technicolor extravaganza *Heaven Can Wait* with Don Ameche as the student and Swedish Signe Hasso as the "governess." However, as a tale of a young man's sexual inititation, self-discovery and education in the secrets of love, *Lição de amor* profits from its wonderfully controlled direction and excellent performances.

Lillian Lemmertz as the "fraulein" governess and Marcos Taquechel as Carlos, her student, give sensitive performances. When their affair is consummated, the conclusion of the film is very predictable. Of course Carlos's father, a wealthy Brazilian land baron, Felisberta Souza Costa (Rogerio Froes), settles enough money on this hard-edged German expatriate to return to her country. Lemmertz plays the fraulein's role with culture and charm. When she leaves the film, we lose our best performance. However, director Escorel has made a stunningly light, well-decorated sex comedy that is worthy of our attention. Too bad it had none of the Lubitsch spark! But it does have those gorgeous settings done by Anisio Madeiros, one of the best set designers of Brazilian cinema.

NOTES: Born in 1945 in São Paulo, Eduardo Escorel was a student of Sweden's great documentary filmmaker Arne Sucksdorff. He later worked with Brazilian director Joaquim Pedro de Andrade and as an editor of the *Cinema Nôvo* group before directing *Lição de amor*, his debut feature. His only other notable feature is *Act of Violence*, about a man who commits the same crime twice at an interval of ten years — an absorbing and suspenseful noir melodrama. Escorel continues to live and make films in Brazil.

Like Water for Chocolate see *Como agua para chocolate*

The Lion's Den see *La boca del lobo*

144. Lo que le pasó a Santiago (What Happened to Santiago).

Jacobo Morales. Puerto Rico, 1989. 105 min., Color. Spanish.

COMMENTARY: Popular television actor Tommy Muñíz stars as Santiago Rodríguez, "a recently retired, lonely widower whose life is rejuvenated when he unexpectedly falls in love with an enigmatic younger woman named Angelina (Gladys Rodríguez), whom he meets during one of his strolls in a local park. The woman agrees to see him on the condition that he not inquire about her past or personal life. Curious and unable to deal with the strain that this anonymity imposes on their growing relationship, Santiago hires a private investigator, who uncovers some unsettling truths about the woman's past. Much of the pleasure of this film comes from director Jacobo Morales's decision to linger over and savor the quiet yet often painful moments that Santiago shares with his two grown children as they struggle to understand a relationship undertaken so late in life." (Program notes — Chicago Center Theater.)

Santiago, whose three children are all problematic (of the two daughters, one lives abroad and the other is currently separated from her husband; his only son is an outpatient of a mental clinic in a local hospital), deserves something better in his now empty life. When he meets Angelina, his life begins again, but his children cannot accept the relationship.

The director capitalizes on his location settings, having Angelina meet Santiago in the plazas and parks of Old San Juan. Although the film contains a "mystery" to be discovered at the conclusion, it is inconsequential as far as the plot is concerned. The film is a mature work with a charm and sensitivity, avoiding the cloying sentimentality of its predecessors like José Garcí's nostalgia-laden *To Begin Again* (1980), which dealt with a similar theme (and won an Oscar in 1981). Morales avoids all the Hollywood

clichés, and the actors, who have been playing on Puerto Rican television for years in a soap opera called "The Garcías," more than reprise their roles here. They give new meaning and depth to their movie personages by focusing on the complete development of one major character in the space of nearly two hours, unlike their TV roles in which they reveal one new quality or plot twist per episode. Their restrained and beautiful performances in the round give this film its *raison d'être* and make it worthwhile for all audiences.

145. Lo que vendrá (Time Will Come or What Is to Come). Gustavo Mosquera. Argentina, 1987. 98 min., Color. Spanish.

COMMENTARY: A debut feature by Gustavo Mosquera, *Time Will Come* stars that wonderful actor from Eliseo Subiela's *Hombre mirando al sudeste*, Hugo Soto, playing the extraordinary role of Galván, an innocent bystander shot down in a riot during a political demonstration as repressive police try to quell the protest. (Of course there are many reverberations here regarding Argentina's own political climate, but Mosquera makes no overt commentaries. He lets his "impersonal camera" do all the speaking and commenting for him. It should also be noted that the real death of a young boy shot in the head inspired the director to make this "allegory of crisis" or grim satire of a modern-day South American police state, perhaps today's Argentina.)

Galván has a head injury and is able to think while all around him there is chaos. He is taken to a hospital, where the authorities try to hush up the incident. Meanwhile, the cop who fired the shot, Morea (Juan Leyrado), is put on the carpet and rebuked for his constant use of brutal measures. It is interesting that this particular military dictatorship of the future prefers to use brain control (through medication) rather than overt violence. Nevertheless, Galván is protected by a male nurse (who pretends to be a doctor and is also an ambulance driver) played by Charly García (one of Argentina's top rock musicians, the Tom Waits of Argentina), who engineers Galván's final escape from the beautiful nurse (Rosario Blefari) who administers drugs to control our surly patient.

Galván is driven to a remote dock area by the guardian angel ambulance driver, and it is on this empty, rust-colored set that the final shoot-out between Galván (who has finally gained some modicum of real expression) and Morea, his dreaded nemesis, finally takes place. You can guess the predictable outcome of *Lo que vendrá* in more ways than one.

The film is shot in a new, bold, experimental style, reflecting on the future by using the past as a point of departure in a present that is somewhat dark and desolate, marked by the certainty that the future will come — but what kind of future will it be? Mosquera provides some profound moments here.

There are echoes of Stanley Kubrick's *A Clockwork Orange* when we watch anonymous punks beating each other in dark alleys without explanation. Also, when Galván, wearing his stereo headset, is fired upon by Morea in a sudden burst of anger because of the demonstrators, the camera follows Galván's eyes and we fall upside down with him. We watch what he watches, upside down — another disturbing, Kubrickian surreal steal.

The film is exciting because it is glossy, fast-paced, with ingenious camera angles, fascinating faces of new actors and sets and illogical plot twists and turns that give viewers a rush for their money, like a great video game set in the future. It's not *Star Wars*, but a kind film noir with science-fiction overlay and ambiguous mystery-detective overtones, a kind of Wellsian *Lady from Shanghai*,

with brunette Hugo Soto as its centerpiece — not the gorgeous Rita Hayworth whose beauty cried for color but was immortalized by her director in black and white. Perhaps *Lo que vendrá* is closer to the science fiction noir film *The Terminator* because of its color and technical innovations, but it is closer in spirit to the darkness of the Orson Welles product because of its delineation of the "mean-spirited black characters" on the Argentine pampas of the future.

146. Lola. María Novaro. Mexico, 1988. 92 min., Color. Spanish.

COMMENTARY: "On a lonely Christmas night, Lola and her five-year-old daughter, Ana, await Omar's return. He doesn't show. Once again, he is on tour with his rock group. The break up between them is imminent and even though they try to avoid it, it happens. The relationship between mother and daughter becomes more fragile; the duality of love-hate feeling intensifies. Lola evades her responsibility as a parent. She feels guilty and tries to assume her role, only to fall apart and evade the issue again. Alone with the little girl, Lola tries to change, to fall in love, to forget, but she can't. Her loneliness overcomes her, and she decides to leave Ana with her mother, Chelo, who receives them doubtfully. Chelo doesn't dare put her questions into words because her own relationship with Lola is strained.

"Mexico City is the backdrop of the story. Still in rubble after the 1985 earthquakes, it resembles the people who inhabit it: hurt and vital, hard and loving, broken. Lola's friends are like that: El Duende, Dora, Mudo. These friends are street vendors; they take over the sidewalks with their wares and are constantly harassed by policemen in civvies. Yet they are back day after day, trying to establish their right to be on the streets. Together with her friends, Lola goes on a trip where she finally learns that she is stronger than she thought. Before a human panorama of beach vacationers, poor and full of a love that they are not even aware of, we receive along with Lola a brief but deep lesson on human emotions. Love wins over loneliness, and Lola goes back to her daughter. At the end we see Lola, if not different, at least with a strong purpose and a firm heart." (Press book.)

Lola is a significant first feature by María Novaro, a small and impressive film that explores new territory in depicting the fragile world of an imperfect modern woman — one who must fend for herself and her daughter in the absence of the traditional family unit. Lola lives her marginal life as best she can, selling irregular-sized clothing on the streets of Mexico City.

Leticia Huijara as Lola gives a terrific performance as an abandoned single mother. She is ably helped by Alejandra Vargas as her daughter and Martha Navarro as her own mother. The color photography by Rodrigo García is ravishing, capturing the steet life of Mexico with its assembly of characters, and the editing by Sigfrido Barjau is fast, effective, sometimes jarring, like the subversive life depicted on the streets, constantly interrupted by the *tamarindos* (cops). María Novaro is certainly a new Mexican feminist to watch in the future.

147. Lolo. Francisco Athié. Mexico, 1992. 99 min., Color. Spanish.

COMMENTARY: Lolo is the name of the leading character in the film, beautifully played by Roberto Sosa. A seventeen-year-old foundry worker without any other education, Lolo complains to the foreman about his low pay. He is summarily beaten and robbed by the bosses, and after spending time in a local hospital recovering from his wounds, he is fired for his "vacation." Having nowhere to go, he returns home to his mother, Doña Rosario (strongly acted by Lucha Villa, one of Mexico's leading actresses), who has only insults for her son.

Searching for any sort of job, Lolo works for the hurdy-gurdy player, Alambrista, and meets Sonia, a local girl with whom he falls in love. But happiness is short-lived because of the local *pandillas* (gangs). Here the plot becomes somewhat convoluted and a bit hysterical. Because Lolo's mother needs money to survive, she pawns her watch. Lolo sees this as an opportunity to steal the money-lender's cash and the watch as well, but instead, Lolo murders him and leaves evidence pointing to Alambrista as the real murderer. The neighborhood gangs intervene and want to get to the bottom of the mystery. Do we find out the real truth — who is the perpetrator of the crime — or will we witness the enactment of the Darwinian concept (survival of the fittest)? It seems Alambrista (played effectively by Alonso Echanové) has been a victim before.

The film's conclusion is quite predictable. Even though Lolo has been treated unfairly, in a candle-lit church scene, he admits to the killing below a statue of the Virgin, an act of faith in keeping with the goodness of his character. One can never know why he went berserk and murdered the money-lender, but director Athié prefers to tell Lolo's story in a straightforward manner with a redemptive ending. It's Nicholas Ray's 1949 film *Knock on Any Door*, a smart, melodramatic film noir making facile social points, recycled to Mexico City in the 1990s. *Lolo* makes the same points, but in color.

The Lost Republic (Parts I and II) see *La república perdida (partes I y II)*

Love Is a Fat Woman see *El amor es una mujer gorda*

Raquel Revuelta as the 1895 "Lucía" in Humberto Solas's epic Cuban film of that name (1969). As Lucía walks through the streets, she is hiding a dagger with which she will soon kill her Spanish lover who betrayed her own love and killed her brother.

Love Lesson see *Lição de amor*

Love Lies see *Mentiras piadosas*

148. Lucía. Humberto Solas. Cuba, 1969. 160 min., B&W. Spanish.

COMMENTARY: Humberto Solas' *Lucía* is a masterpiece of Cuban cinema. It is a three-part epic of love and revolution that begins in 1895, moves to 1933 and ends in the 1960s. It is about three different Lucías, played (in chronological order) by Raquel Revuelta, Eslinda Núñez and Adela Legra as the film progresses to the present. The three men in their lives are Rafael, Aldo and Tomás, respectively played by Eduardo Moure, Ramon Brito and Adolfo Llaurado.

"Part One: 1895. With Cuba's fight against the Spanish oppressor decimating the male population, the aristocratic

Lucía (Revuelta), like most of her companions, seems certain to die an old maid. She is overwhelmed when Rafael, a handsome stranger, courts her and soon proposes marriage. She smothers him with love and girlish confidences, but will never take him to the mountain plantation which figures in many of her childhood reminiscences, since it is in fact the headquarters of the rebel army in which her brother Felipe — officially studying abroad — is an active fighter. The news that Rafael already has a wife and child in Spain drives Lucía to a frenzy of despair. But despite an ominous warning, Lucía eventually goes to a secret tryst with Rafael, becomes his mistress and, in an excess of passion, agrees to elope with him to the plantation. As they approach it, they are overtaken by Spanish-paid brigands. Rafael flings her from the horse they are sharing and rides away. Lucía witnesses the massacre of the rebel army and later finds Felipe dead among the casualties. Back in town, Lucía sees Rafael in Spanish uniform and stabs him to death in the town square.

"Part Two —1933. Alone with her ill-tempered mother on their island summer house and oppressed by the latter's suspicions about her husband's fidelity, Lucía sees a wounded man being put ashore one night. She discovers his hiding place, learns that he is a revolutionary named Aldo, and — after a period of separation and some more family squabbles — leaves her bourgeois home to live with him in Havana. She takes a job in the same cigar factory as Flora, the wife of Aldo's comrade Antonio, and joins her in a woman's protest march against Machado's regime as Aldo, Antonio and an associate gun down a number of policemen inside a music hall. Machado is deposed, and when Antonio and Aldo are both given important jobs, Lucía — now pregnant — is obliged to spend time alone in the city of Havana. The disil-lusioned Aldo quarrels with Antonio, whom he sees helping to make the new regime as corrupt as the old. Returning to revolutionary action, Aldo is killed in the Havana streets, and Lucía must identify his body in the morgue.

"Part Three: 196–. Obsessively jealous, Tomás refuses to allow his young bride, Lucía, to return to work in the fields and keeps her locked up alone in his house all day. His jealousy increases when — as part of the government's literacy campaign — Comrade Angelina and the local assembly insist that a handsome young teacher from Havana be billeted in the house to teach Lucía to read and write. Beaten up by Tomás for allowing her mother into the house, Lucía follows the teacher's advice, leaves Tomás and goes to work. They are utterly miserable apart, and Tomás eventually comes out to the salt quarry to convince Lucía of his love and to continue their quarrel over the role of wives in a revolutionary society." (Press book.)

Lucía is the best Cuban film this viewer has seen to date. It explores in human terms the spirit of each era in the development of the Cuban nation. Although it is panoramic in nature, it is also personal, since it reveals and informs us about the foibles of each of the Lucías we see on screen.

Our 1895 Lucía is an aristocratic, romantic personage. She is betrayed by love, betrayed by Spain as the whole nation was in a state of military insurrection due to Cuban resistance that led to the blowing up of the battleship *Maine* and to the Spanish-American War a few years later. Lucía's betrayal precipitates Spain's defeat by America and freedom for the Cuban nation. This section of the film is so full of bravura scenes of battle set against its highly romantic love story that it leaves the viewer breathless.

The 1933 Lucía, by comparison, is also romantic, but more modern than her 1895 predecessor. Betrayed by her aristocratic background and the falsity of their hollow value system, this Lucía is quite liberated since she seeks an idol of her own — a revolutionary who dies for his cause, but leaves his young wife to fend for herself in a society where class values no longer count. This Lucía cannot return home again; she will always be prey to the dominant political group because she will always be an outsider. She will spend her life raising her child in a Cuba ruled by a succession of regimes more repressive and corrupt than even the Machado one, against which she and Aldo fought and lost.

Our 196– Lucía is the simplest creature, the happiest woman, the most liberated, perhaps because she is the most uneducated and also the most sensual of the three women in the film. She is frank, candid, at peace, too good for the macho husband who adores her and wants to possess her mind and body. But with the massive literacy campaign organized by the Castro regime after the 1959 revolution, this new Lucía represents the "new" Cuban woman, literate, an equal, completely liberated and modern, embracing the social struggle, critical of her nation, her husband and herself. Solas wants her autocritical spirit to persevere.

Perhaps Humberto Solas is really the three Lucías rolled into one. Solas is expert in feminine psychology. What drives the first Lucía to murder is not only the death of her brother but the fact that Rafael neglected to tell her he was already married and used Lucía to gain information that destroyed her brother and the local Cuban insurrectionists. Our 1933 Lucía is Solas himself, striking out in a new direction, finding a cause (his career as a filmmaker) in a society that did not readily encourage a life in the arts. Philosophically, Solas would like to become the third Lucía, because she incarnates a true freedom of spirit that her truck-driver husband can never

share — and yet Solas was able to make this terrific film in Castro's Cuba. In interviews, he has even said that his intentions were "to show the epoch not through historical facts but through a narrative which allows one to feel the spirit of the time. It is the time as it was lived by people, real people and the atmosphere that grew out of it, and not as a moment of history that I wanted to capture."

On its initial release in 1969, *Lucía* and its then 26-year-old director won international acclaim and a number of film prizes, too many to recount. Although it was briefly shown in America in the early seventies, it deserves wider exposure because of its epic greatness. It is still the single, best and most cohesive and cinematic feature ever to come out of Cuba.

149. Lúcio Flávio. Hector Babenco. Brazil, 1977. 124 min., Color. Portuguese.

COMMENTARY: In this true story, the child of a middle-class family of Rio de Janeiro grows up to become one of the most famous bank robbers in Brazil.

The police arrest and torture many outlaws in their search for information about this robber, Lúcio Flávio. Once imprisoned, Lúcio Flávio is brutally tortured, but, thanks to his connections with some policemen, he manages to escape. However, he is aware that if he reveals all he knows, he will not survive for long.

The underworld intrigues, as well as Lúcio Flávio's connections with the corrupt police, are quite clear in this film, which is based on facts that stirred the city in the '70s, and on the book by José Louzeiro.

Lúcio Flávio is arrested many times but always manages to escape, until at last he dies in prison, murdered by another outlaw. Nevertheless, he is able to denounce all he knows, mainly his clandestine connections with the police. (Press book.)

Hector Babenco made *Lúcio Flávio* just before making his most famous international success, *Pixote*. But *Lúcio Flávio* was a huge commercial success in Brazil because of the bank robber's notoriety. He was called the John Dillinger of Rio, and the film has that 1930s gangster sensibility, although it does contain many scenes of male frontal nudity (something never seen in American films of that era) which gives it a far more contemporary look. The film is chock-full of violence — death squad murders on the side of the law balanced with violent murders by bank robbers and opposing gang members. In fact, because they were based on fact, the death squad sequences aroused public indignation and fomented political change in Brazil in the late seventies. The film is an astute reminder of Brazil's outlaw past and its death squads.

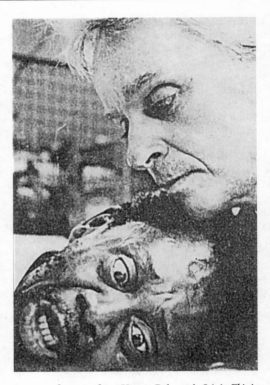

A scene of torture from Hector Babenco's *Lúcio Flávio* (1977).

150. Un lugar del mundo (A Place in the World). Adolfo Aristarain. Argentina, 1992. 120 min., Color. Spanish/Yiddish.

COMMENTARY: This film was produced, directed and written by Adolfo Aristarain, who obviously prefers total control over the process of filmmaking. If only he had a more interesting story to tell us! As it is related in flashback by Ernesto (Gaston Batyi), a doctor who has returned from Spain to Argentina to visit the valley where his father was buried, the movie loses its dramatic force because its tale is a bit convoluted.

Ernesto is visiting his past, his teenage years, when his father, Mario (played over the top by Federico Luppi), ran a country school for all the provincial children, trying to combat illiteracy, and his Jewish mother, Ana (Cecilia Roth), was the local doctor who tended to the needs of children and adults alike. They are idealists, perhaps Spanish "communists" who left that country to return to their native Argentina, begin a new communal life and find their place in the world.

The rest of the film revolves around a love story between Ernesto and Luciana (Lorena del Río), whom he meets clandestinely to teach her to read against the will of her foreman father. The father, called Zamora (Hugo Arana), works for Andrada (Rodolfo Ranni), a cattle rancher who is buying up all the land he can around him, trying to break the cooperative enterprise set up by

Mario and Ana and a renegade nun, Nelda (Leonor Benedetto), who refuses to wear clerical garb.

The entire plot becomes amazingly clear when Hans Meyer, a Spanish engineer with a German name (played too, too broadly by José Sacristan), comes to the valley to examine it geologically and determine the feasibility of building a hydroelectric project in this desolate valley about 100 miles outside of Buenos Aires.

If you remember the opening scene, in the present, you will recall Ernesto looking at an undeveloped valley. Therefore everything that follows this scene is gratuitous — since the greed of Andrada, the cattle baron, does him no good even if he buys up all the land and succeeds in breaking the hold of the cooperative on the valley. But Aristarain wants to have his story both ways. Hans Meyer, the geologist, reveals the reason for his presence early on in the film: He wants the members of the cooperative to adore and sympathize with him while he breaks the backs of the people there in the name of progress for an unidentified European conglomerate whose only interest is money, not real progress.

Many critics may feel that the film's idealism is heady stuff— that three people with burning idealism can make a difference in the world and that the characters' emotions are revealed to be larger than life against a tumultuous political and social canvass. Nevertheless, one cannot escape the inevitable failure of their plight from the film's inception, the stereotyped kinds of idealists they represent or the crushing conventions of plot devices that undermine any real magic or idealism the film could have held for us.

First, there is a dreadful "macho-inebriation" scene between Mario and Hans that takes the film down several pegs. Their "release" in Buenos Aires from their problems is certainly not

spiritual or idealistic, just alcoholic. (It was one of the worst drunk scenes between Latin men that this viewer has ever witnessed on screen.) Secondly, it is not material objects as "gifts" that serve to link people but the emotional weight those gifts carry. Hans' gifts of telescopes and lanterns to Ernesto and his insistence that the latter not wait for the train to leave seem like scenarios written out of some poor forties American westerns. And finally, if Ernesto was really in love with Luciana, he would have braved the fires of hell and come back to rescue her (perhaps through marriage) from that hellish life she was programmed for in the Argentine outback. All we have is Ernesto's nostalgia as he runs his hand over a Hebrew proverb he carved into a wooden gate, a symbol of his idealism and love for Luciana — so when she would see it, she too would remember and strive harder for personal fulfillment. Ernesto's little pony-tailed hairdo, his jeans and leather jacket provide us with a vision of a smug macho male, not the product of a socially realist background but of a pseudo-sophisticated screenplay of little political or social resonance.

There is one, only one, golden moment in the film — when at the gravesite we see the 20-year-old Ernesto and his father in the same frame, separated by the undeveloped valley; Ernesto recounts that his father, indeed, had found his own place in the world. Ernesto grapples with the very same thought as the end-title emerges and the credits roll to the sound of a familiar but undistinguished music score.

NOTES: Adolfo Aristarain was born in Buenos Aires in 1943 and is a film director of much talent. He did film work in Spain and America, obtaining experience on such diverse films as *Once Upon a Time in the West*, *A Touch of Class* and *The Adventurers*. However, he is really known for his Argentine political

Cover of press book of Arturo Ripstein's *El lugar sin límites* (*Hell Hath No Limits*, 1977) showing a rare still of Roberto Cobo dancing in drag in a local Mexican cantina.

films, especially *Tiempo de revancha* (1981), *Los últimos días de la víctima* (1982), and *Un lugar del mundo*, which was nominated for the Best Foreign Film Oscar in 1992. He continues to work internationally, not bound by the concerns of the Argentine film industry.

151. El lugar sin límites
(Hell Hath No Limits / Without Limits / The Place Without Limits). Arturo Ripstein. Mexico, 1977. 110 min., Eastmancolor. Spanish.

COMMENTARY: As a *Variety* film critic said in his review of the film in 1978, "This may be a daring film for Mexico, with its putting down of 'machismo' and its humanization of a transvestite in a small village...."

Based upon an original story by Chilean novelist José Donoso, the plot is amazingly simple: "Drag queen La Manuela (Roberto Cobo) lives with his daughter in the whorehouse they own at the edge of a dying town in rural Mexico. Both are attracted to — yet afraid of — he-man truck driver Pancho (Gonzalo Vega), a violent man who has never understood the passion he feels for La Manuela. When Pancho brutally torments the daughter (Lucha Villa), La Manuela comes to the rescue and emerges a true, rare hero. He bursts into the room, offering himself seductively in an amorous and diabolical dance. For a few moments, sordidness and enchantment merge together and the two men's instincts are stripped naked: the homosexual stands erect and recaptures the freedom denied him for generations by a hypocritical and repressed society; the macho abandons his mold, his unconscious play to appearances, and they form an ephemeral couple of subversive lovers. Before the silent crowd, they surrender to one another in the fury of a shameless and oblivious kiss. However, Octavio (Julian Pastor) shakes Pancho back to his confused and mediocre reality. La Manuela runs away, and the two men chase him in their truck. In the end, Pancho traps the transvestite and kicks him to death — a desolate vision of the most terrible and contradictory passions." (Press book.)

Certainly way ahead of its time, this film offers an amazing and truly masterful performance by Roberto Cobo (of *Los Olvidados*) as La Manuela. From Cobo the film derives its energy, its compulsive (for some, convulsive) beauty, its capacity to move the audience, its high irony and its final explosion — macho vengeance.

The director said of the film: "I had to make it very cheaply, under miserable conditions. ... Manuel Puig didn't want to sign his name to the film. He thought I might not take the subject seriously and make a caricature out of homosexuals. After the film was released (and successful), he wanted his name put back in the credits...but it was simply too late. Puig didn't want to be thought of as a homosexual writer (despite the success of *Kiss of the Spiderwoman*)."

Uncredited screenwriter Manuel Puig said about Ripstein: "I owe [him] the pleasant memory of *El lugar sin límites* [and] the equally happy experience of our association in 1983, when he directed the play version of *Kiss of the Spiderwoman* in Mexico. Once again, Ripstein showed a great deal of talent in respecting the rules of my work as a team." (MOMA program notes.)

Some of the great faults of the film are its static camera combined with a very slow, almost padded script. Yet it is a surprisingly sensitive film, again, quite ahead of its time, and might be viewed differently today. It contains perhaps Roberto Cobo's greatest and most operatic performance, after Jaibo in *Los olvidados*, the second role of a lifetime.

152. Macario. Roberto Gavaldón. Mexico, 1960. 91 min., B&W. Spanish.

COMMENTARY: Overwhelmed by a lifetime of semi-starvation, Macario (Ignacio López Tarso) is determined that for once in his life he will have all he can eat. This determination is triggered by the sight of luscious turkeys being prepared for the household of Don Ramiro (Mario Alberto Rodríguez) and the knowledge that at least some of the feast will be offered to the dead. He vows never to eat again until he can satiate his hunger for the first time in his life.

At last his wife (Pina Pellicer) steals and roasts a turkey for him alone. When he is about to start on his long-awaited banquet, a handsome gentleman (José Galvez) approaches and offers to fulfill all of Macario's wishes if he is invited to share it. Macario refuses, as he guesses that this man is the devil.

Next, an old gentleman (José Luis Jiménez) approaches and asks to be invited. Macario instantly sees God in this old man, and very humbly demurs, pointing out that this meal is the only really satisfying event in his life. He then changes his mind and turns to offer some — but the old man has disappeared.

There comes a third interruption — that of Death (Enrique Lucero), who appears as famished as Macario. Macario promptly divides his turkey in two parts, knowing that while Death is busy eating half, he himself will at least stay alive long enough to eat the other half. Death is grateful and repays Macario with a vial of water that will heal the sick, but with the stipulation that Mario may use it only if Death is standing at the feet of the ill one. If Death stands at the head, Mario must allow the person to die.

Using this water, Macario becomes a famous healer. But as Macario's fame spreads and his wealth increases, the Inquisition intervenes, asking whether Macario's power comes from God or the devil. Then Macario's own son falls ill — and Death stands only at the head of the sick boy. Macario pleads for the boy's life, which means his own, to no avail. He flees, and in his frantic run through the forest, hides in a cave — but it is the cave of Death, who shows him some candles that represent human lives. Macario again flees, but the voice of Death follows him.

It is now the voice of his wife, full of anguish, calling him. Macario is found lying by a tree with a smile on his face and in front of him, half of the turkey he shared with death." (Press book.)

Macario is a visually stunning film, photographed in glorious black and white by Gabriel Figueroa, Mexico's master cinematographer. Based upon a story by B. Traven (more famous for his screenplay of John Huston's film *The Treasure of the Sierra Madre*), *Macario* is a beautifully told allegory, unusual in the simplicity of its narrative and perceptively acted by its principals. The direction is remarkably fluid and strong, rich in human revelations and vivid pictorial qualities. Ignacio López Tarso simply shines in the title role, with a range of expressions from dumb country bumpkin to enlightened father and caring husband. Pina Pellicer is equally adept in her role, sympathetic and appealingly sensitive. The film is full of wonderful ensemble acting, and all the allegorical figures do well in their roles. The candlelight scene in Death's cave is the most memorable in the film and will linger years after you have seen it, owing to Gabriel Figueroa's brilliant photography combined with Manuel Fontanals' gorgeous set design — they are one of the best artistic teams in Mexico's film industry, and *Macario* is the delightful result of their collaboration. *Macario* was the recipient of many awards presented internationally at a number of film festivals, including the well-deserved Special Jury Prize at Cannes in 1961.

NOTES: Director Roberto Gavaldón has made his reputation only in Mexico

Unidentified actors in Joaquim Pedro de Andrade's "picaresque fantasy," *Macunaima* (1969).

and has directed some of that nation's best films, including *La rosa blanca*, his most "political" and controversial film since it deals with the nationalization of Mexico's oil industry and its effects on the people. Ignacio López Tarso starred in *La rosa blanca* and had supporting roles in many well-known Mexican films such as *La cucaracha*, *La desconocida* and *Nazarín*. His co-star, Pina Pellicer, appeared in many Mexican films such as *Nazarín* and *Los ambiciosos* but gained international fame in the Marlon Brando–produced and directed western, *One-Eyed Jacks*. The stress in her personal life caused her to commit suicide while she was in her early thirties.

153. Macunaima (Macunaima: The Characterless Hero). Joaquim Pedro de Andrade. Brazil, 1969. 90 min., Color. Portuguese.

COMMENTARY: Based upon a book by Mario de Andrade written in the 1920s, this is a picaresque fantasy. The film contains serious political and social statements scattered throughout, hidden in the dialogue and incorporated into the burlesque situations that form the screenplay. The critical barbs are isolated within the compendium of folk tales spun by Macunaima, the film's central character, a lazy and egoistic folk hero of sorts. He is assisted by Saci, a one-legged comic character, a totally worthless trickster and a speedy runner despite his handicap. Together, they embark on a series of episodes of a comical nature. The characters do not advance the action or plot of the film, which is its strength and also its weakness, depending upon one's point of view. Much of the humor, based on puns, is intended for Brazilian audiences, lending a hermetic quality to the screenplay.

The film is really about the eccentric Macunaima and the memorable (or unmemorable) incidents that occur throughout the film, which is loaded with magical, fantastic and animated creatures and incident that defy description or synopsis. (See Randal Johnson and Robert Stam's attempt to explain the wacky, detailed plot in their *Brazilian Cinema*, pages 179-181.)

As an epic burlesque, say Johnson and Stam, "the film is filled with encounters and incidents revealing the boisterous and overflowing life of a dynamic country ... [while] the director is criticizing it with ... savagery. ... Although the film is couched in the fantastic plot of a 1920s Brazilian novel and comic in style, it is deeply political. Every character and situation is a synthesis of themes ... the cinematic double-entendres, in blending Marx Bros.–like comedy (some might say Woody Allen–like) with the serious criticism of Brazil...make the film a remarkable work." *Macunaima* is brilliant cinema. It is also Andrade's metaphor for the Brazilian character, a parable and portrayal of the bizarre side of the Brazilian people. The story is an acrid contemporary political allegory. It has to be seen to be believed.

NOTES: Director Joaquim Pedro de Andrade was born in 1932 in Rio, spending his entire career working on films in Brazil. He began making documentaries — *The Poet of the Castle* (1959) and *Garrincha, alegría do povo* (1963) — which led to his first feature, *The Priest and the Girl* (1966). After *Macunaima*,

he made films on a variety of themes judging by their titles: *Os inconfidentes* (1972), *Guerra conjugal* (1974), *Contos eroticos* (1977), *O homem do Pau-Brazil* (1981, about the life of writer Oswald de Andrade) and *Vida mansa* (1982). He continues to live and work in Rio.

Macunaima: The Characterless Hero see *Macunaima*

154. Malabrigo. Alberto Durant. Peru, 1985. 84 min., Color. Spanish.

COMMENTARY: A suspense thriller and Durant's second film that he also co-wrote, *Malabrigo* takes its name from a small fishing port in which most of the action takes place. Sonia (Charo Verastegui) is traveling to Malabrigo to meet her husband, who works in a fish-processing factory. While on the road, the bus is held up by two masked men, who take off a passenger and shoot him. Upon arrival, Sonia discovers her husband has not been seen or heard from for two days. She receives little help from the clerk of the hotel where her husband had been living, the local police or other villagers. She does hear about a mysterious explosion that took place a couple of days before her arrival at the processing plant. With the help of a local reporter, she begins to unravel the mystery of her husband's disappearance and a pattern of corruption among the locals, wanting to hush up matters. Also there is evidence of a possible insurance scam since her husband worked as an accountant for the plant and an insurance adjuster (Luis Álvarez) also arrives to investigate the scene.

The mystery is resolved in an unconvincing manner, perhaps as a consequence of a screenplay that cannot decide whether to concentrate on the banality of the plot or on the larger social issues of corruption and the abuses of money and power by greedy industrialists.

The film is loaded with atmospheric glimpses of the village, but its overly talky finale between the factory owner and the insurance adjuster turns the solution of the mystery into an anticlimax. If only the director had stuck to the politics of the story, trying to show something of the life and corruption in a small fishing village, and had not gotten bogged down by an inept mystery that worked at cross-purposes to the ideology behind the film! Even the leading actress seems unconvinced by the conclusion and looks amused by everything going on around her. The film could have had greater impact if the director had stuck to his original intentions of making a political statement, not a so-so mystery with political nuances.

There is an unintentional pun on the title that is worth mentioning in the context of the film. Perhaps Durant feels his characters are marginal people, lucky enough to remain free in Peru of today, although while they try to survive, they are *malabrigado*— unfit but always alive, living for the future.

Malandro see *Opera do malandro*

155. Malayunta (Bad Connection). José Santiso. Argentina, 1985. 92 min., Color. Spanish.

COMMENTARY: Based upon a play by Jacobo Langsner, *Pater Noster*, and co-written by the director, *Malayunta* is a dark, gripping, provocative and cruel allegorical drama reminiscent of Buñuel and Torre Nilsson. The plot is very deceptive.

An upright couple, Bernardo (Federico Luppi) and Amalia (Barbara Mujica), rent a room from an anti-social sculptor named Nestor (Miguel Ángel Sola) who lives alone in a huge, cluttered Buenos Aires apartment in center city. Taking a parental interest, the couple force their way into the sculptor's life, at first snooping through his belongings, then becoming more actively intrusive, attempting to structure his unconventional ways to meet their notions of decent living. Presenting themselves as typically Argentine (they cherish mementos won in a tango contest twenty years earlier), they reveal themselves to be as typically authoritarian, imposing repressive measures in the name of morality. Later, however, their facade of normalcy crumbles when pressures of their pasts surface in the present. A man questions them about his disappeared brother, and they show a tendency toward violence. Their cruel regulatory measures, are followed by remorse, as they beg the sculptor "not to forgive, but to forget." However, Nestor turns insolent and contemptuous towards them. Resentful, Bernardo and Amalia decide to assert themselves when Nestor reveals his affair with Amalia and possibly Bernardo. Since there seems to be no compromise, this *ménage à trois* becomes a violent clash of youth versus fanatic intolerance. Since Nestor refuses to change his own ways, they decide to get rid of him. (MOMA Program Notes.)

While filming in 1986, director José Santiso said, regarding the idea of reconciliation during the political debates, that "one needs neither to forgive nor to forget, but to disconnect — a bad connection can blow the whole system." In this statement rests the allegorical connection with the film.

Obviously it is the menace of Bernardo and his possible guilt for having assisted the regime during the era of the *desaparecidos* that Santiso is referring to. Also his repressive, authoritarian nature, overtly religious but hiding a multitude of secrets, is under scrutiny here. Bernardo's character within this battle of wills between Amalia and Nestor suggests many political and social interpretations in this renaissance of Argentine cinema, seeking to reexamine the past and find cures for old ailments. José Santiso has given us a deeply probing and humanistic portrait of three people caught in the vortex of one of Argentina's saddest moments in its long history.

156. Malclovia. Emilio "El Indio" Fernández. Mexico, 1948. 105 min., B&W. Spanish.

COMMENTARY: Beautifully photographed in black and white by Gabriel Figueroa, *Malclovia* is a love story concerning indigenous Mexicans. For director Emilio Fernández, it is a continuation of the theme that he began with *María Candelaría* four years earlier.

Set before the Mexican Revolution on the island of Janitzio in the state of Michoacán, the story deals with poor fisherman José María (Pedro Armendáriz), who wants to marry Malclovia (María Félix), the beautiful daughter of the village chief. Malclovia's father opposes the union, while a corrupt official, Sergeant Garza (menacingly played by Carlos López Moctezuma), tries to arrest the fisherman so that he can have the girl for himself.

The director plays the drama to the hilt — Armendáriz is arrested but breaks out through steel doors in a fierce display of might as the army races to dispatch the evil sergeant just as he is about to seduce Malclovia. The story ends happily, although the audience witnesses overplayed scenes of physical and emotional endurance. If one can look past the overacting, there is much to enjoy: beautifully lit night scenes, candlelight celebrations, folkloric dances, fishing on the ocean, scenes that leave the viewer breathless from their sheer beauty of tone and composition. Despite the hackneyed, utterly predictable plot and the broad playing of the photogenic actors, the film is directed with the same skill, nobility and care that graces every Emilio Fernández production. However, it is Gabriel Figueroa who is always the real star behind these films, because of his luminous photographic talent. ¡Qué viva Figueroa!

157. A Man, When He Is a Man. Valeria Sarmiento. Costa Rica/Chile, 1985. 66 min., Color. Spanish.

COMMENTARY: Called by *Variety* a "mesmerizing documentary detailing the universal stud" and by *Film Comment* "an imaginative documentary that sent audiences howling at [Sarmiento's] wicked deconstruction of the all-too-familiar macho mystique," *A Man, When He Is a Man* takes its title from an interview that the director had with an elderly pharmacist who said, "A man is a man when he works and tries to make something of himself. And when he is with a woman, he shows that he is a man by trying to conquer her. If she gives him a chance, he kisses her and wins her over. But if she is willing and he doesn't take her, that woman will think that he isn't a man, she'll feel let down."

In an interview, Sarmiento said about the film: "Now that I have the distance [living in Paris as a Chilean exile], I can reflect on what it means to be a Latin American." And so after making several other documentaries on a variety of subjects, she embarked on this interview film in Costa Rica. Zuzana M. Pick, in her book *The New Latin American Cinema*, spends five pages reviewing the film, its "interviews with males of all ages [that] alternate with folk dances, mariachi bands, film clips, coming out parties and weddings." She concludes that "to the extent that 'machismo' is sanctioned in discourse and mediated by representation, it is an issue that Latin American women cannot afford to ignore. ... the film indicates the crucial role that 'machismo' plays in the construction of social and subjective identities."

NOTES: Director Valeria Sarmiento, a native of Chile, now resides in Paris with her husband, film director Raúl Ruiz. She has experience in making documentary films. Her first, *Color-Tainted Dreams*, was made in Chile about nightclub strippers working in a local cabaret. In 1979, she filmed *People from Everywhere, People from Nowhere*, about the lives of immigrants living in Parisian suburbs. After the success of *A Man, When He Is a Man* (1982), she made a film biography of Corin Tellado, a romantic writer of women's fiction called *Our Marriage* (1984). Her most recent work is the 1990 film entitled *Amelia López O'Neill*. Many of these titles can be found on 16mm and video cassette in the "Women Make Movies" series, a collection that since 1972 has featured work of filmmakers from Peru, Chile, Nicaragua and Colombia.

Man Facing Southeast see *Hombre mirando al sureste*

The Man from Maisinicú see *El Hombre de Maisinicú*

Man Looking Southeast see *Hombre mirando al sureste*

158. La mano en la trampa
(Hand in the Trap). Leopoldo Torre Nilsson. Argentina, 1961. 90 min., B&W. Spanish.

COMMENTARY: At the film's conclusion, the feminine lead, Laura (Elsa Daniel), remembers a quote from St. Augustine: "When one puts one's hand into a trap, one must carry the trap around forever."

Torre Nilsson and his wife, Beatriz Guido, have written an almost gothic-style screenplay around this phrase which is very critical of the Argentine upper bourgeoisie. The tale focuses on two sisters and one of their daughters, Laura Lavigne. Laura is home from the convent boarding school for her annual visit, to the dismay of the nuns, who worry about the effects of idle hands in a small town. And indeed, once away from convent influence, Laura's imagination runs free, and in her mother's and aunt's dark, baroque house, she uncovers a melodrama of deceptive appearances and suppressed sexuality. The upper-class sisters spend their time sewing trousseaus for others and caring for the family's "shame," an aunt seduced by a local playboy, who for her indiscretion has been shut away in an upper floor for the past twenty years. The other women, too, are shut in, their doors closed against knowledge of a changing outside world, intent on maintaining a façade of their former social prominence. Laura resists their immobility, somberly exploring the town, her sexuality and the family's mystery. But as the film's closed-in, claustrophobic framing and repeated use of close-ups suggest, one can be trapped in many ways — within one's home, by social conventions and gender roles, by love and lovelessness. (MOMA program notes.)

When the aunt's former lover, Cristóbal Achaval (played moodily by Spanish actor Francisco Rabal), discovers the shut-away aunt twenty years later, she dies of shock. Laura discovers both mysteries and ends up with her "hand in the trap," becoming Achaval's mistress without any way out as long as she feels for him and wants him even though this is a possibly incestuous relationship.

There is a wonderful sense of provincial puritanism dispelled by actress Elsa Daniel's heady sensuality. It gives the film, with all its darkness, a breath of fresh air. Elsa Daniel has become expert in playing the "professional virgin" who gives in to a crumbling, decadent Argentine Catholic household, as she did in other Torre Nilsson films, especially *La casa de Ángel*. The mustiness of the film's atmosphere comes through strongly, and we are clearly in Ingmar-

Bergman-cum-Edgar-Allan-Poe country for nearly 91 glorious and glamorous minutes. Curiously, however, the film fails to grab the viewer's emotions, perhaps because it is set in a time and place both long ago and far away.

159. María Antonia. Sergio Giral. Cuba, 1991. 102 min., Color. Spanish.

COMMENTARY: Sergio Giral is one of Cuba's most gifted black directors, and it is amazing to see how his career has spiraled downward after watching his latest release to come from Cuba — a sleazy, sweaty portrait of barrio life with low characters and a melodramatic plot that is hardly worthy of description.

Alina Rodríguez has the title role, a prostitute who reclaims her lover Julián (Alexis Valdéz) after he served time in a local prison. But Julian is more interested in a boxing career and breaks with María. The latter then takes up with a married man who is extremely jealous of Julián. After this man poisons Julián, sets his hotel room on fire and tries to stab María because of her former affair, María goes back to her life as a prostitute, into the bars and pool halls, without one word of redemption or penitence for her murdered lover.

Two interesting notes: The film is evidently set in the fifties, because at a local movie house, they are showing Richard Burton as John Boothe in *Prince of Players*, a 1955 Fox film directed by Philip Dunne in CinemaScope (perhaps Giral's nod to something literary). Also, Daisy Granados, the wonderful Cuban actress with many serious roles on the Cuban screen to her credit, has a shockingly good time by playing a local hooker with the incredible name of Nena Capitolio. One hopes Giral will do something more serious in the late nineties.

160. María Candelaría. Emilio "El Indio" Fernández. Mexico, 1943. 96 min., B&W. Spanish.

COMMENTARY: The first and best of all those native Mexican films by Emilio "El Indio" Fernández, *María Candelaría* is exemplary cinema because of its superb casting, its flawless story, its tight direction and its wonderful cinematography and music score.

Dolores del Río plays María Candelaría with a luminous beauty and humility that intoxicates the audience. She is an Indian peasant who tries to earn a living selling flowers in Xochimílco. She lives in a community that previously had stoned her mother for posing nude for an upper-class bourgeois Mexican portrait painter. María is tainted by her mother's "sinful" behavior, as is her suitor, Lorenzo Rafael (played capably and with great reserve by Pedro Armendáriz), who wants to marry her but cannot afford to buy her a wedding dress from the local town merchant, the cunning Don Damián (Manuel Inclán), who has plans to seduce María for himself. (Fernández's 1948 film *Malclovia* echoes with a similar plot but starred María Félix.)

The film's story is told by the painter (Alberto Galán), entirely in flashback. Because María needs money to live (Don Damián even threatens to take her prize pig), she agrees to pose for "el pintor." When she realizes she has to pose nude, she runs away during the modeling session. The painter uses another body for the painting, unknown to María Candelaría. The latter, believing she has her pride intact, continues working until she is felled by a sudden attack of malaria. Don Damián controls the rationing of quinine necessary to cure her. He refuses to give Lorenzo María's dosage. Lorenzo breaks into the store on a particularly rainy night, steals the quinine (and money and a wedding dress to boot) and saves María's life. Just as they are about

María Candelaría (Dolores del Río) lies dead, stoned by an angry crowd. Beside her sits Lorenzo (Pedro Armendáriz), who literally broke down his cell door to stop the angry mob but to no avail in this scene from Emilio Fernández's *María Candelaría* (1943).

to marry, Damián interrupts, accusing Lorenzo of theft.

María goes back to the artist for financial help, then finally to her priest (played with aching sympathy by Rafael Icardo), who only gives her consolation. What María does not know is that another woman, Lupe (Margarita Cortez), has seen the new "nude" portrait of María and has set all the women of the village against María Candelaría.

In one of the most brilliantly photographed torchlight chase scenes (the mob's pursuit of the Frankenstein monster in James Whales' 1932 film of the same name is the other), we follow María Candelaría's escape over land and canal to the town where Lorenzo Rafael watches her through his jail cell window as she is stoned to death by the ignorant, vicious mob. He bursts through the steel

locks just in time for María Candelaría to die in his arms.

The painter has related this to a woman reporter who has asked why he refuses to sell this particular painting. The story of the entire film is his response and our good fortune.

Once again, the miracle cinematographer Gabriel Figueroa gives the Mexican landscape a participating role in the film, capturing impressively in blacks, whites and greys (along with many other tonalities) the spectacularly beautiful waterways of Xochimílco, even the fragrance of the flowers in the air. He makes Dolores del Río (then about 38 years old) look like a woman of nineteen, dressing her in Indian costumes and capturing the beauty of her bone structure. The skyscapes, with those rolling clouds over the plains, are pure poetry on the screen, brilliantly photographed and aided by the sensitive music score of Francisco Domínguez.

The only things detracting from this viewer's enjoyment are the film's ponderous dialogue and quiescent humility. Sometimes the repetition of names out of respect seems risible, although it was customary and very proper for its era. These minor irritations generally pop up at huge screenings in America. But when *María Candelaría* is shown in a Spanish-speaking country, it is treated reverently, a real classic!

161. María de mi corazón

(**Mary My Dearest**). Jaime Humberto Hermosillo. Mexico, 1983. 100 min., Color. Spanish.

COMMENTARY: Based upon a screenplay co-written by director Hermosillo and Gabriel García Márquez, *María de mi corazón* is one of the most charmingly bizarre films to come out of that sector of independent filmmaking in Mexico in decades. The plot is droll and full of unexpected twists and surprises.

"A petty thief, Hector (Hector Bonilla), has just returned to his apartment and finds María (María Rojo) there, asleep on a couch in a wedding dress. She explains she was jilted, an act that made her realize how much she hurt Hector when she left him. María is a magician by profession and performs at children's parties. She encourages Hector to give up his life of crime and perform with her as a team called Lothario and Eurydice. Renewing their love relationship, they get married, buy a van and prepare to tour.

"Hector has gone on ahead to secure bookings while María follows in their van, which breaks down one rainy night. Searching frantically for a telephone, Maria comes upon a sanitarium. The doctors believe Maria is an inmate because she seems to be ranting just like the lunatics housed there. Hector himself becomes crazed when Maria doesn't show up, believes she left him again and despairs until he finally traces María to the asylum. Hector comes to visit María in his tuxedo and cape as María had sworn he would. He sees her among the insane; the doctors warn him of her funny obsessions like trying to call him on the telephone. María reacts to Hector's visit hysterically. And now her husband begins to really believe that she will begin to lose her mind and so, somewhat sadly, he leaves María there." (Press book.)

The film effectively mixes a somewhat naturalistic, sociological view of everyday Mexican society with some bizarre and fantastic elements that lead to a horrifying if somewhat incredible conclusion. María will be a prisoner for life; she cannot escape. The cruelty and insensitivity of the institution ends up annihilating her. This thought is tremendously disturbing, as are other scenes—like Hector setting María's wedding dress on fire after mistakenly thinking that she walked out on him, or María suffering at the hands of the head nurse, Xochtil, a lesbian transvestite whose cruelties send shivers down one's spine. The film is really part fairy tale, part nightmare. It is Hermosillo's black humor, his penchant for irony and the fantastic as part of reality, that gives the film its cutting edge and makes *María de mi corazón* a gripping experience.

The Maria Soledad Case see *El Caso de María Soledad*

162. El mariachi.

Robert Rodríguez. Mexico/U.S., 1992. 81 min., Color. English/Spanish.

COMMENTARY: The plot of *El mariachi* is deceptively simple, revolving around a case of mistaken identity. The Mariachi (balladeer) of the title arrives in a Mexican border town just as Azul (Reinol Martínez), a vicious thug and

Carlos Gallardo walks down a country road, directed by Ricardo Rodríguez, in *El mariachi* (1992).

drug dealer, escapes from a jail run by corrupt police. Both men are dressed in black and carry guitar cases, though the Mariachi's contains only his guitar while Azul's is an *estuche* (weapons carrier). Azul carries everything, from automatic weapons to brass knuckles. He is bent on exacting revenge because of a double cross perpetrated by the menacing Moco (Peter Marquardt), a drug kingpin and the film's real villain. Moco is a suave drug dealer who always wears white and has his nails filed by a bikini-clad girl-friend at poolside. Moco gives orders to his henchmen to kill Azul on sight, but they mistake the friendly Mariachi (played winningly by Carlos Gallardo) for the gangster. Azul and the Mariachi converge in the only bar in town, run by *femme fatale* Domino (Consuelo Gómez), and it is there that guitar cases are mistakenly swapped and both men realize there are two "Mariachis" in town. To prove his identity to Domino, the real Mariachi sings her a love song he wrote, earning her sympathy, her pro-tection and her love.

The story becomes a chase thriller with amusing jokes. For example, when the Mariachi looks for a singing job, a bartender rolls out an electronic keyboard, his one-man Mariachi. The singer asks, "What happened to the days when Mariachis were gods?" It also becomes a love story. Apparently, Domino is fronting for Moco and is his mistress. But as in all neo-noir films of the nineties, Domino is caught in a shootout, killed intentionally by Moco for her betrayal. Moco also kills Azul in the same scene, and the Mariachi, who has been beaten and wounded, summons up the energy to shoot Moco. He then climbs aboard Domino's motorcycle with her pit bull, remembering the past but declaring, "Now I'm prepared for the future."

Sources say *El mariachi* was made on a bare-bones budget for $7,000. It must have been a labor of love, since the director had total control over the script, editing and production. Apparently Columbia Pictures laid in a new soundtrack and blew it up to 35mm for commercial release, which accounts for the film's graininess in color. Besides being a take-off on film noir conventions, Rodríguez's film has spirit and the advantage of using appealing unknown actors in the principal roles. It is skillfully photographed (there was no money for retakes), although it is visually primitive, having a home-movie look. But the film has wonderful villains, a decorative gun moll, a *femme fatale*, artful camera work (an overuse of zooms and slow-motion), dream sequences and best of all, spirited humor. It is pure pulp, but without being a conventional send-up of noir as is Carl Reiner's 1982 spoof *Dead Men Don't Wear Plaid*. In any case, it certainly entertains. Robert Rodríguez is a Chicano film director on the way up.

NOTES: Robert Rodríguez is a Texan of Mexican extraction. He has been making films since age thirteen, and *El mariachi* is his debut feature. To eke out a budget, he earned $3,000 as a guinea pig in a research hospital and wrote the screenplay during his stay there. Most of the actors in the film are family members, but he recruited Peter Marquardt (Moco) at the hospital. His best friend, Carlos Gallardo, who plays the title role, was a student pal when he and Rodríguez were at a seminary boarding school as teenagers. *El mariachi* was produced by Gallardo and shot in 14 days in Acuna, Mexico, just across the Texas border from Gallardo's hometown. Rodríguez later made a sequel to *El mariachi* entitled *Desperado*, which was released by Columbia Pictures in 1995 and starred Antonio Banderas and Joaquim de Almeida. He also directed a film titled *From Dusk till Dawn* starring the actor-director Quentin Tarantino (of *Pulp Fiction* fame) about two thieves who stumble into a biker bar whose regulars happen to be the "undead."

163. Mariana, Mariana. Alberto Isaac. Mexico, 1987. 110 min., Color. Spanish.

COMMENTARY: Based upon a novel by José Luis Pacheco entitled *Battles in the Desert*, *Mariana, Mariana* is a film about one boy's memory of his best friend's mother and their relationship in Mexico City of the 1940s. The story is told in flashback, as the two grown men, riding in a car, trapped in a traffic jam and the smog of Mexico City, remember the past. The mature Carlos (played by Pedro Armendáriz, Jr., son of the leading Mexican actor of the forties) tells his friend about Mariana (beautifully played by Elizabeth Aguilar).

The film is more successful in the flashbacks because the young Carlos is acted sensitively by Luis Mario Quiróz. Carlos has a schoolboy crush on Mariana, a woman of dubious virtue, rich, the mother of Jim (Juan Carlos Andrews), Carlos' best friend. Apparently Jim is illegitimate and Carlos' parents constantly discourage any association with him or his mother. But Carlos is attracted by the freedom he feels in Jim's presence and begins cutting classes, to the consternation of his bourgeois parents. On one particular day, Carlos climbs over the school wall, goes directly to Jim's house and declares his love for Mariana. We never find out what happens after the declaration scene, but we suspect the ambiguous ending suits the writer, since his real mission is to show how disaffected Carlos is by the double standard he must deal with — one set of rules for children, another for adults who constantly violate their own codes of honor. The film represents a subtle awakening of Carlos in a cryptic, confused, disturbing world — Mexico City circa 1940.

164. Martín Fierro. Leopoldo Torre Nilsson. Argentina, 1967. 136 min., Eastmancolor. Spanish.

COMMENTARY: Basing his story upon the 1872 epic gaucho poem by José Hernández, Torre Nilsson has not filmed a recreation of the original. He has done away with a ponderous narrator and made a straight action film, reportedly over four hours but cut to just over two for commercial release.

Retaining some lines from the original poem into the dialogue, and avoiding the folklore elements of a gaucho-western, Torre Nilsson has made a credible film version of the gaucho epic, with strong visuals and excellent acting, especially by Alfredo Alcón in the title role and Lautaro Murua as Cruz, his friend in arms.

The narrative is basically straightforward. Martín Fierro is a good gaucho, married, the father of two sons, who is drafted into the army to fight against the local Indians in a frontier outpost on the pampas. However, he becomes a farmer-rancher, not a soldier, working for the military commander. Unpaid and kept a prisoner by the army, he deserts and rides home, only to find his ranch in ruins and his family gone. In his search for them he becomes desperate, drunk and gets into a fight with a Negro, whom he kills in self-defense.

Now he is an outlaw, and the military is ready to apprehend him when Cruz, a gaucho turned soldier, helps him escape because he admires Fierro's bravery in fighting. They team up, become friends and kill most of their pursuers. Because they cannot go back to civilization as they know it, they live among the savages, where white men are accepted in a state of barbarism.

Cruz dies, and Fierro decides to return to civilization together with a captive woman he has freed from the Indians. He finds his sons (inexplicably) and is ready to begin life again when he is challenged by the brother of the Negro he killed years before. Fierro has no choice but to fight. He wins again and repeats his life as a fugitive, this time with his sons in tow, as well as the son of Cruz. They realize they must split up or risk capture by the police. So they rendezvous and decide, on horseback, that each man will start riding in a different direction, to the four corners of the pampas.

The color photography by Aníbal di Salvo is glorious. The film's music score by Ariel Ramírez, with additional folkloric sounds from the pampas, is equally impressive. What director Torre Nilsson has done so well is to keep alive the myth and symbol of Martín Fierro — the classic Argentine symbol of rebellion against injustice.

Mary My Dearest see *María de mi corazón*

165. Matar al abuelito (Killing Grandad). Luis César D'Angiolillo. Argentina, 1993. 114 min., Fujicolor. Spanish.

COMMENTARY: *Matar al abuelito* has a plot reminiscent of the kind of 1930 or 1940 American comedy film that has been recycled recently in the United States (Kirk Douglas as a septuagenarian in the 1994 comedy *Greed*) and has now found an audience in Argentina.

The story is quite conventional. Grandad, Don Mariano Aguero (played winningly by Federico Luppi), is a widower, bedridden, ill and miserable since his wife's death. His large family is waiting for him to die to get their inheritance. However, his servant, Ramón (Emilio Bardi), throws a wrench into the entire situation, bringing his stepsister, the luscious Rosita (Inés Estevez), on the scene.

Rosita brings Don Mariano back to life, spending time with him, even slipping into bed with him for an occasional sexual encounter. After several therapeutic sessions, she really falls in love with the old man. To the chagrin of the family, Rosita's therapy brings the old man joy and the possibility of spending his entire bank account. The family members, at that point, plot to get rid of Rosita, who is young enough to be Don Mariano's granddaughter. In an ending very reminiscent of Ridley Scott's *Thelma and Louise*, the couple makes a lyrical escape from the menace of Don Mariano's greedy relatives.

The film is very entertaining, and the casting is perfect. Luppi avoids the Kirk Douglas style of overacting, and Inés Estevez is suitably charming. The family members are all capably acted, and there is a subplot of one granddaughter who has a lesbian lover, making it a very "nineties" script. But the film is still a trifle, with scenes of sex and nudity that will insure its commercial appeal. Although the Kirk Douglas film, *Greed* had Michael J. Fox in the role of his son for box office insurance, the American version flopped badly. Federico Luppi's film should do much, much better.

166. Mauvaise Conduite (Improper Conduct). Nestor Almendros

and Orlando Jiménez-Leal. France, 1984. 110 in., Color. Spanish/French/English.

COMMENTARY: *Mauvaise Conduite* "is an inquiry-film in essay form. Twenty-eight Cuban exiles are interviewed. They often speak in Spanish and sometimes in French. We found them scattered around the world: in Paris, New York, Madrid, Rome, Miami and London. They come from different milieus; we met writers, dancers, painters, doctors, transvestites, workers, students. Two foreigners, former sympathizers of the Cuban revolution, each give an account from the point of view of the outsider. An interview with Fidel Castro, done in Havana in 1979 for French television, serves sometimes as counterpoint." (The directors.)

Mauvaise Conduite is a filmed investigation that sheds light on the Cuban revolution's shadowy side. The film begins in Paris, when ten members of Alicia Alonso's Cuban National Ballet decided to defect. They tell their stories of oppression and Castro's hard line against the "anti-social elements" of the Cuban population.

The most affecting interviews come from the seasoned exiles like gay writer Reinaldo Arenas, imprisoned and now considered a "non-person" despite his international fame as a novelist; poet Armando Valladares, who tells of his 22 years spent in prison and relates an affecting story about a 12-year-old boy, imprisoned for a minor offense, tortured by guards and raped by inmates; novelist Cabrera Infante, who talks about the persecution of homosexuals of both sexes and how hypocritical leader Fidel Castro is married to the revolution, to Cuba, not to the ideal of the bourgeois family. Even Susan Sontag, a former supporter of the revolution, when she became enlightened about the persecution of homosexuals, felt "how much the Left needs to evolve."

Mauvaise Conduite is the best documentary of its kind — an intellectual attack on Fidel Castro's Cuban revolution. It is a rare film and utterly compelling because it shows the contradictions of daily Cuban life, the loss of individuality in a now completely regimented society. It correctly denounces the repression of a regime that clearly deserves to be out of power.

NOTES: Spanish by birth (Barcelona, 1932), Nestor Almendros was a citizen of the world career-wise, although he did spend most of his life in Havana before the onset of the Castro revolution. He had a doctorate from the University of Havana and also studied filmmaking at CCNY, in Rome, later working as a cinematographer before making his own films. His collaborations with François Truffaut, Eric Rohmer, Barbet Schroder and Robert Benton are too numerous to mention. However, it was the 1978 film *Days of Heaven* that confirmed his greatness as a cinematographer and gave him international success. *Mauvaise conduite* (1983) and *Nadie escuchaba* (1988) are the only two films he directed in his long career. He died in 1992.

Orlando Jiménez-Leal was born in Havana in 1941 and began making documentaries when he was fourteen years old. Apart from his collaborations with Nestor Almendros, he is known primarily in America for his 1980 film *El super* and since then has lived in the United States. He continues to make documentary films in America and abroad.

167. El mégano (The Charcoal Worker). Tomás Gutiérrez Alea and Julio García Espinosa. Cuba, 1955. 65 min., B&W. Spanish.

COMMENTARY: Originally made in 16mm, *El mégano* is one of the first socially disturbing short films ever made in Cuba. It was particularly annoying to the Batista regime because, as a social-problem film, it depicted (in the Italian neo-realist style of Rossellini and De-Sica) the miserable working and living conditions of coal miners in northern Cuba. It was a scathing exposé of the exploitation of these miners and stands as a landmark of Cuban social cinema. Its very viewing incites feelings for reform of these incredible living conditions. It aggravated the Batista regime so much that it was confiscated and suppressed. When the Castro regime came to power, the film was revived and its directors so lionized by Castro himself that the dictator was inspired to create ICAIC — the Cuban Institute of Art and Film (El instituto cubano del arte e industria cinematográficos).

168. Memorias del subdesarrollo (Memories of Underdevelopment). Tomás Gutiérrez Alea. Cuba, 1968. 104 min., B&W. Spanish.

COMMENTARY: Based upon the very successful 1967 Edmundo Desnoes novel *Inconsolable Memories*, Alea's film captures the era just before the missile crisis of 1961 and those early years of the onset of the Castro revolution.

Sergio Corrieri plays Sergio, a bourgeois intellectual who elects to stay in Cuba while his family flees to Miami. He lives off the rental of his apartment to the Castro regime and decides to discover his own identity. He reflects on his past, his sexual fantasies about his cleaning lady, his alienated wife, his career, his future as a European intellectual in Castro's Cuba. He seduces a young woman who puts her faith more in the revolution than in Sergio's intellectual pursuits. Accused of rape by her family, Sergio is finally acquitted, then left bereft just as the missile crisis erupts in the country.

There are some interesting moments in the film. For example, Sergio attends a writer's conference, a roundtable of Marxists (including the author Desnoes) who push words back and forth, revealing very little. Sergio says, "Words

Sergio (played by Sergio Corrieri), the bourgeois intellectual, holds a copy of *Lolita* in his hands as he moves through a Havana bookstore in Tomás Gutiérrez Alea's *Memorias del subdesarrollo* (*Memories of Underdevelopment*, 1968).

devour words and leave you in the clouds." Obviously the authors are not up to the ideals of the revolution. Also, Sergio gazes from the balcony of his apartment, a spectator in a land of revolutionaries and counterrevolutionaries, nothing more. This is a privileged moment in the film, which reveals the lack of scrutiny of the screenplay or censorship by the Castro regime because it does not force Sergio to embrace party politics. Sergio is benumbed by the revolution, the missile crisis, by life in general. He seems to play the role of a disaffected outsider. It is strange that Alea, who is committed to the revolution, would choose to make a film about Sergio, the weak intellectual, a doomed species in a new Cuba. Perhaps this is ultimately Alea's message — that there is little room, if any, for individuals, for disaffected intellectuals.

Memories of Underdevelopment
see *Memorias del subdesarrollo*

169. Mentiras piadosas
(White Lies / Love Lies). Arturo Ripstein. Mexico, 1988. 110 min., Eastmancolor. Spanish.

COMMENTARY: Israel Ordóñez (Alonso Echanové), the owner of a small business, is married and the father of three children. He works with Matilde (Ernesto Yáñez), a well-known homosexual artist who is bent on building a mechanical exhibit of store dummies with Mexican costumes. Israel then meets Clara (Delia Casanova), a health inspector who comes to fine the grocer for some violations; later, she thinks she has found the love of her life. Israel and Clara abandon their families to live together in an apartment under the store. But their relationship is troubled immediately by their lack of trust. Matilde, who now lives with Israel and Clara, watches them fight violently — Always against the backdrop of old, unsentimental, yet beloved Mexico City. Clara and Israel are both torn by guilt, and Israel becomes pathologically jealous of Clara. They are forced to separate but make plans for the future in their now bleak *ménage*.

The film is always on the razor's edge between the sublime and the ridiculous. Ripstein's pathetic, but moving characters cling to the little they have. Thus *Mentiras piadosas* is a lucid metaphor of what Mexican cinema is today. It's a tale of little people whose only hope lies in the cards and each other — and even then, the deck is stacked against them.

Ripstein himself said that these films "deal with survivors. These are characters that are very dear.... To observe things which happen around a person, which move and motivate them — that is the way to a clear understanding. I make films about things that fascinate me, and there are so many things that fascinate me here that I sometimes feel like a stranger." (MOMA Program Notes.)

Mexican Bus Ride see *Subida al cielo*

170. Mi querido Tom Mix

(My Dear Tom Mix). Carlos García Agraz. Mexico, 1991. 120 min., Color. Spanish.

COMMENTARY: Agraz built this comedy-adventure, his first feature, around the character of an old lady in love with a screen idol. Set in rural northern Mexico in the 1930s, the film stars veteran actress Ana Ofelia Murguía as the sexagenarian Joaquina, who lives with her nephew, a small-town doctor (Manuel Ojeda), and his wife. Joaquina sneaks out to see Tom Mix at the local cinema, writes fan letters to him and imagines him riding through town on his white horse. At one point, the rural population is threatened by local bandits. So Joaquina sends for Tom Mix. Instead, an aging cowboy drifter (Federico Luppi), who is on the side of law and order, comes riding into town to right the wrongs of marauding bandits.

Luppi's acting is broad, especially in the gun-drawing scene in front of a mirror. "Are ya talkin to me?" he says, somewhat comically, looking into the camera. Luppi is the hottest Argentine actor of the nineties, playing all these "older man" roles to the hilt. Despite an unthreatening kidnapping scene with Joaquina as the victim, the film ends happily. Like many newer films from Mexico, it is keenly aware of the cinema idols of the past and uses them adroitly.

171. Milagros en Roma

(Miracles in Rome). Lisandro Duque Naranjo. Colombia, 1988. 80 min., Color. Spanish.

COMMENTARY: Based upon a short story by García Márquez entitled "The Long Happy Life of Margarito Duarte," this Colombian film is a charming rendition of a fantastic tale.

The plot is modest for a García Márquez short story. Margarito Duarte (Frank Ramírez), a modest employee of the local court in a small Colombian town, suddenly loses his seven-year-old daughter, Evilia (Amalia Duque García), who had never been ill one day in her life. Twelve years later, he exhumes the body and discovers the cadaver intact. She looks as young as the day she was buried, although the coffin is rotted all around her. The townspeople are so moved that the local bishop (played by Santiago García) orders the body to be interred once again.

The townspeople, however, declare Evilia a saint and send the father and daughter to Rome for a blessing called the "Miracle of the First Colombian Saint." Completely alone, Margarito braves the international flight with his daughter in tow as "carry-on luggage." (There is a comical luggage x-ray scene by Vatican security.) But basically, Margarito is dignified, waiting for his papal interview, confronting the fate of the Pope's decision as he too must deal with astute politicians, diplomats and police officials who want to cash in on Evilia's sainthood.

It is a very moral tale, full of human interest and pathos and charmingly played by the entire cast.

Miracles in Rome see *Milagros en Roma*

172. Miroslava. Alejandro Pelayo Rangel. Mexico, 1992. 100 min., Color and B&W. Spanish.

COMMENTARY: Miroslava Stern (1930–1955) was a leading actress known primarily in Mexico for her role in Luis Buñuel's 1955 film *Ensayo de un crimen*. She was seen in America in Robert Rossen's 1951 film *The Brave Bulls* and Jacques Tourneur's 1955 western *Stranger on Horseback*, but although by age 25 she had appeared in 27 films, her career quickly evaporated because she had no real star power. She committed suicide in 1955. She was 25 years old.

Miroslava, Rangel's fourth documentary, is a biography of this troubled star. The director speculates on her past, her family's escape from Czechoslovakia and the Nazi threat. Troubled by the deaths of her mother and grandmother (because of cancer and the war), she cannot seem to find love easily. After a failed first marriage, an affair with bullfighter Luis Dominguín leads her to depression and suicide.

Miroslava, who always projected a serious and sweet image, is played in this film by French actress Arielle Dombasle, who captures the doomed actress's personality, replicating the cold surfaces that were always apparent in the real actress' films. One wonders why the director chose to elevate Miroslava to the pantheon of "famous" Mexican actresses, unless he was fascinated by her Jewishness or her star appeal. She remains, sadly, a minor constellation in both the Hollywood and Mexican heavens.

173. Miss Mary. María Luisa Bemberg. Argentina, 1986. 100 min., Color.

COMMENTARY: In a luxurious house in Buenos Aires, two little girls, Carolina and Teresa, are saying their prayers with Miss Mary, their English governess, before going to bed. Their parents come into the bedroom to wish them good night before going to a party in honor of the military *coup d'état* of 1930, which overthrew the constitutional government of Argentine president Yrigoyen.

The next scene opens on October 16, 1945, and Miss Mary (played winningly by English actress Julie Christie) is in her bedroom in Buenos Aires. She is about 45 years old and dressed with simplicity. While she is arranging her belongings in a trunk, voices shouting, "¡Viva Perón!" can be heard through the window. She has read in a newspaper the announcement of Teresa's wedding when she had just arrived from England to live with the family who just hired her as the governess of their children.

In flashbacks, Miss Mary, newly arrived from England, acclimates herself in the huge English-style house to the everyday life of the aristocratic family with whom she will live while she works as their governess. Carolina, Teresa and Johnny (Donald McIntire) are the children of Alfredo, a "father figure," strict and authoritative. His wife, Mecha, is melancholic and submissive. Ernesto, Mecha's brother, is a fascist who marks on the map the victories and defeats of General Franco during the Spanish civil war. The grandparents live totally isolated from the rest of their family in their world of memories.

At the end of the day, Miss Mary writes a letter to her mother in England, and she invents for her a colorful world that doesn't exist. As she weeps with loneliness, Johnny watches her through a window.

Once again in the present (1945), Miss Mary has a brief conversation with the doorman. He warns her about the tense political situation in the country. The workers want the freedom of Colonel Perón, who has been detained by the military forces associated with the oligarchy.

Miss Mary remembers again the party for the Catholic missions organized by Mecha on the estate, where numerous large ceremonies like baptisms, weddings and first holy communions took place in the past. In a flashback to the party, Perla (Lucinda Brando) is introduced. She is the widow of a rich rancher and former manicurist of the exclusive Jockey Club. That night, Perla is overcome by the seduction of Alfredo, and Mecha clumsily fires a gun several times at them, scaring the children. Miss Mary tries to calm them down, and at that moment, Carolina asks, "Do you think my family is crazy? Do you think we have enough money?"

Returning to 1945, Miss Mary attends Teresa's wedding. During the ceremony, Johnny is the only one who recognizes her, and she discreetly gives him her card.

Johnny visits Miss Mary in her apartment. While having tea, he tells her about the life of the family members during the past seven years. Teresa had been found making love for the first time to a young man she doesn't love and had to marry to save the family honor. Carolina is currently under psychiatric treatment because she couldn't subjugate her rebellious personality to all the social conventions with which she had to live.

Johnny got married and is an officer in the marines.

Meanwhile, the intimate climate that is created on this occasion becomes tense, almost unbearable. Miss Mary and Johnny come back to the same memory — when Johnny turned 15. His uncle Ernesto gave him a "present": He took him to the village brothel for his sexual initiation. After having completed his "male obligation," Johnny comes back to the house in a rainstorm. The car gets stuck on the road, and he has to walk back home. Covered with mud and with tears in his eyes, he suddenly walks into Miss Mary's bedroom. Then a beautiful scene takes place where the desire and the strict moral beliefs of the governess fight against each other in a battle that ends in a very touching, lovely moment.

Johnny's mother, Mecha, discovers what has happened the next morning and fires Miss Mary, while the children, locked in the bathroom by their mother, call her name. They never see Miss Mary again and assume she left for England.

At this point, Miss Mary and Johnny return to the present from the joint memory of the past. Timidly, Johnny reminds Miss Mary of the emotions they shared that night, but Miss Mary severely cuts him off. They part forever. Later, Miss Mary's trunk is loaded by a crane in the Buenos Aires harbor aboard a transatlantic ship. Simultaneously, a new page in Argentina's history begins: the era of Juan Perón. (Press book.)

Julie Christie gives a wonderful performance as Miss Mary, modulated, subtle, well-defined, strong, cool, respectable and appealing. She shows her compassion for the family, which is mainly obsessed with problems of honor and appearances. But the director's interest is not Miss Mary's story. María Luisa Bemberg uses the screenplay only as a ploy to present the historical panorama of Argentina from 1930 to 1945,

Jack Lemmon rehearses a scene from *Missing* (1982) with Sissy Spacek and director Constantine Costa-Gavras standing behind her.

recreating the costumes and mores of the era that led to the ascension of Juan Perón as Argentine president. It seems that the director couldn't make up her mind whether to tell Miss Mary's story or recreate the history of Argentina, resulting in a kind of opaque film.

Also the film suffers from faults in continuity and an excessive amount of flashbacks and flashforwards that tend to confuse the viewer. Except for some brief scenes of nudity and profanity, the beautifully technicolored film offers little to afford, but also little in the way of political insight into the era and its people. It is just a tender story about memories — a recreation of the past, not an American past like *Summer of '42*, but an Argentine past as seen through the eyes of an English governess. Though

Julie Christie is ever the consummate actress, it seems the director of *Camila* has lost the cutting edge of her feminist wit, humor and passion which she so amply displayed earlier in her career.

174. Missing. Constantine Costa-Gavras. Chile/U.S., 1982. 122 min., Color. English.

COMMENTARY: Inspired by a real event, the disappearance of Charlie Horman in Chile, director Costa-Gavras reveals the participation of the United States in the *coup d'état* that brought Salvador Allende to power in 1973. It is a piercing, factually based drama about American-sanctioned political atrocities in post–Allende Chile. Conceived as a political thriller, the film is a powerfully corrosive indictment of fascism and the

Jesuit priest Father Gabriel (Jeremy Irons) leads the Guaraní Indians in prayer as they resist Portuguese troops in *The Mission* (1986).

collusion of the American government, which places the interests of business over the protection of individual citizens. The film also affirms the need of international human rights groups to be aware of political acts that engender dire consequences — in this case, the probable death of Charlie Horman.

Although the film was made essentially on Mexican locations, by a director based in Greece and Paris, and produced with American backing by Universal Pictures, the atmosphere of the film is achingly Chilean. Jack Lemmon plays the role of his life as the Christian Scientist father who steadfastly believes in the American way until he comes to terms with the realities of American bureaucracy and his son's probable death. (The real Ed Horman sued Henry Kissinger and other United States officials for complicity in his son's death, but to no avail.) Sissy Spacek plays the role of Charlie Horman's wife, convinc-

ingly searching with his father for her husband's remains. But it is John Shea as Charlie, seen in flashbacks as an American writer sticking his nose where it doesn't belong, who is remembered long after the film ends, because it was at the cost of his life that American involvement in the Chilean coup was discovered and revealed to the world. *Missing* is driving, chillingly dramatic, political cinema at its best.

NOTES: Born in 1933, Costa-Gavras has always made successful, politically oriented suspense thrillers. In 1965, he made his debut with the French film *The Sleeping Car Murders* with Yves Montand. *The Confession* (1970), *Z* (1972), *State of Siege* (1972, which dealt with the Pinochet regime), *Special Section* (1975), *Missing* (1982) and *The Music Box* (1990) are among his best political thrillers.

175. The Mission. Roland Joffe.
United Kingdom/Colombia, Argentina,

Paraguay, Brazil, 1986. 128 min., Color and CinemaScope. English/Spanish/Portuguese.

COMMENTARY: Set in 1750 when Portugal and Spain were arguing over the territorial boundaries along the Parana River at Iguazú, the story is mainly about Father Gabriel (forcefully played by Jeremy Irons), who establishes a mission in the rain forest as a refuge for native Indians. The mission becomes their sanctuary, where they are educated in letters and religion, treated for illness and shown respect for their own cultures. Robert De Niro is cast in the unlikely role of Mendoza, a Portuguese slave trader who abducts Indians at will for profit. Having just killed his brother (Aidan Quinn) for seducing his girlfriend, Mendoza does penance, carrying a huge cross up river to Father Gabriel's mission, helping the latter build and establish himself further in the rain forest. Mendoza and Father Gabriel are caught in a political vortex. Both the Spaniards and Portuguese want the lands claimed by the Jesuits to establish their boundaries; both countries want to continue the slave trade and diminish the power of the Jesuits. The action of the film culminates in the destruction of the mission by fire and the deaths of Father Gabriel and Mendoza, the former slave trader turned postulate.

Written by playwright Robert Bolt and photographed by Chris Menges with a richly symphonic score by Ennio Morricone, *The Mission* cost over $23 million to make. Sixteen weeks were spent in Colombia on location shooting, and three weeks were devoted exclusively to photographing the rivers and cataracts of Iguazú. The glory of the film rests in its photography. It is as stunning visually as Herzog's *Aguirre* or *Fitzcarraldo* and Babenco's *At Play in the Fields of the Lord*. The most memorable and remarkable scene occurs at the opening of the film when a priest, strapped to a cross,

is sent over Iguazú Falls as an act of martyrdom (or insanity) by the Indians. The firing of the mission, like Babenco's scene of destruction of the Indian village after an epidemic, is equally thrilling. *The Mission* captures the feeling of the eighteenth century visually, as well as in tongue and in spirit. If it was supposed to be spiritually uplifting or proselytizing for the Catholic church, it missed its mark on this point. Above all, it is a physically impressive picture, scenically stunning, though curiously uninvolving emotionally.

NOTES: Roland Joffe is an English director, born in Manchester in 1945. He is skilled at location shooting, and his films usually have some kind of documentary background. He has worked in Vietnam for *The Killing Fields* (1984), South America for *The Mission* (1986) and India for *City of Joy* (1992).

Mr. President see *El señor presidente*

176. Modelo Antiguo (Classic Model). Raúl Araiza. Mexico, 1992. 95 min., Color. Spanish.

COMMENTARY: The program notes call this one a "three-handkerchief melodrama about a lonely upper-class woman who gives romantic advice on the radio." That description offers little insight into the woman herself, Carmen (lovingly played by Silvia Pinal, Buñuel's favorite actress in the 1961 *Viridiana*), who has just learned she has one month to live. She leaves her job and rides around in her fifties-vintage Cadillac, the "classic model" of the title, and reexamines her life, her memories that we see in flashback, about her incestuous love for her brother which caused multiple family suicides and resulted in her inheriting a small fortune. (Director Raúl Araiza was wise to use another actress, Stephanie Salas, to play the "young" Pinal character of Carmen. He also uses his own son to play Gabriel, her handsome brother.) Now, while riding around, Carmen meets a cab driver named Juan (played in macho fashion by Alonso Echanové) who falls in love with her and abandons his sexy, young girlfriend, Laura (Daniela Durán). The two of them, the dying radio advice expert and the lowly cabbie, fall in love and spend their days together in her car, visiting museums, four-star restaurants, salsa clubs, the night life of Mexico City. The film comes to an abrupt ending with the death of Carmen, unexpected by all except the audience. Pinal plays the role with excessive melodramatics and nostalgia for the past. Like Bette Davis in *Dark Victory* or Susan Hayward in *Back Street*, Carmen nobly faces the grim reaper. Even in an unabashedly slurpy tearjerker like this one, it is always a pleasure to watch the talented Silvia Pinal on the screen, who has aged gracefully and is still a vision of charm and loveliness — the perfect actress to give life to the role of a dying radio star.

177. Mojado Power (Wetback Power). Alfonso Arau. Mexico, 1980. 90 min., B&W. Spanish.

COMMENTARY: More than ten years before achieving international fame as a leading Mexican film director with the 1991 release *Como agua para chocolate*, Alfonso Arau made *Mojado Power*. Considered a satirical, socially appropriate film about illegal immigrants in the United States, it did not have the same impact of Gregorio Nava's *El norte* which preceded it by three years.

Mojado Power combines comedy, music and political satire in order to reflect on the sudden changes of fortune of an immigrant mechanic who goes to work in Los Angeles, dealing with conditions of discrimination and margination that he suffers along with other Mexicans who try to cross the United States border illegally. It is a funny film,

full of humor about a humorless subject. Imagine seeing a humorous version of *El norte*!

The film stars director Alfonso Arau as Neto, a wise-guy Chicano, whose almost picaresque adventures we follow from Mexico to Los Angeles, where he takes up residence and begins to explode because of all the discrimination against him and his fellow immigrants. He creates a solidarity movement and gathers his fellow *mojados* under a banner that reads, "Mojado Power." But the Mexicans are not organized enough even to support Neto's minor show of strength. However, the Americans grab him for dealing drugs, a trumped-up charge to get rid of the protester, and Neto is returned to Mexico. There he is thrown into jail for the same false crime, and all continues to go badly for Neto; he has to fight off a rival prisoner who has unified his own gang under a banner that reads, "Chicano Power."

Intercut into the film are various songs and dances which serve the plot and accentuate the political slant of the film. Arau as director mixes humor with drama, satire with emotion. The fact that a Mexican actor-director could make a humorous film about a serious situation is the most revealing aspect of *Mojado Power* and makes it deserving of wider distribution.

The Mole see *El topo*

Muddy Waters see *Las aguas bajan turbias*

178. Muerte al amanecer (Death at Dawn). Francisco José Lombardi. Peru/Venezuela, 1977. 113 min., Eastmancolor. Spanish.

COMMENTARY: Dealing with the theme of capital punishment, *Muerte al amanecer* tells the story of a drifter suspected of the serial killing of young children in a small Peruvian town. We watch the man's speedy trial, his imprisonment and finally his execution in a harsh island prison, where inexperienced guards, scheming politicos, unctuous civil servants, nosy reporters and vulgar wardens gather for the event. As the victim goes down screaming he is innocent, the film makes a plea for the end of capital punishment. Gustavo Rodríguez, William Moreno and Jorge Rodríguez turn in credible performances.

179. La muerte de un burócrata (Death of a Bureaucrat). Tomás Gutiérrez Alea. Cuba, 1966. 84 min., B&W. Spanish.

COMMENTARY: A repairman dies in an accident while working and is buried with his labor card as a symbol of his proletarian condition. When his widow goes to secure her pension, they demand the dead man's card. A duplicate cannot be made unless the worker is present, so it is necessary to disinter the body. But this is only possible two years after the burial.

The widow's nephew tries to solve this problem by hiring several grave-diggers, who perform a clandestine exhumation in order to retrieve the dead man's labor card. But now the nephew's biggest problem is to have the body buried again. He goes to many offices and argues with a lot of bureaucrats; little by little, he realizes these obstacles will lead him to an act of violence or turpitude.

Finally, a bureaucrat's death provides a solution. The bureaucrat's burial procession and his uncle's will cross paths on the way to the cemetery. At last, with a switch of bodies, the repairman will find eternal peace. (Press book.)

La muerte de un burócrata is a high-spirited, somewhat quirky, satirical comedy whose target is the red tape that can strangle a society — in this case, Castro's revolutionary Cuban society. Ironically, the dead man is a pseudo-sculptor and

inventor, whose machine (which killed him) turns out mass-produced busts of national hero José Martí. (They used to call him the "poor man's Michelangelo.") Another gag-fest is the slapstick custard-pie-and-flowers battle that takes place at the cemetery when the nephew tries to bury his uncle without the proper forms and the officials start to dismantle the hearse of the undertaker. Alea is a student of American cinema and adept at using comic examples from Laurel and Hardy, Harold Lloyd and the Three Stooges. For example, there is also a scene on a narrow ledge in front of a large clock high above the street as well as the eternal banana peel to be stepped on — farce *de rigueur*. The way the nephew deals with bureaucracy echoes many similar incidents in the films of Ingmar Bergman and Luis Buñuel.

The acting by all parties is extremely adroit. Salvador Wood plays the nephew, harrassed constantly as he travels from one bureaucrat's office to another without satisfaction. Silvia Planas is perfect as the poor widow trapped by red tape. But the honors go to the director, Alea, who, somewhat in the manner of Hal Roach, has produced a film whose lunatic comedy scenes dispel the outrage of a society choked by functionaries.

180. Muerte de un magnate (Death of a Tycoon). Francisco José Lombardi. Peru, 1980. 112 min., Color. Spanish.

COMMENTARY: Few crime films come from Peru, and *Muerte de un magnate* is perhaps not the best example of the director's style. Nevertheless it has performances by Orlando Sacha, Marthe Figueroa, Pablo Tezen and Hernando Cortés that are worthwhile in the context of the film.

The nub of the plot is this: an Indian boy working for a tycoon is jealous of his mistresses, his wealth, his position, his handsome figure. The son of the

Tomás Gutiérrez Alea, director of *La muerte de un burócrata* (*Death of a Bureaucrat*, 1966).

magnate's caretaker, he wants to have it all — the material benefits, the sex affairs, the power of the tycoon, the possessions, even a face-lift. After stealing money from the tycoon, the Indian lad comes upon the man himself and his mistress-secretary. He proceeds to rape the secretary and kill the tycoon, then goes to his room to await the police.

The film is apparently based upon a real event in which the secretary and Indian boy were in the plot together (each received six years in jail for the tycoon's murder). Director Lombardi had no political intentions in churning out this crime film for the Peruvian audience. Although it is suggested that the tycoon is not in touch with his workers and that his interests may be "nationalized" by the government, he comes off as a cardboard stereotype, as do all the characters ex-

cept the Indian boy, who displays real terror in the killing scenes and twisted emotion as he retreats into his introverted personality waiting for justice.

181. El muerto (**The Dead One**). Hector Olivera. Argentina, 1975. 105 min., Color. Spanish.

COMMENTARY: Based upon a wonderful short story by Argentine novelist Jorge Luis Borges, *El muerto* is about a man, Ortalora (Juan José Camero), who flees Buenos Aires after killing another man in a knife duel. He looks for refuge in Montevideo and joins a gang of smugglers led by Bandeira (Francisco Rabal). They smuggle cattle and weapons, but Ortalora is not satisfied. He wants to take over the gang, Bandeira's henchmen and his mistress. After letting him think he has succeeded, Bandeira has Ulpiano

Julio Alemán and Sandra Riva hold their son (Raúl Martín) as he writhes in pain from a snake bite in Armando Robles Godoy's *La muralla verde* (*The Green Wall*, 1969).

(Antonio Iranzo) kill the ambitious Ortalora, who becomes "the dead one."

It is Francisco Rabal's performance that makes the film an absolute delight. A seasoned Spanish actor, Rabal has just the right amount of charm, wit and intelligence to play an old man who is still master in games of power. The short story has been opened out considerably, with wonderful cinematography in new and exotic locales — the landscapes of Tacuarembo (northern Uruguay). The percussion score by Ariel Ramírez also lends a lot to the ambiance of the film. *El muerto* is even available on video for students of Borges and Olivera.

NOTES: Director Hector Olivera was born in Buenos Aires in 1931 and has worked in the Argentine film industry since 1947. With producer Fernando Ayala, he co-founded the company Aries Cinematográfica in 1956 and has made a wide variety of films into the nineties. His most popular ones are *La Patagonia rebelde* (1974), *Los viernes de eternidad* (1981), *No habrá más penas ni olvido* (1983), and *La noche de los lápices* (1986). He continues to live and work in Buenos Aires.

182. Una mujer sin amor (A Woman Without Love). Luis Buñuel. Mexico, 1951. 85 min., B&W. Spanish.

COMMENTARY: Considered by many a melodramatic potboiler, the film is actually one of the better efforts of Luis Buñuel during his "Mexican" period. The film is an adaptation of Guy de Maupassant's story "Pierre et Jean" and is essentially a story of a young wife's betrayal of her middle-aged husband. The wife, Rosario (Rosario Granados), falls in love with an engineer, Julio Mistral (Tito Junco). They consummate their affair, but she will not leave her husband, the antique dealer Don Carlos Montero (Julio Villaroel). Twenty-five years later, one of Don Montero's sons, Carlos (Joaquín Cordero), is left a fortune by a rich Argentinian, which creates all sorts of problems for the family. Don Montero reminisces over his old friend who saved little Carlitos from drowning at a dam site. Carlos, now grown, realizes he is illegitimate and calls his mother a prostitute. The inheritance tears the family apart, creating all sorts of jealousies between Carlos and his other brother Miguel (Javier Loya). Unbelievably, all the threads of the plot weave into a happy ending. When the mother becomes a widow, the sons realize their foolishness as Rosario secretly looks at an old photograph of Julio, her lover, now dead. She has loved and lost twice, she thinks as she clutches her crucifix and Bible and remains completely dressed in black in the closing shot of the film.

One cannot take this soap opera really seriously, but it does show a world of inverted values — where immorality is morality and the only heroes are the anti-heroes, the constructive characters with their feet on the ground, like the engineer who dies alone. But passion has no place in the bourgeois world of Rosario, and we suffer with her as she returns to her prison while her children replicate the sins of their parents.

We would have adored watching Bette Davis or Joan Crawford or Ann Sheridan play the role of Rosario. The film resembles that 1940 Bette Davis tearjerker directed by Anatole Litvak called *All This and Heaven Too* where Davis does not even get to consummate her love for Charles Boyer and goes back to her cage of "schoolmarm." The same spirit of pointless rebellion encases

Rosario at the conclusion of *Una mujer sin amor*.

183. Mujer transparente (Transparent Woman). Hector Veitia/Mayra Segura/Mayra Valasi/Mario Crespo/Ana Rodríguez. Cuba, 1991. 100 min., B&W. Spanish.

COMMENTARY: Essentially this is a compilation film about five women. Each short tale is directed in the descending order of the director's names that appear above, giving us five different views of the modern Cuban woman.

"Isabel" is the story of a mother who has lived for her children and has finally rebelled. "Adriana" is about a spinster who has lived alone since the revolution until she is visited unexpectedly by a telephone repairman. "Julia" is about a woman whose husband deserts her for another woman. Disconcerted, Julia herself takes another lover but would prefer the return of her husband. "Zoe" is about an alienated art student who lures a conservative classmate into bed. "Laura" deals with the problems of exiles as the title character tries to renew a friendship begun some fifteen years earlier. She is ignored by the hotelier in favor of foreign tourism.

The entire film is fascinating in conception, and in the aggregate, it shows a different kind of Cuban woman, with human foibles, not the "revolutionary" types we expect or have seen before in those agit-prop films of the seventies and eighties. What this viewer liked most was the ambiguity of the endings in several of the stories. The film is essentially a showcase for the five young Cuban directors represented. We hope they do well in feature presentations. Their short films do show that they are not without talent.

184. La muralla verde (The Green Wall). Armando Robles Godoy. Peru, 1969. 110 min., Eastmancolor. Spanish.

COMMENTARY: A young couple in the Peruvian jungle, Delba (Sandra Riva) and Mario (Julio Alemán), tenderly embrace beneath their mosquito netting, listening to the pelting rains while their six-year-old son, Rómulo (played by Raúl Martín), sleeps in a nearby nook of their cabin.

After the stormy night, the new day opens with events that threaten their dreams and their fortune. Their calm is challenged by surveyors who tell Mario that the Land Reform Commission is planning changes in the area that will affect the property — a patch of cleared jungle that, after six years of struggle and discouragement, is finally beginning to have some real significance.

After chasing the surveyors off his land, Mario leaves his wife and son and starts the long journey through the jungle towards the neighboring city of Tingo María to straighten matters out. As he treks along, his thoughts flash back to his beginnings as a salesman in Lima, his courtship and amorous moments with Delba, his burning desire to escape from the big city, and the red tape he had to cut through in order to get a land grant in the jungle.

To complicate matters, on the same day, the president of Peru, who is on tour of the region, is scheduled to arrive in Tingo María. Preparations for his arrival are apparent everywhere, and Mario's mission is of little consequence in the flurry of all this excitement.

Meanwhile, Delba is going about her household chores, and Rómulo is playing in a miniature village complete with waterwheel that Mario built over the stream near the house. As Rómulo occupies himself with his toy city, Delba's thoughts turn to earlier days — the joys of her courtship with Mario, their wedding night, her fears of the jungle and its strangeness and the moment of ecstasy when finally they were in each other's arms

on a piece of land they could call their own.

Suddenly, her happy dreams are shattered when Rómulo is bitten by a venomous snake. Delba races towards Tingo María with the child. As they reach the town, Mario spots them and they rush Rómulo to the hospital.

At the hospital, they are told that the director, who has a new antivenin under lock and key, is at a reception for the president and Mario fights his way through the crowds, finally reaching the director. They get back, the serum is administered — but too late.

The next morning, Delba and Mario silently begin their journey to Rómulo's final resting place: the burial grounds at the end of the river, reached by canoe. Word of Rómulo's passing has reached the children of the other settlers along the river bank, and one by one, in their canoes, they form a funeral cortege accompanying Delba and Mario down river.

When they reach home, Delba dazedly carries on with her household chores. Meanwhile Mario's attention is drawn to a strange tinkling sound which he discovers comes from the watermill in Rómulo's toy village. After Mario's departure for the city, Rómulo had hung a broken glass over the wheel, which the wheel strikes with each full turn, creating a melancholy, haunting sound.

Full of rage, Mario kicks the wheel, wrecks the mill and breaks down. Some time later he realizes the damage he has done and what he has silenced. Slowly he begins to repair the mill. At last he returns to the house with the melancholy sound from the water wheel tinkling in the quiet of the jungle as night falls.

Mario is sitting at the table, and soon Delba places her hand on his shoulder and falls into his arms. Without a word, they embrace. Their life will go on, as the water will keep flowing in the stream and Rómulo's mill will keep turning. (Press book.)

La muralla verde was the first film from Peru to gain attention in America because it is based partially on some real experiences of the director and his wife who, twenty years earlier, tried to break down the "green wall" of the jungle to homestead. Robles Godoy has presented his viewers with a lush setting, rich with the realities of people's lives, making the film a pure pleasure to watch. The family's tragedy is touching. And the director shows us the threatening snake early on, traveling towards the small boy until Rómulo is finally bitten. He uses flashbacks and intermingles them within the thoughts of his characters in present time. Although many observers of the film may attribute these shifts in time to the director's sense of style, the somewhat rambling structure is necessary to provide background and impel the forward action of the film, whose plot is really quite minimal.

Robles Godoy uses his camera wonderfully, with close-ups that intimidate and zoom shots that focus in on the action. His use of filters colors our emotions during certain scenes, and freeze frames augment the horror of Rómulo's death as he cries out soundlessly. The director also made interesting use of source music, mostly Bach, to bring a modicum of "civilization" into a jungle setting. The Mexican actor Julio Alemán was perfectly cast in a film that otherwise included only Peruvian professionals. His co-star, Sandra Riva, provided the right blend of sensuality and motherliness. Even the little boy, Rómulo, played by Raúl Martín, was perfectly cast, trying to keep up with his parents but defenseless against the dark threats of the jungle.

The film cost some $200,000 to make and took fourteen weeks to shoot. The director reconstructed the home he and his wife lived in during the fifties for the *ménage* of principal actors. The jungle scenes were photographed superbly by Gianfranco Annichini, who also caught the horrors of the "urban" jungle in his shots of Lima. The film has been a prizewinner internationally and deserves worldwide distribution. It is still timely, since human beings will always struggle with their environment.

NOTES: Born in 1923, Armando Robles Godoy has worked mainly as a director in Peruvian cinema since the mid-sixties. He was a short story writer, journalist and even a film critic before he went into filmmaking. He began making documentaries but is internationally known for *La muralla verde*, his third film. Titles of his other films are *Ganarás el pan* (1965), *En la selva no hay estrellas* (1966) and *Espejismo* (1973). Although he spent the first ten years of his life in New York City, he makes his home in Peru and continues to film there, making documentaries and features for television.

185. El muro de silencio
(The Wall of Silence). Luis Alcoriza. Mexico, 1976. 100 min., Color. Spanish.

COMMENTARY: "Regina, who is nearly thirty, lives in a provincial Mexican city with her son, Daniel, the product of an unhappy love affair with a married man who was killed in an auto accident. Daniel's father had not allowed Regina to legalize their union, nor had he recognized Daniel as his son. Regina's fortunes are worsened by local gossip, murmurings and prejudices of a small, vulgar, hypocritical society. She even loses her job as a teacher in the local school and has to set up a shop as a seamstress to earn her living.

"Fearing that the townspeople's dislike would harm her son, Regina decides to educate him herself at home. Meanwhile, she keeps herself beautiful, and another man starts courting her. Although she falls in love with him, she rejects him, realizing her son does not want her to belong to anyone but him.

"The years go by, and Regina's overwhelming love for her son ends up practically destroying him. To keep from being possessed by his mother, Daniel tries to find the answers to his cloistered existence in his own world. However, he finds nothing but a tissue of lies and loneliness.

"Daniel finally becomes a totally insensitive being. Not even does he go to his mother's aid when she, stricken by a heart attack, calls out to him in anguish. He is no longer affected by anything. Mother love has destroyed him." (Press book.)

The film stars Fabiola Falcón in her debut role as Regina and Brontis Jodorowsky as Daniel. Claudio Brook played Marcos, Daniel's deceased father. All the actors are capable in this Mexican potboiler of the seventies. You could not ask for a more melodramatic situation between mother and son. Regina's death scene recalls a contorted version of Herbert Marshall's demise in William Wyler's 1941 film *The Little Foxes*, where Bette Davis (who played a southern belle also named Regina) pretends not to notice as husband Marshall collapses on a staircase, begging for medicine for his angina.

Whenever we watch a film by Luis Alcoriza, we are generally in for florid melodrama. Alcoriza, a native Spaniard, made his career in Mexican cinema, preferring to excel in this type of film rather than the neo-realist films with which he began his career such as *Tiburoneros* (*Shark Fishermen*) (1962). *El muro de silencio* is his usual product: melodrama without art.

NOTES: Luis Alcoriza was born in Badajoz, Spain, in 1920 and died a Mexican citizen in 1992. He began his career as a European stage actor and became a lead in Mexican films. However, his claim to fame is as scriptwriter for Luis Buñuel, his compatriot. Together they had a wonderful collaboration which produced nine glorious films, from *El gran calavera* (1949) to *El ángel exterminador* (1962), all directed by Buñuel. He usually wrote his own scenarios for the films he directed after he ended his association with Buñuel. They are all melodramas. His last film, *Lo que importa es vivir* (1989), was made a few years before his death. Alcoriza directed several films in Spain but none with real distinction.

My Dear Tom Mix see *Mi querido Tom Mix*

186. La nación clandestina
(**The Secret Nation**). Jorge Sanjinés. Bolivia, 1989. 125 min., Color. Spanish/Aymara.

COMMENTARY: *La nación clandestina* is photographed and directed in the same style as *Yawar mallku*, and the director reworks a great number of the themes that have appeared in his early films. In flashbacks, he tells the story of an Indian named Sebastian — how he wronged his wife, his mother and the entire village and then was cast out.

Seeking redemption, he returns carrying on his back an ancient costume and head gear. He intends to atone for his corrupt past by dancing in a sacred ritual, a homage to the last Aymara great dancing lord. He knows that when he performs the ritual dance, it will cost him his life. He sets off for La Paz, where he intends to perform the dance, smarting under the weight of the costume and head gear. As he walks, he relives his past. He remembers how he met his wife, his father's death, his estrangement from his brother and family after joining the army. He meets a communist sympathizer escaping from the police and thinks about his betrayal of the villagers. Apparently he sold out to the gringos, preventing the villagers from joining their miner comrades who were engaged in fighting against the military. Sebastian also stole United States aid money from the village.

The area is now flooded with soldiers, who kill an intellectual they had been hunting. On his trek towards La Paz to atone, Sebastian is confronted with resistance groups, peasants and workers.

The three key historical markers in Sebastian's past — the revolution of 1952, the Barrientos coup of 1964 and the onset of power of the Banzer regime in the mid–1970s — coincide with memories of his impoverished youth and life as a servant in La Paz, his military service and his role as a Bolivian national (demanding the villagers give up their arms) and his role as a civilian para-military, becoming the village leader, his betrayal and their expulsion of him for stealing aid. Finally, his exit from the village on the road to redemption takes place in present time, during the Meza coup of 1980. It is after coming to terms with himself, through his memories, that Sebastian is inadvertently shot and killed by an army convoy, mistaken for one of the impoverished Indians whose destiny in poverty and death he now shares.

La nación clandestina is Jorge Sanjinés's eighth film. Despite a totally amateur look (grainy photography, an excessive use of shaky hand-held camera shots, untranslated Aymara dialogue), the film is a sincere effort, beautifully shot on the severe *altiplanos* of Bolivia. The color photography by César Pérez recaptures the majesty of Bolivia's terrain, and the music score by Cergio Prudencio, with its indigenous rhythms, blends well with Sanjinés's efforts to recapture his protagonist's past. Sanjinés continues to be one of the most serious Chilean filmmakers, always stressing the power of the Indian — how he can survive alone and in a community, how he survives the city and lives on the plains, how he survives continual colonization

by Spaniards and Americans, how he triumphs over poverty and each new military regime that comes to power. The body of Sanjinés's films itself is a commitment to the fulfillment of the dreams of the downtrodden. His films are more than educational experiences; they are political statements that demand our action.

187. Nadie escuchaba (Nobody Listened). Nestor Almendros and Jorge Ulla. U.S./Cuba, 1988. 117 min., Color and B&W. Spanish/English.

COMMENTARY: Writing for the MOMA program notes, Almendros and Ulla said that *Nadie escuchaba* "is not exactly a documentary about prison atrocities in Fidel Castro's Cuba. ... In fact, the story isn't a single story at all, but rather the collective experiences of men and women who were victims of oppression. ... Our goal ... was to walk a fine line: it could neither be a documentary that buries its emotional impact under stacks of data, nor one that unnecessarily heightens the drama to the extent of numbing the senses. We present the candid and often disquieting testimonies of some 30 people who were direct or indirect victims of oppression. Through them we would like the audience to experience the circumstances in Cuba on various levels: historical, political and above all, emotional. ... Its protagonists are people who are alive today, and their testimonies are the tools with which we can render judgment. ... [W]ithout them, historical research would find it difficult to uncover what is revealed today."

Somewhat like its predecessor, *Mauvaise Conduite* (1983), *Nadie escuchaba* is another documentary record of the systematic violation of human rights in Cuba. Word is out, internationally, about the evils of the Castro regime. The 30 survivors of torture and oppression in Castro's jails tell their own heartrending and true stories about the reign of

Ignacio López Tarso scolds his mistress, Marga López, in Luis Buñuel's *Nazarín* (1958).

terror, Cuba's undeniable tragedy. If the world had only known — hence the title of the film. The international world had been denied the knowledge of the island's atrocities.

Very much like Claude Lanzmann in his 1985 nine-hour epic *Shoah*, with testimony by Holocaust survivors, directors Almendros and Ulla have fashioned a documentary with heavy emotional impact. Survivors like Huber Matos and Armando Valladares repeat their tales of torture and unjust incarceration for merely being critical of the Castro party line. The camera never wanders from the face of the interviewee. Only occasional zoom shots break the monotony and emphasize a particular shocking moment during the testimony. Orson Ochoa's simply lit photography, with occasional

zooms, lends credence to the riveting words of the former "victims." Both Almendros's documentaries, together with Carlos Franqui's 1983 film *The Other Cuba*, present unshakable, irrefutable testimony that one hopes will bring about dialogue and imperatives geared for social change.

188. Nazarín. Luis Buñuel. Mexico, 1958. 94 min., B&W. Spanish.

COMMENTARY: Based upon the celebrated nineteenth-century Spanish novel by Benito Pérez-Galdós, with a screenplay by Buñuel and Julio Alejandro and photography by the celebrated Gabriel Figueroa, *Nazarín* burst onto screens in Mexico and around the world to plaudits and controversy because of its anti-religious themes.

The film is set in Mexico in 1900. "Porfirio Díaz is the reigning dictator, supported by a land-owning class, a military clique and a very conservative clergy. Among craftsmen, beggars, muleteers, thieves and prostitutes lives Nazarín (played by Spanish actor Francisco Rabal), in a slum dwelling owned by Señora Chanfa (Ofelia Guilman). The priest lives mainly by alms; he asks nothing of his fellow man but is continually mocked by them. In his daily life, Nazarín only obeys the lesson of Christ: compassion, love and forgiveness.

"In the same slum dwelling lives Beatriz (beautifully played by Marga López), a victim of hysteria and a sense of guilt who has been abandoned by Pinto (Noe Murayama), the man she both desires and rejects. Andara (Rita Macedo) is a whore whose primitive kindliness is lost under the flashy colors of her trade. The destinies of these two women weave together after Andara kills another prostitute in a brawl and hides, wounded and bleeding, in Nazarín's shabby room. They are all linked by fate—Andara is running from the police; Beatriz, from herself; and Nazarín, from poverty. Both women decide to follow Nazarín, whose money and clothes were stolen in the slum. Believing that only in pilgrimage among the nameless poor can he fulfill his ideal for goodness and undo the wrongs of others, the three of them set out on the road for another small town.

"In a rail junction, workmen repel him because he would rather work for food than a salary. In a small village, ignorant religious women believe Nazarín can work miracles because he saved a young boy from death after his fever broke. In another town struck by cholera, two lovers in the throes of death prefer sexual passion and refuse religious comfort. In another small town, a humiliated dwarf comes to love the prostitute Andara. In all of Nazarín's travels, he finds an unjust society which will not be moved by his example of pure Christianity.

"Pursuing guards catch up with Andara and Nazarín, her protector. Both are thrown into prison. Nazarín is jeered and struck by a child murderer. The images of failure cloud Nazarín's eyes when a church-thief and fellow inmate asks, "What's your life worth? You on the good path, I on the bad path…We're both worthless." Nazarín realizes neither his words nor his goodness will change the world.

"In the final scenes, Nazarín is walking, shackled, bruised, spat upon. Doubt becomes stronger than faith, and because he doubts, he accepts his destiny and his failure with a new resignation—no longer humble, but rebellious. We hear drum rolls. When offered a pineapple, Nazarín grabs it and bites voraciously into it on this last walk, on the path that leads to the scaffold reserved by society for rebels." (Press book.)

A few years after *Nazarín*, Buñuel made his anti-Catholic film, the classic and controversial *Viridiana*, whose message is that in the modern world it is indeed impossible to lead a Christian life (an intending nun ends up in a provincial *ménage à trois*). *Nazarín* was certainly a preparation for Buñuel's strident attack on the church, but in this earlier film the director sticks to the confines of the novel and stays within the realm of the mores of early twentieth-century Mexico. His message is still strident, but more ambiguous. Buñuel shows how faith can be a useful weapon against injustice. Virtue exists at the edge of real faith, and the truly dispossessed reveal their true natures, but not through prayer.

The film's message is hard to take, but engaging and rewarding. It is a moving indictment of a world that cannot allow simple religion to survive. Even

Buñuel said: "One can be relatively Christian, but the absolutely pure being, the innocent, is condemned to defeat. He is beaten in advance." Curiously, the film won the International Catholic Cinema Office award in 1958, but its successor, *Viridiana*, was placed on the index of films banned for all Catholics.

Buñuel's anti-religious sentiment can be seen throughout his career — as early as 1928 in (*Un Chien andalou*) right through his very last film in 1977 (*That Obscure Object of Desire*). *Nazarín* is a step in a creative process that has led to Buñuel's long refutation of organized religion and the Catholic church. Somewhat milder than most of his anti-religious films, it is a definite link in a long career of creative intransigence. ¡Viva Buñuel!

Nest of Virgins see *El rincón de las vírgenes*

The Nets see *Redes*

189. Nicaragua, no pasarán
(**Nicaragua, They Shall Not Pass**). David Bradbury. Nicaragua/Australia, 1984. 73 min., Color. English.

COMMENTARY: John Corry, in his November 2, 1984, review of this film called it "a love letter to a revolution. It looks on the Sandinistas and finds them good. It is possible this is so; it is possible that their struggle is just." Obviously, the filmmaker's sympathies lie with the Sandinistas, in power since 1979. Bradbury interviews two leaders: Tomás Borge, a charismatic character (and the minister of interior) who freely talks about his rise to power and his tortures under the Somoza regime; and Eden Pastora, a dissident Sandinista, now a Contra himself who is critical of the Sandinistas.

The film tries to give a quick rundown of Nicaraguan history — the American invasion of 1927, the murder of leader Augusto Sandino, the years of Spanish colonialism, British influence, civil wars, dictatorships, attempts to bring about free elections, the overthrow of the Somoza regime, an examination of the Miskito Indian problem and the plight of the Sandinistas and Contras. There is a kind of palpable anti–Americanism and adherence to Sandinista orthodoxy that gives the film a kind of simple-minded view of a very, very complex situation. It is clear that Bradbury should have just let the images he photographed speak for themselves.

For example, one of the best scenes is the Pope's visit; trying to spread peace everywhere, the pontiff, when greeted by cries of "We want peace!" becomes visibly angry at the crowd's impertinent behavior. Also the Sandinistas smile very easily and willingly for the camera, and some of them play the guitar at the drop of a hat. Even the Miskito Indians sing a song on camera at the urging of interior minister Tomás Borge. Also, sometimes the camera just wanders, focusing on the ordinary citizens of Nicaragua in a marketplace, discussing their discontent with the Sandinistas, food shortages, and others debating the good the Sandinistas have done for the country.

Obviously, *Nicaragua, no pasarán* has its assets as an up-to-the-minute documentary. It may not be the kind of tough-minded news reporting we've seen from other parts of the world, but it is definitely a valuable document in tracking the revolutionary fever of Nicaragua of the early eighties.

NOTES: David Bradbury is an Australian documentary filmmaker who was nominated for an Academy Award for the documentary entitled *Frontline*, about a photo-journalist in Vietnam during the war. He continues to live and work in Australia and on foreign locations.

Nicaragua, They Shall Not Pass see *Nicaragua, no pasarán*

The Night of San Juan see *La notte di San Juan*

The Night of the Pencils see *La noche de los lápices*

190. No habrá más penas ni olvido (A Funny, Dirty Little War / There Shall Be No More Sorrows or Forgetting). Hector Olivera. Argentina, 1983. 79 min., Color. Spanish.

COMMENTARY: "Argentina, 1974: a small village in the province of Buenos Aires. In the last days of the Peronist dictatorship, fights are blazing up between the right and the left wings of the party. The command to remove the delegate Ignacio Fuentes (Federico Luppi), who is wrongly accused of harboring left-wing sympathies, reaches the village and creates an uproar. Even the best of friends become enemies when it comes to swearing their allegiance to the official right-wing political faction. Violence hangs in the air; murder and torture are the order of the day. The delegate barricades himself in the town hall and energetically resists the attempts of Guglielmi, the mayor (Lautaro Murua), to arrest him. The readiness with which even the soberest citizens resort to violence is a symbol of the nightmare which haunted Argentina during that time. But Peronism still remains a force to be reckoned with in Argentina today, and this is far from being merely a historical film. What it has to say about 1974 is still relevant a decade later, in spite of the changes in government." (MOMA program notes.)

No habrá más penas ni olvido, a savagely ironic anti-war satire, looks at the phenomenon of Peronism with a brutal sense of the absurd as the small town erupts into opposing factions and self-destructs in this pitch-black comedy. Based upon a novel by Osvaldo Soriano, the plot is quite simple and comical but with dire consequences.

In the town of Colonia Vega, Suprino (Hector Bidonde) is the local Peronista who plots with the county mayor, Guglielmi, and the local union leader to remove deputy mayor Fuentes (Luppi) from office. Fuentes is told to fire his assistant (José María López) because he is a Marxist, but the deputy mayor defends the man, and Suprino brings in the police chief (Rodolfo Ranni) to intimidate him. Fighting for even what Perón would have thought was true, Fuentes turns his office into a fortress, resisting many police assaults. The county mayor (Murua) calls in the death squadron to use heavy gunfire in an aerial attack, but Fuentes has another pilot ward off the gunfire by spraying clouds of insecticide in the air and later use manure in a bombing run. The police chief is abducted by Fuentes's supporters, but to no avail. The rightists, supporters of Suprino, kill all Fuentes's supporters. Fuentes himself is tortured and killed as well as the aerial sprayer. While there is much of Laurel and Hardy in the antics of the battle, suddenly the comic war play becomes serious and we begin to notice everyone is using real bullets. Neighbors who have known each other all their lives die in a kind of civil war. The creation of methods of torture and killing, originally thought to be funny, come back to haunt the participants. The message, obviously, is the ridiculousness of war, especially between people who have no idea of what is right or left or Marxist or Peronist.

The use of manure in a bombing run on the enemy is a bit forced, risible but grotesque in its humor. Even the other shootings, maimings and tortures, especially the demise of Fuentes in a schoolroom filled with portraits of the founding fathers of Argentina, are clearly too dehumanizing and against the grain. One might think the Argentines never took their politics seriously (Perón's ascendance to power), but it was Perón

Poster art for an Argentine film by Hector Olivera, *La noche de los lápices* (*The Night of the Pencils*, 1987).

who did them in, and politics became no laughing matter, as the second half of the film tells us. Clearly the film is meant to be some sort of parable, farcical, outrageous, profane in its depiction of Perón's second coming as a chapter of stupendously botched history. Splendid, vulgar, lunatic, and invigorating are other adjectives that may describe this film. While slipping on a banana peel is humorous, breaking your neck dilutes the humor. Olivera loves this kind of film cliché and turns it around to his advantage, but to the detriment of audience enjoyment. When does death stop being funny, even in this imaginary town?

191. ¿No oyes ladrar los perros? (Do You Hear the Dogs Barking?). François Reichenbach. Mexico/France, 1974. 85 min., Eastmancolor. Spanish.

COMMENTARY: Set in Chiapas and based on a story by Juan Rulfo (adapted for the screen by Carlos Fuentes), this film examines the internal dialogue a Tzotzil Indian man has with his tribal myths and deities. As he carries his deathly ill son in search of modern medical assistance, the man reflects on collective tribal life. The film is of real folkloric interest and aptly describes the conflict of the multi-faceted society of modern Mexico. (Program notes.)

Filmed by a French documentary maker, *¿No oyes ladrar los perros?* is the director's first venture into fiction. Sometimes dwelling too long on folkloric scenes, Reichenbach does capture the true feeling of outrage the father feels after carrying his mortally ill son on his back only to see him die, leaving the father alone in rage, screaming his despair. Perhaps the filmmaker is using the literary device of Rulfo's short story to focus on Indian problems. The film has much in common with a later work, the Peruvian film by Robles Godoy entitled *La muralla verde*, in which a father treks through the jungle after his son is bitten by a snake; the boy dies because of a bureaucratic foul-up, and also because there is no aid in the jungle. It is hard to take the revisionist character out of Reichenbach's first "literary" film.

NOTES: François Reichenbach was born in Paris in 1922 and is known primarily as a director of documentaries using a *cinéma vérité* style. His forte is the short documentary, and he has made dozens of them on a variety of subjects. His Oscar-winning short seen worldwide is *Arthur Rubenstein: Love of Life* (1970). His last film, *François Reichenback's Japan*, was filmed in 1983.

Nobody Listened see *Nadie escuchaba*

Nobody's Wife see *Señora de nadie*

192. La noche de los lápices (The Night of the Pencils). Hector Olivera. Argentina, 1987. 95 min., Color. Spanish.

COMMENTARY: This is a true story based on the testimony given by Pablo Díaz, the only survivor of the incident to which the title refers: a tragic episode that took place in 1976 in the city of La Plata, the capital of the province of Buenos Aires. Security forces kidnapped seven student leaders, aged seventeen on the average, who led a demonstration in support of cheaper transportation for high school students on public buses. Pablo was jailed for four years; the other 6 student leaders are among the 238 adolescents who were kidnapped during the military dictatorship and to this day are still missing. (Press book.)

The film deals primarily with the teenagers who led the rowdy campaign for bus discounts, which were granted during the presidency of Isabel Perón. When the latter was ousted from power, the military was given strict orders to curb student unrest. The bus fare agitators were singled out for distributing leaflets and painting slogans in public areas. Hooded police abducted the leaders from their homes. They were taken to unknown isolated destinations and were beaten, tortured, interrogated and punished until they "confessed" their supposed relationships with enemy guerrillas.

Much time is spent exacting these so-called confessions from the victims, as the interrogators degrade and humiliate the student leaders, eventually breaking their dignity. There is much graphic realism in scenes of torture of nude boys with electric cattle prods — but the boys, though terrified, do not submit easily to their oppressors. No cowardice is ever shown on screen, which gives the audience an emotional jolt — like the torture scenes in American World War II films, where United States soldiers would rather die bravely than submit to the Japanese menace. We feel compassion for the victims and wonder if we will ever know what happened to them.

Alejo García Pintos plays Pablo to perfection. He is a typical adolescent but somewhat savvy about Argentine politics. He is warned about the dangers of dissent by his girlfriend, Claudia (Vita Escardo). But how could teenagers be expected to know the dangers of dealing with such irrational enemies? We watch the society crumble around them as the military junta overthrows Isabel Perón and the students, too, are seen in transitional scenes after tortures, echoing the worsening political conditions with blood-stained faces, emaciated bodies, and soiled, threadbare underwear. The military uses loud music while electroshocking Pablo, hiding his cries of pain. We watch the kids dragged from their filthy, adjoining cells, their faces in close-up, showing desperation and tremendous fear. The singular note of hope

is sounded by Pablo when he asks Claudia to go steady at the film's conclusion. Pablo is a survivor. The film may need this conventional Hollywood ending, geared to nostalgic sentiment and youthful optimism. However, it is more satisfying to stick to the grim facts and the bleak realities, to leave the audience shocked by what they just saw so they will press for political redress. *La noche de los lápices* is a tough film, very hard to take and Argentine revisionist cinema at its best. But worst of all, the *desaparecidos* continue to be lost.

193. El norte (The North).
Gregory Nava. U.S./Mexico/Guatemala, 1983. 139 min., Color. Spanish/English.

COMMENTARY: *El norte* has been called a Latino *Grapes of Wrath*. Just like that 1940 predecessor, the film is epic in its presentation of a Guatemalan family making their way from their little village, through Mexico, to the border and finally into the urban life of Los Angeles.

The film is divided into three sections, each about 45 minutes in length. They are simply called "Guatemala," "Mexico" and "Southern California." We watch the family in native dress (probably speaking maya-quiché) as they work in the fields, picking cotton and coffee, until a military coup forces them to seek refuge to the north.

After losing their parents in the insurrection, Rosa and Enrique suffer many incidents of deprivation, discrimination and lawlessness before they finally arrive at the United States border, anxious to cross. The most harrowing scene in the film is their night flight through an underground sewer system infested with rats. Brother and sister finally make it to Los Angeles. Rosa works as a maid to a rich Los Angeles family, and Enrique becomes a waiter at a plush Hollywood restaurant. But the *migra* (immigration authorities) are constantly in pursuit.

Director Gregory Nava prepares the next shot of *El norte* (*The North*, 1983), while producer Anna Thomas looks on.

Rosa is caught; she has developed typhus from a rat bite. Enrique must leave her for the promise of work in Chicago. We expect Enrique to grab his big chance and take the job as a factory foreman in the cold, cold climate of Chicago. But in the next scene, Enrique has missed the plane and his big career opportunity; he is at Rosa's bedside. In her delirium, Rosa speaks of the moral of the film: "We are homeless [in Guatemala] and are not even accepted here [in America]." The film ends somewhat tragically and beautifully since Rosa dies and is seen back in Guatemala, united in death with her parents. But for the immigrant without a green card, there is little hope.

Zaïde Silvia Gutiérrez as Rosa and David Villaplando as Enrique play their roles with ease and conviction. They carry the action of the film forward to its harrowing conclusion. But along the way, there is some humor. In the Los Angeles section, Rosa cannot figure out how to work a clothes dryer, so she takes the laundry outside and lays it on the grass surrounding the pool to dry. Rosa then begins to wash some other soiled pieces on stones, using the water in the pool, to the horrified consternation of her Los Angeles employer.

The scope of the color photography by John Glennon is absolutely breathtaking, especially in the "Guatemala" section. The soundtrack contains some beautiful pre–Colombian flute music that sets off the dramatically underscored passages with source music by Mahler, Barber and Verdi. But unlike Robert M. Young's *Alambrista* (1978) or John Ford's *The Grapes of Wrath* (1940), *El norte* is curiously uninvolving. We have watched these characters move through cataclysmic events in their lives, on a giant geographical and sociological canvas, yet we feel empty, detached. Perhaps it is the smallness of this theme, elevated to such grandiose and colorful proportions, that is at odds with our emotions. Often, gigantic production values can diminish our intellectual and aesthetic pleasures. *El norte* has won our sympathies, even with its very melodramatic ending, but in the pantheon of immigration films, it does not stay with us. Perhaps it needed tighter direction and real star power (and a more realistic ending) to make it more memorable.

NOTES: Gregory Nava was born in California in 1949 and studied filmmaking at UCLA film school. In 1973, he made his first film, *The Confession of*

Amans (using costumes from *El Cid*), about a wandering minstrel in Europe. The film won first prize at the Chicago International Film Festival in 1976. His other films include *The Haunting of M* (1979), *The End of August* (1982) and *A Time for Destiny* (1988). Unlike Mira Nair, the director of *The Pérez Family* (1995), Nava used Chicano actors like Jimmy Smits, Esai Morales and Eduardo Jaime Olmos in his 1995 film, at first titled *East L.A.* but released as *Mi familia* (*My Family*), which scored a resounding success at the box office. He is married to Anna Thomas, a producer and screenwriter who has worked on many of his films.

The North see *El norte*

194. La notte di San Juan
(La noche de San Juan / The Night of San Juan). Jorge Sanjinés. Bolivia/Italy, 1971. 90 min., Color. Spanish.

COMMENTARY: *La notte di San Juan* is a historical re-construction of a massacre that took place in Bolivia on the night of June 24, 1967. The authors of this documentary film lived through that terrible night and escaped death only by a miracle. Thus they tell the story as a first-hand experience, talking about their hopes for the liberation of their country and the bitterness of everyday life there. The film reveals the exploitation of Bolivian workers, particularly the miners. The mines are a major national asset, providing raw materials for the United States space program, while the Bolivians who work them are treated like animals, die of silicosis and other pulmonary diseases. This is one of the situations that has encouraged the guerrilla movement in Bolivia, which seeks to help and defend these men in the face of government repression. The film, which was produced by Italian television (RAI) with the assistance of the Ukamau group of Bolivia, attempts to shed some light on Bolivia's social and political problems and on the people's anguish and need for liberty.

The film opens with a massacre of miners that took place in 1942. These sequences are followed by the depiction of six other workers' massacres that occurred between 1942 and 1967. This part of the film serves as an introduction; it seeks to explain the reasons behind these events and to single out those who were responsible. The photographs of the survivors of the 1967 San Juan massacre come alive, and one by one, they tell the story of the events leading up to the fateful night.

Federico Vallejo is a miner. Domitilla Chungara is the leader of the Women's Movement. Felicidad Coca García is the deputy head of the miners. Eusebio Giranda is a university student. The scenes of the "night of San Juan" portray reality as closely as possible and are therefore at times both violent and cruel. (Press book.)

Believing that making films like this is a real way to help the Bolivian people become politically aware and attain freedom, Sanjinés made *La notte di San Juan* as a strong revisionist film. It takes hard positions on human rights, encouraging miners to organize, demonstrate and strike justifiably to improve the quality of their lives. Sanjinés condemns the outright killing of miners as governmental repression and casts blame on United States imperialists anxious about their own interests in the tin industry. He reconstructs these events with a group of some professional and mostly non-professional actors. The director had the advantage of filming in isolated mining areas of Bolivia, in and outside of mines as well. He has pushed all the buttons to show his fellow Bolivians as downtrodden and deserving of a better life. *La notte di San Juan* is great social-revisionist-dramatic filmmaking at Sanjinés's best.

Ocho-A see *[Eight]-A*

Odd Number see *La cifra impar*

The Official Story see *La historia oficial*

195. Old Gringo. Luiz Puenzo.
U.S./Mexico, 1989. 119 min., Color. English/Spanish.

COMMENTARY: To make this film based upon the Carlos Fuentes novel *El viejo gringo*, Columbia Pictures employed Argentina's award-winning director Luis Puenzo (*La historia oficial*), his Argentine screenwriter-collaborator Aida Bortnik and a Hollywood cast including Jane Fonda, Gregory Peck and Jimmy Smits, eventually spending over $24 million to produce a small, confusing romantic drama on a grandiose scale with locations in Mexico.

The story concerns the real-life journalist Ambrose Bierce (Gregory Peck) and a fortyish, unmarried American schoolteacher, Harriet Winslow (Jane Fonda), both swept up into the Mexican revolution of Pancho Villa. One of Villa's generals, Arroyo (Jimmy Smits), falls in love with the schoolteacher and must divide his loyalties between her and the revolution. Ambrose Bierce forms the third side of the amorous triangle. Gregory Peck plays his part crustily, paternally, wearily, as he played his Oscar-winning role in *To Kill a Mockingbird* some twenty-five years before.

The real excuse for making the film is the recreation of the Mexican revolution scenes and the settings of turn-of-the-century Mexico. Although the color is superb and the location photograpy is striking, the film itself misses the mark emotionally. It seems the Argentine director and screenwriter who were so good together making *La historia oficial*, a very serious film about the *desaparecidos*, missed the dramatic nuances of the Carlos Fuentes novel, making it into something of a light comedy — which is not their forte. Puenzo and Bortnik had their chance to do a big Hollywood production, but unfortunately, it came off exceedingly lifeless and empty. Perhaps they should stick to the kinds of scenarios they do best in Argentina.

196. Los Olvidados (The Young and the Damned / The Forgotten Ones). Luis Buñuel. Mexico, 1951. 99 min., B&W. Spanish.

Pedro (Alfonso Mejía) is a young boy, abandoned by his mother (Estela Inda), who lives in the sordid slums on the outskirts of Mexico City. He falls in with a gang of delinquents led by Jaibo (played by Roberto Cobo in his first professional acting role), a sadistic bully. He becomes bound to Jaibo by being an unwilling witness to the brutal murder of Julián, a bricklayer supporting his family. (Jaibo originally thought Julián to be a *soplon*, a police informant, and killed him.)

Pedro tries to do the right thing by becoming a knife-maker's apprentice. Jaibo comes on the scene and steals a knife. Pedro is fired. The police come for Pedro, thinking he is the thief, and his mother sends him to the reformatory. Earning the trust of the warden, Pedro is given a 50-peso note to buy cigarettes. He meets Jaibo, who steals the money and follows Pedro back to the Mexico City slums. As Pedro attempts to recover the money in a fight with Jaibo, the latter inadvertently drops the stolen knife and Pedro reveals, in his anger, that Jaibo killed Julián. Jaibo escapes and vows revenge.

Meanwhile, Pedro runs off to get a job pushing horses on a merry-go-round. Coming back one night to rest, Jaibo meets Pedro again in the barn where Pedro sleeps. Jaibo bullies and dominates him and finally kills him. Jaibo then escapes, only to be killed in a hail of police bullets after being informed upon by a "blind" man. Pedro's body is stuffed into a sack and dumped on a garbage heap outside of the slum area. (Press Book.)

There are two wonderful surreal dream sequences in the film. In the first, Pedro dreams about hunger. His mother offers him some meat, but Jaibo comes out from under the bed and steals it. The murdered Julián is seen as well, with a blood-spattered face, trying to get his hands on Pedro; he disappears before Jaibo appears on the scene.

The other surreal sequence appears in Jaibo's dream as he runs to escape the shower of police bullets that eventually kill him. Running down a wet street, Jaibo is struck by a bullet, and as he loses consciousness, a wet dog continues running on the same street glistening with rain. Jaibo lets go of consciousness and enters the vortex.

Los olvidados was made by Buñuel in 21 days. It won (deservedly) the Cannes Film Festival Award for Best Picture in 1951. The film is almost a documentary of poverty and violence in the slums, while on another level it has the nightmarish, erotic, hallucinatory quality of the world of the subconscious. *Los olvidados* is a disturbing work, probing, amoral, devastating, with, in the Italian neo-realist style, many layers of meaning.

Roberto Cobo is simply brilliant as Jaibo. He plays the savvy street kid led into murder with a glibness and charm that is frightening. He shows naiveté and tenderness when he is seduced by Pedro's mother, then the right amount of *machismo* that makes him a frightening and sympathetic villain. Alfonso Mejía as Pedro has just the proper mixture of innocence, purity and streetwise attitude. His revolt in the reformatory, killing the roosters, is very real and understandable. Mejía plays a victim with skill and compassion.

Though someone in the film declares, "it's the parents that should be locked up, no one watching Estela Inda as Pedro's mother can help feeling sympathy for this beautiful but steely-hearted woman, though she hates her son with such venom that she refuses to feed or protect him, preferring to have him institutionalized, because his father left her pregnant when he disappeared.

Miguel Inclán plays the vicious, gluttonous, lascivious blind man who informs on Jaibo after the latter cruelly mistreats him. He says at one point in the film that all the children "should be killed before they are born."

All the other actors, among them Alma Fuentes as Meche and Francisco Jambrina as the warden, are very capable in their roles. But it is the young actors, principals Cobo and Mejía, who move the drama forward into a tour de force, making *Los olvidados* one of the best of Buñuel's films and one of the best treating the subject of slum poverty. More acerbic than Buñuel's 1960 Spanish film *Viridiana* and a brilliant forerunner of Hector Babenco's *Pixote. Los olvidados* belongs in the pantheon of one of the world's 25 best films ever made.

On the Empty Balcony see *En el balcón vacío*

One Way or Another see *De cierta manera*

197. Opera do Malandro

(**Malandro**). Ruy Guerra. Brazil, 1985. 105 min., Color. Portuguese.

COMMENTARY: *Opera do Malandro* ("Malandro's Opera") is the first musical to come out of Latin America in the last thirty years. Although its plot and characters are taken from Bertolt Brecht's *Threepenny Opera* (which goes uncredited), the film's source is Chico Buarque's musical play "Opera do Malandro."

The story begins late in 1941, in Rio de Janeiro. Populist dictator Vargas has declared Brazil the *Estado Nôvo* or New State and thrown his full support behind the aspiring fascist empires of Hitler and Mussolini. On the street, however, among the pimps, thieves, smugglers and hustlers, the war in Europe couldn't be more irrelevant.

Max, a smooth, zoot-suited *malandro* (pimp) with a talent for seduction and con games, is too preoccupied with his own survival and status to think about war or politics — that is, until Japan attacks Pearl Harbor. Max responds to the Japanese strike with an act of patriotic duty: With a few American sailors, he orchestrates a "retaliation raid" on a cabaret owned by a German man, Otto Strudell. Unfortunately, the raid results in the firing of an employee named Margot — Max's current interest and constant meal ticket. Max connives the ultimate revenge: the seduction of Ludmilla, Strudell's comely daughter. (Press book.)

Edson Celuari as Max, Elba Ramalho as Margo, Claudia Ohana as Ludmilla (fondly called "Lu") and Fabio Sabag as Otto Strudell all enact their roles with grace and verve. The film contains many visual allusions to *Scarface* and *Casablanca*. Its dance numbers are sensational.

Opera do malandro is a film of wit and imagination melding political satire and lusty melodrama. Unlike a Gene Kelly musical full of nostalgia, this one combines a Hollywood vision with a unique critique of eighties Brazilian politics that will both stimulate and entertain.

198. Orfeu negro (Black Orpheus).

Marcel Camus. Brazil/France, 1958. 106 min., Color. Portuguese/French.

COMMENTARY: Starring Bruno Mello as a trolley conductor named Orpheus and Marpessa Dawn as his girlfriend, Eurydice, the film is a shameless takeoff of the Orpheus legend. Orpheus is

Claudia Venturini plays the adolescent Oriane and Luis Armando Castillo plays the sexy Sergio, who may be the illegitimate son of her Aunt Oriane, in this Venezuelan biography-cummystery film by Fina Torres entitled *Oriane* (1985).

betrothed to another woman, Mira, who is jealous of his real love. At carnival time, Eurydice is pursued by Mira and the figure of Death. During the frenetic, frenzied carnival, she is killed among the noise of the dancing. Mello goes down to the Underworld to find his lost love in the predictable, sentimental ending.

Filming in Brazil with a completely black cast, the director uses the Orpheus myth to demonstrate not only its universality but the splendors of Rio — its exoticism, its poetry, its gay carnival atmosphere. During the fifties, *Orfeu negro* was one of the few French films to be made in Brazil to become an international hit and show off the beauties (and some of the problems) of life in Rio. More than a mere location setting for its mythical story, it catches the raw spirit of the Brazilian people in one of its proudest displays of color and energy, at carnival. It should not be missed.

NOTES: Director Marcel Camus was born in France in 1912 and died there in 1982. He had a distinguished career in French cinema and worked with some of the best talents (Luis Buñuel, Jacques Feyder, Henri Decoin) before he made his debut as a director with *Fugitive in Saigon* (1957). *Orfeu negro* (1958) was his second film, which starred his wife, Marpessa Dawn. Although he tended to shoot his subsequent films on exotic locations, *Orfeu negro* was his most renowned film to date. His last production, *The Pastors of the Night*, was made in Brazil in 1977.

Oriana see *Oriane*

199. Oriane (Oriana). Fina Torres. Venezuela, 1985. 88 min., Color. Spanish.

COMMENTARY: Marie, after living in France many years with her husband and young son, returns to Venezuela after her Aunt Oriane's death to sell the house and the *hacienda* (farm) she has inherited. Wandering around the old dusty mansion (in a terrible state of disrepair), she slowly remembers a period of her adolesence that she spent there in the company of Aunt Oriane. Oriane lived all of her life in that house, never leaving the hacienda. Remembrance of things past, now that she is an adult, bring Marie a new understanding of her aunt's life. The fragments of the past gather together under Marie's eyes. The film is a series of inside flashbacks, like Chinese boxes. An older Marie gazes out a window and sees herself twenty years earlier, on her first visit to Oriane's house. It is these kinds of Proustian shifts of memory, some based on visual stimuli, others based on other senses, that are the style of the entire film.

But mood and atmosphere are not enough. Although the director is expert at conveying textures — night winds, sensuality, the sultry obscurity of the woods contrasting with the fresh clarity of the beach just a few yards away — she takes too long to tell a simple story because of her insistence on this kind of stylistic flight.

The theme of the film is incest. The missing link to the mystery of Oriane's life is that she has a son living in the house, fathered by her brother, Sergio, who was beaten to death by Oriane's father because of their incestuous relationship. Moreover, Fidelia, the maid, poisoned the father's water as he rode away on horseback, then stayed faithful to Oriane, a shut-in, for the rest of her life. Marie's discovery that Oriane's son still lives seems almost anticlimactic as she returns to France with her family, firm in her resolution never to sell the house and to keep the mystery of Oriane a dark family secret. There is also the possibility that Oriane has an incestuous relationship with her own son and

that this obsessive spirit of incest continues to haunt and weave its spell on Marie in the present.

As a film about memory and the recapturing of the past — like William Wyler's *Wuthering Heights*, Anatole Litvak's *All This and Heaven Too*, Alfred Hitchcock's *Rebecca*, Carlos Saura's *La prima angélica* and Volker Schlondorff's *Swann in Love* (based upon Proust's fabulous novel of "recherche") — *Oriane* misses the mark. It is minimalist, feminist cinema, obscured by stylistic excesses of sometimes unmotivated flashbacks and structural inconsistencies in the screenplay that make it a turgid film to watch, despite its enormous sensitivity and beautiful color photography. It won the Cannes Festival Camera d'Or Award probably because it had a courageous theme, represented the debut of a new woman director from Venezuela (a country on the edge of a burgeoning film industry) and was *au courant* with a spate of women's films from foreign locations (Claire St. Denis's *Chocolat*, for example). Financed with French money and chock-full of French sensibility, Fina Torres is still a new Venezuelan director of note, and her film deserves to be seen internationally.

NOTES: *Oriane* is Fina Torres' debut film. She is a Venezuelan filmmaker who was born in Caracas in 1951 and was a journalist and photographer for many Venezuelan magazines. In 1973 she studied filmmaking at IDHEC in Paris. She spent some time working in French, Colombian and Venezuelan television before making her first feature. She made one shorter film before *Oriane* called *The Other Side of the Dream*, about Veronique Sanson, in 1978. She continues to live and work in both Europe and South America.

The Other Francisco see *El otro Francisco*

200. El otro Francisco (The Other Francisco). Sergio Giral. Cuba, 1974. 100 min., B&W. Spanish.

COMMENTARY: Adapted from the book by Anselmo Suárez y Romero—the first anti-slavery novel ever written in Cuba—*El otro Francisco* deals brutally and realistically with the first half of nineteenth-century Cuba and its practice of black slavery. The film (with a screenplay by the director) concentrates not on the original, sentimental drama of a slave couple deprived of the most minimum conditions to continue their own human relationship, but on the historical motives behind slavery, as well as the motivations of its opponents.

The image of the slave presented by Giral is a romantic one. The film opens in a Cuban literary salon presided over by Domingo del Monte. The latter has invited Englishman Richard Madden to read Suárez y Romero's new novel. Madden is in Cuba investigating violations on a treaty between Britain and Spain on the suppression of the slave trade. As Madden investigates, he meets the characters in the novel in his travels around the island. The film cuts back and forth between the literary salon discussions and the unrelieved exploitation and mistreatment of the Cuban slaves.

With daring camera work, Giral reproduces scenes of revolt, blood-spattered slaves in contrast with the sentimental drama of Romero's novel. The film is artful, beautifully photograhed and scored by Leo Brouwer, and is within the agit-prop realm of product made by ICAIC under Castro's regime.

Outlaw Love see *El amor bandido*

Painted Lips see *Boquitas pintadas*

201. País Portátil (Portable Country). Ivan Feo and Antonio Llerandi. Venezuela, 1978. 103 min., Eastmancolor. Spanish.

COMMENTARY: Based on a very famous Venezuelan novel by Adriano Gonzáles León, *País Portátil* tells the story of three generations of a revolutionary family, the Barazartes, in the backlands of Venezuela, from the turn of the century, through occasional flashbacks to 1925 and 1933, to the present day of the film, 1977.

We witness the family's victories, their personal and political failures and their final comeuppance in the political situation of the late seventies. Through flashbacks, we learn about the past of the youngest family member even as he travels to a shoot-out and his imminent death at the hands of the corrupt police. The directors use a common gimmick of magical realism by having the boy's ancestors hand him ammunition for the ultimate face-off with the cops, a kind of silent symbolism. Perhaps the film's message is that the youngest, too, must bear arms against the politicos, evening the score for the government's past evils against the revolutionaries of old.

All the actors play the family members to perfection: Hector Duvachelle as Salvador, Ivan Feo (the director) as Andres, Eliseo Perera as León, Eduardo Gil as Nicolascito and Ibsen Martínez as José Eladio Barazarte. Silvia Santelices as Ernestina and Alejandra Pinedo as Delia do very well in the few feminine roles of the film. Very much like the novel, with its time ellipses, the film's flashbacks and flashforwards tend to confuse. But the exotic Venezuelan location settings and the political message couched in the title make the film an interesting experience to decode. It is a pity that *País portátil* had such a short run in America. Its message about a group of Venezuelan pioneers who rejected authority and dictatorship way back when and do battle with modern police forces of the seventies is something to behold.

NOTES: Antonio Llerandi is a stage actor and director of the new Venezuelan cinema. He made several short films before he directed *País portátil* with fellow actor Ivan Feo. Since 1976, he has made *Adiós Miami* in 1984 and *Profundo* in 1986. He is also the director at the film school at the Ateneo de Caracas.

202. Palomita blanca (White Dove). Raúl Ruiz. Chile, 1992. 122 min., B&W. Spanish.

COMMENTARY: Although this film was shot in Chile in 1973 by the director, it took nearly 20 years to reach Chilean screens. Based upon a novel by Enrique Lefourcade, it is about María, a high school girl who lives in a poor tenement, and Juan Carlos, a Chilean playboy who lives in the lap of luxury in a suburban mansion. The two meet and fall in love against the background of 1970 Chilean politics — Salvador Allende's election and inauguration.

Raúl Ruiz uses overlapping dialogue, an improvisational style of camera and a cast composed of a mixture of professional and non-professional actors to tell his poor-girl-meets-rich-boy story. His directorial technique reminds the viewer of Hollywood's Robert Altman, although this film in no way resembles such films as *Nashville* or *Short Circuit*. The film is a fair transposition of the novel to the screen but is not the kind of fascinating cinema with which Ruiz has sometimes dazzled us since his exile.

203. The Panama Deception. Barbara Trent. Panama/U.S., 1992. 94 min., Color. Spanish/English.

COMMENTARY: If not for the Empowerment Project, an organization based in North Carolina that supports national screenings for controversial political documentary films, *The Panama Deception* would not have been seen in the United States. However, with that organization's support, the film, without an established distributor, was seen by more than 50,000 people in 25 cities during its first four months of release. Apparently, word got out that this documentary is a political powerhouse because of its many revelations.

The Panama Deception examines the 1989 American invasion of Panama and pursuit of General Noriega. The images of Panama being destroyed in an illegal raid by American troops are alarming and disarming. They have been carefully chosen and edited to show not the rape of Panama, but the corrupt politique behind the invasion. Director Barbara Trent and writer and editor David Kasper convincingly marshall all their facts to prove conclusively (1) that the American troop movement, subsequently condemned by the United Nations, was illegal; (2) that the American news media cooperated with the United States government to suppress and censor news from Panama and present only the Bush administration's point of view; (3) that General Noriega was a puppet for United States politics gone out-of-control with illegal drug trafficking, (4) that the United States fully intended to destabilize Panama, militarily and politically, so that the United States could re-negotiate the Canal Zone treaty and cancel the promised proprietorship in the year 2000 granted by President Carter; and (5) that the Bush administration had a plan to take control of the drug cartel in Third World countries in Central and South America, with the invasion of Panama as the first link in the chain.

We watch a parade of witnesses — politicians, journalists, historians, poor Panamanians whose houses and lives were destroyed by the invasion. Many of them lived for nearly a year in air hangars converted into shelters. Those who were killed during the invasion were buried in mass graves, later uncovered by government officials and international rightist groups. The actress Elizabeth Montgomery narrates the entire film, but the images alone tell a serious story of illegalities and a life-death situation that threatens the democratic foundations of the United States. The policies of the Bush administration deserve reexamination in light of the proofs elucidated in *The Panama Deception*. With a classic sense of irony, Barbara Trent juxtaposes images that prove exact opposites visually and verbally. Let there be no mistake about the perpetrators of the Panama deception: The Americans here are the villains, specifically George Bush and the Republican leadership in Congress. This revelation is hard to take, but the shrewdness of the filmmakers' observations are worth the price of admission alone. Barbara Trent has made a strong documentary that surpasses anything this viewer has seen from Panama in many a year. It is unfortunate that Panama has virtually no film industry of its own and that the country, because of American intervention, is still in a gruesome state of disrepair.

Parting of the Ways see *Lejanía*

The Party Is Over see *Fin de fiesta*

204. Pasajeros de una pesadilla (Passengers of a Nightmare). Fernando Ayala. Argentina, 1984. 95 min., Eastmancolor. Spanish.

COMMENTARY: The Schocklender family made headlines in Buenos Aires in the early eighties when the family's two sons murdered their parents. One of the sons, Pablo, wrote a story of the affair, which producer-director Fernando Ayala optioned for the screen. The film is a series of flashbacks based upon this true-life double murder.

For the film, the family name has been changed to Fogelman. The younger son (Gabriel Lenn) tells scenarist Jorge Goldenberg how the story began. It seems Mr. Fogelman (Federico Luppi) married a non–Jewish girl (Alicia Bruzzo) and had three children: a daughter (Gabriela Flores) and two sons. (The elder son is played by German Palacios.)

Years go by; the children are teenagers and the father, an engineer, has amassed a great fortune selling arms to the Argentine military and others. Then their lives go haywire. The mother becomes alcoholic and takes a series of lovers. The father comes out as a homosexual with his wife's approval. Their relationships with their children begin to deteriorate, becoming episodes of neurotic behavior. At one point, the mother has an incestuous affair with the younger son. The boys want to escape the household and leave for Israel to live on a kibbutz, but the mother refuses to consent.

When the bodies of the parents are found in the trunk of a car, dripping blood in a tony section of Buenos Aires, the boys cannot be found by police. At last the youths are tracked and found horseback riding near Mar de la Plata. They are captured and supposedly brought to justice. However, it is discovered that the father was the agent of a British munitions company and may have been double-dealing with the Argentines. Although we are never told directly who shot the parents, whatever their familial crimes, the film suggests that professional killers were employed from the para-military.

Federico Luppi is especially good as the father, although one cannot understand or trace his motivations for coming out. Nor can we fathom the mother's behavior, but Alicia Bruzzo acts her role aggressively, showing Mrs. Fogelman's very erratic and at times vicious alcoholic personality. The boys are effectively played, and the film succeeds commercially as a potboiler with larger

Still from Hector Olivera's *La Patagonia rebelde* (*Rebellion in Patagonia*, 1974).

pretensions. And it is the larger impli-
cation — the corruption of the military
regime — that seems to be the unspoken
theme behind this Argentine drama.
The film also has the feel of a docudrama, cast very much in the mold of
Richard Brooks' 1967 film *In Cold
Blood*, based on Truman Capote's do-
cunovel about two midwestern killers
who wipe out an entire family. It is not
as visceral as John McNaughton's 1986
film *Henry: Portrait of a Serial Killer*, but
it has its own haunting power in light of
Argentine history.

NOTES: Fernando Ayala was born in
Argentina in 1920 and is probably one
of that nation's most prolific producers
and directors. With Hector Olivera and
Leopoldo Torre Nilsson, he founded
Aries Cinematográfica and made some
of the most socially relevant films to
come out of Argentina in the sixties and
seventies. In the decade of the eighties,
he seems more interested in commercial,

mass-appeal movies. Besides *Pasajeros*,
some of his best films are *Ayer fué pri-
mavera* (1955), *El candidato* (1959),
Plata dulce (1982), and *Sobredosis* (1986).
Having made over thirty films, he continues to work with his favorite co-producer and director, Hector Olivera.

Passengers of a Nightmare see
Pasajeros de una pesadilla

205. La Patagonia rebelde
(**Rebellion in Patagonia or Uprising in
Patagonia**). Hector Olivera. Argentina,
1974. 107 min., Eastmancolor. Spanish.

COMMENTARY: Based upon Osvaldo
Bayer's book *The Revengers of the Tragic
Patagonia*, Olivera's film depicts a massacre of workers that actually occurred in
this southernmost outpost of the rural
part of Argentina. The workers are striking for better conditions. The landowners are furious, and since they represent
the great wealth of foreign interests, they

advise the politicos to send in the troops to put down the rebellion.

Hector Alterio brillantly plays the turncoat Lt. Commander Zavala. He wishes the workers well after signing the first labor pact in Patagonia; then, summarily, coldly, he slaughters them. The film covers a great deal of ground, beginning with Zavala's death in 1923 when he was assassinated as he left his home for work, and in flashback describing the events that led to his assassination. Most of the action takes place on the spacious plains of Patagonia and shows how the communists and anarchists successfully organized the sheep farmers.

The film has several Argentine actors playing labor leaders, including Luis Brandoni in the role of a Spanish activist and Pepe Soriano as a German idealist. Federico Luppi plays an Argentine named José Font who is used as a pawn by Lt. Zavala. Font believes that Zavala is on the side of the workers, since he settled the first strike. The strike scene itself is very colorful — black flags representing the anarchist interests and red flags, the sindicalists. Many Chileans and foreign workers are drawn into the vortex and slaughtered by the wily commander. Supposedly 3000 souls perished in the massacre, leaving the workers worse off than before. The workers are seen always in a sympathetic light, the bosses as evil villains incarnate. When the film ends quietly, it is a powerful indictment of the corrupt rich and the military who keep the masses downtrodden. In his best agit-prop manner, director Olivera is seeking redress for the proletariat. In light of the numerous military coups taking place in Argentina, he did not have long to wait. This film, like its Bolivian predecessor, the 1973 Jorge Sanjinés propaganda piece *La notte di San Juan*, is pushing for social change. But unlike the Sanjinés epic, Olivera's film shows the politics, strategy and irony behind the rebellion in Patagonia.

206. El patrullero (Highway Patrolman). Alex Cox. Mexico, 1992. 91 min., Color. Spanish/English.

COMMENTARY: Roberto Sosa plays Pedro Rojas, a young graduate from Mexico's national police academy who is assigned to the isolated territory of Matimi in Durango where drug traffic is rife. He meets Griselda (played by Zaïde Silvia Gutiérrez of *El norte* fame), a local girl whom he marries and makes pregnant. He soon regrets his choice when his wife starts to complain that his salary is too low. His situation becomes more difficult when he meets Maribel (Vanessa Bauche), a hooker with a heart of gold. He starts to have an affair with her and pays for her cocaine habit and the expenses of her two children.

Falling into the pattern of local corruption, made desperate by his obligations to two women, Pedro begins taking the bribes he originally turned down. While thus trashing his life, he comes up against some drug runners who refuse to pay him the usual bribe. In the film's most exciting scene, a car chase, Pedro's police car fails him and his partner, Anibal (Bruno Bichir), is shot by the drug dealers. Pedro follows Anibal's bloody tracks into the desert and reaches him a few minutes before he dies in his arms. Anibal's murder pushes Pedro over the edge, and he becomes a fanatical cop, a one-man crusader against the drug trade in Durango.

The ghost of Pedro's dead father always shows up in the frame at critical moments, reminding Pedro he should have been a doctor and not a bribe-taking cop. Pedro does become a solid citizen at the film's conclusion.

The director has given the audience a picture of gringo-based corruption south of the border. What is more daring, this British-born, American-educated director made the film, perhaps his best, in Spanish! *El patrullero* is a wonderful "black" comedy, its underlying vision more melancholy than bitter. Everyone south of the border seems casually corrupt, and Alex Cox has caught the ambience very well on film. Using a hand-held camera, mostly long takes, and making fewer than 190 cuts in the whole film, Cox shows up expensive Hollywood production teams with a film that celebrates the arid landscapes, the mountain chaparrals and the harsh environment in his efforts to explore a real social problem with flair and verve. With the aid of expert camerman Miguel Garzón, he has succeeded.

NOTES: Born in Liverpool in 1954 and coming from a theater background, Alex Cox studied filmmaking at UCLA. But it was his job with a car repossession company that stimulated him to make his first film, *Repo Man* in 1984. When that film proved a resounding success, Cox was inspired by the life of Sid Vicious to star Gary Oldman in *Sid and Nancy* (1986), which become another cult favorite in the United States and abroad. In 1987, he worked on two films, *Straight to Hell* and *Walker*. But it was *El patrullero*, daringly made in a language foreign to him, that put Cox's directing career into high gear.

207. The Pearl. Emilio "El Indio" Fernández. Mexico, 1947. 69 min., B&W. English.

COMMENTARY: Set on the western coast of Mexico, this film is yet another wonderful collaboration between the director, his leading actors and their favorite cameraman, Gabriel Figueroa. It is the story of what happens to a poor Mexican family when sudden wealth comes to them in the form of a huge, flawless pearl. Its discovery brings the greed of evil men, danger and death to some before the family, realizing it is better to live without the pearl, returns it to the sea.

Based upon the John Steinbeck novel of the same title, *The Pearl* is a truly exceptional film, a tragic folk tale, bleak in its conclusion about the covetousness of men, the inability of the poor to cope with great fortune and the happiness to be found in the simple (but impoverished) life.

Pedro Armendáriz plays the pearl diver with conviction and strength. When he discovers the pearl, he is sure its value will release him and his family from a lifetime of poverty and ignorance. But the pearl brings only misery, including the murder of his son.

Although the role was tailored for Dolores de Río, María Elena Márquez plays Juana, the wife of Kino, the pearl fisherman. She does an effective job in a difficult supporting role, and her acting is simple, fluid and luminous. Fernando Wagner plays the pearl buyer with all the bluster and brutality he can muster.

The entire film is a wonderful transposition of art, from Steinbeck's prose to the images of Gabriel Figueroa's camera. Figueroa has caught the suspense, tragedy and beauty within Steinbeck's tale with his simply stunning camera work. Those gleaming night scenes of glistening water, vast stretches of moonlight cast on beaches, against waves rolling on to the shore, the splendid use of light and shadow and probably filtered lenses that create startling beautiful images of black, white and grey in his compositions of sea and landscapes are extraordinary. But most amazing, the film was made in English, though shot completely in Mexico with a Mexican production company and director. It is one of the most beautiful and powerful Mexican films ever made.

208. Pedro Páramo. Carlos Velo. Mexico, 1966. 118 min., B&W. Spanish.

COMMENTARY: With a screenplay by

Mexican novelist Carlos Fuentes from the famous Juan Rulfo novel and a cast that included American John Gavin in the title role, *Pedro Páramo* is a surreal fantasy that has a lot going for it.

Essentially it is about a young man, Pedro, who is searching for his father in revolutionary Mexico of the 1900s. The story is told in flashbacks and ace cameraman Gabriel Figueroa has made Mexico come alive once again during this era of blood and guts. His camera work is flamboyant, and although Gavin's performance is not magnetic enough to hold the audience, the film does succeed in capturing the symbols, the allegorical modes, the mystical influences on the main character.

Mexican character actors Pina Pellicer as Susana and Ignacio López Tarso as Fulgor do extremely well in supporting roles. But the unexpected surprise is John Gavin as Pedro, speaking fluent Spanish and giving his all to play the heroic Rulfo character. (Gavin became the United States ambassador to Mexico some years after.) The Rulfo novel is so popular in Mexico that is was the subject of another film version made in 1976 by director José Bolanos.

209. Pedro Páramo. José Bolanos. Mexico, 1976. 173 min., Eastmancolor. Spanish.

COMMENTARY: Adding another hour to the 1966 black and white version by Carlos Velo from a script by Carlos Fuentes, the same Juan Rulfo novel has been completely redone, expanded and rewritten by the director and lovingly photographed in Eastmancolor.

Once again, we are back in the Mexican revolution in the year 1900 and our protagonist, Pedro Páramo, arrives at a deserted Mexican village to seek out his father. Apparently the director, José Bolanos, is more concerned with the storyline in this version. It seems Pedro Páramo (Manuel Ojeda), a landowner,

develops an uncontrollable passion for a widow, Susana San Juan (Vanetia Vianello), and finally marries her. But memories of her deceased husband interfere with their life and she dies soon after, grief-stricken.

The lead actor plays his scenes, happy and sad, with the same sombre expression throughout this talky, nearly three-hour film. Actually all the actors are caught in the same trap of awe and profundity, speaking their lines in a halting manner as if out of respect for the greatness of the novel. Even the music score by Ennio Morricone becomes humdrum as it repeats the same thematic signature over and over again, and the overall sound quality is poor. Most important, the continuity of the film is disrupted so frequently that the viewer is frequently lost trying to catch the thread of the narrative. Hampered by poor lighting, even the color photography did not help to improve on the luminous black and white version made ten years earlier. Although this is the director's third film, sometimes it is better not to tamper with a classic novel.

210. La película del rey (A King and His Movie / The King's Movie). Carlos Sorín. Argentina, 1985. 88 min., Eastmancolor. Spanish.

COMMENTARY: A young director, David Vass (Julio Chaves), is determined to make a film on the life of an obscure Frenchman named Orellie Antoine de Tounenes, who declared himself king of Patagonia and Araucania in 1860. As the story of Vass and his movie unfolds, it becomes a tale of obsession — the obsession both of the would-be king and of his would-be biographer.

When the film project runs into financial difficulties, Vass refuses to face reality and instead follows his vision so singlemindedly that he doesn't see the cost to others. As he heads for

Patagonia for location shooting, the obstacles to realizing his project mount.

Vass is gradually abandoned by cast and crew, and for pure absurdity his venture soon competes with that of his hero. As his vision becomes increasingly surreal, obeying a logic of his own creation, the parallels to authoritarian regimes become inescapable — but always within the context of a comedy of mythmaking in the grand scale of filmmaking. (MOMA program notes.)

When the director cannot find a suitable actor to play the king, he picks up a street vendor (probably wanted for some petty crimes by the police) to play the leading role. Sorín continually lampoons the process of choosing actors. He even makes fun of movies as Vass' producer runs off with the monies to finish the film. The vendor also flees when he suspects the police are after him and shaves off the beard necessary for the role.

The actors themselves are as tawdry a collection as you can imagine — an enormous giggling whore, a gay dancing instructor, a street vendor — nonprofessionals all. In the orphanange where the budget-strapped film crew is staying, the gay dance instructor gets them all in trouble because of his seductive behavior with the children. Director Vass wants to complete his film before all the money and actors disappear. And so, in one scene, he even uses dummies standing in for Araucanians — very surreal.

To relax and get away from the situation, the director goes to a revival theatre and watches John Ford's 1939 classic *Stagecoach* for inspiration. When he has to do a scene with an actor who cannot ride, he uses the Ford film as an example in his own pursuit of filmmaking. Other in-jokes include a burlesque of a television interview show, the taping of a film shoot on location where the self-absorbed crew is oblivious to the TV cameras, and a series of hopeless screen tests to find a man with a "great presence."

Of course, the final film that director Vass makes is a disaster, reflecting the absolute chaos of the location shooting. Vass tried to do a real film, but it turned into the caricature of a film within a film. Following the images in Vass' head of John Ford's Monument Valley, the cast goes off to the wind-howling, somber landscapes of Patagonia. It's too bad we couldn't see the film-within-a-film that Vass (Sorín) made, since *La película del rey* draws a fine line between fiction and reality as what unfolds behind the cameras begins to resemble the mad tragedy played in front.

Sorín apparently based the film, his first feature, upon some real (or surreal) experiences of his own concerning a real film he never completed about Orellie Antoine de Tounenes. He may also have drawn inspiration from the experiences of Werner Herzog, especially the difficulties he faced in making *Aguirre* and *Fitzcarraldo*. Whatever the source, he certainly turned his ideas into one of the most imaginative films about moviemaking to come out of Argentina in the mid-eighties. *La película del rey*, above all, turns out to be a satire on a filmmaker's daring to film an impossible subject.

211. Perfume de gardenias (Scent of Gardenias). Guilherme de Almeida Prado. Brazil, 1992. 116 min., Color. Portuguese.

COMMENTARY: Very much as he did in the 1984 film *A dama do cine Shanghai* the director sends up the film noir genre, but this time he includes television soaps (*chanchadas*) and melodramas as well. The story concerns Daniel (José Mayer), a cabdriver who kills a couple who tried to rob him one evening. Switching to the day shift without telling his wife, Giza (Christiane Torloni), of the incident, Daniel suffers guilt. At the same time, Giza is spotted by a movie crew on a shoot and is selected as an extra for a popular soap opera. Giza becomes a television star and leaves Daniel and their small son for fame and fortune. Angered by these twists of fate, Daniel plans revenge. Of course, we dream along with him as he plots, but it turns out that the film is an entirely imaginary scenario in the mind of Daniel.

Perfume de gardenias is funny and tense at the same time. It mixes Hollywood genre conventions to produce an entertainment that is light, bubbleheaded but draws a fine line between dream and reality. There are some hilarious moments, and the acting is all very professional. Compared with Fritz Lang's 1944 great film noir *Woman in the Window*, this film is the Brazilian flip side — noir at its most shallow.

La perla see *The Pearl*

212. Perro de alambre (Wire Dog). Manuel Cano. Venezuela/Spain, 1980. 120 min., Color. Spanish.

COMMENTARY: With a cast of mostly unknowns, *Perro de alambre* tells the story of a fictional country where a communist dictatorship is obviously in power. The theme of the film is repression.

The film consists of a series of chases, captures, torture and prison scenes in which the good guys are obviously caught by the bad guys and there seems to be little hope for survival unless international help is forthcoming.

After this heavy dose of idealism, the final roll-up at the end of the melodramatics consists of quotations from Amnesty International, relating to unlawful imprisonment everywhere in the world, though obviously its intended target is Cuba.

The film was written by the director and by Carlos A. Montaner, a Cuban exile and professor of literature now working in the United States. The film is long on rhetoric, melodrama and propaganda. Besides more accurate and grammatical titles in English, the film is in serious need of cutting. A more discernible narrative approach would minimize the great number of incidents shown, instead provide fewer such scenes in greater depth.

213. Perros de la noche (Dogs of the Night). Teo Kofman. Argentina, 1986. 85 min., Color. Spanish.

COMMENTARY: "The Argentine cinema has established a reputation for sophistication [because of] its focus on the sophisticated middle-class of Buenos Aires. As rare as it is to find a film set outside the capital, it is even rarer to find one set outside of the Argentine middle-class milieu. Thus, Teo Kofman's choice to make the Enrique Medina novel *Perros de la noche* into a movie attracted particular attention. The novel itself had been banned during the years of the military dictatorship. Its setting is the demimonde of Argentina's slums and seedy outposts, a world of marginality which Kofman took on with full vigor in his filmmaking debut. ... Told in a brutally straightforward style, *Perros de la noche* follows its characters through the increasingly degraded circumstances of their existence." (MOMA program notes.)

After their mother's death, Mingo (Emilio Bardi) begins a life of petty crime, while his sister, Mecha (Gabriela Flores), struggles to keep their heads above water by taking menial jobs for low, low pay. When Mingo is finally sent to jail after committing a crime, he meets a group of gangsters there who give him the idea to use his sister as a singer and prostitute in a provincial bar. Mingo starts using his sister in this manner, and they travel the provinces until one day Mecha meets Ferreira (played by Hector Bidone). He is much older, but he really cares for the girl. He gives her the courage to break relations with her brother, which she eventually does and starts to live life on her own terms, without her brother's influence.

Some may see parallels with the films of Hector Babenco and Luis Buñuel when they watch *Perros de la noche*. Kofman's film certainly echoes the work of these directors, as do most films about social conditions, especially the plight of slum children. Shot on real locations, the film has a graininess and edge that give it a kind of super-realism. The only faulty moment in the scenario is the ending. Both *Pixote* and *Los olvidados* have harrowing conclusions. Not that it is not possible to escape slum conditions, but the film suffers from a synthetic, saccharine ending which apparently differs from the book's original downbeat conclusion. Be that as it may, *Perros de la noche* is remarkably vivid, beautifully photographed by Julio Lencina, and it tells a fascinating, if predictable, story. The acting by both Emilio Bardi and Gabriela Flores is especially good, as they age and become more aware of their lives as adults in the demiworld outside of the capital. The recreation of the nightclub and strip-joint milieu is especially well caught by Kofman's engaging use of a wandering and intrusive camera. You can almost see the clients' beads of sweat and smell their cheap perfume in the roadside joints, even feel the rot and dust of the shantytowns that still exist today outside of Buenos Aires.

214. La peste (The Plague).

Luis Puenzo. Argentina, 1992. 146 min., Color. English.

COMMENTARY: Using the 1947 Albert Camus novel *La Peste* as his basis, after the disastrous American film experience with *Old Gringo*, Luis Puenzo decided to film in English again, but this time in Buenos Aires, his home base. He wrote the screenplay and produced the film as well.

The new story is set in South America, year 199–. In yet another film about the practices of military dictatorships, we see public officials herding Argentines into cattle pens, declaring martial law. William Hurt plays Dr. Rieux, who relates the action of the entire film in flashback. The plague is identified as bubonic, and Hurt, together with a cast of international actors, seems to stem the tide of disease, death, philosophizing and overacting by a great many participants in the film.

French actor Jean-Marc Barr plays Jean Tarrou, a TV camerman who becomes a medical volunteer. He fights the plague along with Sandrine Bonnaire, playing Martine Rambert, a professional woman who lends authority to the almost entirely male cast. Americans Raúl Julia and Robert Duvall, as a profiteer and statistician respectively, play their roles with grace and depth.

Death is always in the air, and there is much philosophizing about it as the bluish-gray smog descends over the protagonists, aiding them in their moods of profundity and stretches of ponderous dialogue. The film runs terribly long, despite the relatively short novel it is based upon. Yet director Luis Puenzo has put together a seriously entertaining film. It is beautifully photographed by Félix Monti but sorely in need of a lofty music score.

215. Piel de verano (Summer Skin). Leopoldo Torre Nilsson. Argentina, 1961. 96 min., B&W. Spanish.

COMMENTARY: The story of *Piel de verano* is deceptively simple and clever: A young girl, Marcela (Graciela Borges), is persuaded by her wealthy, loose-living grandmother (Franca Boni) to play up to the dying son of the older woman's lover — the girl's reward to be a year in Paris and a Dior wardrobe. The son,

Brazilian singer Marila Pera plays a prostitute to young actor Fernando Ramos Da Silva's juvenile delinquent in Hector Babenco's 1981 international success, *Pixote*.

Martín, actually falls in love with the girl, and through their love he achieves a cure. But the girl, her aspirations fixed on café society life in Paris, tells him the truth about her grandmother's "deal," and the young man shoots himself. The title refers to the girl's virtue, which peels from her like "summer skin." (Press book.)

Winner of the International Film Prize at the Cannes Film Festival in 1961, *Piel de verano* is a very sultry Argentine reflection on the theme of corruption of one's morals and sentiments. As played by Graciela Borges, Marcela is beautiful, spoiled and empty. She may be young and warm-blooded, but with her desire focused on luxuries, her spirit is cold and calculating. Poor Martín is dying of an incurable chest disease, and his father would like to buy him time and a "relationship" at any price. It is a pity Marcela is moved to revulsion, not rap-

ture, as Martín is slowly cured through love. The other actors — Luciana Possamay as Adela, Martín's nurse who takes care of his "sexual" needs, and Juan Jones as Marcos, a male nurse who bullies everyone in sight, are both effective in supporting roles. But it is the Torre Nilsson-Beatriz Guido screenplay, full of that sixties theme of alienation (so well utilized by Italian director Michelangelo Antonioni), that is new to Argentine society and cinema. Thus Torre Nilsson and his wife made another daring art-house cinema film, revealing of contemporary Argentine society, something they had not dared to do before.

The Pig's War see *La guerra de los cerdos*

216. Pixote (Pixote — Survival of the Weakest). Hector Babenco. Brazil, 1981. 125 min., Color. Brazilian.

COMMENTARY: Revolted by the violence and injustice to which they are subject in a reformatory for the underage in the city of São Paulo, a group of street children — Paulo, Dito, Lilica, Chico and Pixote — breaks away. To survive in this underworld of outlaws and prostitutes, they take to performing a series of petty crimes. Eventually they become involved with a drug dealer who commissions the gang to make a drug delivery in Rio de Janeiro. But the boys get double-crossed, one of them is killed, and Pixote commits his first murder.

They set up a partnership with a hooker called Sueli, mugging her customers at gunpoint. An affectionate relationship develops between the children and the whore, a substitute for the familial affection they have never known. But this does not last long. The group breaks up, and Pixote starts off on his own. (Press book.)

Director Babenco made the following comments about the film: "It did not start off by being called *Pixote.* ... [A]t the start, some 500 children are shown. ... [L]ittle by little, some characters emerge ... someone who starts being called "Pee-wee" (Pixote), a real ten-year-old street child played by Fernando Ramos Da Silva, the macho kid Dito (Gilberto Moura) who falls in love with the effeminate Lilica (Jorge Juliao), who throws him (her) over for Debora (Elke Maravilha), an aging São Paulo streetwalker. The story unravels without a hero. ... From an anonymous group emerge naturally certain individuals. ... The film is not a social document. On the other hand it does not deny that the boys can in part be explained through their social origins; the film never stops showing the social milieu and illustrating the problem ... called hooliganism.... The film was not made to cater to the psychologist, the sociologist or to the politician. The film is poetry only, because it shows at every moment, love

is most important...." (MOMA program notes.)

Pixote is a slice of life, a trenchant look at juvenile delinquency in Brazil of the eighties. Like *Los olvidados,* it is hard to take. It has a despairing view, namely that there is no future for these kids. In reality, the star, Fernando Ramos Da Silva, fathered an illegitimate child and returned to a life of street crime, to be killed by Brazilian police in 1987. But the film is truly a work of art. The performances are all outstanding, especially by Marila Pera, who played the worn-out prostitute Sueli. She is the streetwalker with whom Pixote bonds near the conclusion, becoming his mother-lover figure before she turns him out into the streets, alone again, contemplating a life of crime. *Pixote* has the force of an Émile Zola novel, unremitting in its tale of desperation. It has all the elements of Italian neo-realist cinema, as devastating as Visconti's *La terra trema* or De Sica's *Umberto D,* because of its total caught-in-the-act sense of reality, which devastates the viewer. It would be a far more bleak film if Babenco had made it in black and white. But color helps to contrast the real squalor of São Paulo's slum world with other location shooting in a brighter city like Rio, which at times also appears equally squalid as Babenco's camera probes its own demimonde. *Pixote* is astringent, unsentimental, ruthless cinema at its best.

Pixote — Survival of the Weakest see *Pixote*

A Place in the World see *Un lugar del mundo*

Place Without Limits see *El lugar sin límites*

217. ¡Plaff! ("¡Plaff! Demasiado miedo a la vida" / "Plaff! Too Afraid

of Life"). Juan Carlos Tabio. Cuba, 1988. 110 min., Color. Spanish.

COMMENTARY: One of the first farces to come out of Cuba in years, this one stars Daisy Granados as Concha, a disciple of the African-based Cuban religion known as *santería*, who wants to use this influence to break up the marriage between her baseball-player son, José Ramón (Luis Alberto García) and his engineer wife, Clarita (Thaïs Valdés). After the couple moves into Concha's house, someone mysteriously begins pelting the facade with eggs (making the onomatopoeic sound — "plaff" — of the film's title). Meanwhile, widowed Concha is easy prey for taxi driver Tomás (played by Raúl Pomares), but she prefers to take solace in the joys of *santería* rather than remarry.

The film is full of in-jokes and satire that sometimes wear thin. But it is best when *¡Plaff!* takes aim at its true targets — *santería* and other religious cults, soap opera, government control, bureaucracy and the art of filmmaking in the Third World — and hits them hard (*plaff!*). For example, there is a filing cabinet full of unnecessary letters blocking an office door, but to remove it, a mail sack full of "necessary" letters must be written, then stored in the same inconvenient space. The director is also fond of cinematic jokes, like always admitting to the presence of the camera in scenes with mirrors, or throwing in props, gags or the sight of camera crews doing bumbling work to give the impression that the film is a disaster and that Third World cinema is indeed inefficient and unworkable.

The director is trying to make a screamingly funny farce with a happy ending. But despite the intentional bad editing, continuity fluffs, acting histrionics, hyperbolic use of sound, visible camera booms and props just thrown on to the set by intrusive crews caught in the frame, the film cannot hide a very conventional morality, which sadly puts the kibosh on its venture towards something fresh and free and makes the film rather sane and even nauseating in its moral outlook. It looks as if the director was trying to do a Preston Sturges comedy in Cuba, but the zaniness was suppressed and he had to return to political reality — and to being the real Juan Carlos Tabio, gifted but controlled by the practiced hand of the censor. One day Tabio's gifts will soar beyond official Cuban artistic controls.

Plaff! Too Afraid of Life see *¡Plaff!*

The Plague see *La peste*

218. Plata dulce (Easy Money). Fernando Ayala. Argentina, 1982. 90 min., Color. Spanish.

COMMENTARY: "Made during the waning days of military rule and opening in Buenos Aires just one month after the Malvinas War, *Plata dulce* reveals the economic chaos and ethical turpitude that accompanied the junta's downfall.... Its portrait of everyday life in 1981–82 may toe the line for its time (in presumed deference to censorship parameters, for instance, there is no mention of politics or the 'disappeared'), yet it constitutes a perfect snapshot of what was going wrong. ... A prelude to the kind of filmmaking that would follow the democratization of Argentine society in the following year, *Plata dulce* suggests just how far it was possible to go so long as certain obvious truths were avoided." (MOMA program notes.)

Plata dulce is the first satirical comedy to come out of Argentina in years. It is merciless, using comic strategies to picture the economic and moral disintegration of the period. The twisted lives and lowered moral ethics of the period are beautifully captured in the screenplay by Oscar Viale and Jorge Goldenberg.

Federico Luppi plays Carlos Bonifatti, and Julio De Grazia plays Rubén Molinuevo. They are married to two sisters, Ofelia (Adriana Alzemberg) and Cora (Flora Steinberg), and are partners in a factory that produces medicine chests, whose business is destroyed by Taiwanese imports. Rubén, the actual maker, is hardest hit, while Carlos, the accountant for the firm, takes another job as the head of a real estate and lending company. For a while, Carlos lives high on the hog, taking spending trips to Miami, going on wild shopping sprees, taking a new lover (his niece Patricia, played by Marina Skell). But Carlos discovers he has been a victim of a gigantic swindle engineered by Arteche (Gianni Lunadel), his old friend, who escapes with the money and the girl to live in the United States while Carlos goes to jail.

The comedy behind the real economic circumstances is quite dark for Argentines. In fact, the film exposes how the economic reforms of 1976 opened the doors of the financial market to many swindlers and created unemployment and colossal indebtedness through the artificial underevaluation of the dollar and the substitution of imports for local products.

The actors do very well in this hilarious but painful comedy. Luppi as the duped former industrialist, de Grazia as his former partner and Lunadel as the treacherous Arteche give excellent performances. The women are also good, especially Marina Skell as the sexpot Patricia, willing to seduce her uncle but at all times keeping her eyes on the money. *Plata dulce* is another wonderfully satiric film, produced by the Ayala-Olivera team, that makes Argentine cinema one of the most exciting and engaging to watch because of its international perspectives. It is possible *Plata dulce* could take place in the United States!

219. Pobre mariposa (Poor Butterfly). Raúl de la Torre. Argentina, 1986. 118 min., Color. Spanish.

COMMENTARY: "The story takes place in Buenos Aires in 1945, from the last days of Hitler and the fall of Berlin until the rise of Perón to total power in Argentina. Clara (Graciela Borges), a well-known, attractive radio broadcaster, is married to a surgeon, Julio (Lautaro Murua), twenty years older than she is; they have three daughters. Her tranquil existence is disrupted when she learns of the death of her father, Boris Somoloff, a socialist journalist of Russian-Jewish origin. Clara is confronted by memories of the world she belonged to until she was ten years old, her father's world, with his Jewish roots and progressive realities. It appears her father did not die of natural causes. His investigation of the infiltration of top Nazi leaders into Argentina's circles of power leads him to a violent death. Along with the rediscovery of this world — her grandmother's language, the rituals surrounding her father's burial, the encounter with her first love, her cousin José (Victor Laplace), the dreams of her uncle Sholoime (Pepe Soriano), her husband's fear of aging — she is also confronted by the disquieting question: "What does it mean to be a Jew?" Just as Argentina, the naive country of light entertainment, is entering a new phase of its history, so is Clara. While she tries to reconstruct the past and comprehend the present, Clara is putting her future in jeopardy." (MOMA program notes.)

Pobre mariposa is a visually stunning film, photographed by Marcello Camorino in gorgeous Technicolor that recaptures the era of Nazi Germany in the forties before the film shifts its focus to Buenos Aires. Graciela Borges gives a nicely modulated performance in the role of Clara. As she begins to discover the mysteries of her past and the death of her father, she reminds one of Norma

Aleandro in Luis Puenzo's *La historia oficial*, for both women make discoveries that severely alter their lives. Just as Norma Aleandro is jettisoned out of her smug, bourgeois world into the conflict and uncertainty of a growing military dictatorship, so is Graciela Borges made aware of the reality of what is to be Perón's Argentina and his support of facism. One wonders if Clara's father was killed by Nazis who fled the European war to live in Argentina under Perón's protection. Was it just coincidental that she received the news of her father's death on the day of a public demonstration supporting Juan Perón's ascendancy as dictator of Argentina? The subplot of Nazi-hunting Jews takes on a new meaning for us in light of the development of Clara's persona and her eventual illumination. The director has sought to recreate Clara's entire world and its disintegration, not to make a thriller like Franklin Schaffner's 1978 *The Boys from Brazil*. The wonderful thing about *Pobre mariposa* is its calm, its intellectual appeal, its story that overwhelms by its utter simplicity. It is a tour de force for its director, Raúl de la Torre, and certainly deserving of international attention and acclaim.

Poor Butterfly see *Pobre mariposa*

220. Las Poquianchis. Felipe
Cazals. Mexico, 1976. 115 min., Color. Spanish.

COMMENTARY: Based upon true incidents taking place in Mexico during the period 1951–1964, the film's screenplay, written by author Tomás Pérez Turrent, was taken from a novel by Jorge Ibargüengoitia. Its main theme is white slavery and prostitution.

The opening scene takes place at a decrepit old house in the country. The police uncover a group of abused and trapped girls who were forced into prostitution by three sisters who ran this place as a bordello. Several graves of girls are found in the courtyard. The film then uses flashback to tell how two young girls (played by Diana Bracho and Tina Romero) were lured away from their peasant father, an impoverished farm laborer (Jorge Martínez de Hoyos), by the sisters who owned the bordello, the Poquianchis. The film does not spare the details of how the girls were beaten and starved into submission to become prostitutes.

The girls were originally promised room and board and work in a large city when the Poquianchis paid their parents a pittance for them. Instead, the girls were used as brothel slaves, lived on a rigorous diet of spiced beans and were so roughly beaten if they did not take as many clients as possible that they were eventually killed and buried in the backyard by their whoremasters. While depicting this terrible exploitation of the girls, director Cazals also develops a subplot taking place during the López Mateos regime, showing how peasants are losing their land to cattle barons. When they try to reclaim the land, they are killed by the barons. These peasants are also the parents of the girls who sold their daughters in the hope of bettering their lives. The public prosecutor (Alejandro Parodi) discovers an insidious pattern that undermines the lives of the Mexican poor.

The film is an indictment of the ignorance of rural peasants, the land barons who exploit them and the city-run brothels that exploit the daughters of the poor. When some of the girls are asked why they didn't escape from the brothel, their response was to ask where could they have gone to find life any better.

The film is harsh, mixing black and white scenes with color to emphasize the graphic nature of the subject. Adding to the stark realism, the film uses some non-professionals, real Indian and Mexican peasant faces, lending a documentary-like air to the production. The filmmakers have pulled out all the stops, for they want you to remember the evil exploitation committed by two sisters, the Poquianchis, who deserve a worse fate than the law allows. There is a sense of hopelessness in the faces of the peasants, and one wonders if true evil like this, as depicted in the film, will ever be redressed.

Portable Country see *País portátil*

Portrait of Teresa see *Retrato de Teresa*

221. La primera carga del machete (The First Charge of the Machete). Manuel Octavio Gómez. Cuba, 1969. 84 min., B&W. Spanish.

COMMENTARY: "In October 1868, an uprising against Spanish domination on the island of Cuba takes place. The cry of "always faithful to Cuba" is heard everywhere. The insurgents take hold of Bayamon, one of the main cities. The Spanish general sends columns of the colonial army to retake the city and smash the rebellion. The Cuban troops force one of the columns to retreat through military strategy rather than direct confrontation.

"The second column is destroyed at the doors of Bayamon in a quick attack using machetes. It was the first of a long series of charges with this weapon that provided victories and made possible Cuba's triumph in their wars for independence from Spain. The initial attack was led by a Dominican called Maximo Gómez." (Press book.)

This spectacular film is a chronicle, analyzing cinematically the methods used by Maximo Gómez, who first converted the machete into a decisive weapon against the Spanish colonials. It

is a grandiloquent historical film, using a documentary method with very modern techniques (including interviews, direct sound, and hand-held cameras). For example, a group of Cubans are interviewed in Havana about their "opinions" concerning independence and its significance for them. Also, Spanish soldiers who have survived the machete charges tell of their terror while escaping from the battle. There is also a balladeer, Pablo Milanés, who comments on the action of the battle as the film reaches its conclusion.

La primera carga del machete is Cuban experimental cinema at its best. The film not only recaptures the past, but brings its anti-war and proud nationalistic message home to the present. It is a worthy cinematic experience.

222. Primera crónica (First Chronicle). Patricio Guzmán. Chile, 1971. 100 min., B&W. Spanish.

COMMENTARY: A fascinating prelude to Guzmán's monumental *La batalla de Chile*, *Primera crónica* deals with themes such as the nationalization of the copper mines and textile mills, the plight and problems of the Mapuche Indians of southern Chile, Fidel Castro's visit, and problems emanating from interviews with workers, miners and peasants, showing their dissatisfaction in the first fourteen months of President Salvador Allende's Popular Front government.

Primera crónica displays Patricio Guzmán's gift as a documentary filmmaker. His camera probes the events as he captures the emotional reactions of those interviewed while the political scene unravels around them. Guzmán seems an impartial observer, perhaps able to foresee the overthrow of the Allende government, which goes unsuspected in this earlier documentary. But dissatisfaction was certainly in the air, and *Primera crónica* captures the feeling through its

Italian actor Renato Salvatori (left) as a mulatto is shaking hands with Evaristo Márquez, playing a revolutionary leader, as American actor Marlon Brando (playing an English diplomat) stands between them in Gillo Pontecorvo's film *¡Quemada!* (*Burn!* 1970).

seemingly steely, unemotional filmmaker. It is worthwhile to see this film before attempting the gigantic and overpowering *La batalla de Chile.*

The Promised Land see *La tierra prometida*

223. Pubis angélical (Angel Hair). Raúl de la Torre. Argentina, 1982. 117 min., Color. Spanish.

COMMENTARY: Set in the 1970s and adapted from a novel by Argentine writer Manuel Puig and starring Graciela Borges in the leading role of Ana, the film deals essentially with Ana's life, which oscillates between life and death, dream and reality.

After convalescing from a cancer operation in Mexico City, Ana must return home to Buenos Aires. Reality and fantasy mix constantly with pres-

ent and past as Ana seeks to rebuild her life.

This is the main drama of the film, and the director, with his unique insights into feminine psychology, portrays Ana as a woman on the periphery, trying her best at self-discovery.

The film version of the Puig novel is perhaps more successful than its original. More of an art house cinema discovery, *Pubis angélical* did not succeed with American audiences, but it is finding new fans in its video version.

224. ¡Quemada! (Burn!). Gillo Pontecorvo. Italy/France, 1970. 132 min., Color by Deluxe. English.

COMMENTARY: To a wonderful musical score by Ennio Morricone, enhanced by beautiful camera work by Marcello Gatti, Marlon Brando and Renato Salvatori star in this fascinating film made on location on islands near Venezuela. The story concerns a diplomat, Sir William Walker (played somewhat dazedly by Brando), who is sent to an unnamed Caribbean island to break the Portuguese sugar monopoly but becomes involved with revolutionaries who want to free the island from the colonials.

Evaristo Márquez plays José Dolores, the uneducated revolutionary who at Walker's urging foments violence against a British sugar cartel and takes control, letting the mulattoes led by Teddy Sánchez (Renato Salvatori in unconvincing black makeup) run the island. Actually, Walker's instigation is a ploy to rid the island of former Portuguese intervention so the British can keep the profits themselves and share the wealth with the natives. But Portuguese influence assumes a threatening stance ten years later, and Walker is sent back to repeat his instigator role for the British. However, the revolutionaries have grown wiser and do not need a middle-man when they can enjoy the profits themselves. Walker is killed by one of Dolores' henchmen in a bloody battle.

Although the acting is at times wooden, even laughable, the settings and scenic design are marvelous in color. Location shooting proved an obvious bonus for a somewhat shaky "historical" rendition of a semifictional event. As in *Battle of Algiers*, Pontecorvo wanted *¡Quemada!* to echo his feelings regarding the self-destructive nature of colonialism. The film succeeds on this level, but not as well as his remarkably realistic evocation of Algerian resistance against the French in 1966. Perhaps he was beginning to run out of revolutionary rhetoric.

NOTES: Gillo Pontecorvo is an Italian filmmaker born in Pisa in 1919. He worked internationally with Brazilian Alberto Cavalcanti and Dutch Joris Ivens in the fifties before making an international success with *The Battle of Algiers* in 1966. *¡Quemada!* followed shortly after in 1969, and his last film to date was made ten years later, entitled *Operation Ogro — The Tunnel.*

225. Quilombo. Carlos Diegues. Brazil, 1984. 127 min., Color. Portuguese.

COMMENTARY: "This is the story of a Negro community called Quilombo dos Palmares, which held out for over a century and which was formed by slaves who had run away from European violence, domination and persecution.

"Under the leadership of Ganga Zumba, the nation of former slaves develops its own economy and establishes the genuine structure of an independent state. Ana de Ferro, a French prostitute, becomes a refugee in the community. She becomes not only Ganga Zumba's lover but also advisor to the king of Palmares. Kidnapped by the whites while still a small child, Zumbi, Ganga Zumba's godson, escapes back to Palmares and becomes the community leader. But Ganga Zumba and Zumbi disagree as to which politics to adopt in dealing with the whites: Ganga Zumba accepts the white people's proposal to discuss a treaty of peace, but Zumbi believes there can be no harmony as long as there are slaves. The white men's cannons are then used to destroy the community of Palmares, in the northeast of Brazil." (Press book.)

Before its destruction in 1694, Palmares lasted nearly one hundred years. Deservedly, the story of this Utopia receives epic treatment in *Quilombo*. (It was also the subject of director Carlos Diegues' very first film made in 1963, entitled *Ganga zumba*.) It is splendidly acted by Toni Tornado as Ganga Zumba, Antonio Pompeo as Zumbi, Vera Fischer as Ana de Ferro and several hundred extras who appear in the film's bloody conclusion of startling battle scenes, as the Portuguese (who have just defeated the Dutch) invade the mountains and defeat the former slaves.

The film has an exotic flavor because of its beautiful color photography by Lauro Escorel Filho and Pedro Farkas and is aided by the wonderful music score of Gilberto Gil, whose use of native rhythms is spectacular. *Quilombo* reminds one of an earlier Diegues film, *Xica da Silva* (1976), another story about black power in a colonial setting. Yet *Quilombo* is more triumphant as a film because it idealizes its characters and places them on a pedestal — they are already a part of Brazilian history, and they are to be respected and revered. This kind of historical perspective sometimes gives the film a static quality, but this is a minor point in a relatively fascinating film that assumes panoramic proportions. It is a story of how great heroes are forged by fire through terribly epic events, and how they triumph spiritually even in their loss. This is the essence of *Quilombo* and why it fascinates.

226. Raíces (The Roots). Benito Alazraki. Mexico, 1958. 85 min., B&W. Spanish.

COMMENTARY: *Raíces* is a small, beautiful film that contains a collection of four stories by Francisco González. In the first, "The Cows," a mother becomes a wet nurse to support her family. In the second, "Our Lady," an American anthropologist becomes aware that the Indians she lives with are not savages. In the third, "The One-eyed Boy," a badly treated, almost blind boy finds happiness when he beomes totally blind. In the fourth and last story, "The Filly," a Mexican girl is bartered by her parents to an American anthropologist who receives a higher offer to let her go and marry a Mexican.

Of all the episodes, the first is the strongest because it shows how impoverished the Mexicans really are. When a spoiled city couple comes by car to find a wet nurse, offering a ridiculous sum of money for an Indian woman to nurse their baby instead of her own, the Indian mother puts her baby in her husband's arms and says, ironically, "Now you have a cow." There is righteous anger here. The director is trying to show how the Mexican Indians are rooted to their land, how the sun smiles down upon them, how the idea of a God gives them sustenance — they are like potted plants surviving from the earth and spiritual elements. But Alazraki also shows the misery of the Mexican Indian's condition, and Francisco González's short stories tend to magnify the condition of the rootedness, almost as a protest to end these unbearable circumstances of the fifties.

NOTES: Benito Alazraki was born in Mexico in 1923 and worked with Emilio Fernández on many of his films, especially as co-scenarist on the latter's *Enamorada* (1947). In 1955, he won the International Critics Prize at the Cannes Film Festival for *Raíces*. His subsequent films have generally been potboilers and have attracted little worldwide attention. His last Mexican film was entitled *Los pistoleros* (1961) and in 1962 he made one in the United States under the pseudonym Carlos Arconti called *The Time and the Touch*, an insignificant B film.

227. Raíces de sangre (Roots of Blood). Jesús Salvador Trevino. Mexico, 1976. 100 min., Color. Spanish.

COMMENTARY: Like Martin Ritt's 1979 film *Norma Rae*, *Raíces de Sangre* covers the problems of workers in the garment industry. However, Trevino's film is a Chicano problem picture concerning the female garment industry in an American-owned plant just south of the Texas-Mexico border. Throw in some other problems like *los mojados* (wetbacks) and the usual traffic in illegal drugs plus a section on racial pride, and *Raíces de sangre* contains all the possibilities for Third World propaganda.

The film stars Ricardo Yniguez as Carlos Rivera, who has cut his Mexican roots to obtain a degree in law from Harvard and live the high life in a San Francisco suburb. While working for a community action group called Barrio Unido in Mexico one summer, Carlos rediscovers his roots and his people.

The film also tackles divisiveness among proles in the movement for solidarity, the temptation of the American dollar to Mexican workers who would betray the union movement, the reluctance of parents to become involved politically, conflict among radical youths who yearn for power, and strategic problems of organization against the political powers that be.

Raíces de sangre is wonderful Chicano-style cinema. It is beautifully shot in color by Rosalio Solano and has an excellent music score by Sergio Guerrero which aids the dramatic action onscreen. Jesús Salvador Trevino had total control over the film, writing, producing and directing it. Although there are some gaps in continuity, it is a solidly made Chicano problem film that excels in its call to political activism.

228. Raoni. Jean-Pierre Dutilleux. France/Belgium, 1978. 82 min., color. French.

COMMENTARY: A fascinating documentary with a spoken French soundtrack and Brazilian music by Egberto Gismonti, *Raoni* takes its name from an Amazon Indian chieftan who meets with a Brazilian Indian agent and asks for help before there is civil war among the tribes, threatening that they may direct their anger against the white men in charge unless their conflicts are resolved.

The conflicts are never made specific, but civilization is impinging upon the tribes as roads are built into their part of the jungle. Apparently the Indians are angry about the loss of their lands, and the government has done nothing to assuage their anger.

As their representative, Raoni (who has a disked lower lip like the Ubangi tribes) presents the Indian problems as best he can on his own terms in his native habitat. Dutilleux is careful to include lots of extra footage of Indian life and customs of this particular Amazon group, but the film lacks drama and penetration into the everyday life of the inhabitants in this part of the Amazon jungle. It does satisfy, though, as a sociological exploration into the declining rain forest of the Amazon and the problems therein for both Amazonian Indians and Brazilians alike. Apparently there was another soundtrack made expressly for American audiences with the voice of Marlon Brando, the actor and Indian activist, narrating the plight of the Indians.

The Rattlesnake see *Cascabel*

The Realm of Fortune see *El império de la fortuna*

Rebellion in Patagonia see *La Patagonia rebelde*

The Red Light Bandit see *O bandido de luz vermelha*

229. Redes (The Wave / The Nets). Paul Strand and Fred Zinnemann. Mexico/U.S., 1937. 57 min., B&W. Spanish.

COMMENTARY: Set in the tiny fishing village of Alvarado in the state of Vera Cruz, *Redes* seeks to explain the fishing methods of Mexican natives. Unjust working conditions and lack of solidarity among fishermen are portrayed as social themes of the film, but they are incidental to the travelogue nature of the footage. The photography by Paul Strand is utterly spectacular and combines readily with the liberal agit-prop in which the film seems to indulge.

There are wondrous skyscapes and seascapes, beautiful contrasts of light and shadow that are reminiscent of Sergei Eisenstein's magnificent *¡Qué viva Mexico!* (1932) but anticipate the beautiful camera work of Mexico's photographic genius, Gabriel Figueroa, especially in the 1947 film *La perla*.

Although the film indulges in too many close-ups of beautiful but inexpressive native faces and ends somewhat abruptly after suggesting some kind of revisionist social reform, we are left in the dark, literally and figuratively, wondering why this film was made at all — as some kind of socialist propaganda piece, or as an excuse for a scenic tour of Mexico's gorgeous eastern coast? In retrospect, the film certainly did not hurt the career of European director Fred Zinnemann, who began his ascent with the MGM studios shortly thereafter.

NOTES: Fred Zinnemann was born in 1907 in Vienna. He made his film debut with *Redes* in 1937 as a co-director of the documentary and made a great number of fascinating films through the mid-eighties. His most enthralling ones for this viewer are *High Noon* (1952), *A Nun's Story* (1959), *A Man for All Seasons* (1966) and *Julia* (1977). His autobiography, *A Life in the Movies*, was published in 1992.

Paul Strand was born in New York in 1890 and died there in 1976. He was mainly a still photographer but made some wonderful films, notably *Redes*, *The Plow That Broke the Plains* (1936), *The Heart of Spain* (1937), *Return to Life* (1938) and *China Strikes Back* (1939), documentaries all.

230. Renuncia por motivos de salud (Resigned for Reasons of Health). Rafael Baledon. Mexico, 1976. 95 min., Color. Spanish.

COMMENTARY: In this film about corruption in government, Ignacio López Tarso plays Don Gustavo, a scrupulously honest engineer and construction chief for twenty-two years. In a position that lends itself to favors and taking bribes, Gustavo is forced to struggle with his conscience at the sight of a *mordida* or bribe. His son-in-law, an ambitious functionary in the same ministry, encourages Gustavo to look the other way concerning overcharges. But Gustavo reevaluates his conscience.

With pressure from his daughter, Gustavo realizes he is working in a rudderless world, where colleagues betray each other for material gain. When he asks his son, a college drop-out, for his opinions on bribery, the son answers that there is no conscience these days and no one cares about it. In a final confrontation scene with his boss, the minister, Gustavo reveals the bribe scheme, risking his reputation and his own job security. The film ends with both men trying to effect as much change as they can in an already corrupt bureaucratic system.

Ignacio López Tarso plays Don Gustavo with much more dignity than the role deserves. His long-suffering wife as played by Carmen Montejo gives him the kind of emotional support Don Gustavo expects, hand-wringing and teary-eyed, on the edge of depression, but without a word towards a concrete solution to his ethical problems.

The rest of the cast fares as well as the leading actors, but tighter direction would have made this a more memorable social-problem film rather than just another family melodrama with governmental trappings. The message, however, is loud and clear: there is corruption everywhere, not only in official life, but in business, in society, in the family, as well as personal corruption. We must break the chain of corruption so that the Mexican nation will survive.

The film ends with Don Gustavo rolling up his sleeves, making a beginning, hoping the next generation will continue the fight for honesty.

231. Reportaje a la muerte

(**Reports of Death**). Danny Gavidia. Peru, 1993. 95 min., Color. Spanish.

COMMENTARY: One of the first prison films to come out of Peru, based upon a real incident in 1984, this is the director's debut film. It is a suspense thriller with an incredible ending, but it keeps its audience very well entertained.

The film takes place in a Lima prison during the eighties, where rival gangs of terrorists and radicals are housed together with the expectation that there will be a riot in the future. A visit by a political entourage, which includes a woman ambassador (Marthe Figueroa) from Venezuela, triggers the violence. During the riot, she is taken as a hostage along with two other visitors and a prison guard.

The film then shifts gears. Local media executives believe live televison coverage of the event is necessary and send a news team consisting of Anel, a female reporter from Caracas (Marisol Palacios),and Alfredo, a local cameraman (Diego Berti). There is instant rivalry between the two of them. Alfredo strikes a male chauvinst pose, and Anel talks about her former lover, another cameraman, who lost his life in the line of duty. The two become closer emotionally as they proceed with the coverage of the riot.

Meanwhile, the film continues with predictable scenes of violence caught by the television camera. The script condemns the violence but also the manner of coverage since the prisoners have access to televison and can watch their own exploits. Although the concept of "riots as entertainment" wears thin, the action scenes are staged with verve and suspense. The Peruvian gang leaders are in top form, with names like "El Conde" and "Alcaide" that show leadership of sorts. But the director is interested in more than depiction of the riot itself. He is protesting violent entertainment as a part of television coverage. Directors like Don Siegel did not care a whit about this concept when he made *Riot in Cell Block II* in the fifties. Hollywood prison riots were always fun to watch on screen. But Davidia's rendition of a Peruvian prison riot is sometimes as frightening as the real thing.

Reports of Death see *Reportaje a la muerte*

Republic of Sin see *La Fièvre monte à el pao*

232. La república perdida, partes I y II (The Lost Republic, Parts I and II). Miguel Pérez. Argentina, 1983, 1985. 278 min., Color and B&W. Spanish.

COMMENTARY: *La república perdida, parte I* is a documentary of Argentine history from 1930 to 1976 — a period which includes Perón's first presidency, the liberal movement of Frondizi and the military governments of Onganía and Lanusse, and ends with Perón's return from exile for a second term, succeeded by his third wife, Isabel. Using salvaged archival footage, Miguel Pérez structures his history in terms of the conflicts between the oligarchy and the masses, perhaps not surprisingly since the period he analyzes begins and ends with military coups. Released in Argentina just before the democratic elections, *La república perdida, parte I* was heavily attended and hotly debated

La república perdida, parte II continues the history through 1983, probably the country's darkest period, when it suffered under a reign of state terror unprecedented in Latin American history. What is revealed here seems a cross between Hitlerian reality and Kafkaesque fiction. Following the overthrow of Isabel Perón's conservative democracy, the military was able to establish its repressive rule with such statements as "Democracy is the sign of a healthy nation; ours is too sick for it," and "Our society is insane, so orders must be followed without question." The congress and the supreme court were put out of business; kidnappings, torture, summary executions and the (now) well documented "disappearances" followed. Pérez interviews survivors and relatives, interweaving their recollections with footage of government propaganda and choice quotes from the likes of General Videla. The Malvinas War is portrayed as a clever move to unite the nation, but it was not long before the Plaza de Mayo again filled with outraged citizens. The return of democracy with the election of Raúl Alfonsín marks an almost suspiciously upbeat end to what has been so consistently a tragic story. (MOMA program notes.)

Director Pérez hurtles image upon image on the screen until the viewer is simply overwhelmed. He has a strong narrative sense and is skillful in weaving in propaganda material and many political leaders' reactions to it. Even by quoting famous Argentine politicos he tends to ridicule them, lending clever insights into their roles in Argentine history. As the film moves from dictatorship to democracy, it loses its downbeat factuality and becomes almost joyful in concluding its cogent rendering of over fifty years of Argentine history. Ambitious, sweeping, informative, urgent, torrential, overpowering — these are some of the adjectives that best describe the two-part film *La república perdida*. It will stand the test of time and is a worthy companion to other great Latin American documentaries like Patricio Guzmán's *La batalla de Chile* or Fernando Solanas's *La hora de los hornos*,

which deal with the yoke of oppression and the revival of democracy.

Resigned for Reasons of Health see *Renuncia por motivos de salud*

233. Retrato de Teresa (Portrait of Teresa). Pastor Vega. Cuba, 1978. 103 min., Color. Spanish.

COMMENTARY: Women's liberation in Cuba twenty years after the revolution is the theme. The story revolves around Teresa, who works in a textile factory, and her marriage to Ramón, a TV repairman. Teresa is the chief organizer of her factory's dance group, which, partly through her efforts, has become good enough to compete on a national level. Despite this activity and her job duties, the traditional family situation leaves Teresa with the primary responsibility for taking care of the home and their three children.

Although already overburdened with the housework and her factory job, Teresa nevertheless enjoys the dance group, her chance to develop outside of her family and job roles. But Teresa's involvement with the dance group irritates her husband. He complains that she is disregarding her sacred duties as wife and mother. In frustration, Teresa shouts, "What about my life as a human being?" and slaps him in the face.

Teresa goes to her mother for advice but gets no support. Ramón becomes more and more annoyed. He wants out, and leaves Teresa with the house, the kids, her job and her responsibility to the dance group she won't give up.

Ramón begins an affair with another woman, but he is miserable and tries repeatedly to come back. At one point, he and Teresa go to bed together; but when he returns thereafter, Teresa won't have him. Later she changes the lock on the door, making clear the new definition of the relationship.

Ramón attempts a final reconciliation

"An artistic and dramatic success ...Beautifully played...

In Daisy Granados's extraordinary performance... We see nothing less than the evolution of the Women's Movement."

MOLLY HASKELL/MS.MAGAZINE

There's a little of Teresa in every woman.

Directed by Pastor Vega/Starring Daisy Granados & Adolfo Llaurado

A UNIFILM RELEASE

1550 Bryant Street
San Francisco, CA 94103
Phone (415) 864-7755

419 Park Avenue South
New York, NY 10016
Phone (212) 686-9890

Advertising flyer for Pastor Vega's Cuban film *Retrato de Teresa* (*Portrait of Teresa*, 1978) showing Daisy Granados gazing in a mirror and realizing how different she is since her marriage.

with Teresa, and meets with her to discuss the possibility of their living together again. She confronts Ramón with her knowledge of his extramarital affair and questions the fairness of his double standard. Clearly, Teresa has grown into a new role. Faced with the choice between her life with Ramón and the life she now leads, she chooses to define herself in terms that may not include him. (Press book.)

At their last meeting, Teresa (Daisy Granados) asks Ramón (Adolfo Llaurado) what he would do if she had an extramarital affair. Ramón does not answer, and Teresa walks off into the crowded streets of Havana as Ramón follows, somewhat surprised, puzzled, thinking and trying to catch her.

Worthy of mention is Alina Sánchez, who plays Ramón's pragmatic lover. Ramón makes a romantic fool of himself trying to say goodbye to her when their affair ends, since his paramour is ready to go on to another man. Sex is not that important to her, but real love is. Also Raúl Pomares, who plays Teresa's factory supervisor, is a terrific actor and a terrific character who gives Teresa the best, fatherly advice and impels her to go on with her own life, whatever the cost.

Retrato de Teresa is a wonderfully made film, tightly directed and beautifully acted. Although it may teeter on the edge of television sit-com, it has a very serious message about defining men's and women's roles, not just in Cuban society, but universally. In his debut feature, director Pastor Vega has come up with a commercially appealing film that should play far beyond the borders of Cuba.

NOTES: Pastor Vega was born in Havana in 1940. Coming from a theatrical background, he began filmmaking in 1961 and directed his first documentary that year. His best-known documentaries are *Viva la república* (1972), which is a historical compilation about Cuba,

and *Panama: The Fifth Frontier* (1974), which explores the problem of ownership of the Panama Canal and debates the difficulties of control. *Retrato de Teresa* is his first fictional feature. He is married to actress Daisy Granados, and their three children appear in the film. Granados worked for a short time in a textile mill to prepare for her role.

234. El rincón de las vírgenes (The Virgin's Corner / Nest of Virgins). Alberto Isaac. Mexico, 1973. 99 min., Color. Spanish.

COMMENTARY: *El rincón de las vírgenes* is a quirky tragicomedy based upon several stories by Juan Rulfo, most notably "Anacleto Morones" and "El Día Derrumbe." Set in the 1920s, the film features Emilio Fernández as Anacleto Morones, a small-time pedlar who passes himself off as a miracle man, later to be declared "venerable" on his way to sainthood. The film shows us that the pedlar has achieved more status by sexual means than by religious; that his sidekick, Lucas Lucatero (Alfonso Arau), is an immoral opportunist who once narrated rural showings of silent films; and that his daughter, Leona (Rosalba Brambila), is a strange combination of lyricism and promiscuity (she later marries Lucas, who thinks he is coming into saintliness but is really betrothed to a whore). The province in which the trio works their "magic" or con games is presided over by a governor (Hector Ortega) who is pompous and ineffectual, unable to control the group of swindlers.

The film always plays illusion against reality through its flashback structure. The director reaches beyond satire to present a portrait of the grim ironies of life that astounds us. There are also several surprising scenes of frank nudity as well as some folkloric songs that add to the ambience of the film. The film is full of Mexican social and cultural references and shafts of biting humor that find their targets easily. Isaac crucifies the rural classes, with their false morality. He attacks (thru Rulfo's stories) the ignorance of the church with its need for ritual, as well as government agencies with their bureaucratic postures. The film is beautifully photographed, and one can appreciate its ironic title only after seeing it.

Rodrigo "D": No Future see *Rodrigo "D": no futuro*

235. Rodrigo "D": no futuro (Rodrigo "D": No Future). Victor Gaviria. Colombia, 1988. 90 min., Color. Spanish.

COMMENTARY: "From a top floor window of a building in central Medellín, Rodrigo, who is not more than twenty, interrupts the city's normal tempo by trying to jump out. Unemployed, reduced to wandering about aimlessly, bewildered and perplexed, Rodrigo is a lonely, indigent being who prefers to die rather than be obliged to kill. From the window he shouts to the city to listen to him, to take him into account. His attitude is a reaction to apathy and a call to life." (Press book.)

The film presents a slice of life as we follow Rodrigo and his teenager friends over a several-day period, exploring their world and surviving as best they can. Rodrigo (Ramiro Meneses) can't sleep at night. He has headaches and thinks about his mother, who died sometime previous to the film's story. He is also looking for a drum kit so he can start a punk band with his chums, who sell cocaine to school kids, steal cars, listen to raucous punk music or just hang around. The story is unsettling, more often for things unsaid. Rodrigo's suicide becomes an existential decision in the face of a hopeless future. (MOMA program notes.)

Based on a real story about a teenager named Rodrigo Alonso, who leaped from a downtown building in Medellín, this naturalistic film is as powerful as it is bleak. Medellín is probably the most dangerous city in the world, and life is so precarious there. In fact, three teenagers who acted in this film are now dead, violently killed because of the drug situation.

When an audience watches *Rodrigo "D"* they feel very much on the outside, since Medellín is like no other city one knows. There is constant danger in the air; Rodrigo and his friends are always in pursuit or being pursued, looking for a good night's sleep in a safe place. The soundtrack constantly uses the grating, high-pitched sounds of punk rock to disturb the viewer. When the film ends with Rodrigo's suicide plunge (which you suspect but don't really see), you are glad the film is over but feel as if you were assaulted by the soundtrack, the images and the director's relentless pursuit of his points about Colombian youth and society — jobs, education, affluence, but no drugs. The soundtrack is turbulent, the photography restless and edgy; the film is genuinely disturbing, but what a fantastic experience. This is *Pixote* for the nineties. *Rodrigo "D"* is a revolutionary piece of filmmaking, a vibrantly kinetic work about a murderous teenage culture.

NOTES: Born in 1955 and a native of Medellín, Victor Gaviria studied filmmaking with Spanish director José Luis Borau and others. He worked in Colombian television and has made many, many short films, but *Rodrigo "D": no futuro* is his first feature production.

236. Romance da empregada (The Story of Fausta). Bruno Barreto. Brazil, 1988. 100 min., Color. Portuguese.

COMMENTARY: This is a woeful tale of a woman who lives with her truckdriver husband in a slum in Rio, with no where to go except down, down, down.

Ramiro Menenses plays the dysfunctional teenager holding drum batons and looking down dejectedly in a slum area of Medellín in Victor Gaviria's trenchant first film from Colombia, *Rodrigo "D": no futuro* (*Rodrigo "D": No Future*, 1988).

Fausta (Betty Faria), a woman in her forties, is exploited in her job and humiliated and despised by her husband (Daniel Filho), who is an alcoholic and usually unemployed. Their teenage son (Brandão Filho) follows exactly in his father's footsteps, and their dwelling is under constant threat of collapse because of the floods.

The only light in Fausta's life is an old man (Antonio Pedro) who gives her small gifts. She becomes obsessed with him, always taking his money. As she victimizes the old man, so Fausta herself becomes a victim. The film ends on a disastrous note. There is no way out of this Rio slum for any of the protagonists.

This is one of the best films Bruno Barreto has made in years because he is dealing with a very serious subject — how poverty can shape one's moral choices. This is one Brazilian film that is a downer — no music, no love, no hope. It is, surprisingly, available on video in the United States, a serious film from a director known principally for *Doña Flor e seus dois maridos*, a florid but charming sex comedy starring Sonia Braga, and also *Gabriela*, again with Miss B. Barreto does have a serious side, and *Romance da empregada* shows it to good advantage.

Romelia's Secret see *El secreto de Romelia*

The Roots see *Raíces*

Roots of Blood see *Raíces de sangre*

237. La rosa blanca (The White Rose). Roberto Gavaldón. Mexico, 1961. 100 min., B&W. Spanish.

COMMENTARY: "Written in 1929 by the mysterious itinerant storyteller B. Traven (*Treasure of the Sierra Madre*), *La rosa blanca* falls into Traven's style of populist anecdotal novels. Set in the late thirties, the film depicts the personal and national tragedy of the destruction of Mexico's land and traditional values by the rampant exploitation of multinational companies. The film, while politically favorable to the Mexican government, was made in 1961 but was banned until 1972. The polemical opening and closing were not part of Traven's original work, yet the film still dramatically presents the harrowing plot and story of one of Traven's best novels. Cinematographer Gabriel Figueroa and Traven were very close friends, and this film represents their second of three collaborations." (MOMA program notes.)

Not to be confused with a 1983 color film with exactly the same title about dissident students in Munich during World War II, this 1961 *La rosa blanca* is a true Mexican potboiler, cliché-ridden, melodramatic, but seriously affecting nevertheless. It stars Ignacio López Tarso as the owner of a hacienda named *La rosa blanca*. Life is blissful for himself, his wife (played with goodness and light by Rita Macedo) and his family until the day they find oil on his land. Tarso's character wants to continue the bucolic life but is convinced by an overseer for a big American oil company to go to Los Angeles and listen to the offer made for his very valuable land.

Claudio Brook plays the cigar-smoking imperialist Yankee oil magnate with relish. The hacienda owner appears with great humility before him. An irresistible offer is made, but the owner refuses. On his way back by car to Mexico, he is killed by the greedy overseer for the company. Back at the hacienda, his wife becomes frantic with her husband's disappearance. He is finally found, murdered by an unknown assailant, but because he left no will, the oil company moves on to the land and with tractors destroys la rosa blanca.

The film begins and ends with documentary evidence of these illegal expropriations, but for the characters in the

M'an Tine (Darling Legitimus) talks with José (Garry Cadonant) after a day of work in the cane fields in *Rue Cases Nègres* (*Sugar Cane Alley*), directed by Euzhan Palcy (1983).

film, there is no redress. Although the film is a very heavy-handed and naïve exercise, with Americans seen as despoilers and imperialists, liquor-laden and whoremongering, without an ounce of conscience, the Mexicans are presented as honest and foolish victims, too good to be true. Their white clothes never get soiled even after working a full day in the fields — that's how good and clean and true they are. Despite their cardboard portrayal, the film still succeeds as a tearjerker. It had some theatrical releases in America in the early nineties and is also available on video. It is worth a viewing, especially for Ignacio López Tarso's performance and Gabriel Figueroa's beautiful camera work.

238. Rue Cases Nègres (Sugar Cane Alley or Black Shack Alley).
Euzhan Palcy. France/Martinique, 1983. 103 min., Color. French/Creole.
COMMENTARY: Martinique, summer

1931: On a lush plantation lie two rows of tumbledown shacks on a dirt track called Sugar Cane Alley. While their parents toil in the fields, the alley belongs to the children. For them the summer is a holiday, a time for mischief and games.

But this will be their last carefree summer. Soon the children's paths will separate according to the results of their school exams. Some will follow their parents into the back-breaking cane fields. Only the best of them will have a chance to go to high school in the capital, Fort de France.

José, an 11-year-old orphan, knows better than anyone what the stakes in the game are. He is a gentle and appreciative witness of the experience of those around him. He watches the world through the eyes of five other characters: M'an Tine, his grandmother, who raises him and sacrifices all she has to insure his education; Old Medouze, his spiritual father, who dies one night in the cane field; Mr. Roc, his teacher, who teaches him that "education is the second key to freedom"; Leopold, his classmate, who is the illegitimate mulatto son of a wealthy white landowner; and Carmen, a handsome young boat pilot and houseboy, who dreams of being a Hollywood star.

José wins his scholarship, and he and M'an Tine move to a packing crate on the outskirts of Fort de France. At his new school, José is confronted with the sons of Creole aristocracy. Carmen, the naive libertine, shows him the way into this new world. Thanks to one of his teachers, José gets a larger scholarship, which allows M'an Tine, for the first time in her life, to stop working.

One evening, M'an Tine returns to Sugar Cane Alley to buy a suit from the tailor "who needs our money more than the city tailors do." When she doesn't return, José rushes after her. He finds her very sick, and also learns that his friend Leopold has been arrested for breaking into the plantation offices, trying to prove the owners, including his father, have been cheating the workers.

Leopold is taken away by two gendarmes. M'an Tine dies, exhausted by her life of constant labor. José returns to Fort de France to the education that is his comfort and his inspiration. M'an Tine, like Old Medouze before her, has now gone back to "Africa." José will tell their stories for them and for all of those from Sugar Cane Alley. (Press book.)

Rue Cases Nègres is a marvelous, magical recreation of life in Martinique from a perceptive child's point of view. It is a stunning and powerful film that shows off the director's home island and is also an homage to the black workers in the sugar cane fields, to their vitality and dignity. The concept of racism is never addressed; instead, Euzhan Palcy concentrates on a story about upward mobility and sacrifice. The film could have fallen into the realm of the melodramatic

and the maudlin because of its thematic material. But the director rises above the obvious and gives us a film that reflects the mores and people of Martinique of the 1930s, a sort of novelized memoir that takes us into the realm of French colonial history and stands out as a portrait of its era as well as an extremely subtle piece of filmmaking. One can easily see the similarities to Claire Denis' 1988 evocation of her childhood in the French Cameroons in *Chocolat*, a devastating portrait of black and white relationships in the complex era of French colonialism. *Sugar Cane Alley* won the Silver Lion at the Venice Film Festival in 1983 and the French Cesar for the Best First Feature of 1984.

NOTES: Born in 1955 in Martinique, Euzhan Palcy worked on French television on the island, produced radio programs and made her first short film there in 1974 called *La Messagère*. She moved to Paris the follwing year and worked as an editor, making another short film before she debuted with *Rue Cases Nègres* in 1983. She is also a composer of children's songs and has recorded two albums.

239. Salt of the Earth. Herbert J. Biberman. U.S., 1953. 94 min., B&W. English/Spanish.

COMMENTARY: "In Zinc Town, New Mexico, Mexican-American zinc miners are out on strike against the Deleware Zinc Corporation. An accident in the mine caused by inadequate safety precautions precipitated the strike. The miners demand equality with the Anglo-American miners, who receive better wages and were not required to work under dangerous conditions. The miners' wives want plumbing in the huts built on company premises. Despite bitter opposition from their husbands, they set up a ladies auxiliary and add their demands to the strike grievances. Ramón, the union president, particularly

Scene of the striking wives of zinc miners in Herbert J. Biberman's Chicano film *Salt of the Earth* (1953).

resents the independent action of his wife, Esperanza. The company refuses to negotiate and succeeds in getting a court injunction forbidding the miners from picketing. To save the strike, the women take over the picket line — and stay, despite violence and tear gas bombs. Esperanza and the other leaders of the women are arrested and thrown in jail. They make such a nuisance of themselves that the authorities are glad to release them. Esperanza immediately calls a meeting of the women. She and Ramón quarrel fiercely over her independence. More attempts are made to break up the strike. Ramón is savagely beaten. When Esperanza's baby is born, the company refuses to send the company doctor. At the baby's christening

party, deputies arrive with a repossession order for Esperanza's radio. Later, police come with an eviction order but are scared away by the presence of a sullen, angry crowd. Meanwhile other unions have supported the strikers with gifts of money and food. Eventually the company is forced to give in." (Press book.)

Salt of the Earth is based upon a real incident that took place in 1951-52, but the film was not intended as a documentary record of that particular strike. It stars Juan Chacón, a non-professional actor, as union leader Ramón Quintero and Rosaura Revueltas, a professional Mexican actress, as Esperanza. The American character actor Will Geer plays the local sherrif, who seems to hate his job but must follow the company line even though he sympathizes with the Chicanos. The film is as highly charged, emotional piece of cinema as ever appeared on the screen and is frequently shown on public televison. It had only one nationwide theatrical showing (in 1954) and was later put into general release (1965) because of the controversy it stirred, mainly because of its filmmakers, producer Paul Jarrico, writer Michael Wilson and director Herbert J. Biberman. All three were accused of communist affiliation by HUAC and were subsequently blacklisted in Hollywood. The film has been viewed as shrewd propaganda, intended to show that there are no civil liberties in America and that America is a fascist country which brutally oppresses the darker peoples in the service of capitalism. Of course, the McCarthy influence was rife when the film first appeared, and reviewers concentrated mostly on decoding the politics behind the film. Seen in the nineties, *Salt of the Earth* shows much about the treatment of Chicanos. It is a very persuasive film, completely realistic, with excellent camera work, always proving its points about discrimination. It remains to this day a terrific, socially adept and movingly mature cinematic experience.

NOTES: Herbert J. Biberman was born in Philadelphia in 1900 and came from a theatrical background. He worked as a director of many Hollywood "B" films such as *Meet Nero Wolfe* (1936), *The Master Race* (1944) and *New Orleans* (1947) before he ran afoul of HUAC and was blacklisted. His best film is, undeniably, *Salt of the Earth* (1953). He was married to actress Gale Sondergard and died in 1971.

Paul Jarrico was born in Los Angeles in 1915, and like Biberman, he worked on many "B" films in Hollywood as well as some "A" productions like *Song of Russia* (1944) and *The Search* (1948). His Hollywood career was also cut short by

blacklisting. His most recent film is *Messenger of Death*, made in 1988.

240. Salvador. Oliver Stone. U.S./El Salvador, 1985. 123 min., Color. English/Spanish.

COMMENTARY: *Salvador* was inspired by the real-life story of reporter Richard Boyle and his stay in El Salvador in the early eighties, during which the journalist came to realize his own position and the interference of the United States in Central American life and politics. A controversial docudrama of a photojournalist in Central America, the film is designed to expose as many outrages, injustices and human tragedies as possible as it narrows in on the activities of the Salvadorean military, the death squads and United States backing or tolerance for some of these excesses. Several events — the assassination of Archbishop Romero, the aftermath of a rape and murder of American nuns, a battle between the government's militia and the rebels — are reconstructed based on reported news.

The film is a vivid depiction of these and other events in its search for the truth behind the El Salvador situation. Robert Richardson photographs the scenes with historical accuracy, lending both energy and urgency to the story of what is going on in the country, although location shooting obviously took place elsewhere in Latin America. The human story about Richard Boyle's recovery from alcoholism and his return to idealism is merely incidental to the the political and dramatic themes of the film, although James Woods gives an incredibly good, kinetic performance as Boyle, and is ably assisted by John Savage, Michael Murphy and James Belushi in various roles. The film is supposed to spark controversy and discussion, like its contemporaries, Haskell Wexler's 1985 film *Latino*, about Green Berets in Nicaragua, and Robert Spottiswoode's

1983 effort *Under Fire*, about the 1979 revolution in Managua. All three films deal with the problems of social injustice in Latin America and warrant the viewer's attention.

NOTES: Oliver Stone is a New Yorker and was born in 1946. Beginning as a screenwriter, he later became a director of some of Hollywood's most controversial films. A few of his best known works are *Midnight Express* (1978), *Platoon* (1985), *Born on the Fourth of July* (1989), *The Doors* and *JFK* (both 1991). His 1994 film *Natural Born Killers* deals with murder and the media. A three-hour film entitled *Nixon*, about the life of the former Republican president as "visualized" by Oliver Stone, was released in 1995. Stone continues to write, produce and direct projects in the United States and around the world.

241. Sandino. Miguel Littín. Spain/Chile/Nicaragua, 1990. 136 min., Color. Spanish.

COMMENTARY: Shooting entirely on location in Nicaragua, Miguel Littín has made a biography of Augusto C. Sandino, the Nicaraguan leader after whom the Sandinista military group was named. Joaquim de Almeida plays Sandino, whose only weaknesses are beautiful women and deceitful politicians. His wife, Blanca, is played by Spanish actress Victoria Abril; another Spanish actress, Angela Molina, plays his mistress, Teresa. The film explores American policies towards Nicaragua since 1912 and moves to the year 1933, when Sandino was betrayed by Somoza, duped and killed. Although his body was never found, director Littín shows Sandino murdered with his aides and buried in unmarked graves.

The film also features Kris Kristofferson as Tom Holte, an American journalist (and friend to Sandino), and Dean Stockwell as Hatfield, the caricature of an American military officer circa 1930.

With its incredible scene of a baby's delivery in mid-jungle, various staged jungle battles that alternate with sexual scenes, and a dashing hero who cannot handle his women or the political environment, *Sandino* is a worthwhile commerical effort whose audience may want to know more about the man and why he was so revered as a Nicaraguan revolutionary.

242. Santa. Antonio Moreno. Mexico, 1931. 81 min., B&W. Spanish.

COMMENTARY: "*Santa* is a landmark film in Mexican history for at least three reasons. It was the first 'real' sound film made in Mexico and the foundation of that industry. It solidly established a genre of popular melodrama which continues even today: that of a small-town girl, exploited in the name of love, then jilted and left to her own devices in a society which rejects 'used' women. It also introduced Lupita Tovar, a lovely young actress who would capture the hearts of every moviegoer in the country. [Miss Tovar went on to star in the Spanish version of *Dracula* that same year.] The theme song 'Santa' became one of composer Agustín Lara's most memorable and popular themes." (MOMA program notes.)

Santa is based upon the Frederico Gamboa nineteenth-century novel of the same name, a naturalist love story that also condemned prostitution. It was first made into a silent film after World War I and was remade in 1932 by actor-director Antonio Moreno. Having seen both versions, this viewer can safely say the sound one is a classic of sorts, although it was badly reviewed by *Variety* film critics in 1932, chiefly because of its poor visuals and soundtrack. But the film, with its classically trite story, conjures a romantic spell that is worth experiencing.

Lupita Tovar plays Santa, an innocent country girl, seduced by the love of a young military officer in the cavalry who carries her off and leaves her after an extraordinary affair. When her parents discover this, she is thrown out of her home and has no other way of living but to find work in a house of prostitution in the capital, Mexico City.

Beautiful and sensuous, she has a variety of lovers, among them a wealthy lothario (and bullfighter) who wants to marry her but discovers her with her former lover, the military man (Carlos Orellana), and summarily throws her out.

Santa, the saintly one, has no idea about the specter of venereal disease that haunts her until she becomes deathly ill. The pock-marked, blind piano player (Donald Reed), who has always adored Santa from afar, takes care of her and loves her until she dies. He has also composed the beautiful song Santa sings in the film. In the last scene, we are at Santa's gravesite, and our heart breaks with the composer's as he runs his fingers over the gravestone with the letters S-A-N-T-A.

One note about the silent version— it was half the length of the sound one, had intertitles that were cliché-ridden and one very, very long scene in a hospital where Santa is being operated on for some kind of "cancer" and dies beautifully, but agonizingly. This is one time the audience could appreciate the arrival of sound—for Lara's wonderful score, and for the ambience of nightclubs and bawdy houses, which is very well caught in the 1931-32 version.

NOTES: Antonio Moreno made his career in Hollywood as a dashing leading man in silent cinema of the twenties. Born in Madrid in 1886, he died there in 1967 and had an extraordinary career, working with D.W. Griffith, Pola Negri, Gloria Swanson and Greta Garbo. He appeared in many, many silent films, the most famous of which was *The Temptress* (1926) with Greta Garbo, and also in

many sound films up through 1956, when he was last seen in John Ford's *The Searchers*. *Santa* was the only film he ever directed.

243. Santa sangre (Holy Blood). Alejandro Jodorowsky. Italy/Mexico, 1988. 118 min., Color. Spanish.

COMMENTARY: "*Santa sangre* was inspired through personal meetings the director had with a Mexican criminal he met some twelve years ago. The man recounted how, in his younger years, he had killed 30 women and buried them in his garden. The murderer, now in his sixties, married with children living in Mexico City, spent ten years of his childhood in a mental asylum. He escaped, killed 30 women, was captured and spent 20 years in prison. Jodorowsky verified this amazing story by checking the police records. This was the genesis of what would become his return to filmmaking and the story of *Santa Sangre*." (Production notes.)

The plot of the film is quite outrageous: Fénix (Axel Jodorowsky) is a young man raised in a world of conflicting values, from the sexual debauchery of his father to the religious fanaticism of his mother. His childhood is spent at Circo Gringo, his father's circus in downtown Mexico City. The young boy's father, Orgo (Guy Stockwell), is a vain, brutal man, prone to drunken bouts of violence and cheating on his wife. Wearing a blonde wig and makeup in a futile attempt to stay young, Orgo seduces women by hypnotizing them. Fénix's mother, Concha (Blanca Guerra), is a woman driven by an overpowering obsession for her self-anointed "image saint," Santa Sangre, a young woman brutally raped by two men who then cut off both her arms and left her dying in a pool of blood.

When Concha catches her husband in the arms of the tattooed lady, she succumbs to her jealous rage and splashes acid on his groin. Orgo, enraged beyond reasoning, grabs a knife and cuts off both of Concha's arms. Then, in blind desperation, he slits his own throat.

Traumatized by the horror he has witnessed, the eight-year-old Fénix is committed to a mental asylum. He remains incarcerated and degraded, sleeping in a dog's bed and refusing to eat anything but raw fish for the next 12 years. Now, at age 20, Fénix escapes from the asylum to his mother.

Touring the downtown theatres, performing a bizarre and original act, Fénix becomes his mother's arms. This symbiotic relationship permeates Fénix's soul to the extreme; he is trapped in her dark world of demands and twisted imagination — a world that leads to indescribable pain, madness and murder.

Fénix's salvation reappears in the form of Alma (Sabrina Dennison), a young deaf-mute who befriended him in childhood. She is determined to rescue him from the stranglehold of his mother and the torment of his soul. (Press book.)

With a plot like this, *Santa sangre* cannot help being a cult favorite and a sensational piece of filmmaking. Bizarre, bizarre. Something like a cross between the 1935 Peter Lorre classic *Mad Love* (aka *The Hands of Orlac*), Tod Browning's 1927 *The Unknown* and Alfred Hitchcock's 1960 *Psycho*, *Santa sangre* is startling cinema, way over the top. How a mother can use her son's arms to maim, murder, knife, and strangle her opponents is beyond the realm of logic. But Jodorowsky has reached a new high in filming the grotesque. The sight of an elephant's trunk gushing blood as Orgo and Concha reach orgasm is one example of this. *Santa Sangre* is oddball filmmaking, feverish, garish, lunatic, and never boring.

NOTES: Alejandro Jodorowsky is of Polish-Russian descent, born in 1930 in Chile. He studied mime with Marcel Marceau, became a theater director and then began his career in film, making his debut with the extraordinary *El topo* in 1971. After the failure of his second film, *Holy Mountain* (1973), he returned to filmmaking triumphantly with *Santa sangre* and later made *The Rainbow Thief* (1990).

244. São Bernardo. Leon Hirszman. Brazil, 1972. 110 min., Color. Portuguese.

COMMENTARY: "Based upon a novel by Graciliano Ramos concerning the development of a man from the backlands of the Brazilian northeast who dedicates his life to the accumulation of money, *São Bernardo* is about a landowner whose selfishness destroys everyone around him, including himself." (Press release.)

Othon Bastos plays Paulo Honorio, a powerful and brutal plantation owner who narrates the story of his growth and demise in the first person. We are witness to his start as a humble laborer, his growth, his marriage to a schoolteacher named Madalena (Isabel Ribeiro), her suicide, the loss of his empire — the São Bernardo estate — as he narrates the story of his own paranoia in a decaying mansion. "The truth is I never knew which were my good deeds and which were my bad deeds...everything was for the land...I can't ever change myself."

The film is a kind of Brazilian morality play about Paulo's total dedication to capitalism — the singleminded dream of a land exploiter. (Had Warner Bros. made the same film in the sixties, it would have starred Zachary Scott as a conniving southerner seeking to expand his empire, with Dorothy Malone at his side as the wifely schoolteacher, moral but distant.) We never see the violent acts on the screen; they are reported in the dialogue. We have only beautiful visuals with a painterly sense of color and composition, recalling the work of

French director Robert Bresson, who uses long shots and a quiet narrative style on the soundtrack. Sometimes there is a lack of continuity — for example, one is not certain if Paulo and Madalena had a son — but this kind of ambiguity adds to the literary flavor of the film.

Director Leon Hirszman is an artist, and he has chosen a very literary subject, Graciliano Ramos' novel, to make a very beautiful, literary film.

NOTES: Leon Hirszman was born in Rio in 1938 and became one of the founders of *Cinema Nôvo* in the fifties. He made several short documentaries in the early sixties, but his first real feature was entitled *A falecida* (1965) followed by a musical called *The Girl from Ipanema* (1967). *São Bernardo* followed and was a prelude for his controversial feature *Eles não usam black-tie*, made in 1981.

245. Sargento Getulio (Sergeant Getulio). Hermano Penna. Brazil, 1982. 90 min., Color. Portuguese.

COMMENTARY: Sergeant Getulio is a killer hired by a politician. His mission is to take a prisoner, his boss' enemy, from the village of Poco Verde to the city of Aracaju in the Northeast of Brazil. It is a long trip through a poverty-stricken area.

The bullet-riddled, beaten-down jalopy drags down the awful dirt road. The prisoner and the driver are forced to listen to all the stories the sergeant has to tell them.

All of a sudden, representatives of the politican arrive in the hinterlands with a message: There has been an upheaval in politics in the northeast, and the prisoner has become troublesome for the politican, who wants him released. The sergeant cannot understand these political changes. Obsessed by loyalty to his boss, the sergeant refuses to obey new orders and sets out to bring the prisoner in for justice.

Pursued and abandoned, Getulio fights for survival, even against units of his own party, while looking within himself for answers to his questions. In spite of the orders given by his boss, the sergeant goes on to his delirious destiny. "I don't want the world to change; it makes me restless, and I don't know what to do." Getulio gets this off his chest. The trip becomes the meaning of his existence. (Press book.)

Starring Lima Duarte as Sergeant Getulio, the film is based upon a novel by João Ubaldo Ribeiro. It is set in the 1940s in northeastern Brazil, in the state of Sergipe, and concerns the struggle between two political parties for power. Getulio is a sergeant at the service of the PDS Party; the man he must escort is a prisoner taken from the rival UDN Party.

The film reminds one of Hollywood westerns in which the prisoner must obey the lawman even though the situation has changed. It is a rough-and-tumble film about human rights and respect for the law. Originally made for television five years earlier, the 16mm print was blown up to 35mm. Law and order was definitely a top theme in Brazil in the eighties, and *Sargento Getulio* is a film that deals with it intellectually and heroically. More than a TV sit-com, it's a worthy Brazilian entry into the genre of morality westerns.

NOTES: Hermano Penna is a documentary filmmaker born in Brazil in 1945. Beginning his career in 1968, he made several short documentaries on various subjects, including Brazilian independence, the film director Cavalcanti, the author Valderez, Africa, the Brazilian Indians and conservation. He made his first fiction feature film, *Sargento Getulio*, in 1982.

Scent of Gardenias see *Perfume de gardenias*

The Secret Formula see *La fór-mula secreta*

The Secret Nation see *La nación clandestina*

Secret Wedding see *Boda secreta*

246. El secreto de Romelia

(Romelia's Secret). Busi Cortes. Mexico, 1989. 100 min., Color. Spanish.

COMMENTARY: "For her first feature film, Busi Cortes chose Rosario Castellano's novel *The Widower Roman*. Unlike the novel's linear development, Cortes uses a parallel cutting structure in two time periods: the late thirties and the present day. The story concerns an old woman, Romelia [Dolores Beristain], who guards the story of a family divided by education, politics, religion and sexuality. Three generations of women return to a provincial town to collect an inheritance from a recently deceased doctor. Romelia dominates this visit with her remembrances of the past. Who was the doctor? What was Romelia's relationship to him? While these stories are compared and contrasted, we discover a cycle of life which crosses emotional and historical boundaries. In a quiet way, *El secreto de Romelia* evokes the social changes and cultural contrasts that have marked Mexico's development." (MOMA Program Notes.)

The screenplay and director seriously take the trouble to obfuscate the time frames and various uses of symbolism to confuse the audience. Some critics might call that style, but the viewer would prefer clarity. The film suggests many themes: honor, the nature of sexuality, voyeurism, revenge, politics, women's roles in the thirties and now and finally, the roles of students. Attitudes on these concepts vary in flashback and present-day scenes.

Despite occasional lapses in makeup and continuity, the film is beautifully photographed by Franciscoi Bojorquez, and the set design of Leticia Venzor catches the spirit of the thirties and the sixties. *El secreto de Romelia* is compelling viewing, a sad and intricate tale that seems to drift by. Its performances by the lead actors make it a worthwhile piece of old-fashioned women's cinema with some new twists.

247. Secuestro: A Story of a Kidnapping.

Camila Motta. Colombia, 1993. 92 in., Color. Spanish.

COMMENTARY: "In Colombia, a kidnapping occurs every seven hours; in 1985, 20-year-old Sylvia Motta was abducted by ten armed men. Director Camila Motta, the victim's sister, recreates the harrowing three months during which Sylvia was chained to a bed while her father negotiated for her life. Motta builds a riveting story around remarkably candid interviews, including one with Juan, a construction worker moonlighting as one of Sylvia's guards, and through actual recordings of the negotiation, which begins with a $450,000 price tag. Motta uses Sylvia's voice, sometimes overlapping with other interviews, to create a vivid portrait of the psychological torment of her captivity. Footage of daily life in Colombia makes palpable the underlying extremes of wealth and poverty that have given rise to a turn of events in which the bizarre has become common-place. (Since the completion of the film, it has become illegal for civilians to negotiate with kidnappers.)" (Press release.)

Secuestro is a very strong film. Photographed by Camila Motta's husband, Barry Ellsworth, the film fascinates because it is a real story; it really did take three months to secure Sylvia Motta's release. In dealing with the kidnappers, the parents were generally cool and calm, keeping their heads in the face of constant death threats. The film wanders around the city of Bogotá and notes the

Advertising flying for Camila Motta's Colombian *cinéma vérité* film *Secuestro: A Story of a Kidnapping* (1993).

sore division between the upper-class neighborhoods and the urban slums. The soundtrack is constantly riddled with short conversations between the kidnappers and the family, asking for money, threatening action. Sometimes the titles translate the telephone voices; other times the words spoken in the reenacted scenes, sometimes both at the same time — on the top and bottom of the frame.

Secuestro does not suffer from its grainy color photography by Barry Ellsworth but rather profits from the color's contrasts with certain black and white scenes that are the reenactments of Sylvia's abduction. One wonders how Sylvia survived nearly three months chained by one of her legs to a metal bedpost. There is a lot of pleasant source music on the soundtrack, which makes

the scenes of captivity more frightening since the reality of what is happening is always ominous and ironic.

Secuestro: A Story of a Kidnapping is a powerful documentary with a happy ending. It is one of the most emotionally compelling films ever made on this subject, without being emotional itself. The coldness of its objectivity and its crude home-movie cinematography give it a super-realistic edge that is both entertaining and horrifying.

248. El señor presidente
(Mr. President). Marcos Madanes. Argentina, 1970. 130 min., B&W. Spanish.

COMMENTARY: Based upon the celebrated novel by Guatemalan writer Miguel Ángel Asturias, *El señor presidente* is about political corruption. The film may have been intended as an incisive portrait of a politician, but it turned out to be a pure melodrama from which the author tried to dissociate himself.

The plot, told in mini-flashbacks, concerns a local bumpkin (played by Nathan Pinzón) who gets pleasure from ringing church bells in the tower and becomes the target of a sadistic army colonel (Zelmar Guenol). One day the fool accidentally kills the colonel, and the dictator-president (Pedro Buchardo) tries to cast blame on his political opponent for the murder. But the president's chief henchman, Miguel (Luis Brandoni), falls in love with the political opponent's daughter, Camila (Alejandra Dapassano), tries to overturn the dictator's actions and provokes a mini-revolt of the oppressed poor, even gaining the sympathy of the upper classes.

The film tells a very minor story over a long period of screen time in which the essential theme of justice over tryranny gets lost in the director's innocent attempt to tackle the hefty problems of poverty, revolt and political dictatorship. Ángel Asturias' novel deserved better interpretation. The director's intention was to introduce the archetype of dictator-president on the screen in a kind of imagined country, showing the usual exploitation, repression and social injustice. He partially succeeded in bringing some of the elements of the novel to the screen.

249. Señora Bolero. Marilda Vera. Venezuela, 1992. 101 min., Color. Spanish.

COMMENTARY: The suicide of her 25-year-old son is the trigger for Amanda Contreras (Carlota Sosa) to reexamine her entire life, beginning with the fifties, when she was a bolero singer.

In multiple flashbacks, we are witness to the rise and fall of dictator Marcos Pérez Gómez. We also learn of Amanda's relationship to Pedro (Marcelo Ramo), who later becomes her husband, and Alejandro (Hector Myerston), a media personality and political activist who was her lover.

When the political machine was overthrown in the fifties, Alejandro left Amanda and fled to the United States. He and Pedro had worked in the underground to bring about the demise of Pérez Gómez. Amanda remembers that era, the love triangle that involved her and how she was betrayed by both men, since she discovers that Pedro, who is now a middle-aged lawyer in a campaign for a top political office, has sold out to the corrupt regime now in power. Indeed, history repeats itself, and Amanda has to find a way to cope (somewhat melodramatically) with these events, finding a new identity, restructuring the present by investigating the past.

The film is beautifully photographed by Hernan Toro to present a panorama of thirty or more years of Venezuelan history on the screen. Carlota Sosa makes good sense in her role, which is not to obscure the historical facts but to personally interpret their meaning and how they relate to rediscovering the life of Amanda Contreras. The traumatic event of her son's suicide and her husband's mere acceptance of the death give her this cinematic cause to reflect and the audience a very enjoyable film to watch.

Very much in the vein of Luis Puenzo's *La historia oficial* and María Luisa Bemberg's *Miss Mary*, here is another feminine character, searching her past and the events that shaped her, to discover what the future has in store. Although the film lacks the lyricism of her compatriot Fina Torres' moving *Oriane*, *Señora Bolero* is another Venezuelan product that adds to the lustre of that country's now burgeoning movie industry as it thematically indulges itself in recapturing time past.

250. Señora de nadie (Nobody's Wife). María Luisa Bemberg. Argentina, 1982. 90 min., Color. Spanish.

COMMENTARY: "*Señora de nadie* is a film about a woman's search for identity. When an upper middle-class woman, Lenora (Luisina Brando), accidentally discovers her husband's affairs, she leaves him and her two sons. It is an act born of integrity, a refusal to live a lie, but as her encounters with family and economic institutions reinforce her social nonexistence, it becomes a gesture of active resistance. She will be "nobody's wife." The story of Lenora's move — from family, home and a blind life centered on pleasing others, to a desire to create life outside "the system" — clearly grew out of feminist critiques of patriarchy. Bemberg struggled for four years to have her script approved by censors critical of her depiction of the family. The first half of the film sensitively focuses on Lenora; her husband (Rodolfo Ranni) is most notable for his absence. But his presence is felt in all her encounters — whether her mother (China Zorilla) urges her to forgive and forget, or her employer refuses her a loan because she does not have credit in her name. Made in 1982, under the military regime, Bemberg's critique was seen by Argentines as extending from family to state, and her protagonist as a symbol of rupture." (MOMA program notes.)

The film is most explicit as it reveals the hypocrisy of the Argentine upper-middle class, picking it apart as we watch Lenora's painful but ultimately rewarding transition to independence — from the down-side, sleazy men to supportive friends, group therapy and finally, on the upswing, finding and moving in with her new best friend, a gay man (Julio Chávez). *Señora de nadie* is a remarkable film because Luisina Brando gives depth to the character of Lenora, especially in her scenes with Julio Chávez, who plays the young, unhappy homosexual whom she ultimately befriends and with whom she is willing to share her life. Gabriela Acher is also very good in the role of the happily promiscuous girl with whom Lenora shares an apartment after leaving home. As in the recent thriller *Apartment Zero*, Buenos Aires is used as a terrific backdrop to the marital drama of Lenora. By the film's conclusion, Lenora has learned to laugh at herself, and "Mrs. Nobody" has become "Mrs. Somebody" again.

251. Sensaciones (Sensations). Juan Esteban Codero and Viviana Codero. Ecuador, 1991. 80 min., Color. Spanish.

COMMENTARY: Apparently one of the first films made in 35mm in Ecuador, *Sensaciones* is about a musician named Zacarías (played by director Juan Esteban Cordero) who returns to Ecuador to make a new record album using folk rhythms and local jazz routines. Viviana Cordero, the film's other director, plays Chiara, the necessary *femme fatale*, who intrudes on the jazz group that is trying to create a new sound, using their own folkloric music and combining it with Western sounds and technology.

The film is intelligent, beautifully shot in color by Iván Acevedo, especially those stunning panoramas of the Andes mountains in the background. It also has the modern advantage of DTS (digital sound technology) going for it. Very much like its counterpart United States productions as far as storyline is concerned, here is a drama of Ecuadorian youths who want to gain international success. Their music is their life, and the actors are all very appealing in their roles.

Sensations see *Sensaciones*

252. Sentimientos: Mirta de Liniers a Estambul (Feelings: Mirta from Liniers to Istanbul). Jorge

Coscia and Guillermo Saura. Argentina, 1986. 100 min., Color. Spanish.

COMMENTARY: A two-part film, based on a true story and directed by two directors, *Sentimientos* is a story about two Argentine student-lovers who become exiles in Sweden and later, Turkey. Mirta (played by the 22-year-old Argentine actress Emilia Mazer) is an uncommitted student at a Buenos Aires university who falls in love with a political activist, Enrique (played by Norberto Díaz). The military is setting up a police state, and their repressive actions against university students force Mirta (from the Liniers working class section of Buenos Aires) and Enrique to flee into exile.

The second part of the film takes place in Stockholm and was photographed there. Not being able to adapt easily to European ways, Mirta meets a Turk, also an exile (Saim Urgay). She falls in love with him, and they communicate with each other in Swedish. Mirta moves on to Istanbul (Athens was the substitute location for the filmmakers) with her lover into a new life, leaving Argentina far behind.

Sentimientos is a sensitive drama, first portraying the political realities of Argentina of the early eighties among university students and then the sad life of exiles abroad, speaking languages they hardly understand. Although the film may appear disjointed, so does real life: Sudden change can lead you into new horizons, in work, in love, in geography. For those of us who have ever lived and loved in a foreign country or have ever been forced from their homeland, *Sentimientos* will have a special appeal.

Sergeant Getulio see *Sargento Getulio*

Shoot to Kill see *Disparen a matar*

So Feared a Hell see *El infierno tan temido*

Solitary see *El apando*

Song of Chile see *Cantata de Chile*

The Sons of Martín Fierro see *Los hijos de Martín Fierro*

South see *Sur*

The South see *El Sur*

The Southern Cross see *La cruz del sur*

The Story of Fausta see *Romance da empregada*

Strawberry and Chocolate see *Fresa y chocolate*

The Strong Arm see *El brazo fuerte*

253. Subida al cielo (Mexican Bus Ride or Ascent to Heaven). Luis Buñuel. Mexico, 1951. 85 min., B&W. Spanish.

COMMENTARY: Perhaps the lightest of Buñuel's films made in the early fifties, *Subida al cielo* has a deceptively simple plot. As in a ship-of-fools tale, a load of Mexican passengers make several detours through their lives as a consequence of this bus ride.

Esteban Márquez plays Oliverio, who has just been married to Alvina, his peasant bride (played lovingly by Carmen Gonzáles). Just as the village wedding ends, Oliverio's mother (Leonor Gómez) beckons him from her deathbed to return home to ratify her will so that she can thwart her two covetous sons, Oliverio's brothers, Juan and Felipe (respectively, Roberto Cobo and Roberto Meyer).

The bus ride is remarkable for the numbers of characters it introduces as well as for the way it shows off the spectacular mountainous Mexican countryside. The ride is also a series of chance encounters with people and events that determine their destiny. A baby is born to a pregnant passenger; Oliverio is seduced on his wedding day by Raquel (an heir of Buñuel's *Susana*), played by Lillia Prado. In fact, Raquel hands Oliverio an apple and he begins to eat it in a scene foreshadowing their lovemaking on the bus, which occurs as they make their "ascent to the heavens."

Other passengers include a local politico, Don Eladio (Manuel Donde), who is given to making grandiose speeches as the drop of a hat. The bus driver (played with comic élan by Luis Acenves Castañeda) is lackadaisical and not averse to sleeping whenever the feeling overtakes him, even though Oliverio urges him to speed on homeward.

Of course the bus gets stuck in a muddy river and all sorts of efforts are used to get it out, even a tractor. But a child leading a pair of oxen does the job admirably, and Oliverio arrives home — to his already dead mother. However, he takes her dead fingers and presses them to the will, keeping her intent alive and documented.

As in most Buñuel films, there is an obligatory "dream sequence," and this one is a surreal pip. Oliverio is asking permission from his mother to have sex with Raquel. In the dream, he is watching his mother knitting on a pedestal, and the mother suddenly becomes Raquel, holding an apple peel, who in turn metamorphosizes into Alvina, his bride. Oliverio seems to be attached to all the women by his mother's yarn and Raquel's apple peel which ends in his wife's image — perhaps it is one huge umbilical cord. But there is much room for interpretation here, and Buñuel's "light" film is still replete with the usual themes of eroticism, gags, death, dream symbolism and the games of chance. Finally, a remarkable, huge oval mirror loaded on the bus seems to encapsulate all of these colorful, captivating characters as if the mirror itself was a reflection of their unconscious (surreal) desires, especially Oliverio's repressed sexual ones. *Subida al cielo* is a fascinating excursion into the sexual and social mores of Mexican peasants, with mystical detours that satisfy this filmgoer. It is available on video cassette in the United States and is definitely worth a viewing.

A Successful Man see *Un hombre de éxito*

Sugar Cane Alley see *Rue Cases Nègres*

The Summer of Miss Forbes see *El verano de señora Forbes*

Summer Skin see *Piel de verano*

254. El Super (The Super).
Leon Ichaso and Orlando Jiménez-Leal. U.S./Cuba, 1978. 90 min., Color. Spanish/English.

COMMENTARY: Not to be confused with the 1991 Joe Pesci film about a slumlord with the same English title, this *El super* is a remarkably different film, dealing with a Cuban exile trying to cope as a building superintendent in a Queens tenement. With a soundtrack in English and Spanish, the film stars Raymond Hidalgo-Gato as El Super; Zully Montero as his long-suffering wife, Aurelia; Elizabeth Peña as his Americanized daughter, Aurelita; and Reynaldo Medina, Efraín Lopez-Neri and Juan Granda as his pals, Pancho, Bobby and Cuco. Finding no solace in American life (or the cold winters), El Super and his pals recall the sultry days and beaches of Havana and their wartime experiences around the Bay of

Pigs invasion. At last they realize they are strangers in a strange land — the borough of Queens.

After much trivial incident — conversations with building inspectors, the usual linguistic misunderstandings in Spanish, Spanglish, Cuban and other dialects, including fractured English — El Super resolves to make a new life for himself and his family in Miami, which is closer to his own Cuban climate and lifestyle.

The film has its poignant moments, since the entire family is clearly a group of exiles who were caught in the Castro revolution and had to leave to survive. Now they are Cuban-Americans in search of their own dream in America, which they hope they will find in Florida.

The film has a very grainy quality and poor color when projected on the theater screen, perhaps because of limited budgets. Nevertheless, directors Leon Ichaso and Orlando Jiménez-Leal have put on the screen the first film of its kind, with crossover appeal for American and Spanish-speaking audiences alike, and an enjoyably warm comedy at that.

NOTES: Orlando Jiménez-Leal makes his American directorial debut with this film. He has usually been associated with Nestor Almendros, the cinematographer with whom he co-directed a devastating anti–Castro documentary.

The Super see El Super

255. Sur (South). Fernando Solanas. Argentina, 1988. 127 min., Color. Spanish.

COMMENTARY: Made by Fernando Solanas as the companion piece to his aching portrait of exile, *Tangos: l'exil de Gardel* (1986), *Sur* charts the agony of a return to Argentina after years of imprisonment. It also marks a return home for the director of *La hora de los hornos*,

since this is Solanas' first film shot in Argentina in over ten years. In the film, a man imprisoned for subversive activities is released after five years. Desperate to see his wife, Rosi (Susu Pecoraro), again, Floreal (Miguel Ángel Sola) must first undergo a nocturnal reckoning with the past. He wanders through Buenos Aires, strolling down dreamlike streets strewn with banners and leaflets celebrating the return of democracy. Images arise to meet him: ghosts of his past, the events and people of his broken life. Suggestive and sensual, the poetics of *Sur* make this film a deeply humanistic and probing portrait of the collective memory of modern Argentina, and indeed any country which has known oppression. (MOMA program notes.)

Solanas received the 1988 Best Director award at the Cannes Film Festival for this poetic film about a prisoner of the Argentina military regime (1976–83), who is released to confront the effects of that regime on his country and himself. His wife has been through her own hell during Floreal's imprisonment. In her desperation and loneliness, she has become the lover of Floreal's best friend, Roberto (played eloquently by French actor Phillipe Léotard), a Corsican who has found love, friendship and purpose to his life in Argentina.

A blend of memory and fact, scored with the quintessential Argentine tango music of Astor Piazzola, the film is a dazzling, emotionally involving portrayal of Floreal's memories. Running quite long, it is beautifully photographed by Felix Monti and superbly acted by Miguel Ángel Sola, Susu Pecoraro and Phillipe Léotard, with that favorite actor from Hector Olivera's films, Ulises Dumont, in the small role of Emilio. Like all of Solanas' films, *Sur* is involving and very meaningful even if you are not Argentine. It is almost any man's experience after returning home from exile. It is Solanas' cinematic *paseo* (stroll) through life and death, desire and fear, rancor and love, a stroll on which he discovers himself, going "south."

256. El sur (The South). Carlos Saura. Spain/Argentina, 1992. 60 min., Eastmancolor. Spanish.

COMMENTARY: Spanish director Carlos Saura's film *El sur* does not run the risk of being confused with Victor Erice's 1983 Spanish film or Fernando Solanas' 1987 film with practically the same title. Saura's source is fiction, a short story by famed Argentine writer Jorge Luis Borges, called "El Sur."

Photographed by the great Spanish cinematographer José Luis Alcaine, the film, taken from a two-page story, is about Juan Dahlman (Oscar Martínez), a librarian who dreams he is stabbed to death at his family home in the south, a place he has wanted to revisit since childhood. One day, as an adult, he experiences a head injury in a fall, undergoes surgery and is ordered by his doctors to get complete bed rest. Consequently, he decides to go "south," where he meets his fate.

The director has added many extra elements to the story — such as a mother figure, Doña Rosaria Flores (Nini Gambler), who could be a biographical element taken from author Borges' own life — and has also updated the film from the thirties to the nineties. Besides the doctor (Luis Tasca), a pastor (Jorge Narrale) also appears in the film.

The director himself sees the film as experimental, with a precision-mounting, dreamlike ending that echoes elements in his own work in Spanish film over the past twenty years — films like *Cría, Elisa, vida mía* and *La prima Angélica,* "memory" films he made in the sixties and seventies in Spain.

Saura's films are always thought-provoking mood pieces, usually slowly paced and quite emotional. *El sur* was conceived in very much the manner of his past Spanish cinematic successes — emotionally appealing memory films about life and death. Whether he is on location in Buenos Aires, Barcelona or Madrid, Saura is an expert director, always given to frank stories of obsessional behavior. He has found his niche in Latin America with Borges' story "El Sur."

257. Susana (Demonio y carne / The Devil and the Flesh). Luis Buñuel. Mexico, 1951, 82 min., B&W. Spanish.

COMMENTARY: Susana (as played by the beautiful blonde Rosita Quintana) is first seen as a juvenile delinquent in a filthy prison cell, where she prays to God to be free of this bondage. During a rainstorm, a flash of lightning reveals the shadow of a cross cast through the bars of her cell. As Susana is about to kiss the shadow, a spider crawls from the spot where the shadow has fallen, and Susana, frightened, escapes miraculously through the bars of the cell.

As she wanders through the countryside seeking shelter, she comes to a wealthy *hacienda*, presided over by the landowner (Fernando Soler), his wife (Matilde Palau) and their "intellectual" son (Victor Manuel Mendoza). Hired by the family as a maid, Susana uses her erotic charms to seduce every man she lays her eyes on, finally, the loving husband and head of the household.

Of course, virtue must triumph — and in a wonderful confrontation scene, the Catholic wife and mother tells Susana that she will get her just desserts. The overseer informs the police of Susana's whereabouts, since she is an escapee from the local reformatory. The family goes back to its conventional Christian way of life as police lead Susana back to a life in prison.

Susana is a very well played, conventional film, loaded with obvious Christian symbolism and a wonderful vehicle for director Buñuel to take aim at his favorite targets: the Catholic church, the bourgeois family, the inexperienced intellectual, unbridled sexuality. It is a potboiler production made on a shoestring budget, but not without interest. It is available on video cassette here in the United States.

258. Tango: baile nuestro

(**Tango: Our Dance**). Jorge Zanada. Argentina, 1988. 69 min., Color and B&W. Spanish.

COMMENTARY: *Tango: baile nuestro* is the result of director Zanada's research about the actual dancing of the tango nowadays. From 1983 to 1984, Zanada observed the activity of the *milongueros* (amateur popular dancers). He witnessed the *machismo*, the individualism and the competition — sometimes self-destructive, but almost always creative because of the sensual inspiration and passionate feeling that feed the dance. The film traces visually the links between the *milongueros* and some of the great dancers: Juan Carlos Copes, María Nieves, Raquel Rossetti and Julio Bocca (also Vladimir Vassiliev, the ballet genius–choreographer, who dances the tango differently but identifies himself as an Argentine through his movements and cadence). The film avoids folklorism and gives a more personal, subjective and interpretative view of tango. Shot from 1984 through 1987, it includes musical compositions by Daniel Binelli as well as classical tango recordings. Argentine actors Oscar Martínez and Arturo Bonín appear in the film as well as American actor Robert Duvall. (Press book.)

Shown at the Montreal Film Festival in 1988, *Tango: baile nuestro* is a wonderful blend of stage and screen footage, showing off the tango and its role in Argentine life. This was the first film by Zanada, who studied filmmaking at the University of La Plata. Zanada tries to link the dance to the mores of the Argentines by using non-professional dancers, which gives the film a personal touch towards individual interpretation. Dance classes are also visited, something the director learned from Carlos Saura's evocation of the flamenco in his 1986 Spanish film *Carmen*. But *Tango: baile nuestro* is painfully short and will probably do better in the video market than on the wide screen.

Tango: Our Dance see *Tango: baile nuestro*

259. Tango Bar.

Marcos Zurinaga. Argentina/Puerto Rico. 1988. 90 min., Color. Spanish.

COMMENTARY: *Tango Bar* is sort of documentary on the tango combined with a love story. Beginning with the origins of tango, featuring Carlos Gardel, the film takes us through tango history in film, from the twenties through the eighties. We watch Charlie Chaplin, Rudolph Valentino in *Four Horsemen of the Apocalypse*, Laurel and Hardy, Gene Kelly in *Anchors Aweigh* and even the Flintstones do the tango in America. Some counterparts in French films are shown as well. All this leads us into the main love story of the film.

It seems tango singer Antonio (Rubén Juarez) left Argentina when censorship directives came from the military junta then in power, affecting the verses of the tango. He left his partner, Ricardo, also a tango singer (played by Raúl Julia), as well as his girlfriend, Elena (Valeria Lynch), together in Buenos Aires. Naturally the latter two fall in love, but when Antonio returns, there is talk of possible reconciliation on all levels.

The love story is only an excuse to show off the evolution of the tango. The cast from the Broadway success *Tango Argentino* is used throughout the film in the numbers that best illustrate the transitions of the tango. Julia and Juarez accompany the dancers in some thrilling

Two musicians play tango music for an Argentine tango dancer (perhaps the personification of Gardel) in a surreal Parisian sequence from Fernando Solanas' *Tangos: l'exil de Gardel* (*Tangos: The Exile of Gardel*, 1985), a French-Argentine co-production.

numbers. The love story of the triangle of actors comes to a satisfactory conclusion, but the film really belongs to the stage performers. Argentine director Marcos Zurinaga handles the whole affair with agility and charm and has made a very polished film, worthy of his subject.

Tangos: El exilio de Gardel see *Tangos: l'exil de Gardel*

Tangos: The Exile of Gardel see *Tangos: l'exil de Gardel*

260. Tangos: l'exil de Gardel (Tangos: el exilio de Gardel / Tangos: The Exile of Gardel). Fernando Solanas. France/Argentina, 1985. 130 min., Color. Spanish/French.

COMMENTARY: "Recipient of the Special Jury Prize at the Venice Film Festival in 1985, *Tangos* is an elegant, romantic drama about a group of Argentine political exiles in 1980s Paris. Open-ended and occasionally surreal, the style poignantly evokes the emotional contradictions of exile while affirming the beauty of Paris, the exuberance of the young performers, and the dazzling intensity of the tango. Solanas made the film during his own exile in Paris, which ended in 1984 after the restoration of democracy." (Press release.)

"Exile," Solanas has observed from the vantage point of harsh experience, "is a long introspective journey — a deep and paralyzing crisis which reaches every part of your life." The director, who had to leave Argentina himself in 1976 because his radical opinions were endangering his life, used many of his personal experiences in shaping this film.

Tangos: l'exil de Gardel is narrated by the twenty-year-old María (Gabriela Toscano), who relates the story behind an Argentine troupe of actors, dancers and empresarios producing a show about themselves called "Gardel's Exiles." Carlos Gardel was a top tango star in the thirties in Paris and the United States but died tragically in an auto accident at the height of his fame. The show, a tribute to Gardel, is being written in Buenos Aires and sent to Juan Dos (played by Miguel Angel Sola), the star. Juan Dos is also a composer and the lover of Mariana (Marie LaForet), the female star of the show and the mother of María, the narrator. Incidentally, María's father, a prominent Argentine lawyer, was murdered by a right-wing death squad, and María and her mother have to cope with this trauma while dealing with all the usual frictions between parent and teenager. María's mother, Mariana, is also in love with Pierre (played engagingly by Phillipe Leotard), the producer of the show. Pierre is the foil of Florence (Marina Vlady), his former theater partner, who is dubious about committing herself to an "unfinished" production called "tango-dy."

Also in the cast of the show-within-the-film are Gerardo (Lautaro Murua), an intellectual whose daughter is one of the *desaparecidas*, and Miseria, a dancer whose specialty is calling Buenos Aires on public telephones free and ripping off the Paris telephone company. The show links the lives of the characters in the presentation of the "tango-dy," a blend of dance, drama and comedy that will allow them to vent their feelings.

All the threads of the plot move in parallel sequence as the mounting of the show takes place, and all are resolved when the final show is presented to the film's audience. And what a show it is — a dazzling display of tango dancing aided by a wonderful Astor Piazzola score of tango rhythms and syncopations. The film does not make any overt political statements about exiles, but there is a recurring image of mannequins strewn among the dancers — a forceful reminder of the emptiness of the exile's existence.

With most of the interiors shot in Buenos Aires after Solanas' return and the exteriors shot in Paris, *Tangos* is the first French-Argentine co-production to come to international screens, with terrific acting by the principals themselves, Miguel Ángel Sola (also the lead actor of Solanas' *El sur*) and the beautiful French actress Maríe LaForet. But the real star is the brilliant choreography and dancing.

Tangos has been made with a great deal of lyricism and imagination, a fusion of poetic images with musical and dance images as the director searches for his own destiny in Paris. Solanas built his reputation chiefly on his political epic *La hora de los hornos*, and *Tangos*, too, makes a subtle political statement (about the past tumult of Argentina and the plight of those forced to leave their homeland). However, *Tangos* seems largely bent on bringing a playfulness and sense of the absurd and comedic to the screen — a welcome, zestful change for director and audience alike.

261. Tanguito. Marcelo Pineyro. Argentina, 1993. 121 min., Color. Spanish.

COMMENTARY: Another film about repression by the Argentine military junta during their "dirty war," *Tanguito* is the story of a fairly famous rock singer (played by Fernando Miras) who makes his own lyrics and music without following the official party line and consequently is arrested by the police, tortured with shock treatments and killed.

There is an incidental love story when Tanguito meets Marianna (Cecilia Dopazo). She is a rich colonel's daughter; he, a poor slum kid who can sing. They overcome their class differences through their passion, though hardly a word is spoken between them. There are also the obligatory prison scenes interrupting the love story, with the wonderful Argentine actor Hector Alterio playing Lobo, a deceptive cop who offers Tanguito protection if the singer will discuss his political liaisons.

With a script by Aida Bortnik directed by the producer of *La historia oficial*, *Tanguito* is a strong film, powerfully reenacting an individual's fruitless struggle to be free under an oppressive military regime. It is good political cinema, made in the style of Alain Resnais or Costa-Gavras, and has a relevant message, but with a cast of mostly unknown actors portraying the life of a singing star known only in Argentina, it does not seem destined for international commercial success. However, the "truthfulness" of Tanguito's story is quite appealing as directed by Pineyro and played by Fernando Miras, and the film is a worthy product of a "new" Argentine effort to expose past evils in cinematic redress.

262. La tarea (Homework).
Jaime Humberto Hermosillo. Mexico, 1990. 121 min., Color. Spanish.

COMMENTARY: A woman invites a former lover to her home for a little romance, but he discovers she is secretly taping their encounter as a classroom project.

A two-character film starring María Rojo (from *Danzón*) as Virginia and José Alonso as Marcelo, her ex-husband, *La tarea* is a variation on Steven Soderbergh's 1989 award winner *sex, lies and videotape*, with the woman as the filmmaker and the man as the sex object. It also reminds one of Alfred Hitchcock's 1948 color classic *Rope* because of its use of a stationary camera and single long takes of 25 minutes. In fact, Virginia's video camera is placed under a chair, and when her husband places his coat on the chair, the camera's view is obliterated. Hitchcock would change "reels" when an object would cover the camera's eye — the

director had run out of film. Here, the actress just moves her lover's coat and lets the video camera record — possibly up to two or more hours.

The film ends happily even though Marcelo discovers his ex-wife's ruse. In fact, he lets her use the tape to advertise his burial business in her "homework" film. There is much nudity and sex, which some viewers might consider on the edge of pornography. But Hermisillo is a very courageous director and is trying to give Mexican cinema a gigantic push forward into the international arena.

Interestingly enough, *La tarea* was followed by a sequel entitled *La tarea prohibida* (aka *Forbidden Homework*), an 80-minute film made in 1992 by the same director with the same cast. The publicity blurb reads: "Very different from, yet still a variation on *La tarea*, a young woman invites a friend and an older woman (María Rojo) to take part in a video project, but the woman learns all too quickly that the friend will not be showing up." The sequel, presented at the "New Trends in Mexican Cinema" series in New York during the summer of 1993, was introduced at its initial screening by its star, María Rojo, but was sparsely attended and never even reviewed by the press. So much for the fate of sequels.

What made *La tarea* so interesting was María Rojo's delivery of lines like, "I feel like someone is watching us," knowing full well she has placed the video camera under a chair as she pushes her ex-husband always into the range of its lens for a really graphic take. When she finishes her project and presents it at its premiere showing at school, she says, "Using men as a sexual object is a woman's best revenge." *La tarea* takes its audience into yet another realm of the director's daring to approach contemporary subjects on a frank, open, even at times controversial level. Hermosillo, like other international directors before him who liked to amuse or shock us, certainly deserves our praise for his courageous (even if not always likable) filmmaking.

263. Técnicas de duelo (Dueling Techniques). Sergio Cabrera. Colombia/Cuba, 1988. 97 min., Color. Spanish.

COMMENTARY: A film critical of *machismo*, government bureaucracy, honor and religious duty, *Técnicas de duelo* is indeed a surprise. It begins as a comedy of manners, set in a small Andean town, where two former best friends, a teacher (Frank Ramírez) and the town butcher (Humberto Dorado), spend their last few hours in preparation for a duel to the death, without telling the audience the reasons or meaning behind the event.

There are a few scenes where the men are individually seen paying off their debts, ordering coffins, making final farewells to loved ones. There is much *jaleo* (bluster) among the townspeople, who place bets on the outcome (which will go unrevealed in this review). Even the local chief of police and mayor are speculating with cash. But the real victory of the film goes to the director, Sergio Cabrera, because he has dared to criticize the pettiness of bureaucracy and the small-mindedness of Latin American society in his beautifully photographed, well-paced, marvelously acted satire. Recalling Ridley Scott's 1977 film *The Duelists* from a Joseph Conrad short story entitled "Point of Honor," *Técnicas de duelo* transfers the locale, from Poland and Russia to an unspecified Latin American country, but makes similar points about *machismo* and honor.

Tempest see *Barravento*

264. Terra em transe (Earth Entranced / Land in Anguish). Glauber Rocha. Brazil, 1966. 115 min., B&W. Portuguese.

COMMENTARY: Made in 1966 but not released until 1970, *Terra em transe* is a monumental film work about a poet and journalist, Paulo Martins (Jardel Filho) and his mistress, Sara (Glauce Rocha), who become involved in the top political affairs of the nation. While driving away from the headquarters of Felipe Vieira (Jose Lewgoy), the governor of the province of El Dorado, Paulo is shot by the police because he has dared to confront the governor, another corrupt politician, who he finds incapable of leading the people. "El Dorado" is Rocha's imaginary country, where fascist demagogue, political reformer and intellectual all co-exist, act out their lives in similar fashion, though with different behavior patterns. Rocha makes constant references to the social, political and economic situation of Latin America and the conflict between traditional Spanish values and those of the Third World. He sees Latin America as a continent ready to explode, a continent whose own values are continually threatened by a "civilized" world.

As Paulo dies, he tells his girlfriend the story of his shifting political involvements — how he first attached himself to a senator named Porfirio Díaz (played by Paulo Autran), a mystic and reactionary politico who behaved like a demigod, and then to Vieira, a corrupt populist politician who engineered the journalist's downfall. There are multiple flashbacks of gigantic political rallies, spectacular orgy scenes after a candidate's winning a political bid, sensitive scenes where the hero has a breakdown, realizing he is too soft for dirty politics, and lewd semipublic behavior in the risqué sexual scenes. Paulo tries to extricate himself from the permanent state of madness the country seems to be experiencing, and *Terra em transe* is a vigorous denunciation of this very madness since the 1964 *coup d'état*.

The style of the film is very *Cinema*

Nôvo, very Orson Wellesian — striking black and white images, jump-cuts, shock montages, ironic uses of the samba on the soundtrack (reminiscent of Bernard Herrmann's underscoring), film-within-a-film techniques (like the "News on the March" documentary in Welles' 1940 masterpiece, *Citizen Kane*). It is Rocha's first film, devoid of the mystical and surreal evocations he used in the 1961 *Barravento*, the 1964 film *Deus e o diabo na terra do sol*, and the 1969 film *Antonio das Mortes*. *Terra em transe* is Glauber Rocha's most comprehensible, straightforward contemporary film and has just been restored, retranslated and resubtitled by American director Martin Scorsese. It is simply fascinating cinema, a whirlwind that displays the greatness of its director and focuses on one point in the episodic history of Brazil's quirky political past.

265. The Terror and the Time. Rupert Roonaraine. Guyana, 1979. 70 min., Color and B&W. English.

COMMENTARY: The time is 1953; the terror is British colonialism and Cold War imperialism. "*The Terror and the Time* is the story of the Guyanese people's fight for independence and self-determination. The film examines the events of 1953 in Guyana: the first universal adult suffrage elections, the victory of the leftist People's Progressive Party at the polls, the subversion of the constitution, military invasion, and a prolonged state of emergency imposed by the colonial masters — the British. The filmmakers chose the events of this period as paradigmatic of the systemic nature of colonial domination and as crucial to an understanding both of subsequent political developments in the country and the present neo-colonial conditions.

"Scenes of present-day Guyana, still photos, newspaper headlines, and newsreel footage (of Guyana in 1953 and of contemporaneous international liberation struggles) situate the struggle of Guyana in the international context of Cold War politics. The more insidious forms of everyday economic and cultural repression employed throughout colonialism's long history — the impoverishment of the working people, feudal labor conditions and social relations, the government's stranglehold on the press and media — are also documented.

"The 'script' of the film centers around nine poems of Martin Carter's 'Poems of Resistance,' written in Guyana in 1953. The cinematic treatment of the poems is intercut with historical sections (newsreel footage and headlines from local newspapers) and interviews with Guyanese politicians and workers involved in the struggle in 1953. The film treats the poetry as an aspect of the overall cultural production of the period, a vigorous part of the fight for independence, providing the people with 'wider perspectives of reality.'" (MOMA program notes.)

The only truly worthwhile film ever to surface in America from Guyana, *The Terror and the Time* is a brilliant documentary about how British colonialism can distort, disfigure and destroy an already oppressed people, emptying their collective brain of all form and content. Although materials have been collected to continue the documentary — an analysis of neo-colonialism in present-day Guyana as well as a section on the working people's movement for liberation from 1953 to the present, this continuation of *The Terror and the Time* has not been accomplished as yet. The film does share the Latin American's plight of resistance against repression and the struggles of oppressed people throughout the Americas. It is, unfortunately, rarely seen, but it can be viewed through the New York–based distributor, the Victor Jara Collective, named after the Chilean poet and singer who was killed by the military junta after the fall of the Allende regime. It is a wonderfully informative documentary about one of the "colonialized" countries of South America where the native language is English.

That's the Problem see *Ahí está el detalle*

There Are No Thieves in This Village see *En este pueblo no hay ladrones*

There Shall Be No More Sorrows or Forgetting see *No habrá más penas ni olvido*

They Don't Wear Black Tie see *Eles não usam black-tie*

This Strange Passion see *Él*

Those Days in June see *Los días de junio*

Three Crowns of the Sailor see *Les Trois Couronnes du matelot*

Three Sad Tigers see *Tres tristes tigres*

Throw Me a Dime see *Tire die*

266. Tiempo de morir (Time to Die).
Arturo Ripstein. Mexico, 1965. 90 min., B&W. Spanish.

COMMENTARY: Juan Sayago (José Martínez de Hoyos) returns to his hometown after having been in jail eighteen years for the death of Raúl Trueba. He is now 48 years old and trying to forget the past, looking forward to a quiet and peaceful old age. But an adverse destiny awaits him: Raúl Trueba's sons have been sworn to avenge the death of their father. But Juan is not bothered by this danger. The only thing he yearns for is

to see Mariana (Marga López), who was to have been his bride and from whom he never heard in jail. She has become a mature but still very beautiful woman, distinguished and sober, who keeps a posture of severe mourning and is not willing to let a ghost stir up the ashes of the past.

Surrounded by impending danger, Juan starts to pick up the threads of his life and begins to rebuild his home. Convinced that his enemies will not kill him as long as he does not yield to their provocations, Juan endures, with incredible calmness, the insults and humiliations of Julián Trueba (Alfredo Leal), the oldest of the two sons bent on revenge. Pedro Trueba (Enrique Rocha), the younger brother, has learned the real motive behind the death of his father and admires the courage and self-control of Juan Sayago. Meanwhile, Mariana, who can no longer hide her feelings, ends up telling Juan she still loves him. Mariana insists, however, that it is too late to recover lost time, and she feels she and Juan cannot be happy as long as the Truebas exist. Faced by that ultimatum, Juan Sayago does not hesitate to go forth and battle his enemies, once and for all, to decide his destiny. (Press book.)

This was the first film Ripstein directed. Based upon a screenplay by Gabriel García Márquez as adapted by Mexican novelist Carlos Fuentes, the film is really a Mexican western in which all the action is nearly dominated by reflection — a confrontation between the past and present. García Márquez said it was an idea he had for many years, "born from the image of an old sharpshooter who learned how to knit through long years of seclusion." Ripstein found the Colombian novelist's screenplay fascinating and liked its flashback structure. He made the film because he liked it, not because it means anything.

Tiempo de morir is a classic western

story of vengeance and revenge with a tendency towards the creative use of symbolism. It is a very good first effort for a young Mexican director, who has since made his mark on Mexican cinema with such great films as *El lugar sin límites* (1972) and *El imperio de la fortuna* (1985).

267. Tiempo de morir (Time to Die). Jorge Ali Triana. Colombia/Cuba, 1985. 94 min., Color. Spanish.

COMMENTARY: This *Tiempo de morir* is the same story previously filmed by Arturo Ripstein, based on the very same screenplay by Gabriel García Márquez but set, this time, in Colombia, with Triana making his directing debut. Starring Gustavo Angarita as Juan Sayago, it is less symbolic than Ripstein's version, but with more of a denunciation of Latin American *machismo*.

García Márquez is haunted by his own prophetic words. He once said, "The only thing worse than the fear of dying is the fear of killing." Building on this concept, writing some of the dialogue with the assistance of Carlos Fuentes, García Márquez produced a screenplay reminiscent of his novel *Chronicle of a Death Foretold*.

A Colombian film, photographed by Cuban cameraman Mario Garcia Joya and shot on location in the Colombian town of Armero, *Tiempo de morir* is beautifully lensed, a bit slow-paced but with a wonderful performance by Gustavo Angarita as Juan Sayago. Like the Ripstein predecessor, it resembles the classic American western. It is revenge drama not just about Juan Sayago but also Julián Trueba, a common man who is in touch with the passionate universe — one that has a moral, rigid, eternal code — when he decides to avenge the death of his father and fulfill his own inevitable destiny.

This version of *Tiempo de morir* owes much to Fred Zinnemann's 1952 classic western with Gary Cooper called *High Noon*, but taken on its own terms, it is an impressive first film for its director and perhaps the best film made of a Gabriel García Márquez screenplay. It is one of the late eighties film, like Lisandro Duque's *Miracles in Rome*, that is giving stature and new life to Colombian cinema.

NOTES: Born in Colombia in 1942, Jorge Ali Triana studied filmmaking in Prague in the mid-sixties. He had vast stage experience during the fifties and sixties, founding experimental groups and workshops. He began making short documentaries in 1977 and directed an episode in the long feature film *Las cuatro edades del amor* before before directing *Tiempo de morir* in 1985.

268. Tiempo de revancha (Time for Revenge). Adolfo Aristarain. Argentina, 1981. 113 min., Color. Spanish.

COMMENTARY: "Pedro Bengoa (played by the prolific Argentine actor Federico Luppi) is a demolitions expert with an active background in Argentina's radical labor movement. Now in his mid-forties, he feels it's time to settle down, earn some money and live quietly with his wife of 25 years, Amanda (Haydee Padilla).

"Bengoa has work papers forged and obtains a position with Tulsaco, a multinational corporation. As foreman of the crew at an isolated mining camp, Bengoa sets out to give his new life a try, but Bruno Di Toro (Ulises Dumont), a friend from livelier, more idealistic days, is a member of the demolition crew. Bruno already detests the camp's life of long hours, hard work and virtually no contact with civilization. In addition, Bengoa soon discovers that Tulsaco is intentionally endangering the lives of its crews by using bigger, illegal dynamite charges.

"Di Toro has a scheme to blackmail

the company for enough money to retire and asks Bengoa to join him by rigging an explosion. Di Toro will hide in a niche of rocks and afterwards, Bengoa will make sure his friend is "rescued." Bruno will then pretend the trauma has rendered him dumb. With the help of a mercenary lawyer named Larsen (Julio de Grazia), who knows sordid details about several of Tulsaco's other dealings, Di Toro expects to be paid a sizeable sum to keep the case out of court.

"At first, Bengoa is not interested in the scheme, but the situation worsens; an oversized explosion kills two workers and shortly thereafter, he learns of the death of his father, with whom he had shared many ideals. After attending the funeral in Buenos Aires, Bengoa returns to tell Di Toro that he will join his plot.

"When the appointed day arrives and the dynamite is lit, Di Toro loses his nerve with seconds to go before the blast. Bengoa tries to protect his friend, but Di Toro dies and Bengoa is trapped in the mountain. Located and freed, he opens his mouth to speak and does not utter a sound.

"On her husband's behalf, Amanda contacts Larsen, who was to be Di Toro's lawyer/accomplice. The lawyer prepares his silent client for a meeting with Don Guido Ventura (Jorge Hacker), chairman of the Tulsaco conglomerate.

"Ventura wants to avoid a public court case and almost immediately agrees to pay Larsen's asking price of $300,000. However, Bengoa refuses the settlement, and the board chairman ups his offer to a half-million dollars. To the great consternation of all the businessmen, the ex-labor organizer still won't make a deal.

"Bengoa's sanity and courage are challenged during many months of proceedings as Tulsaco tries to break him. His rooms are bugged, phones tapped and movements monitored openly around the clock. Amanda leaves under the pressure of what it's doing to her

husband. Amidst real and imagined threats, in an atmosphere of mounting paranoia and helplessness, Bengoa must summon all his strength to maintain his demeanor and silence.

"The verdict comes in after more than a year; Tulsaco is guilty; Bengoa is legally dumb. The company's quarry is shut down and a full investigation is ordered. Bengoa shares his joy with his wife, and they intend to leave the country after he splits the $200,000 compensation money, awarded by the court, with Larsen. The lawyer warns of danger from Tulsaco now that the trial is over, and Bengoa quickly is shown that the company is determined to hound and psychologically torture him. But he, too, is determined." (Press book.)

Made under the military regime and under conditions of severe censorship, Aristarain's tightly narrated and powerful thriller dealt with Argentine frustration at the impossibility of avenging the junta's atrocities. Bengoa's struggle to expose the mining company's injustices can be decoded as an allegory for life under the junta, and his silence as the silence of an entire society, but also as the possibility of resisting the regime's seeming impunity — using its own terms.

Tiempo de revancha is one of the best political thrillers to come out of Argentina in the early eighties, preceding *La historia oficial*, another total blockbuster of a film. But unlike the Luis Puenzo film, *Tiempo de revancha* is more in the frame of a Costa-Gavras political thriller, a totally fictional story with a Kafkaesque conclusion, somewhat based on fact, but mostly fiction. It depends on how the viewer sees Bengoa — as a truly rebellious idealist activist and revolutionary, or as a selfish, money-hungry murderer out to shake up the establishment whatever the cost. Perhaps he does achieve a victory of sorts, and his willed silence may prove to be a scream of protest. It's the old story of one man against the system, like *Meet John Doe, Mr. Smith Goes to Washington,* or *Mr. Deeds Goes to Town,* Frank Capra populist films all made in an American democracy. But devastatingly graphic punishments await protesters in Argentina as people disappear, bodies are dumped from blue Falcons and a psychological war of nerves using the media is waged by the police or military junta. Like Gene Hackman in Coppola's great 1974 film *The Conversation,* the Argentine junta is out to get Bengoa, to break him psychologically by using high-tech surveillance techniques to monitor his whereabouts for that final, irrevocable assault.

Aristarain has made a bold, unsettling, irrational film about embattled times, where defiance can cost you your life. Aristarain has had other collaborations with Federico Luppi, and both director and star seem to delight in making films about rebellious spirits. Their 1992 effort, *Un lugar del mundo,* is a commercial success, a gratifying film, not the harrowing, noir-like scenario *Tiempo de revancha,* made in a horrifying era. Aristarain is a director worthy of careful study and future evaluation. He may be one of Argentina's greatest.

269. La tierra prometida
(The Promised Land). Miguel Littín. Chile, 1973. 120 min., Eastmancolor. Spanish.

COMMENTARY: "Set in the 1930s, a small group of landless, out-of-work peasants led by José Durán (Nelson Villagra) learns that south of Chile, there is abandoned land belonging to absent landowners or to the state. Under Durán, this straggling group moves south to Palmilla, the 'promised land,' but the Chilean army tries to stop them. Durán believes a decent life of farming can be achieved if they get to Palmilla.

"Among the group is an intellectual named Traje Cruzado ('Pin-Stripe,'

played by Marcelo Gaete), who worked with the founder of the Chilean communist party in the north and who begins to educate Durán. The group finally gets to Palmilla, putting up houses, clearing land, sowing crops. The first harvest is brought in, and a train driver, Juan de Dios (Aníbal Reyna), is charged with selling the crops for the entire community. Unfortunately, the crops are sold for almost nothing, while everything the group buys is expensive.

"One day, a small red plane arrives in Palmilla, and the pilot announces that there is a new progressive president of Chile named Marmeduke Grove and that Chile is now a socialist republic. Durán is persuaded to go to Los Huiques for a transfer of power for his people. The group leaves Palmilla, arrives after a long journey over the snow-covered mountains and Durán and his men take over the town, organizing the peasants to take over the land from the owners they work for. Although Durán doubts the efficacy of this move, the army starts to move against him, learning that Grove is no longer in power and that Alessandri, a reactionary, has taken over.

"Durán and his group return to Palmilla, but on the hills surrounding the town, the army is waiting. A group of soldiers inform Durán that the man who owned the land they have taken has died in Paris and his family has come to reclaim their property. Durán is ordered off the land.

"The women gather together — led by 'La Meche,' Durán's companion — and urge the men to fight. Durán leads all the farmers of Palmilla into a bloody battle. The massacre is total. It is their deaths that are symbolic. Durán and his friends live on, even now, in the minds of the Chilean people." (Press book.)

La tierra prometida was Chile's first widescreen color spectacular, an epic film ballad combining history and myth,

In this almost surreal still of the aftermath of the Chilean army's destruction of an agricultural cooperative, an unidentified nude actress strolls through the carnage in Miguel Littín's *La tierra prometida* (*The Promised Land*, 1973).

allegory and revolution, spectacle and poetry. It is based on historical events during the 1930s when the world-wide depression created social and economic upheaval throughout Chile and eventually led to the establishment of the first socialist republic in the Americas, short-lived though it was.

The film was shot in the province of Colchagua (about 60 miles south of Santiago) in 1972-73. For more than eight months, the director, his crew and the actors who worked on the film lived with the peasants of Santa Cruz. After the military *coup d'état* that overthrew Salvador Allende, the film was shelved, and there were military reprisals against many of the peasants who acted in it. Some were killed, many imprisoned, and its director escaped into exile, which give the film added relevance to the political situation in Chile. The film itself, therefore becomes a banner in the struggle of

the Chilean people. (Publicity handouts.)

Unmistakeably agit-prop in his approach, director Miguel Littín has created a visually beautiful film against a colorful background of the snow-draped Andes mountains, using real peasants who give his film a *cinéma vérité* clarity that holds our attention up to the final massacre scene. Seeking to tell the story as it happened, Littín interrupts the narrative with allegorical visions of the Virgin of the Carmen, whose symbolic usage is muddied by references to evils of the Catholic church as well as a confusion with her significance as a Joan of Arc figure, worshipped by landowners, peasants and the military. Probably intended as a kind of *Grapes of Wrath* of Chile of the 1930s, the film goes off the track using this heavy-handed symbolism. But otherwise, the director of *El chacal de Nahualtero* has hardly had a misstep in his effort to achieve status and democracy for his native homeland.

270. La tigra (The Tigress). Camilo Luzuriaga. Ecuador, 1990. 80 min., Color. Spanish.

COMMENTARY: Perhaps the very first film made in Ecuador since 1980, *La tigra* is not a "great" Latin American film, but it is one of the few representing the country of Ecuador that has been seen on public television in the United States and is also available on video cassette.

The story is about two sisters, warned by a local medicine man that the younger sister must remain a virgin forever to make amends for the sins of the village or they will have hell to pay. Of course, the girls are very sexually active with the local boys, and the film seems to show small town attitudes about love, sex and superstition in modern Ecuador.

The performances by the girls, Lissette Cabrera and Rossana Iturralde, are very good in a cast that also includes Veronica García, Aristides Vargas and Virgilio Valero. The print of the film, however, was very grainy and the color looked quite streaked. Nevertheless, *La tigra*, a hokey film of sorts, is a first for Ecuador and should be seen to encourage further filmmaking efforts in this tiny country.

The Tigress see *La tigra*

Time for Revenge see *Tiempo de revancha*

Time to Die see *Tiempo de morir (Ripstein)*

A group of Argentine youths standing on bridges, asking train passengers to give them money in Fernando Birri's devastating documentary *Tire die* (*Throw Me a Dime* (1958).

Time to Die see *Tiempo de morir (Triana)*

Time Will Come see *Lo que vendrá*

271. Tire die (Throw Me a Dime). Fernando Birri. Argentina, 1958. 30 min., B&W. Spanish.

COMMENTARY: "Billed by its makers as Argentina's "first social survey film," this now legendary work focuses on groups of children from a marginal community who risk life and limb running along railway trestles to beg money from riders in passsing trains. The act of begging has never been so breathlessly kinetic. In deferring this graphic footage to the end, the filmmakers not only generate suspense but also build an understanding of the economic and demographic imbalances which motivate such desperate dare-devilry." (MOMA program notes.)

Arriving on the banks of the city of Santa Fe, Argentina, Birri films a great number of families living near the railroad station in Mitre, near the section called "Tire die." Filming there, he watched children risk their lives for a ride over a bridge two kilometers long, sometimes falling to their deaths on the tracks.

Tire die is neo-realistic cinema at its best and most haunting. It is truly incredible watching a landmark film as this, showing slum children begging for coins, besieging long-distance train passengers in an effort to survive. For pleasure, the children would ride atop the trains, sometimes getting knocked off by the electrical hangers overhead and killed. Birri captures this on film — how cheap is life in Argentina, and how uncaring the parents. About the film, Birri has said himself that "one must place oneself face to face with the reality with a camera and document it, document underdevelopment. ... Cinema which makes itself an accomplice of that underdevelopment is sub-cinema."

Tire die is probably one of the most frighteningly realistic and tragic pieces of cinema ever made and deserves to be seen as a cue into the human condition of Latin American children. *Los olvidados* and *Pixote* are fictionalized, semi-documentary, artful masterworks, but *Tire die* is absolute reality.

Toffee or Mint see *Caluga o menta*

272. El topo (The Mole). Alejandro Jodorowsky. Mexico, 1971. 123 min., Color. Spanish.

COMMENTARY: Controversial is the best word to describe Alejandro Jodorowsky's film *El topo*. One unidentified critic called it "a work of incomprehensible depth...," but "it is more nearly a work of incomprehensible breadth, and I am not persuaded that the director, any more than the rest of us, altogether knows what he [or the film] is about," said *New York Times* critic Roger Greenspun.

El topo is a phantasmagoric allegory of Western civilization, starring Jodorowsky himself as an avenging gunfighter dressed in black, toting his seven-year-old son, Brontis, with him as he cleanses the Mexican desert of all kinds of bandits in the blood-spattered, Sergio Leone tradition of spaghetti western violence. The film is modestly organized into four sections: Genesis, Prophets, Psalms and Apocalypse — pretentious markers laden with crude allegory and heavy symbolism, but chock-full of vivid and fascinating images that are new and exciting (for example, a legless man riding the shoulders of an armless man into a cave of cripples). The film, however, flounders in the swamp of its own allegory as the director sweeps Christian and Pagan symbolism alike onto the screen. It becomes a pretentious philosophical mess, liberally spattered with blood in homage to Luis Buñuel, Federico Fellini, Sergio Leone and Fernando Arrabal, among other surrealist directors. Nevertheless the film is made with a kind of visionary zeal rare in films of the early seventies and evokes some kind of fascination in its hysterical and operatic modality. *El topo* is a unique, one-of-a-kind experience but certainly will not enhance the art of filmmaking or advance the director's career.

Torments see *Él*

Actor and director Alejandro Jodorowsky, dressed in black, has his own seven-year-old son, Brontis, in tow as he cleanses the Mexican landscape of all sorts of bandits. Some are already hanging from the ceiling in Jodorowsky's monumental Mexican film *El topo* (*The Mole*, 1971).

273. Traidores (Traitors). Grupo Cine de la Base. Argentina, 1973. 110 min., B&W. Spanish.

COMMENTARY: Written, directed and acted by anonymous members of a loose, leftist group of political filmmakers in Buenos Aires called Grupo Cine de la Base, whose aim was to target the right-wing Peronistas who had taken control of the new Perón government, *Traidores* tells the story of the seventeen year rise and fall of the fictional character Roberto Barrera, a Peronista trade union leader who sells out to the ruling-class bosses. Crooked to the core, he has a wife and a mistress, a taste for the high life and absolutely no scruples. Making petty deals all around, he sucks up to management, skims the union treasury and rationalizes these acts before he receives his comeuppance. Another man is first tortured in his behalf and then Barrera himself is finally assassinated, an anticlimax to the realistic detailing of political corruption and bureaucratic policies that have underminded the torturers and the entire nation as well.

The title refers to members of the Argentine labor movement who continued to call themselves Peronistas (even after Perón's ouster in 1955) while secretly collaborating with various regimes that were either military or backed by the military. The film follows Barrera from his first compromise with management to insure his election as union chief (dictator) until his death at the hands of urban guerrillas fed up with the subversion of labor's cause. Although the film avoids outwardly condemning Perón himself, it evinces the kind of disillusionment that leads to despair and finally to terrorist tactics shaping Argentina's world of the early seventies. The film supports the use of violence in its denunciation of the Argentine elite, including the right-wing Peronist part of it. It is a no-nonsense call to arms, to revolution, addressed to the working class — a fundamentally communist film attacking the control-of-power issue in today's Argentina.

Since the actors are amateurs and the film was shot by amateurs, *Traidores* has a pseudo-documentary look about it. But it is very serious about the political issues it attacks, and although it does not have the veneer or professionalism of a Costa-Gavras, Pontecorvo or Solanas film, it has tension, passion, intellectual energy and the power to convince and disarm. *Traitors* is strong, political, revisionist cinema.

A Train to the Stars see *Um trem para as estrelas*

Traitors see *Traidores*

Transparent Woman see *Mujer transparente*

274. La tregua (The Truce). Sergio Renan. Argentina, 1974. 108 min., Color. Spanish.

COMMENTARY: *La tregua* is a remarkably sensitive film about a 49-year-old widower (beautifully played by Hector Alterio) who falls in love with a warm-hearted but unsophisticated 24-year-old girl (perceptively played by Ana María Picchio). A conflict arises with the widower's children — two grown sons and a daughter — when their father (who is an administrator in a small manufacturing company) begins to date to fill the emptiness in his life. The widower cannot comprehend why one son has gay companions or the other resents his dating the young woman, a member of his staff.

Eventually father and employee begin living together on a permanent basis, to the family's chagrin. But love triumphs, and the widower changes from an insensitive, resentful, incommunicative man to a warm and happy individual. This is short-lived, however, since the young woman dies quickly from an unspecified illness, shattering the widower's spiritual beliefs in love and enduring happiness, leaving him to cope once more alone, struggling for survival in the everyday, materialistic world of Buenos Aires.

Hector Alterio went on to play the same sort of role in a 1980 Spanish film directed by Jaime de Armiñán entitled *The Nest*, about a widower who falls in love with a teenager (played wonderfully by Ana Torrent) and comes to a sad end — killed by the Civil Guard. *La tregua* was a rehearsal for Alterio's subsequent role, but Alterio's performance here is equally sensitive, subtle and moving. So are the other actors in the ensemble cast, which includes Oscar Martínez as the homosexual son and Luis Politti as an old, sympathetic friend. Argentine actresses Norma Aleandro, Cipe Lincovsky and China Zorilla contribute cameo roles to the film aided by some wonderful tango music by Julián Plaza and the excellent camera work of Juan Carlos Desanzo. *La tregua* is a small, intimate film, the kind of art film that is insightful, emotional, inspirational, ultimately moving. Based on a best-selling novel by Mario Benedetti, the film was also nominated in the Best Foreign Film category for the Academy Awards of 1974.

275. Um trem para as estrelas (A Train to the Stars). Carlos Diegues. Brazil, 1987. 103 min., Color. Portuguese.

COMMENTARY: A kind of Brazilian film noir, *Um trem para as estrelas* is about a young saxophonist named Vinicius (Guilherme Fontes) who tries to eke out a living through his music, looking for jobs all over Rio. His girlfriend, Nieinha (Ana Beatriz Wiltgen), disappears without a trace, and he starts to search the entire city for her, consulting the police (who believe she became a prostitute), her parents (who are lost in their own world of illusions) and his own mother, the owner of a strip-joint (who offers no help). The film becomes a mystery story that is never resolved. It reminds one of the alienation films of Michelangelo Antonioni, especially his *L'avventura*, where a woman's disappearance foments the action of the real love story that takes place between Monica Vitti and Gabriele Ferzetti.

The entire film is an excuse for the director, Carlos Diegues, to create ambience and make a strong social comment about the poverty-stricken shantytowns of Rio's suburbs. He sees Rio society as full of crime and its participants, the prostitutes, pimps, thieves, drug dealers, strippers and even cops, as true victims of the self-perpetuating system. If one could only truly escape the poverty, ignorance and brutality of this society! If physical escape is not possible, then one must dream and take a train for the stars.

The film has been beautifully photographed by Edgar Moura and has a wonderful soundtrack by Gilberto Gil with a terrific saxophone solo that truly reflects the desperation of the protagonist and the emotional content of the film. *Um trem para as estrelas* is a Brazilian version of the 1950 film noir *Young Man with a Horn*, directed by Michael Curtiz with a New York locale, about a trumpeter from an impoverished background really in search of himself. The 1950 film was pure entertainment, loosely based on the life of Bix Beiderbecke, and had none of the social innuendos, nor the suggestions of bleak horizons in store for the country's youth, that Diegues presents in *Um trem para as estrelas*.

276. Tres tristes tigres (Three Sad Tigers). Raúl Ruiz. Chile, 1968. 100 min., B&W. Spanish.

COMMENTARY: Not to be confused

with the Cabrera Infante novel or the 1961 Mexican film with the same title, *Tres tristes tigres* is Raúl Ruiz's first Chilean feature film, which was released abroad in 1969 but was not seen in the United States till 1989.

Made in black and white and with a restless and shaky hand-held camera, the film is set is Santiago's underworld. Tito (Nelson Villagra) and Amanda (Shenda Román) are brother and sister. He is a middle-aged con artist; she, a strip-tease "artiste" too old to be called "Queen of the Strippers." Tito is likewise too old to be an errand boy for Rudy (Jaime Vadell), who himself works for a con artist and petty gangster who wants to be the godfather of Santiago. Amanda is nothing more than a prostitute, used by Tito for financial gain as she is passed around from man to man.

We follow this group's daily existence, from sleazy apartment to apartment, from hefty meal to meal, from crummy bar to bar. Their existence is patently absurd, living from day to day, ready to cheat on each other as soon as an opportunity arises. Their "work" gives them no real satisfaction, so their illicit sex and wine-drinking bouts become their outlet.

In a particular pitiful scene, brother, sister and Rudy are so stoned that they sit around drunkenly reciting the tongue-twister of the title: "Three trapped tigers trepidatiously tripped through the trees." As we look at the scene, we realize how trapped these people are in their crumbling lives, in crummy apartments, with no sense of hope.

Ruiz would come to be known more for his surrealistically styled films, but *Tres tristes tigres* is still a very ambitious first film. Ruiz even said of it, "I was just trying to show something about my town, the way people lived." *Tres tristes tigres* contains some wonderful, strong imagery and well-defined characters in a seedy environment that displays a neo-realist camera style. *Tres tristes tigres* may not have any of Ruiz's characteristic puzzles, word games, collages of images or disjunctive tales that need decoding or provide enigmatic and hermetic intellectual fodder, but it shows verve, strength and talent. Even as an exile, Raúl Ruiz could not be kept from practicing his best art: controversial filmmaking. And *Tres tristes tigres* is his debut in that process.

277. Les Trois Couronnes du matelot (The Three Crowns of the Sailor). Raúl Ruiz. France, 1982. 117 min., Color. French.

COMMENTARY: The 1984 New York Film Festival program called this film "deliriously unsynopsisable ... 'The Rime of the Ancient Mariner' rewritten by Jorge Luis Borges as a script for Orson Welles of *Mr. Arkadin.*"

The film opens in a port surrounded by fog, where a student (Philippe Deplanche) who has just committed murder is grabbed by a mysterious sailor (Jean Bernard Guillard), who asks him to listen to his tale of misfortune for the price of three Danish crowns. They go to a local dance hall, where the sailor describes his macabre past — how he shipped out of his home port of Valparaiso aboard a vessel that was manned by ghosts, on which he was the only living crewman, bound to sail the seven seas until he found someone to replace him. (The plot sounds very much like the 1951 Albert Lewin film *Pandora and the Flying Dutchman*, with Ava Gardner, who gives up her life to sail the seven seas with James Mason, the erstwhile Dutchman of the title.)

We watch the world-weary mariner recount his past in the demimonde of gangsters, prostitutes, pimps, dockside prophets and other assortments of characters. When a new day dawns, the student beats the sailor to death and takes his place on the ghost ship.

A hostage in a makeshift jail in Jan Lindqvist's documentary *¡Tupamaros!* (1973).

It is entirely possible Ruiz drew his inspiration from the Lewin film cited above or some of the stories of Robert Louis Stevenson, or a Val Lewton film called *Ghost Ship*, or Jack London's *The Sea Wolf*, or any of those films of the thirties or forties, in America or France, where great fog machines were used to create "atmosphere." Whatever the source, Ruiz has come up with a very entertaining work, beautifully photographed by Sacha Vierny in France with location work in Portugal, abetted by a zesty music score by Jorge Arraigada. *Les Trois Couronnes du matelot* is one of Raúl Ruiz's least bizarre films — no baroque imagery, no profound intellectual puzzles, no hermetic offbeat humor. On an intellectual level, it does examine the idea of exile explicitly. (After the Allende overthrow Ruiz was forced to leave his native Chile with his wife, Valeria Sarmiento, who was an ed-itor of this film.) But *Les Trois Couronnes* is also a treat for the eyes, the ears and the mind — totally entertaining.

The Truce see *La tregua*

278. ¡Tupamaros! Jan Lindqvist. Uruguay/Sweden, 1973. 50 min., B&W. Spanish/Swedish.

COMMENTARY: Completed in August 1972, this documentary was secretly carried out of Uruguay because the repressive military took over. One wonders if the Tupamaros leaders are still alive.

The Tupamaros are a small band of urban guerrillas who took power in Uruguay. They state that the prevailing government created violence and, therfore, created them. The aim of this documentary is to educate the public about the abuse of political power, the government's use of torture and repression of all kinds. The goal of the Tupamaros is to take the power and profit that now reside in the hands of a minority and place it in the hands of the majority, thereby combatting unemployment and inflation and strengthening the educational and health facilities of the nation.

The leaders are interviewed in black silhouette against a flag of the National Liberation Movement of Uruguay. One leader takes the director, Jan Lindqvist, with cameras to the People's Prison, where Dan Mitrione, the American police expert in the employ of the repressive military machine, was murdered by the Tupamaros as retaliation against the government.

Costa-Gavras tackled the same theme (less convincingly) in his 1973 French film *State of Siege*, starring Yves Montand, about the CIA confronting the Tupamaros killers and bringing them to justice — done in a thriller format. This documentary, *¡Tupamaros!* is the real story behind CIA participation in Uruguay. It is unfortunate that, like Barbara Trent's *Panama Deception*, it did not get wide showings in the United States. Its clandestine production history and the fact that it was smuggled out of the country should give it a kind of dangerously romantic appeal for distributors. That not being the case, *¡Tupamaros!* is viewed as a valuable supplement to the Costa-Gavras film. But very much like the Argentine documentary *Traidores*, this film is a battle cry for violence until the repression is ended in Uruguay. However, when we see hostages taken in a "people's prison," no matter who they are, no matter how good the conditions, no matter how favorable the interviews with them (we see three in this film), one cannot help wondering if their way is indeed the best and only way. *¡Tupamaros!* shows the activists to be honorable and moral, not motivated by personal profit — but actively seeking to establish parallel power in the nation, to influence the people by constantly questioning the

validity of the regime. If only there was a better way for the Tupamaros to foment change.

279. Ukamau (And So It Is).
Jorge Sanjinés. Bolivia, 1966. 70 min., B&W. Spanish.

COMMENTARY: Andrés Mayta, a young Indian peasant of the native community of Yumani, the Sun Island on Lake Titicaca, lives with his beautiful wife, Sabina Urpi, on the produce of his land and fish from the lake. The two live happily, at peace with their natural environment.

One day Andrés leaves by canoe for the fair at Copacabana, a nearby village. After seeing him off, Sabina returns home to find Rosendo Ramos, the halfbreed who regularly buys farm produce from Andrés and other peasants on the island. Disappointed because Andrés has taken his produce with him to the fair instead of selling to him, Ramos decides to wait for Andrés' return.

Soon, Ramos tries to seduce Sabina. Her stubborn and desperate resistance increases his desire. Eventually Ramos' physical superiority overpowers the woman's resistance, and he takes her. Ramos goes away, not knowing that Sabina has been mortally wounded.

Andrés returns and finds Sabina near death. She manages to whisper Ramos' name to her husband. Andrés attends his wife's burial, utterly distressed. He meets with the community leaders and tells them the killer's name.

Meanwhile, Ramos, certain nobody will ever suspect him in Sabina's death, hushes his conscience and goes on leading an easy and superficial life, alternating entertainments and drinks. Andrés watches him surreptitiously until the day that Ramos must take a journey to his brother's mine to get back some money he is owed. The road is blocked, and Ramos must travel by mule.

One evening, Ramos feels Andrés is

after him. The Indian follows Ramos stealthily. When Ramos gets to the endless pampas, suddenly, as if springing up from the earth, Andrés appears and soundlessly picks up a huge rock. Ramos, realizing why the Indian is there, tries to defend himself. The two men start fighting wildly, and Ramos dies." (Press book.)

The leading actors of *Ukamau* are all professionals and act their roles vigorously. Nestor Cardenas Peredo played the half-breed, Ramos, who after becoming a rich man is killed in a fierce fight with Andrés (beautifully played by Vicente Verneros Salinas) as revenge for raping his wife, Sabina (Benedicta Mendoza Huanca). The director, Jorge Sanjinés, captures the rugged life and colorful detail in the customs of these Bolivian Indians as he weaves his morality tale that also has a just and satisfactory conclusion. Bolivian native Sanjinés is a master filmmaker, and *Ukamau* is among his best folkloric efforts.

280. La última cena (The Last Supper). Tomás Gutiérrez Alea. Cuba, 1976. 110 min., Color. Spanish.

COMMENTARY: "A wealthy and very religious owner of a sugar mill, a count of Havana (Nelson Villagra), is driven by his conscience to perform genuine acts of spiritual goodness. During Holy Week, he visits his sugar mill and gathers twelve black slaves. He washes and kisses their feet and then, in a supper similiar to the one Jesus gave to bid farewell to his disciples, he invites the slaves to join him at his own table.

"During the dinner on Holy Thursday, the count's behavior is alternately arrogant and humble. He converses with the slaves and tells them of an episode in the life of St. Francis, the moral of which is that perfect happiness lies in accepting pain and abuse with humility and joy. They eat and drink wine and, little by little, the initial tension is relieved. The wine helps the count regain his inner peace. He discovers that he feels at ease talking with this group of black men, and this astounds him; he becomes benevolent, happy and communicative. He even begins to speak ill of the overseer. Most of the slaves give way to these feelings and enjoy the occasion.

"On Friday morning, the count returns to his villa. At the sugar mill, the overseer rouses the slaves for work. The slaves tell him that nobody works on Good Friday. Some of the slaves who attended the supper given by the count are convinced that their master will not approve the attitude of the overseer and decide to resist. They hold the overseer hostage and send a message to the count to come to the sugar mill and pass judgment. When the count finds out the slaves have disobeyed the overseer, he is indignant and orders out an armed posse to control the situation. The count puts aside his benevolent and paternalistic attitude to act openly in accord with his real interests. Faced with the attack, some slaves kill the overseer and set fire to the sugar mill before fleeing.

"The count, with his mill in ruins, unleashes a cruel repression; he captures 11 of 12 slaves who attended the supper and orders their heads cut off. Only one slave eludes capture. He escapes into the hills." (Press book.)

The director's first color film, *La última cena* may be viewed as an allegory on Christian liberalism and also the same sort of anti-religious satire that Luis Buñuel was so fond of making. The idea of 12 slaves reenacting the roles of the apostles in a recreation of the Last Supper during Holy Week, then being beheaded by the plantation owner after he has displayed his Christian charity and liberalism, is very caustic humor and quite hard to take. The film does revel in its details as a bit of real history, revealing the intricate social relationships

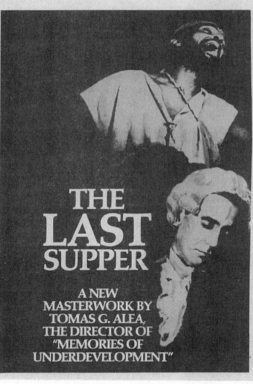
Advertising flyer for Tomás Gutiérrez Alea's *La última cena* (*The Last Supper*, 1976).

of plantation life, the shocking brutalities of black slavery and the African cultural heritage preserved by the slaves. Above all, the film is a provocative and engrossing moral tale dealing with such universal themes as transference of guilt, the avoidance of responsibility and the ceaseless human desire for freedom.

The Cuban Film Institute spared no expense to make this film. It is superbly produced, with period detail in costumes and settings, and luminously photographed in authentic locales. But scrupulous attention to lighting, color and costume design are not enough to make *La última cena* as convincing a spectacle as any Hollywood swashbuckler, which it tries to be. The viewer senses a kind of awkwardness in the acting and a feeling of the director's unease in working with a period piece. We are alienated by the distance between our own feelings and the ultimately propagandistic message of the film, i.e., that Cuban socialism is a better way to live and that there is real danger if you give people freedom, even a little bit of freedom. The Castro regime unfortunately continues its policy of repression, and that is the real message behind Alea's interesting but ultimately flawed *La última cena*.

281. Últimas imágenes del naufragio (Last Images of the Shipwreck). Eliseo Subiela. Argentina, 1989. 127 min., Color. Spanish.

COMMENTARY: Perhaps best described as a unique blend of satirical madness, spine-tingling fantasy and philosophical meditations on the spiritual barrenness of man's existence, *Últimas imágenes del naufragio* is a truly fascinating film by the maker of *Hombre mirando al sudeste*. Very much like that metaphysical parable, this film tells a personal story clearly related to the political realities of modern Argentina.

In the film, the main character, Roberto tells his story to his newborn son as the scenes unfold in flashback before us. A naive, 40-year-old insurance agent, Roberto is bored to tears with his job and trying to write the great novel of his life that will lift him out of obscurity and out of his daily ride on the Buenos Aires metro. One night, Roberto (Lorenzo Quinteros) is picked up in a scam initiated by a hooker named Estela

(Noemi Frenkel), whom he saved as she jumped in front of an oncoming train. Though married, Roberto falls for Estela. He meets her bizarre family and starts to use them as characters in his novel.

As Roberto accompanies Estela on a bus ride to her home outside of Buenos Aires, the spirits of the dead come aboard the bus from a nearby cemetery — Estela's father, her aunt and uncle. Just as metro passengers look like plastic-wrapped zombies to Roberto, these "ghosts" are equally surreal to the incommunicative Estela. As for Estela's living family members, they are completely lunatic. José is a gun-toting psychotic with a grudge against God; Claudio is a withdrawn obsessive who systematically removes words from his dictionary when he no longer has any use for them; another brother provides financial support for the family with his day job, but spends his evenings building an airplane to escape his prison-like existence through "a tunnel in the sky"; Estela's mother is a complete eccentric, bitter about her husband's desertion of her and resentful of Argentina's loss of political greatness.

As the family begins to accept Roberto, the latter starts to fill the place of the philandering father. Roberto also becomes obsessed with transmuting the family's life into his fiction. He becomes depressed at home, leaves his wife, moves into a hotel and begins writing scripts to fill the lives of the family members deserted by their father.

Meanwhile, Estela goes to the local church and has lunch with Jesús, who is always available for inspiration, crown of thorns and all. She receives advice from him on how to seduce Roberto and ultimately succeeds. While making love to Estela, Roberto realizes that she is his only chance for salvation. He continues in the role of novelist manqué as he tells this entire story to his baby son.

Director Eliseo Subiela has made a fascinating film about Argentina, a society in retreat, evoking the despair of abandonment and the joy of salvation through human, not cosmic, error. The performances of all the actors, including Hugo Soto, Pablo Brichta, Sara Benítez, Andrés Tiengo and Alicia Aller, are extraordinary. Subiela is an original, a truly gifted filmmaker with a finely honed sensibility and a unique vision of society that thrills his audience. Sometimes his films tend to enter into stages of metaphysical murkiness, but they are always rescued by his meticulous attention to excellent storytelling and character development, combined with some surreal imagery that is always a knockout. *Últimas imágenes del naufragio* is a film that just flattens its audience, visually and intellectually.

282. Los últimos días de la víctima (The Last Days of the Victim). Adolfo Aristarain. Argentina, 1981. 91 min., Color. Spanish.

COMMENTARY: Produced by filmmaker Hector Olivera, *Los últimos días de la víctima* is yet another collaboration between star Federico Luppi and director Adolfo Aristarain, although this one is not as highly successful because the essential story fails to fascinate.

Luppi plays a professional killer hired by a powerful businessman to get rid of people in his way to the top. Acting more as a security man, Luppi first proves his worth by murdering someone engaged in fraud. He then receives another assignment, but because he now knows too much as the hired killer, the very same businessman has hired another assassin to dispatch Luppi.

There is much voyeurism in this film. Luppi begins spying on his intended victim, watching his sexual couplings. The woman he sees with the victim is, coincidentally, the wife of his last victim. Ready to act after a period of surveil-

lance, Luppi finally bursts into the room of his quarry, only to be greeted by the victim himself, ready and waiting with the news about his gun for hire.

The film is narrated completely from Luppi's viewpoint and very much like Alfred Hitchcock's 1954 voyeur classic, *Rear Window*: We already know who the murderers are, but who will be the next victim? Made strictly as a crime film with some noir pretensions and sexual titillations, *Los últimos días de la víctima* is pure entertainment, beautifully filmed by camera man Horacio Maira, with an unsympathetic performance by Federico Luppi as the assassin turned victim. The supporting players, especially Soledad Silveyra as the promiscuous widow, Ulises Dumont as a nearsighted weapons expert, China Zorilla as the bawdy owner of a cheap hotel and Monica Galan as a highway prostitute, do very well with what little they have to work with.

Let us remember the more successful Luppi-Aristarain collaborations like *Tiempo de revancha* and *Un lugar en del mundo*, two films of intellectual and political significance that were also devastatingly entertaining.

283. Under Fire. Robert Spottiswoode. U.S./Nicaragua, 1983. 127 min., Color. English.

COMMENTARY: The story of three correspondents in Nicaragua becoming involved in dirty politics on both sides and trying to discover the real truth of the war from both Somoza partisans and Sandinistas, *Under Fire* comes close to being the most thrilling fictional feature film made about Nicaragua.

With a cast of thorough professionals that includes Nick Nolte, Gene Hackman and Joanna Cassidy as the reporters and Jean-Louis Trintignant as a mercenary, the film makes strides forward on the meaning of committment to a democratic ideal, the mercenary mentality and the torturous ironies of history.

The plot itself is complex and entirely fictional, making Nolte inadvertently the fall guy for the death of Hackman at the hands of the Somoza militia and also the cause of the death of the Sandinista leader "Raphael," all because Nolte plays into the hands of the deceptive mercenary Trintignant. Most important, *Under Fire* is a thinking man's entertainment, part of a spate of international films — like Peter Lilienthal's *The Uprising* and Miguel Littín's *Alsino y el condor*— which deal with Nicaragua and its military and social problems. Some stock footage from Nicaragua was used in the making of the film but most of the location filming was done in Guatemala. *Under Fire* makes it clear that, to paraphrase Arthur Miller on Nicaragua, "attention must be paid."

284. Under the Volcano.

John Huston. U.S./Mexico, 1984. 109 min., Color. English/Spanish.

COMMENTARY: Based on the very celebrated autobiographical masterpiece by Malcolm Lowry, starring Albert Finney in the role of the dipsomaniac Geoffrey Firmín, with Jacqueline Bisset (looking astonishingly ravishing) as his wife, Yvonne, and Mexican actors Ignacio López Tarso, Katy Jurado and actor-director Emilio Fernández in various minor roles, *Under the Volcano* is a wonderful transposition of the book to the screen.

It is essentially a pessimistic story, about the descent into hell and oblivion of a self-destructive, impotent alcoholic. What better place to film such a story than in Cuernavaca, Mexico, during the yearly Day of the Dead celebration? Huston, himself then a resident of Puerto Vallarta, Mexico, chose all the locations with care, especially the country bullfight scene situated "under the volcano," as well as the tawdry cantina, filled with lowlifes and prostitutes, where Finney meets his destiny.

Never has a location shoot been realized so perfectly; nor have the mores and folklore been brought to the screen with such color, verve and fidelity to custom. When Ignacio López Tarso as Dr. Vigil says, "Only in Mexico is death an occasion for laughter," the film reaches its zenith of credibility. Albert Finney's superb incarnation of his role is a further triumph for Huston in this, his most underrated cinematic success.

Under the Volcano was photographed in color by the great Mexican cinematographer Gabriel Figueroa and had a fascinating music score written by Alex North. Anthony Andrews had the pitiful role of Firmín's brother, the third side of an amorous triangle that broke up Firmín's marriage. Followers of the Lowry novel may cavil over Huston's treatment, feeling that the director wanted to stay on Graham Greene turf, where a cuckolded Englishman drives himself to drink under an exotic Mexican moon; true syncophants of Lowry may prefer a more faithful vision of the consul destroying himself by the apocalypse of his own imagination. In any case, Mexico, not Lowry, is the star here, and *Under the Volcano* is great Mexican cinema.

NOTES: John Huston was a screenwriter and director in Hollywood beginning in the early 1930s and always showed a keen interest in Latin America. Some of his best films in this thematic area are *Treasure of the Sierra Madre* (1947), based upon the B. Traven novel; *We Were Strangers* (1947), about rebels fighting the Machado regime in Cuba; and *Night of the Iguana* (1964), about a group of Tennessee Williams-style misfits caught together in Puerto Vallarta. *Under the Volcano* is his best Latin American effort shot on location; in fact, all except *Volcano* seemed curiously studio-bound projects. Huston also reputedly had a house in the jungle somewhere around Puerto Vallarta for a short period of his life that he spent in Mexico. He died in Ireland in 1987 at the age of eighty-one.

Under the World see *Debajo del mundo*

Unexpected Encounter see *Encuentro inesperado*

Unfinished Diary see *Journal inachevé*

Up to a Certain Point see *Hasta cierto punto*

285. The Uprising. Peter Lilienthal. W. Germany/Nicaragua, 1980. 96 min., Color. Spanish.

COMMENTARY: This feature focuses on the major events of the people's uprising in León, Nicaragua. At the center of the events stands the story of a family which becomes a symbol of the fight for the reinstatement of human dignity and freedom in Nicaragua.

"Nicaragua 1979. In León, a university city northwest of the capital of Managua. The final fighting is taking place between the National Guard of the dictator, Somoza, and the Sandinista Liberation Front (F.S.L.N.). The fighting leads to the overthrow of the government on July 19.

"Agustín, a soldier in a special unit and communication technician of the National Guard, visits his family on a weekend pass. His father and his sister are on the side of the rebels. Agustín witnesses the cruelties committed by the National Guard against the civilian population. He justifies his uniform to his father: His pay as a soldier feeds the family. The parents, with the help of the priest, persuade him to desert.

"Captain Flores, who views Agustín as his personal property, threatens a terror action against the part of the city where Agustín's parents live. This threat is made in order to bring the elite troops safely back to the barracks. Agustín yields to the blackmail.

"Flores, who wants to evacuate his family and belongings to the United States, is attacked at the harbor. The Sandinistas thereby capture their weapons to use in the fight for liberation.

"Unarmed people gather in a church. A letter of protest from the bishop of Managua is read attacking the unchecked despotism of the government. Soldiers seize the demonstrators in the church.

"The women of León gather in front of the barracks. They demand that Captain Flores let their sons go. They are driven away. They organize themselves to learn how to construct bombs.

"After a massacre in the church of León, Agustín decides to desert and support the resistance. His first act is to tap a telegraph line and thereby prevent the arrival of enemy enforcements.

"Agustín finds his sister among the Sandinistas and reconciles himself with his father.

"Firemen supporting the Liberation Front have commandeered a water truck. They fill it with gasoline in place of water and maneuver it to the vicinity of the barracks. With the help of the population, the hose is brought into position, running through the houses. The National Guard takes civilian hostages, among them the uncle of Agustín. His father offers himself voluntarily in order not to endanger the liberation action. The Sandinistas pump gasoline through the water hose and set the barracks on fire. Captain Flores, using the hostages for a shield, breaks out of the camp with his last men. Agustín wants to give himself up to him in order to save his family.

"In the fighting, Agustín and the captain are killed. The population celebrates the victorious uprising of July 19, 1979. A member of the uprising teaches the children to dance and tells them of the fighting." (Press book.)

The film was shot in León four months after the Sandinista victory, using citizens, former guerrilla fighters and units of the F.S.L.N. as the actors. Agustín Pereira plays the soldier; Carlos Catania plays his Sandinista father; María Lourdes Centano Zelaya, his mother; Vicky Montero, his sister; and Guido Sáenz, his uncle. Oscar Castillo, the only professional actor in the cast, plays Captain Flores as a jaded, greedy monster with a slightly homoerotic fixation on Agustín. The non-professionals, with dignity and courage in their faces, reenacted their real-life roles and dedicated this film to the free people of Nicaragua. Consequently, *The Uprising* is a fresh, real documentary, simply acted by the participants in the revolution right after the Sandinista victory.

The film was written by the director and Chilean novelist-exile Antonio Skarméta and marks their second collaboration (their first, the 1976 film *Calm Prevails Over the Country*, was a study of fascism in an unnamed Latin American country. *The Uprising* is a gripping study of daily life during an armed insurrection. Lilienthal and Skármeta have both lived under the Allende regime and have experienced the conditions of repression and revolution. That they chose to make such a thrilling docudrama on the subject is a tribute to their persistent zeal for democracy. *The Uprising* presents no polemics, no background information, no political or economic problems of Nicaragua; only the meaning of heroism and solidarity of people in the face of military repression and tyranny. It is a stirring example of revolutionary psychodrama and one of the best of its kind.

NOTES: Peter Lilienthal was born in Germany but spent most of his life in South America, particularly in Uruguay and Chile. In 1939 his family left Germany for Uruguay, where he spent the major part of his youth. He established himself as a filmmaker in West Germany during the 1960s, then moved to Chile, only to be exiled by the Allende regime. Lilienthal's most popular international success was the 1979 film *David*, a true account of the survival of the Holocaust by a rabbi's son.

Uprising in Patagonia see *La Patagonia rebelde*

286. Valparaíso mi amor
(**Valparaíso My Love**). Aldo Francia. Chile, 1969. 95 min., B&W. Spsnish.

COMMENTARY: The film is about a slaughterhouse worker, fired from his job, who after eight months of unemployment finally steals a cow to feed his many children and his wife. Like Jean Valjean, who stole a loaf of bread in Victor Hugo's immortal novel *Les Misérables*, our worker is sent to jail. His five-year term causes the complete disintegration of his family. When he is released he finds that his children, after trying to make a living honestly, have drifted unavoidably into a life of crime and prostitution.

Made in a very neo-realistic style, *Valparaíso mi amor* resembles the early work of Vittorio DeSica (*Bicycle Thief*) or Luchino Visconti (*Rocco and His Brothers*). There is a kind of revisionist attitude in its depiction of the Valparaíso slums that gives the film a semi-documentary aura. The film is a strong, unpretentious debut for its director.

NOTES: Born in 1923 in Chile, Aldo Francia lived in Valparaíso most of his life. At the age of 45, after practicing medicine for over twenty years, Francia became interested in films and filmmaking. He organized the first Cine Club in Vina del Mar, as well as the whole Chilean arthouse system. He also organized various festivals of Latin American films and became the director of the film department at the University of Valparaíso. *Valparaíso mi amor* is his first feature film, although he did make one short film for television entitled *Pasena*. After the Allende *coup d'état*, he returned to practicing medicine.

Valparaíso My Love see *Valparaíso mi amor*

287. Vampirios en la Habana (Vampires in Havana). Juan Padrón. Cuba, 1985. 115 min., Color. Spanish.

COMMENTARY: *Vampirios en la Habana*, the only animated feature reviewed in this book, deserves inclusion because of its high caliber; indeed, it is one of the best films of its kind to come from Latin America, more particularly from Cuba.

The plot is unique and funny: "A vampire scientist travels to Cuba with his young nephew, after failing in Europe in his experiments on a formula that would allow vampires to withstand the sun. In Havana, in a secluded house, he experiments on his nephew Joseph, who grows in the sun like a normal child, without being aware of his vampire origins.

"In 1933, Cuba is suffering under the tyranny of Machado, and Joseph ('Pepito' to Cubans) fights against it. His uncle notifies the Vampire Group in Europe that he has devised the formula and that he wishes to donate it to all the vampires in the world. The European group has other plans for the formula: to establish a monopoly and sell it under the name 'Vampisol.'

"Elsewhere, the vampire mafia of Chicago (La Capa Nostra), whose business interests include underground beaches and clubs for vampires, is threatened by the marketing of Vampisol because it

means that vampires will begin going to real beaches.

"The European group and La Capa Nostra travel to Havana, one to steal the formula and the other to destroy it, while Pepito and his friends flee the tyrant, Machado's police.

"The Europeans — a German, a Frenchman, an Englishman, an Italian and a Spaniard — broadcast an advertisement on Radio Vampire International, stating they have Vampisol. The Chicago vampires bring in specialists such as Sharpie (who fires silver bullets), Fadeout Johnson and a mediocre Wolfman to destroy the European group and its formula.

"After fighting for the formula, Pepito unintentionally ends up with the formula documents in his possession. His aim is to finish the work of his uncle (who has perished) and give it away, free of cost, to vampires. To do so, he must first confront the police and the two groups of vampires, who chase him all over Havana, until he is finally able to broadcast a song on Radio Vampire International whose lyrics are the manufacturing formula for Vampisol." (Press book.)

Vampirios en la Habana is a lively cartoon send-up of vampire and gangster films, combined with Cuban color that makes it a lively, entertaining film. It is played in broad strokes, in caricature by its animated actors, with satire that targets not just the obvious movie genres but also the Machado regime, American tourism and morally slack musicians. The film is farcical, bawdy, crudely animated and drawn, but rowdy, insouciant, raunchy, recalling the best of Ralph Bakshi films like *Fritz the Cat*. It is full of black humor and has a deliciously witty style. With its cartoon send-ups, from Bela Lugosi to Al Capone, from Düsseldorf to Chicago, *Vampirios en la Habana* is a welcome surprise from a state-controlled film

Scene from the Cuban cartoon feature directed by Juan Padrón entitled *Vampirios de la Habana* (*Vampires in Havana*, 1985).

industry, and a breath of fresh air for Cubans and international audiences alike.

Vampires in Havana see *Vampirios en la Habana*

288. El verano de la señora Forbes (The Summer of Miss Forbes).
Jaime Humberto Hermosillo. Mexico/ Spain, 1988. 88 min., Color. Spanish.

COMMENTARY: "Miss Forbes, a German governess, is hired to look after two children for six weeks while their parents are on a pleasure cruise. Miss Forbes turns out to be an authoritative and repressive woman. She imposes a military discipline on the children to get them to fulfill their obligations and duties. Her attitude, which reminds one of a Prussian sergeant, nourishes a blind, growing hate in the children, leading them to plan her murder.

"Having made up their minds to do away with her, the children begin to spy on her at night, and are amazed to discover a very different Miss Forbes to the cold, dictatorial woman who orders them about and threatens them during the day. They find she is a voluptuous woman who reads porn magazines, drinks like a fish and sings strange songs in German, while parading naked around her bedroom, evoking the name of Achilles, a young man who often comes to the house to play with the children.

"Eaten up by a burning passion, the governess gives free rein to her repressed instincts and seduces the young Achilles. Yet when he answers her ardent call, he is brutally rejected. We now see her obscure split personality. For the children, it is madness, pure and simple. This lover's game of provocation and rejection goes on for some time and has a surprisng denouement. For me, the most striking feature of the story is the split personality of Miss Forbes, which enables the spectator to sympathize with the characters. Another result is that at first, we loathe Miss Forbes; then we understand her, and finally we end up feeling sorry for her. The fright and catharsis produced help attain the level of grandeur and modern tragedy contained in this story by García Márquez." (Hermosillo, press book.)

The governess is beautifully played by German actress Hanna Schygulla who inhabits every inch of the role. The two children, played by Alexis Castanares and Victor César Villalobos, bring a tenacity and conviction to their roles. Francisco Gattorno is adequate as Achilles, the young stud and underwater swimming instructor who wants to bed the governess. The conclusion is quite shocking and leads to the eventual demise of the voluptuary, Miss Forbes.

The film is photographed in a kind of murky Eastmancolor, especially the erotic underwater scenes that intentionally lend a disturbing quality to the narrative drive of the screenplay. Made as part of the García Márquez series "Six Loves," *El verano de la señora Forbes* is black comedy at its most sadistic, though in keeping with the themes of violence and pathos that have shaped Latin American politics — and consequently its cinema — for years. Not surprisingly, it is available, like most García Márquez screenplays, on video in America.

289. Verónico Cruz (La deuda interna / The Debt). Miguel Pereira. Argentina, 1987. 100 min., Color. Spanish.

COMMENTARY: "Miguel Pereira's first feature film is set in Chorcán, in the desolate province of Jujuy where he was born. This beautiful filmed narrative captures the pace and details of life in the isolated region. A young boy, raised by his grandmother as a shepherd, is exposed to a world beyond the mountains when he befriends the new local school teacher. But the education of Verónico is more than sentimental; his exposure to "civilization" coincides with the junta's taking power in Buenos Aires. In Chorcán, the local mayor is replaced by a policeman. While this termination of civil authority may seem largely symbolic, when Verónico and his teacher journey to the provincial capital in search of his father, they find that there the effects of military repression differ only in degree. While the film focuses on Verónico's debt to his teacher, a debt of friendship and education, it shows that the country incurred a debt to its citizens, even in the most isolated regions." (MOMA program notes.)

Verónico is played with conviction and innocence by Gonzálo Morales and his kindly teacher by Juan José Camero. There is an idyllic, ineffable bond that forms between them, almost like father and son, even as both search for Verónico's real father, played in the early part of the film by Fortunato Ramos.

Eventually they come to realize he is one of the *desaparecidos*. Verónico is like every young man, full of aspirations. Always fascinated by water as a child, as soon as he is of age, he joins the Argentine navy, only to die tragically in Argentina's 1982 Malvinas Islands "short" war with the British. The film also deals with the military's repressive encroachment on even the most distant of Argentine territories to assure absolute control and power.

Verónico Cruz is a gentle and genteel film that shows civilization can triumph over primitivism, but at what ironic price — the life of its hero. There is a quiet earnestness in the acting, and the gorgeously silent landscapes serve as a wonderful backdrop to a story really about the plight of simple souls, caught in a political war beyond their control that results in wasted lives. Although the film moves a tad slowly, the conclusion packs an unexpected wallop, especially when we hear Verónico's last letter to his girlfriend, Juanita (who may be carrying his child), read by his teacher and we see his smiling photograph in the closing frame. Verónico is no longer isolated or naive. He paid a real price — his death on the battleship *Belgrano*, sunk by the British — to attain his adulthood.

NOTES: Miguel Pereira, an Argentine by birth, now lives in London. *Verónico Cruz* is his debut film, a British-Argentine co-production. He studied filmmaking in a London film school and is currently working on a new feature, as yet untitled. *Verónico Cruz* won the Silver Bear award at the Berlin Film Festival in 1987.

290. El viaje (The Journey).
Fernando Solanas. Argentina, 1991. 135 min., Color. Spanish.

COMMENTARY: This saga of a man's search for his father (Martín is played by Walter Quiróz) was shot in five Latin American countries, from Patagonia to Mexico. Martín lives with his mother (Italian actress Dominique Sanda) in Ushuaia and decides to bicycle to Brazil, where he heard his father was working. So he goes north. As usual, Solanas peppers the film with allegorical figures, like Tito the Hopegiver and Américo Inconclusive, among others. He takes a political swipe at a George Bush lookalike as a visiting president who genuflects, and another unrealistic swipe at Rana, a "frog" president who wears flippers to address his people during a flood.

Although the film at times is visually striking, Solanas should have stayed in the south in Argentina, where he knows the territory. *El viaje* stretches itself very thin, to include a wide variety of themes, like civilization encroaching on the rain forest and on primitive peoples, but the film is not terribly well focused and the viewer's interest lags. Nevertheless, a journey with Solanas is always an experience, even when not as fulfilling as *Sur* or his best film, *Tangos: l'exil de Gardel*.

291. La vida es una sola
(You Only Live Once). Peru, 1993. 84 min., Color. Spanish.

COMMENTARY: Not to be confused with Fritz Lang's 1937 classic pre-noir Bonnie and Clyde film of the same title, this 1993 film concerns guerrilla warfare now being waged in Peru. Its central character, Florinda (Milagros del Carpio), falls in love with Marcelino (Jillat Zambrano), also a student, who then reveals himself to be a guerrilla on the side of the group called Shining Path. Florinda gives up everything for Marcelino and becomes a guerrilla fighter. When the Shining Path group begins to execute dissident townspeople, Florinda has second thoughts, but when the real military arrive, led by El Tigre (Aristóteles Picho), they are equally punitive, suspecting rebellion everywhere. Florinda finds herself caught in a vortex after being subjected to tests like killing her

In a still from Nelson Pereira Dos Santos' Brazilian film *Vidas secas* (*Barren Lives*, 1963), the father (Athila Iorio) and mother (María Riberio) talk about their lack of food, the heat and the dangers in the backlands.

best friend (who is apolitical) and even her dog.

Although the film is pure melodrama, it does provide an unsentimental — in fact, sometimes frightening — view of guerrilla warfare in present-day Peru. The film reminds us that "you only live once and politics involves everyone." The film is gorgeously photographed in color by César Pérez in the Andean highland town of Rayopampa and concentrates on presenting the indigenous atmosphere of isolated communities as well as more suburban ones. It is set in the year 1983, when the Peruvians were caught in a complex battle between Shining Path guerrillas and the military; there was no middle ground, and one

had to take a stand. *La vida es una sola* shows how one's life depended on the politics of the moment and ultimately, on the correct decision for survival. The film tries to give us some insights into a situation that still permeates the politics of the country.

292. Vidas secas (Barren Lives). Nelson Pereira dos Santos. Brazil, 1963. 105 min., B&W. Portuguese.

COMMENTARY: Probably one of the best Brazilian films ever made and taken from the famous Graciliano Ramos novel, *Vidas secas* has been one of the most influential films of *Cinema Nôvo*, and with it Santos has shown himself to be one of its most brilliant directors.

The plot is quite spare: In the northeast of Brazil, in the year 1940, Fabiano (Athila Iorio), Vitoria (María Riberio), their two children and their dog have left their home to escape drought and famine. Luckily, they find an abandoned house to live in, and in a stroke of good fortune, Fabiano gets a job as a herdsman for the local landowner. But when they go to town for a fiesta, Fabiano is provoked by a policeman (Orlando Macedo), then flogged and imprisoned. He is rescued by a band of *cangaçeiros* (outlaws) who have come to spring one of their men from a prison cell. They invite Fabiano to join them, but he refuses. Drought returns, the water-hole dries up, and the cattle begin to die. The dog falls sick and has to be killed. The family takes to the road again, beneath the burning sun of the *sertão* (plain). (Press book.)

Vidas secas reminds one of the great films about family migration like John Ford's 1940 American classic, *The Grapes of Wrath*, or more specifically any of the great Indian films from Satyajit Ray's trilogy *The World of Apu*. Although the aforementioned may have more lyrical insights and visual power, Dos Santos' film deals with the most elemental problems of survival: how to combat ignorance, bad weather, poverty, petty officials, disease, starvation, each other. Drought is the real antagonist in *Vidas secas*, and the director is pleading with the government to end these barren conditions in Brazil, where life is hard and ruthless.

Vidas secas is one of the great revisionist films of Brazilian cinema, one of the fiercest cries for social reform ever put on film. Its greatness lies in the director's truly dispassionate view, simply letting the camera show the crude conditions and not exploiting the misery and abject poverty of mind and heart of this unfortunate family. Santos wants to change the family's destiny and the destiny of the entire nation of Brazil with this kind of cinema.

Hector Olivera, director of *Los viernes de la eternidad* (*The Fridays of Eternity*, 1980).

In making *Vidas secas*, Dos Santos was partly motivated by the need to make some statement on the perniciousness of Brazilian agrarian policy, and in the film's description of the suffering of the people, the tyranny of religion and bureaucracy, and the passivity with which everything is endured are the roots of revolutionary thinking, not immediately apparent but profound nevertheless. But the director remarked many years later that the film was not a commercial success, even though it was simple, direct and uncomplicated in form and theme. It is still one of the 25 best-made films of all time and deserves to be in that pantheon of great world cinema.

293. Los viernes de la eternidad (The Fridays of Eternity). Hector Olivera. Argentina, 1980. 90 min., Color. Spanish.

COMMENTARY: An Argentine fantasy starring Hector Alterio in a Hector Olivera production that made its way to the United States even on video cassette, *Las viernes de la eternidad* is a slightly amusing story: Two men have killed each other in a duel over a woman named

Zese Motta is the star of Carlos Diegues' historical Brazilian film *Xica da Silva* (sometimes know as *Xica*, 1976). The actor on the right is unidentified.

Delfina (Thelma Biral). One of them comes back to haunt her, Don Gervasio (Alterio), the man she preferred dead. Delfina captures this spectre and tries to use his powers to establish herself as a medium or sorceress.

With similarities to the Bruno Barreto film *Doña Flor e seus dois maridos*, there are appropriate sex scenes of raunchiness and nudity, but the film really has nowhere to go. It is not as amusing as the Barreto film, in which special effects were first-rate and the development of character was a prime concern for the director. *Fridays* suffers in both of these departments, although its principal actors give it some kind of life. It is Olivera's attempt at finding a more international audience in a film that has nothing on its mind but simply to entertain. Unfortunately, the shallowness of its screenplay does the actors and the fine color production in. Yet it has the possibility of being a commercial success, because unlike any other Argentine film at the moment, it has no real problem at its core.

The Virgin's Corner see *El Rincón de las vírgenes*

Waiting for the Pallbearers see *Esperando la carroza*

Wall of Silence see *Un muro de silencio*

The Wave see *Redes*

Way Down on the Rancho Grande see *Allá en el rancho grande*

Wetback Power see *Mojado Power*

294. Xica da Silva. Carlos Diegues. Brazil, 1976. 117 min., Color. Portuguese.

COMMENTARY: *Xica da Silva* is based on a true incident in Brazilian history. It is Carlos Diegues' debut film, an entertaining personality study, comedy and history lesson telling an eighteenth-century story about exploitation, corruption and revolution. As played by Zese Motta, Xica is a charismatic black slave woman who derives her considerable power from being able to drive men wild through her sexuality. Walmor Chagas plays João Fernández, the envoy of the Portuguese king. So overcome is Fernández that he gives her a letter of freedom and makes her ruler over the diamond mining region of Arraial. "Xica becomes the Black Queen of Diamonds, and even orders the building of a vast lake and a luxurious galley to sail on it. Eventually word of what is happening reaches the ears of the Portuguese king. Fernández is forced to leave, and Xica's power is destroyed by the whites." (Press book.) It is an intelligent and exotic film but still a Brazilian comedy, where men pop their eyes a great deal in surprise and sexual pleasure is seen discretely, mostly off screen.

Carlos Diegues said of the film: "It is about a dream of freedom, but it is also about the reality of failure. Liberation is collective—one cannot free oneself if those around you remain bound—and in this film, the established power is always there to destroy the ideal." This is the director's political rationale for making the film, but frankly, it is more of an entertainment than anything else. It is a political work, certainly, but essentially optimistic, not downbeat, as the director might have you think. *Xica da Silva* is marvelous, colorful entertainment. No wonder Xica became a myth and a legend of Minas Gerais; she did represent the creative imagination and sensibility of her people, with her love for poetry and liberty. Carlos Diegues has captured these essences in his wonderful film.

295. Yanco. Servando Gonzales. Mexico, 1961. 100 min., B&W. Spanish.

COMMENTARY: *Yanco* is the first feature by Mexican documentary filmmaker Servando Gonzales, and it is a beautiful, lyrical film—also a curious mixture of realism, mysticism, pagan ritual, even social criticism.

Yanco is the story of Juanito (Richard Ancona), who cannot stand the noise of

Unidentified Bolivian Indian actors walk through the mountains in Jorge Sanjinés's film, *Yawar mallku* (*Blood of the Condor*, 1969).

Mexico City and scampers into the countryside, where he makes music on a homemade violin. Villagers make fun of him because of the loud, discordant noises he makes, and his mother (María Bustamente) takes him to a *curandera* to cure him of this illness — perhaps a highly developed aural sense and a growing musical genius that she cannot comprehend. Actually, Juanito is a musical prodigy.

One day, on a shopping trip, Juanito meets an old man (Jesús Medina), a fiddle-playing candy pedlar who was once a great violinist, who takes the boy on as a pupil. Juanito, an excellent student, is playing in Isaac Stern fashion in a few weeks. Suddenly, the old man dies, and his violin (which is named "Yanco") is found in a pawn shop, expropriated by its owner for some debts. Juanito's mother will not buy it, so Juanito steals

Yanco one night, makes beautiful nocturnal music with it and then returns it on successive evenings.

When the suspicious villagers hear this nocturnal music, they come to believe it is an evil omen. Finally they track down Juanito entering the pawn shop to take the violin on the evening of a religious festival. They organize a lynching party, but Juanito grabs Yanco and begins playing as he goes downstream on the river to his final descent in an Orpheus-like, mystical setting. Juanito drowns in the whirlpool, finally meeting his destiny.

The black and white camera work by Alex Phillips, Jr., is extraordinary, rivaling that of the great Mexican cinematographer Gabriel Figueroa. *Yanco* features beautiful skyscapes, candle-lit scenes, and torchlight parades that add to the great charm and sensitivity of the performances. The film has very little dialogue — some phrases in Nahuatl are not translatable — and relies mostly on its imagery. *Yanco* is a very poetic, spiritual work, photographed in a very realistic manner, pleading for an end to superstitious ways and a sincere attempt to instill mutual understanding through education. You cannot take the documentary sensibility out of the director, even if he calls *Yanco* his first fiction full-length feature.

296. Yawar mallku (Blood of the Condor). Jorge Sanjinés. Bolivia, j 1969. 75 min., B&W. Spanish/Quechua.

COMMENTARY: In the Quechua language, *mallku* means chief or condor, while *yawar* means blood. *Yawar mallku* is supposedly the first entirely Bolivian feature ever released in the United States and is an exposé of American doctors and nurses in Bolivia, working for the Peace Corps under the Kennedy administration, who went about sterilizing Indian women to prevent a (nonexistent) population explosion in the country. The director tells the story of one Indian couple, Ignacio (Marcelino Yanahuaya) and Paulina (Benedicta Mendoza Huanca), who are unable to have more children after their first three have died from an outbreak of plague.

After investigating the reasons his wife cannot conceive, Ignacio discovers the sterilization plan of the Amercians, and with a group of Quechuan Indians from his village, he castrates two of the American doctors and wrecks the medical center. After a wild hunt through some of the most beautiful scenic mountains of Bolivia, Ignacio is caught and shot. The scene then shifts to a hospital in La Paz. Ignacio does not immediately die from his wounds, but because his wife and his brother Sixto (Vicente Salinas) cannot raise some 700 pesos for a blood plasma transfusion, he bleeds to death, slowly and torturously. Sixto and Paulina return to the mountain village to pick up the threads of resistance to a deliberate plan to exterminate the indigenous peoples. The film ends with a lovely shot of Sixto facing the dawn of a new day as the condors fly high in the Andes.

The film was beautifully photographed by Antonio Eguino (who later became a director himself), and he catches all the majesty of the mountains, as well as the customs of the Quechua Indians. Derived from a script by Oscar Soria and the director, the film is supposedly based upon real incidents taking place not only in Bolivia but in other parts of South America as well. *Yawar mallka* is a fresh, first-hand document of what was going on in Bolivia in 1968–69, and it is riveting cinema because it is made by a Latin American (Sanjinés) probing his region's problems with his own eyes, not American or European ones. Not made for commercial purposes, *Yawar mallku* continues to thrill audiences who see it because it is a bold (somewhat anti–American) critique of social practices that must be changed. It is a brilliant piece of revisionist cinema.

297. Yo, la peor de todos (I, the Worst of Them All). María Luisa Bemberg. Argentina, 1990. 109 min., Color. Spanish.

COMMENTARY: Based upon a book by Mexican poet Octavio Paz, this film is set in seventeenth-century Mexico and is a story of religious and sexual persecution. Sister Juana (played by the beautiful Spanish actress Assumpta Serna) has the protection of the viceroy (Hector Alterio) and his wife (Italian actress Dominique Sanda). But because she is a poet and writer, a rebellious spirit, and above all, a woman, she is hated by the archbishop (Lautaro Murua), whose hatred of women is well known — though his hatred for Juana may indicate suppressed sexual lust for her. The film also suggests that the archbishop may be the real father of Sister Juana. Meanwhile, Juana (is she the famous, real Sor Juana de la Cruz?) is loved by the viceroy's wife, who spends too much time with her, indicating a lesbian tendency. When the Spanish viceroy and his wife are recalled to their homeland, Juana's life becomes hellish. The film's title refers to the confession of her sins: "I, the worst of them all...."

Assumpta Serna has the role of her life, graduating from those tedious Spanish films of Pedro Almódovar to a play a part that offers her a chance to express her real beauty and sensitivity. Her performance is intelligent, moving and passionate. The film is also beautifully photographed in seventeenth-century trappings by Félix Monti, the expert cinematographer who also worked on Luis Puenzo's only American film, *Old Gringo*. The film may be a pseudo-biography of Sor Juana de la Cruz, whose passion for knowledge and literature and lack of piety caused her undoing. But the director shows her to be, first of all, a real woman of flesh and blood — one of the first real feminists in the Latin American world. It is in this manner that *Yo, la peor de todos* has a genuine appeal to international audiences of the nineties.

298. Yo soy chicano (I Am Chicano). Jesús Trevino. Mexico/U.S., 1972. 59 min., Color. Spanish.

COMMENTARY: This film recreates the key events of the Chicano experience as viewed from pre–Columbian days to the present. The film discusses solutions to oppression of the Chicanos and has some remarkable interviews with Chicano leaders, including Dolores Huerta, Reles López Tijerina, Rodolfo "Corky" Gonzáles and José Ángel Gutiérrez. The film is narrated by Victor Millian and contains music and songs by Daniel Valdéz.

299. Yo soy Joaquín (I Am Joaquín). Luis Valdéz. Mexico/U.S., 1971. 20 min., Color. English/Spanish.

COMMENTARY: This short film is about the Mexican-American heritage of Chicanos as viewed from the days of the Mayan princes to today's Chicano movement, as told in Corky Gonzáles' poem about the Chicano experience. The film denounces the long history of bondage and exploitation of the Mexican people and the current discrimination against Mexicans living in the United States, which seeks to strip them of their culture.

NOTES: Luis Valdéz is a Chicano born in 1940 in Los Angeles. *Yo soy Joaquín* was his first feature, but since then, he has made *Zoot Suit* (1981) and, most recently, *La Bamba* (1987), a biography of Mexican rock star Richie Valens.

You Only Live Once see *La vida es una sola*

The Young and the Damned see *Los olvidados*

300. The Young One (La joven). Luis Buñuel. Mexico/U.S., 1960. 94 min., B&W. English.

COMMENTARY: Something of a curiosity among Buñuel's works, *The Young One* was shot as a Mexican film in Acapulco, but the setting is the southern United States, and the language is English. Based upon a Peter Matthiessen short story, "Travelin' Man," the film stars Zachary Scott as Miller, the game warden on an island preserve off South Carolina. He lives with a kind old handyman whose granddaughter, Evvie (Kay Meersman), shares the same cabin until she meets up with an escaped Negro named Traver (Bernie Hamilton), falsely accused of rape. When the grandfather dies, Reverend Fleetwood (Claudio Brook) shows up on the island to

Director Luis Valdéz on the set of *Zoot Suit* (1981).

formance has neither grace nor charm as the object of Scott's desire, and only Bernie Hamilton saves the film from tedium with his convincing performance as the runaway prisoner who has consideration for the feelings of others.

What is truly disarming is that Luis Buñuel would take this Tennessee-Williams-*Streetcar*-cum-Vladimir-Nabokov-*Lolita* situation, film it in a Mexican location and manage to get a South Carolina flavor out of it. The Mexican setting is the real star in this melodrama. And melodrama it is, especially when the Zachary Scott character helps Bernie Hamilton to escape the island, profiting from Reverent Fleetwood's rendition of the golden rule. The ending is pat, the characters are all stereotypes, and yet *The Young One* holds a certain fascination for its audience, mostly because it was Luis Buñuel's first and only film directed in English! Why the film received a special-mention award at the Cannes Film Festival in 1960 is still a mystery to this viewer.

take the orphaned girl to a shelter, since the Zachary Scott character is already lusting after her. Traver's arrival on the island foments Miller's racial hate, and Miller begins to track Traver down with bloodhounds and all the necessary "southern" paraphernalia because the Negro dared to be kind to the adolescent Evvie and treated her like an equal. Reverend Fleetwood is quick to grasp the situation of Miller's carnal desire for Evvie as well as Traver's eagerness to escape Miller's persecution.

The film was first shown in the United States in 1961 and was revived, curiously, in New York in the summer of 1993 as part of the "Mexican Cinema and the Literary Tradition" series shown at the Walter Reade Theater in Lincoln Center. Although the film is supposedly a lesson for racial tolerance, Zachary Scott comes off as the worst of stereotyped southerners, Kay Meersman's per-

301. Zoot Suit. Luis Valdéz.
U.S., 1981. 103 min., Color. English/Spanish.

COMMENTARY: Based upon a real incident, the Sleepy Lagoon Murder Mystery, that took place in 1942 in Los Angeles, *Zoot Suit* tells of the railroading of a Chicano gang into lifelong jail sentences on a trumped-up murder charge, as well as the subsequent attempts to free them.

Shot on an eleven-day schedule at a cost of $2.5 million by Universal Pictures, the film stars Eduardo Jaime Olmos as El Pachuco, who plays the zoot-suited foil to Daniel Valdéz as

Eduardo Jaime Olmos as El Pachuco, welcoming the audience in the surreal Chicano film by Luis Valdéz, *Zoot Suit* (1981).

Henry Reyna, the narrator of the action. And the action is sometimes very brutal, showing dramatically the prejudice of Americans against Chicanos as seen in gang wars, beatings, murders and rapes.

All the actors are fine, especially Olmos in the starring role and Tyne

Daly in the role of a lawyer trying desperately to free the boys from jail sentences for crimes they did not commit. The costumes, settings and general design of the production are quite superb, beautifully caught by the Technicolor cameras. Apparently *Zoot Suit* first emerged as a theatrical piece, with musical numbers and choreography. Director Luis Valdéz has succeeded very well in making the transition from stage to screen, and the film has strong drawing power despite its particularly specialized theme. Not necessarily a film just about the Chicano experience, *Zoot Suit* becomes a morality tale about the wrongs of Americans toward Chicanos and succeeds brilliantly in depicting, in a colorful, Hollywood extravaganza style, the plight of the victims. The film may have limited appeal, but it is a strong indictment of prejudice against Mexican-Americans and deserves worldwide distribution.

SELECT BIBLIOGRAPHY

Berg, Charles Ramírez. *Cinema of Solitude*. Austin: University of Texas Press, 1992.

Burns, E. Bradford. *Latin American Cinema: Film and History*. Los Angeles: University of California Press, 1975.

Burton, Julianne. *Short Films from Latin America*. New York: American Federation of the Arts, 1992.

Chanan, Michael. *Chilean Cinema*. London: British Film Institute, 1976.

_____, ed. *Twenty-five Years of Latin American Cinema*. London: British Film Institute, 1983.

Foster, David William. *Contemporary Argentine Cinema*. Columbia: University of Missouri Press, 1992.

Hennebelle, Guy, and Hennebell, Gumucio-Dagron. *Les Cinémas de l'Amérique-Latine*. Paris: L'Herminier, 1981.

Johnson, Randal, and Stam, Robert. *Brazilian Cinema*. Rutherford: Fairleigh Dickinson University Press, 1982.

King, John. *Magical Reels*. London: Verso, 1990.

King, John, et al., eds. *Mediating Two Worlds*. London: British Film Institute, 1993.

Luhr, William, ed. *World Cinema Since 1945*. New York: Ungar, 1987.

Mora, Carl J. *Mexican Cinema*. 2nd ed. Berkeley: University of California Press, 1989.

Noriega, Chon A., and Ricci, Steven, eds. *The Mexican Cinema Project*. Los Angeles: UCLA Film and Television Archive, 1994.

Pick, Zuzana M. *The New Latin American Cinema*. Austin: University of Texas Press, 1993.

Schuman, Peter. *Historia del cine latinoamericao*. Trans. by Oscar Zambrano. Buenos Aires: Ed. Legaza, 1981.

Toledo, Teresa. *10 Años del cine latinoamericano*. Havana: ICIAC, 1989.

Trelles Plazaola, Luis. *South American Cinema: Dictionary of Filmmakers*. Trans. by Y. Ferdinandy. Rio Piedras: University of Puerto Rico, 1989.

A NOTE ON VIDEO SOURCES

The following is a list of video distributors who have large collections of Latin American films. Distributors who may have certain films on 16mm are designated with an asterisk (*). Some of the films may be subtitled in English or other languages. Some dealers may sell only; some may rent; some may do both.

Cinevista Video. 560 W. 43d St., New York NY (212) 947-4373.

Condor Video. 5730 Buckingham Pkwy., Culver City CA (800) 421-4509.

Connoisseur Video. 8436 W. 3d St., Ste. 600, Los Angeles CA (213) 653-8873.

Evergreen Video. 37 Carmine St., New York NY (212) 691-7632.

Facets Video. 1517 W. Fullerton Ave., Chicago IL (800) 331-6197.

Kim's Underground. 144 Bleecker St., New York NY (212) 260-1010.

Movies Unlimited. 6738 Castor Ave., Philadelphia PA (800) 722-8398.

*New Yorker Films. 16 West 61st St., New York NY (212) 247-6110.

*Kit Parker Films. P.O. Box 16022, Monterey CA (800) 538-5838.

RCA/Columbia Pictures Home Video. 3500 W Olive, Burbank CA (818) 953-7900.

TLA Video. 521 S. 4th St., Philadelphia PA (215) 564-3838.

UCLA Film and TV Archive. 405 Highland Ave., Los Angeles CA (310) 206-8013.

Video Visa. 12901 Coral Tree Pl., Los Angeles CA (213) 827-7222.

West Coast Video Distributor. 5750 E. Shields Ave., Ste. 101, Fresno CA (209) 292-2013.

Women Make Movies. 462 Broadway, 5th floor, New York NY (212) 925-0606.

INDEX

References are to entry numbers with the exception that
"**p. 000**" references are to pages with illustrations.